Margaret Russett uses the example of Thomas De Quincey, the nineteenth-century essayist best remembered for his *Confessions of an English Opium-Eater* and his memoirs of Wordsworth and Coleridge, to examine the idea of the "minor" author, and how it is related to what we now call the Romantic canon. The case of De Quincey, neither a canonical figure nor a disenfranchised marginal author, offers a point of access to specifically Romantic problems of literary transmission and periodization. Taking an intertextual approach, Russett situates De Quincey's career against the works of Wordsworth and Coleridge; the essays of Lamb, Hazlitt, and other writers for the *London Magazine*; and discourses of ethics and political economy which are central to the problem of determining literary value. *De Quincey's Romanticism* shows how De Quincey helped to shape the canon by which his career was defined.

CAMBRIDGE STUDIES IN ROMANTICISM 25

DE QUINCEY'S ROMANTICISM

CAMBRIDGE STUDIES IN ROMANTICISM 25

General editors

Professor Marilyn Butler
University of Oxford

Professor James Chandler
University of Chicago

Editorial board
John Barrell, *University of York*
Paul Hamilton, *University of London*
Mary Jacobus, *Cornell University*
Kenneth Johnston, *Indiana University*
Alan Liu, *University of California, Santa Barbara*
Jerome McGann, *University of Virginia*
David Simpson, *University of California, Davis*

This series aims to foster the best new work in one of the most challenging fields within English literary studies. From the early 1780s to the early 1830s a formidable array of talented men and women took to literary composition, not just in poetry, which some of them famously transformed, but in many modes of writing. The expansion of publishing created new opportunities for writers, and the political stakes of what they wrote were raised again by what Wordsworth called those "great national events" that were "almost daily taking place": the French Revolution, the Napoleonic and American wars, urbanization, industrialization, religious revival, an expanded empire abroad, and the reform movement at home. This was an enormous ambition, even when it pretended otherwise. The relations between science, philosophy, religion, and literature were reworked in texts such as *Frankenstein* and *Biographia Literaria*; gender relations in *A Vindication of the Rights of Women* and *Don Juan*; journalism by Cobbett and Hazlitt; poetic form, content, and style by the Lake School and the Cockney School. Outside Shakespeare studies, probably no body of writing has produced such a wealth of response or done so much to shape the emergence of those notions of "literature" and of literary history, especially national literary history, on which modern scholarship in English has been founded.

The categories produced by Romanticism have also been challenged by recent historicist arguments. The task of the series is to engage both with a challenging corpus of Romantic writings and with the changing field of criticism they have helped to shape. As with other literary series published by Cambridge, this one will represent the work of both younger and more established scholars, on either side of the Atlantic and elsewhere.

For a complete list of titles published see end of book

DE QUINCEY'S ROMANTICISM

Canonical minority and the forms of transmission

MARGARET RUSSETT

University of Southern California

CAMBRIDGE
UNIVERSITY PRESS

PUBLISHED BY THE PRESS SYNDICATE OF THE UNIVERSITY OF CAMBRIDGE
The Pitt Building, Trumpington Street, Cambridge CB2 1RP, United Kingdom

CAMBRIDGE UNIVERSITY PRESS
The Edinburgh Building, Cambridge CB2 2RU, United Kingdom
40 West 20th Street, New York, NY 10011-4211, USA
10 Stamford Road, Oakleigh, Melbourne 3166, Australia

First published 1997

Printed in the United Kingdom at the University Press, Cambridge

Typeset in Baskerville   [SE]

A catalogue record for this book is available from the British Library

Library of Congress cataloguing in publication data
Russett, Margaret.
De Quincey's romanticism / Margaret Russett.
p.   cm. – (Cambridge studies in Romanticism; 25)
Includes Bibliographical references and index.
ISBN 0 521 57236 3 (hardback)
1. De Quincey, Thomas, 1785–1859 – Criticism and interpretation.
2. Authorship – History – 19th century.   3. Romanticism – Great
Britain.   4. Transmission of texts.   5. Canon (Literature)
I. Title   II. Series.
PR4538.R64R87   1997
828'.809–dc21   96-52445 CIP

ISBN 0 521 57236 3 hardback

To my parents,
Cynthia and Bruce Russett

There is a genius, which stands in need of learning to make it shine. Of genius there are two species, an earlier, and a later; or call them *infantine*, and *adult*. An adult genius comes out of nature's hand, as *Pallas* out of *Jove's* head, at full growth, and mature . . . [but] an infantine genius . . . like other infants, must be nursed, and educated, or it will come to nought: Learning is its nurse, and tutor.

Imitators . . . though most excellent, and even immortal (as some of them are) yet are still but *Dii minorum gentium*, nor can expect the largest share of incense, the greatest profusion of praise, on their secondary altars.

Edward Young,
Conjectures on Original Composition, in a Letter to the Author of Sir Charles Grandison, ed. Edith J. Morley (Manchester University Press, 1918), 15, 19.

Contents

Acknowledgments

Whether or not all criticism is a form of autobiography, I have been unable to avoid perceiving analogies between the subjects of this book and its composition. A first project and as gradual as most, it emerges into print as the palimpsest of its earlier versions. Given the number and profundity of the impressions I recognize, I must hope that the book achieves the originality of "resurrecting," as De Quincey imagines, the successive inscriptions it has received.

Stripped away layer by layer, my traceable debts go something like this: I thank Jim Chandler for his support and for his shrewd suggestions about final revision. My press-readers, Alan Liu and John Barrell, offered balanced measures of encouragement and perceptive criticism. Peter Manning continues to represent an ideal of collegiality to which I can only aspire. The judicious reader of endless drafts, he has also been much more: a boundlessly generous friend and a one-person intellectual community. Not that I have had to make do with one, for I have encountered sympathetic receptions and genial advice among colleagues in Los Angeles and elsewhere. Those who commented helpfully on chapters include Andrea Henderson, Jim Kincaid, Julia Reinhard Lupton, and Mark Schoenfield. Others, too numerous to name, generated insights with their vibrant conversation.

This book began as a dissertation at Johns Hopkins, where it was indelibly marked by Frances Ferguson, Mary Poovey, and Neil Hertz. Several friends from those days – especially Kim Wheatley and Charles Dove – gave essential help, both moral and intellectual. My greatest influence is undoubtedly Jerome Christensen, whose brilliance inspired, whose admonishment strengthened, and whose coruscating commentary sustained the project from beginning to end. To Paul Fry, however, belongs the praise or blame for determining the direction of my graduate studies in the first place.

During the dissertation phase, a Mellon Fellowship provided the time necessary for my diffuse ruminations to take shape. Grant support and a junior leave from the University of Southern California allowed me to pursue crucial research at a later stage. My thanks as well to the Trustees of the National Library of Scotland, for permission to quote from unpublished manuscripts of De Quincey; and to the Trustees of Boston University for allowing me to reprint a portion of chapter one, which appeared as "Wordsworth's Gothic Interpreter: De Quincey Personifies 'We Are Seven,'" in *Studies in Romanticism* 30 (Fall 1991).

Abbreviations

BL   Samuel Taylor Coleridge, *Biographia Literaria*, ed. James Engell and Walter Jackson Bate, *The Collected Works of Samuel Taylor Coleridge*, VII, 2 vols. (Princeton University Press, 1983).

√ C   Thomas De Quincey, *Confessions of an English Opium-Eater and Other Writings*, ed. Grevel Lindop (Oxford University Press, 1985).

CL   Samuel Taylor Coleridge, *Collected Letters*, ed. Earl Leslie Griggs, 6 vols. (Oxford: Clarendon Press, 1956–71).

CPW   Samuel Taylor Coleridge, *Poetical Works*, ed. Ernest Hartley Coleridge (London: Oxford University Press, 1912).

CW   *The Collected Works of Samuel Taylor Coleridge*, general ed. Kathleen Coburn, 16 vols. (Princeton University Press, 1969–).

E   Charles Lamb, *Elia and The Last Essays of Elia*, ed. Jonathan Bate (Oxford University Press, 1987).

EY, MY, LY   *The Letters of William and Dorothy Wordworth*, ed. Ernest De Selincourt, 2nd edn, 7 vols. in all: *The Early Years*, 1 vol.; *The Middle Years* (parts 1 and 2), 2 vols.; *The Later Years* (parts 1–4), 4 vols. (Oxford: Clarendon Press, 1967–1982).

H   William Hazlitt, *Complete Works*, ed. P. P. Howe, 21 vols. (London: Dent, 1931).

HCR   Edith J. Morley (ed.), *Henry Crabb Robinson on Books and their Writers*, 3 vols. (London: Dent, 1938) vol. 1.

√ J   John E. Jordan (ed.), *De Quincey to Wordsworth: A Biography of a Relationship. With the Letters of Thomas De Quincey to the Wordsworth Family* (Berkeley: University of California Press, 1963).

K	Immanuel Kant, *Critique of Judgment*, trans. J. H. Bernard (New York: Hafner Press, 1951).
LB	William Wordsworth and Samuel Taylor Coleridge, *Lyrical Ballads*, ed. R. L. Brett and A. R. Jones, 2nd edn (London: Routledge, 1991).
LM	*The London Magazine*, 18 vols. (London: Baldwin, Cradock and Joy. London: Taylor and Hessey. 1820–29).
LY	See *EY.*
M	*The Collected Writings of Thomas De Quincey*, ed. David Masson, 14 vols. (Edinburgh: Adam and Charles Black, 1890).
MY	See *EY.*
NLS	Thomas De Quincey, unpublished manuscripts in the collection of the National Library of Scotland.
OE	Grevel Lindop, *The Opium Eater: A Life of Thomas De Quincey* (New York: Taplinger, 1981).
PW	William Wordsworth, *Poetical Works*, ed. Thomas Hutchinson, rev. Ernest De Selincourt (New York: Oxford University Press, 1981).
Prelude	William Wordsworth, *The Prelude 1799, 1805, 1850*, ed. Jonathan Wordsworth, M. H. Abrams, and Stephen Gill (New York: Norton, 1979). Except where otherwise noted, references are to the 1805 version. Cited by Book and line (after the colon).
PrW	William Wordsworth, *Prose Works*, ed. W. J. B. Owen and Jane Worthington Smyser, 3 vols. (Oxford: Clarendon Press, 1974).
R	Thomas De Quincey, *Recollections of the Lakes and the Lake Poets*, ed. David Wright (Harmondsworth: Penguin, 1985). For convenience, the alternative title *Lake Reminiscences* is used throughout the text.
SE	Sigmund Freud, *The Standard Edition of the Complete Psychological Works*, trans. and ed. James Strachey with Anna Freud, 24 vols. (London: Hogarth Press, 1958).

References to prose works are given by volume (where relevant), with page numbers after the colon. Single-volume works are cited by page number alone. References to poetical works other than the *Prelude* are given by page, with line numbers, if appropriate, after the colon.

Where possible, I have included bracketed secondary references for works by De Quincey, Hazlitt and Lamb quoted from *The London Magazine.*

Introduction

> The least things in the universe must be secret mirrors to the
> greatest. (*M* 1:129)

Thomas De Quincey traded in the lives of poets. Above all, he
capitalized on his youthful enthusiasm for William Wordsworth
and Samuel Taylor Coleridge, whom he regarded and helped to
establish as the leading literary figures of his century: the "first
generation" of the family we call "English Romanticism."
Wordsworth he considered "*the* great poet of the age" (*R* 116), and
it was this recognition, rather than his own body of published work
(extending to more than fourteen volumes), on which he staked
his highest pretensions to literary fame. Neither Wordsworth's
confidant nor the first critic to praise him, De Quincey represented himself as the privileged auditor of a "profound secret":
that, as Coleridge claimed, Wordsworth's "*fame* belongs to another
age, and can neither be accelerated or retarded" (*R* 117; *BL*
2:158). For De Quincey, the prospect of that other age was figured
in regress from the age of reason to the condition of minority. His
dispersed autobiographical writings cast him as an epiphenomenon of the Lake School, interpreting the infantilized
abasement to genius as the possession of a precious, albeit thematically limiting, literary property. That gesture is confirmed by his
standing in the academic canon of Romanticism, which, in its
various nineteenth- and twentieth-century permutations, has gradually relegated De Quincey to the secure but secondary position of
a significant *minor* writer.[1] Qualitative judgment meets juridical
classification in an exemplary figure of Romantic "developmental
discourse."[2]

Focusing on the career of De Quincey, this study examines the
category of the minor in relation to the larger cultural project of

1

canon-formation. My interest in this question originated with bemusement at De Quincey's apparently spontaneous recognition of the Lake Poets' "genius": however little explanatory value this notion may possess for the contemporary critic, it evokes a constellation of desires that still seems to me a resonant historical enigma. And while other poets have, since De Quincey's time, joined Romanticism's roster of great authors, the generational *form* and generic hierarchies of that canon have remained substantially the same, and recapitulate terms he adduced to naturalize his own responses. If De Quincey's grandiose humility marks him, therefore, as a writer of putatively diminished powers, it also suggests that to publish another's genius is to replicate oneself, even while instantiating the devious turns of what Pierre Bourdieu calls "reproduction." The English Romantic canon, I argue, takes its shape from Romantic dialectics. Its historical pressures survive in familiar tropes of institutional transmission – genius and talent, first and second generations, primary and secondary texts, even poetry and prose – as well as in the more invidious pairings of wholes and fragments, health and sickness, growth and stunting. The minor writer represents both the negative and the counterpart of the major, whose identification cannot, therefore, be understood purely as the fetish of a belated idealism. De Quincey's imbrication in the cult of self-sustaining poetic genius, on one hand, and the context of periodical writing and proto-professional criticism, on the other, situates him at a historical crux whose symptom, minority, is inextricable from our received narratives of greatness.[3]

Like his contemporaries Charles Lamb and William Hazlitt, De Quincey was a magazine writer whose works have very selectively maintained a presence in teaching anthologies and on collegiate syllabi. In each case the canonical writings are short and oscillate between subjective memoir and objective reportage, limning a domain of prosaically diminished "confessions" and opinionated, "egotistical" criticism. Despite the generic ambivalence of their work, domesticated under the label of the familiar essay, all three writers have been deeply mined for positivistic literary history: Lamb's "Christ's Hospital Five and Thirty Years Ago," Hazlitt's "My First Acquaintance with Poets" and *The Spirit of the Age*, and De Quincey's *Reminiscences* are routinely cited in studies and biographies of the major figures. Yet the sources of this information are also, and without acknowledged contradiction, treated as formally reflexive Romantic texts. Neither a biographer nor a critic in the senses licensed by contemporary practice, De Quincey has traditionally been judged – and found wanting – by the criteria of originality and sustained imaginative intensity to which Romantic culture gave rise.[4] Despite the praise often granted to his "impassioned prose," any evaluation conducted in these terms can be made to stick, and recent variants, while organized by different agendas, have not markedly altered the balance. Yet the unanimity of these judgments also suggests their circularity: critical discourse reiterates the rhetorical structure of the minor text, merging subject-positions with the generic differences abstracted in the facing mirrors of creation and imitation.

I have little interest in recuperating reputations. The giants and dwarves of the *Biographia Literaria* will not change places here. And although I include myself among De Quincey's admirers, it will be an assumption of the following chapters that judgments of quality grounded on the affirmation or denial of an empirical consensus are doomed to unwitting reinscription of what are – to paraphrase de Man – displaced figures of a structural predicament. De Quincey has, in any case, enjoyed a remarkable critical vogue recently, as witnessed by five full-length studies since 1990, as well as supporting roles in several essay collections.[5] It is by no means clear, however, to what degree such studies either reflect or define classroom practice; if long-ignored authors are being taught in some Romantic surveys these days, the content of recent anthologies suggests that the rediscoveries are unlikely to feature such unapologetic exponents of Romantic ideology as De Quincey.[6] The flourishing state of De Quincey studies attests to a convergence of institutional pressures, among them the late-Romantic imperative of originality and post-Romantic skepticism about the ontology of literature. While De Quincey's appeal to historicists, in particular, undoubtedly answers Marilyn Butler's call for "a concern with the external relations of" texts, these studies must be seen as cognate rather than congruent with the much-debated "expansion" or "instability" of the teaching canon.[7]

De Quincey's canonical status remains, I suggest, fundamentally unchanged in the midst of these countervailing adjustments. What continues to change, and hence indicates this study's horizon of influence, is the way professional readers conceive of their relation to the subjects they profess. As Samuel Weber observes, "in recent years the humanistic disciplines have manifested an increasing interest in . . . their own institutional status."[8] This interest ultimately motivates De Quincey's critical popularity as well: De Quincey presents an especially instructive test case for the "historicity" or situatedness of theoretical critique, whether as the augury of de Manian rhetoric or as the unlikely hero of historical materialism.[9] These preoccupations of the contemporary academy will be much in evidence here, for De Quincey *theorizes*, in however displaced and elliptical a way, the minor status that he *elects*. Inscribing material contingency as rhetorical design (and vice-versa), the minor text converts production to consumption in terms that confound allegory and experience, quality and quantity, specular desire and aesthetic discrimination. Thus, although the persuasiveness of an argument so wedded to minutiae demands a willingness to grant Crabb Robinson's view of De Quincey as at least "curious, if not valuable" (*HCR* 273) – or symptomatic, if not transcendent – his career occasions a broader reflection on the tropology and psychoanalytics of cultural esteem.

This claim of theoretical recursiveness poses one significant distinction between my account of minority and the utopian projects outlined by Louis A. Renza and, before him, Gilles Deleuze and Felix Guattari. Whatever the possibility of a text that "short-circuit[s] social production" or even one that reveals an "unregenerate desire for literary finitude," it is precisely the "nondialectical" vision of a "canonically free minor literature" that I contest, since the canon's specific gravity changes in response to the very "process of *becoming*" that these theorists posit as the institutionally elusive movement of minor desire.[10] *Like* minor literature, the canon does not exist; it becomes. While Renza admits that "the conception of minor literary texts" thus demands "a questioning of . . . the act of criticism," I take this questioning to be the telos of literary-historical inquiry.[11] I return to brief engagements with several theorists of minor writing in this book's conclusion; for now it will be enough, by way of heuristic, to evoke a creative or parasitic dependency upon an evolving set of *figures*, at once rhetorical and biographical, more "original," "comprehensive," "spacious," and "powerful" – to quote De Quincey's epithets for Coleridge – than the historical satellites now typically read beside them. Simply stated: majority and minority are mutually constitutive categories, and may indeed be construed as such by writers whose conditions of production situate them in the contours of a family-romance. Even more simply, the minor *articulates* the major canon. The socio-psychic nuances of these articulations are richly and intricately explored by De Quincey, whose diagnosis of Lamb's "essential *non*-popularity" succinctly outlines the themes of his own career. "Even as a crowd of men divides into th[e] . . . majority and minority," De Quincey writes, "a library divides into sections of worldly and unworldly," the latter of which he identifies with the qualities of "childlike simplicity," "shy profundity," and "inspired self-communion." If *non*-popularity suggests failure, De Quincey attributes to Lamb and his ilk "a grace and strength of originality" which "will continue to command a select audience in every generation" (*M* 5:215–17). Minority troped as "childlike" insight elicits the canonical prestige "assessed," according to John Guillory, by "the *limit* of . . . dissemination," that is, by "relative exclusivity."[12]

The minor is to be distinguished, therefore, not only from the major but also from the disenfranchised *marginal* writer, of whom, again, Romanticism presents many examples, ranging from peasant poets like John Clare and James Hogg to then-famous women writers like Felicia Hemans, Mary Robinson, and Ann Radcliffe. The boundaries between classes of production are of course not absolute, and perhaps no taxonomy could accommodate the range and canonical vicissitudes represented by a cross-section of early nineteenth-century writing. It is important, though, to stress how minority – a form of canonical *in*clusion – differs both from the nostalgic simulation of unlettered speech marketed under the names of Clare and Hogg, as well as from the "popularity" that Romantic theory would proscribe on the basis of explicit or disguised generic regulations. Canonical minority offers no privileged access to the "forgotten, lost, or marginal figure" whose "recovery," as Peter T. Murphy suggestively argues, provides a critical "opportunity for the contemplation of loss," itself structurally homologous with Romantic aesthetics.[13] Moreover, if a submerged analogy with *cultural* minority has energized scholarship on poets like Clare or Hemans, their canonization will nonetheless take the "majority" form of an ascription of textual difficulty, the institutional trace of the Romantic reading standard.[14] (This is by no means to argue against teaching or researching the works of these writers, a project in which I also hope to engage.) The minor writer, by contrast – never "forgotten" and in no danger of becoming so – occupies the negative pole of Romantic dialectics without, like the marginal or the "non-canonical" writer, failing to be inscribed in a dialectic of *production*. The minor work forms a "complex continuum" with major works, as well as "works read primarily in research contexts."[15]

The minor writer's shadowy historical presence in scholarship and teaching practice – as illustration, stylistic model, limit-case, comic relief – challenges the schematic division of canonical from non-canonical works that, in nineteenth-century studies, has overlain the doublings of Romantic sociology. The minor Romantic intersects with literary history at the site of its origin and iteration: namely, the scene of instruction where, as Guillory has brilliantly demonstrated, the canon is purveyed as the vessel of elite literacy, or symbolic capital.[16] De Quincey himself is blandly academic in his praise for the "rights of heirship" protected by the university; he merely regrets that "few or none of the Oxford undergraduates" with whom he studied in 1803–08 "knew anything at all of English literature" (*M* 2:18; *R* 114). Privileged as regards literary means, yet circumstantially assigned to the sphere of reception or ends, the minor prose writer represents a vehicle of transmission in *both* respects relevant to the narrative of literary tradition. At once a literary author and a critic or empirical recorder, the minor Romantic both *has* and *is* a particular form of cultural capital, now mainly disseminated in specialized branches of higher education.[17] This ambiguity is also the minor's perceived limitation, confining him to a secondary status in both the chronological and the (Romantically) evaluative senses of the term.

This dual identity is possible in part because English studies had not yet, in the early nineteenth century, been formalized into academic discipline. De Quincey's career unfolded in a milieu where "literary journalism and scholarship form[ed] the ends of a spectrum" in which "authors, editors, publishers and professors changed roles with the greatest of ease."[18] His most explicitly didactic essays, such as the "Letters to a Young Man Whose Education Has Been Neglected," represented only one strain in a discourse of vernacular instruction whose embodiments, actual or imagined, included the periodical reviewer as well as the Coleridgean cleric.[19] This evocation of context, with its reminder of the porousness and internal fractures of the literary "institution," suggests one among several ways in which the minor Romantic's career represents a primal scene of criticism. Considered as the humble vehicle of a mightier tenor, De Quincey prefigures the modalities of response to a monumentalized great tradition. The study of his canonical maneuvers contributes to a historical understanding of literature's theory and practice – the reification of "original talent" on one hand, and the credentialed discipline of criticism on the other. Romanticism (or literature in its "absolute" sense) "inaugurates," as Philippe Lacoue-Labarthe and Jean-Luc Nancy have asserted, "criticism as [the] reproduction" or "second power" of poetic form; this doubly *literary* criticism implies both "the absolutization of the Absolute, a fulfillment of every work in its Work, and the disparity, the surplus, the almost unaccountable excess of one more completion."[20]

The widening of this disparity, a kind of desynonymy, will eventually found the well-known "anxiety of influence"; but De Quincey's unanxious techniques of quotation and *rifacimento* correspond instead with Lamb's admission that "books think for me" and Hazlitt's deference to "Coleridge's better genius."[21] The matter of priority, or influence, never arises because it is precluded by the trope of minority, wherein a "second power" adopts the stance of the younger, smaller, pupil or offspring of a *primary* and "superior organism" – a posture naturalized, in its turn, by the Romantic reverence for "listening infancy" (*Prelude* 5:190).[22] Thus Hazlitt and Lamb, both born within a few years of Wordsworth and Coleridge, take their places with De Quincey in the second *phase* of Romanticism. Their careers, which accelerated in the late 1810s and 1820s, also provide theoretical justification for the familial metaphor that later historians would apply less self-consciously to Byron, Shelley, and Keats. The minors' share in the Lake School's posthumous fame ironically vindicates the Wordsworthian dictum that "the child is father of the man," since, as I show in some detail, they not only codified the canonical terms of appreciation but answered Coleridge's ambition "to win . . . friends among the rising generation" (Goethe, quoted in *BL* 1:3).

To study minority, then, is to study generation. It follows that this study makes no attempt to quarantine its object. The book's dispersion of focus may qualify it as literary history, albeit a history that substitutes involuted analysis for extensive view. Both in my choices of De Quinceyan texts and in my deviations from them, I have embraced as Coleridgean method the eccentricities and errancies of the fragments I half-create. These intertextual fragments constitute both more and less than a synecdoche of De Quincey's "achievement": they have been selected not for their representative but for their *exemplary* status, that is, to illuminate aspects of the relation between literary transmission and the assignment of canonical stature. Further conforming with De Quincey's heterogeneity, I skirt distinctions between the sub-genres of his writing. Instead, I have methodized my tenet that readings evolve through dislocation, so that an apparently non-literary text like *The Logic of Political Economy* is taken to gloss *The Confessions of an English Opium-Eater* (itself, as I argue, the displaced canonization of two poets' "symbiosis"). The consequent peculiarities of emphasis are the less to be regretted in light of the fine recent work, noted above and elsewhere, that has taken a more conventional single-author approach. This book is about reading Wordsworth, repeating Coleridge, writing for magazines, and competing for popularity at least as much as it is about interpreting De Quincey. One of my intentions, indeed, is to demonstrate practically how artificial any isolation of these themes must be, whether the various resulting objects be designated by authors, by genres, or by periods. Thus I bring certain preoccupations of traditional literary history (the nature of a vocation, the characteristics of genius, the possibility of representative voice) into the domain of poststructuralism – less to "deconstruct" or disqualify them than to glimpse the internal dramas of idealism.

The book could then also be seen as the dialectical counterpart of an influence study: emphasizing neither imaginative "origin" nor empirical "reception," and with little regard for De Quincey's alleged debts to Wordsworth or Coleridge, I attempt to trace the *production* of signature Romantic themes, motifs, and rhetorical effects at the contested and undecidably distorting site of *transmission*.[25] At this point, however, a more explicit theoretical statement may be called for. By electing the concept of transmission over the near-synonymous "interpretation" or even "reading," I mean to adopt and endorse Guillory's thesis, in his book *Cultural Capital*, that "canonicity is not a property of the work itself but of its transmission, its relation to other works in a collocation of works." As Guillory (influenced by Bourdieu) has decisively shown, transmission is above all a material fact, conditioned by its "institutional locus." The continued presence of an author in the canon, or idealized horizon of knowledge, thus depends not only on obvious factors of availability and inclusion but also on the transformed materiality of the institutional *habitus*: that is, the rarefied literacy, or "sociolect," that registers the traces of social stratification. "The literary canon," in this account, "has always functioned . . . as a pedagogic device for producing an effect of linguistic distinction" by inculcating a restricted "literary language." Wordsworth's canonicity, for example, follows from his resistance to "the pressure of novelization" through a "co-optation of the language of prose" that indexes a crisis in the vernacular standard.[24]

Entirely convincing in itself, this example also suggests the limits of Guillory's analysis for understanding the deformations effected by, and also conditioning, the transmission of any *particular* work or "author." If, on the one hand, the syllogistic form of the argument (Wordsworth's diagnosis of the canonical crisis makes him canonical) invites further specification of historical accident, Guillory's reluctance in this case to examine authorial "resistance" also elides the consanguinity of literary *transmission* with what he elsewhere acutely names "transference."[25] Thus my own account, while much indebted to Guillory's sociology, attends to contingent details of biography and mode of authorship that are made largely irrelevant by his focus on the *longue durée*. Perhaps more tellingly, I regard transmission as a function of "iterability," which, as Weber observes, "entails alteration as much as it does recurrence."[26] This is to say both that no act of transmission – even simple quotation – leaves its object unchanged, and that every such act produces effects in excess of sheer replication. It is indeed this material excess *of the signifier* which, I contend, sponsors the minor career. That reproduction should be incarnated in the figure of minority suggests, finally, the impossibility of a reading that is not personalized by transference, or the contamination of dialectics by the vagaries of psychology. "The aporetic project" of literary transmission, the project "of *imparting the particular*," is driven by an exemplarity that cannot be abstracted from the personified exemplum, or minor.[27] And just as De Quincey's particularity shades readily into perversion, the means of transmission unfold into the moment of change.

My focus on the exemplary moment has dictated (or justified) a synthesis for which I appropriate the title of poststructuralist biography, modifying the prototypes adumbrated by Jerome Christensen as well as William Epstein.[28] Each chapter begins from a defined point in De Quincey's career, understood both as a simulation of chronology and as the articulation of a theoretical problem. Thus, I repeatedly posit something resembling a biographical stage, often only to violate this unity by intermixing presumptively discrete texts and authors, De Quincey sometimes least in evidence. Although concerned with questions of form, the composition is not formalist. I endeavor in practice to vindicate my largest abstract claim: that the Romantic cult of solitary genius misrecognizes what is in fact a *corporate* mode of production that the minor's "genius for instrumentality" (*CW* 4[1]: 420) both underwrites and unveils.

Each chapter also attempts to define an aspect of the over-determined category "minor." The first offers a genesis of minority from a special case of the oft-remarked "theme of the child." Presuming the heuristic value of psychoanalysis for literary history, chapter one treats the De Quinceyan persona as a case of textual subjection: the "birth" of the readerly identity signifies the "unconscious" of (another) writer. De Quincey's career opens with a letter to Wordsworth in which, describing his first acquaintance with *Lyrical Ballads*, he adopts the lyric voice of the "little maid" in "We Are Seven," so confirming the diagnostics of Wordsworth's "Preface." This conversion is reenacted both in Wordsworth's vocational itinerary and in the form of De Quincey's autobiographies. De Quincey founds himself in a feminized, subjugated, and derivative stance toward the poet, while Wordsworth gains his first professional "client" at the price of appropriation by a dark interpreter. In the origins of minority, intertextual questions converge with the discourse of pathology.[29] Some iterations of this scenario are discussed in the chapter's third section, which, describing biography and autobiography as variations on the act of counting, links impressionistic accounts of De Quincey's arrested development to the accumulated deaths recorded in *Suspiria de Profundis* and his later *Autobiographic Sketches*.

While in the first chapter psychoanalytic terms predominate, the second foregrounds the issues and idioms of political theory. Beginning with the empirical premise of a collaboration among Wordsworth, Coleridge, and De Quincey to intervene in international affairs, this chapter examines the composition of *The Convention of Cintra* as an allegory of political domination and resistance. The imperative of "timely utterance" urged by Wordsworth implicitly contrasts with the temporal diffusion of texts, from Rousseau's 1762 *Social Contract* to De Quincey's 1849 *English Mail-Coach*, in which *Cintra*'s questions of action, reaction, revolution, and invasion are prefigured and replayed. De Quincey, minimally concerned in its intellectual genesis, nonetheless became the scapegoat for the pamphlet's failure. With his demotion from Coleridgean "friend" to casuistical "follower," De Quincey began his separate career, abandoning the Wordsworthian ambition of representative status for the defense of circumstance and idiosyncrasy. Late for the revolution, the minor writer supplements a mythic egalitarian alliance.

The periodical context of De Quincey's literary debut, *The Confessions of an English Opium-Eater*, is the subject of my third chapter, which shifts focus from his vertical affiliations to the horizontal axis of the magazine industry and its writers, particularly Hazlitt and Lamb. Here I attempt to specify the characteristics of an "author-function," the magazinist, which differs from book-market authorship (the primary domain of Wordsworth and Coleridge) in its material conditions, in its thematic preoccupations, and in its relative prestige. Concentrating on the problem of the corporate text's anonymity, which I treat as an expression of anxieties over cultural capital, I show how the essayist's style and persona evolved from the demands of serial publication – even, in special cases, enabling the writer to cross over to the book market. At the same time, the periodical career acts out a logic of imposture that implicitly critiques the specious unity and closure of book-market authorship. The "Opium-Eater" emerges as a candidate for this equivocal fame from a contested field including *Blackwood's Magazine*, the *Waverley* novels, "Table Talk" and the essays of "Elia," and the *London Magazine* contributors T. G. Wainewright, John Scott, and Thomas Hood. All the minor Romantics worked as journalists; this section describes how *some* journalists achieved the preconditions of canonicity.

The following chapter undertakes a Romantic analysis of cultural capital, a term that remarries the divorced discourses of political economy and transcendental philosophy. My focus is De Quincey's *Logic of Political Economy*, which I read as an effort to subject aesthetic reception (Kant) to the discipline of commodity consumption (Ricardo). Whereas the high Romantic artist, exemplified here by Wordsworth, proffers a claim for the *intrinsic* (or "use") value of the literary artifact, De Quincey, in Kantian fashion, locates aesthetic value in a particular mode of reception (or "exchange"). Unlike Kant, though, he draws no line between imaginative presentation and quantified economic value. Reception, then, is redefined as transmission, the site of commodity-exchange and pedagogy: the reader, minor partner in the creation of textual meaning, becomes significant in conducting *power*, or words' worth. The aesthete finds his place at the nexus of dissemination, as the cultural capitalist who reaps ineffable returns on his literary investments. This proposition is tested in a close reading of the *Confessions*, arguing that the dream of Piranesi allegorizes the descent of Wordsworth and Coleridge into the literary market, and an impending rise in their symbolic stock. Mediating this exchange, the Opium-Eater incorporates himself into the Lake School as its agent of reproduction.

Turning then to De Quincey's explicit essays in canon-formation, the 1834–40 *Lake Reminiscences,* I attempt to reconcile Wordsworth's outrage at these infringements of his "single selfhood" with the challenge to literary property posed by the trajectory of canonization. De Quincey deviated from the standard of Johnson's *Lives of the Poets* by writing a memoir of a poet whose manuscript "life," the *Prelude,* was still being revised. Biography, then, apparently sacrifices the empirical person to the posthumous textual *corpus.* Chapter five explores this mode of aggression by reviving the psychoanalytic terms of chapter one in concert with the problematics of literary materiality and copyright law; these issues coalesce in a discussion of De Quincey's unauthorized excerpts from the *Prelude.* Variously depicting the memorialist as would-be daughter, as thieving Arab, as ghostly double, and as the cradle-robbing lover of Wordsworth's daughter Catherine, De Quincey's *Reminiscences* foretell the death and disfigurement of the author which constitute the prerequisites for literary fame.

I conclude with a theoretical defense of the book's punning subtitle, linking questions of judgment (greater and lesser genius; and, behind these evaluative terms, the specters of mass culture and minority taste) to the tropes of miniaturization and diminishment typically invoked by the minor Romantic writer. Here I suggest, with reference to the "gentle-hearted" Lamb and the self-thwarting Hazlitt, that De Quincey's property in the representation and psychology of minors displaces a canonical strategy premised on reading rather than writing. In his appreciation for Wordsworth's "minor poems" (*BL* 1:74) as in his mystification of infancy, De Quincey sketches a "conditional and derivative" relation toward major forms and cultural prescriptions (*R* 162). Like Hazlitt and Lamb, also in their different ways figures of what Harold Bloom might call "incapable" imagination, De Quincey made a strength of his self-confessed frailty. Electing precocity over power, all three scripted exquisite faculties of response that equate neither with self-sustaining "genius" nor with mechanically assembling "talent," as Coleridge divides the republic of letters. Thus, first situating the minor in the context of Romantic dialectics, I then suggest how he anticipates Bourdieu's critique of the "gifted minority" whose possession of cultural capital is experienced as a sense of distinction.

The stance of weakness, ironically construed as powerful feeling, not only complicates the erotics of agon but marks the absence of explicit scenes of instruction in formalist studies of influence. The lapsed discussion of primary poetry and secondary prose indicates, therefore, a site of tension between the claims of genius and the emerging culture of professionalism. In a Romantic restatement of this discovery, I suggest that De Quincey's self-inscriptions enact the practical truth of Kant's abstract challenge to sociology: in other words, that production and transmission can no longer be distinguished even in theory. Romantic dialectics incorporated reception into the aesthetic object, so that prose "reading" could plausibly represent itself as an aspect of poetic *writing*.[30] A shadow cast across Wordsworth's picture of the mind, De Quincey reads the poetic text as his own prefiguration; and in that reflexive genesis he finds both the greatness he values and the unfailing demand for interpretive recurrence. In his career, then, we may read the prehistory of our own practice – the moment when, with the invention of literature, poetry became the allegory of its own transmission.

CHAPTER 1

Conversions: Wordsworth's gothic interpreter

DE QUINCEY PERSONIFIES "WE ARE SEVEN"

Halfway through his revised *Confessions*, De Quincey pauses to ask a rhetorical question – "Was I then, in July 1802, really quoting from Wordsworth?" – and stays to answer, "Yes, reader; and I only in all Europe. In 1799 I had become acquainted with 'We are Seven' at Bath" (*M* 3:302). De Quincey's question and his response characteristically link grandiose posturing with a memory of reading, through apostrophe to the surrogate of his own early wonder. Equally characteristic is the bathetic following sentence, in which he names the poem he read and specifies the date and place of his first acquaintance with it. These details anchor the constitutive De Quinceyan claim that, simply by quoting Wordsworth, he had "taken up one position in advance of my age by full thirty years" (*R* 116). Like a leading from above, "We Are Seven" catalyzes "the unfolding of" De Quincey's "own mind" (*R* 33), as though the encounter described in the poem, where a man interrogates "a little cottage girl" (*LB* 66:5), represented a discovery of vocation. Thus the De Quinceyan reader, wise "by one entire generation" (*R* 118), converts youth and solitude into rhetorical advantage. De Quincey stakes his place in literature on a historical circumstance he interprets as accelerated "intellectual development" (*R* 116): the precocity of a fourteen-year-old who can already read "We Are Seven."

The extent of De Quincey's success may be gauged by the canonical role of the correspondence he began three years later. Regarded as testimonials to Wordsworth's influence on the "pure and innocent mind" (*MY* 1:160) of an untaught admirer, De Quincey's letters have documented the birth of a movement for later generations of literary scholars. In the first and best known, the solitary child "prostrate[d]" himself before the genial author of *Lyrical Ballads*, whose "enchanting volumes" had dwarfed the "eight or nine other poets that I have been able to find since the world began" (*J* 30). This lowly position did not prevent his voicing an ambitious request for Wordsworth's friendship: "with such opinions," as he observed, "it is not surprising that the hope of that friendship should have sustained me through two years" (*J* 30). Whether surprising or predictable, De Quincey's suit for the Wordsworthian title of "friend" launched a series of strategic moves and rhetorical adjustments that eventually won him his problematic inclusion in the Wordsworth circle. The poet responded to De Quincey's opening gambit with a carefully worded letter, warmly inviting him to visit but cautioning that "my friendship it is not in my power to give" (*EY* 400). De Quincey professed himself delighted at this polite rebuff, though he would not actually meet Wordsworth until November of 1807. In the meantime, their correspondence quickly normalized the curious oscillation of intimacy and formality that would characterize De Quincey's interactions with the poet who changed his life.

De Quincey's first extended exercise as an interpreter of poetry occurs in his third letter, which both marks a turn in his campaign for Wordsworth's esteem and rehearses the motifs of his *Reminiscences* and confessional writings. To reorient his attachment to Wordsworth, he fashions an elaborate conversion narrative that pivots, most implausibly, on an often ridiculed "little poem" (*BL* 2:140) in the *Lyrical Ballads*.[1] The letter begins with an apology for the "long interval" that has elapsed since his last, and the explanation that he has lately become unwholesomely absorbed in the "painful employments" of college life. Having removed from Oxford to restore his mind "in some retirement" at Littlemore, De Quincey bestows "the first fruits of returning moral health" on "that circle of human beings in whom half my love, & all my admiration are centred." Already this story has an uncannily Wordsworthian feel, a tone and a plot seemingly caught from "Tintern Abbey." The remainder both deepens and mystifies this effect, as one fable of redemption inexorably yields another, requiring "a sketch of the circumstances attending my first acquaintance with your poems." De Quincey then retraces his journey to Wordsworth from the moment when, "some years ago spending my holidays in Bath I was shewn the poem of We are

Seven which was handed about in manuscript" (*J*36).[2] De Quincey found himself, he implies, in reading "We Are Seven."

"A long time intervened" (*J*36) between this punctual moment and his discovery of the poem's authorship. De Quincey's "long time," less specific than Wordsworth's "five years," nevertheless suggests a rhythm of encounter and reencounter that derives, like his vocabulary, from "Tintern Abbey." Wordsworth, more interested in the structure of revisitation than in what sets it off, barely sketches the period between his first and second visits to the Wye. De Quincey drastically expands this "interval" into a fullblown gothic excursus. Picking up on the poem's faint hints of time ill-spent, he tells a tale of delusion replete with familiar generic features.

gothic

> I gradually came under the dominion of my passions, & from frequent meditation on some characters of our own, & some of ancient story, & afterwards on some of the German Drama, I began to model my conduct & my aims on theirs: by degrees, being dazzled by the glory thrown on such objects by the voice of the people, & miserably deluding myself with the thought that I was led on by high aims, & such as were most worthy of my nature I daily intoxicated myself more & more with that delirious & lawless pleasure which I drew from the hope of elevating my name in authority & kingly splendour above every name that is named upon earth. For I felt myself unable to live in the pursuit of common objects, & unfettered by any ties of common restraint – & I felt, too, or imagined myself able to compass any plans capable of gratifying that stimulating class of desires which I then thought ebullitions of the highest state of moral improvement, but which I now consider as only a less degrading species of sensualism. (*J*37)

Extravagantly self-aggrandizing, this is also extravagantly literary, defeating the curiosity for biographical substantiation that the confessional tone necessarily arouses. While such a passage could conceivably refer to De Quincey's fugitive winter in London, its hyper-tropism suggests an interpretation founded on strictly textual antecedents.[3] Nothing ever happened to De Quincey that he had not read about first. One would need a comprehensive knowledge of eighteenth-century popular literature, but probably not much ingenuity, to find a novelistic or dramatic source for virtually every phrase in the paragraph. The "voice of the people" and the delusive "high aims," for example, are borrowed from Schiller's *Die Räuber*, while the despotic self-elevation sounds like *Vathek* or *Faust*.[4]

From a beginning in imitation of "Tintern Abbey," then, De Quincey's narrative escalates into a gothic fable that exploits a consciousness of its own genre: a gothic about the perils of gothic. On the one hand, the allusion to his literary influences places De Quincey's letter squarely within the gothic tradition. The sense of being "about" its generic requirements, and the notion that literary experience deforms or suspends the laws of reality, are constitutive features of gothic, "the conventional genre par excellence."[5] But De Quincey's plot adumbrates reader-response yet more explicitly than, for example, the novels of Ann Radcliffe do. Its trials and its villains are those of a poetic disquisition – Wordsworth's "Preface" to *Lyrical Ballads* – that De Quincey interprets precisely as a gothic novel about the dangerous effects of gothic novels. Taking personally Wordsworth's sideswipes at "frantic novels, sickly and stupid German Tragedies, and deluges of idle and extravagant stories in verse" (*PrW* 1:128), De Quincey tells how he was seduced into emulating a degraded sensibility. He produces his miniature biography to illustrate Wordsworth's thesis on the pernicious consequences of "gross and violent stimulants" in fiction.

But a tale does not transcend its genre simply by moralizing its stimulus; one moral of gothic is that theoretical critique need not dissipate generic charms.[6] De Quincey's hyperbolic language undercuts even as it draws attention to the Wordsworthian lesson he dutifully reproduces. For all his reverence of *Lyrical Ballads*, he will never abandon gothic thrills for the real language of men. His luridly excessive style coincides with an ingenious misrepresentation of Wordsworth's central premise. In the first place, Wordsworth's analysis is tied to an anti-commercialist polemic on the morale of urban laborers, and Thomas De Quincey, Oxford student and son of a Manchester merchant, cannot be counted among the objects of such reformist concern. By associating himself with the mass of popular readers rather than with the elite readers of Johnson and Gray whom Wordsworth addresses, De Quincey hints at the instability of both those projected social categories. Then too, his assertion that he had "modelled" his behavior on fictional characters distorts Wordsworth's strictures against sensation. The "Preface" never implies that readers could confuse themselves with fictional characters; only that an irresponsible class of literature has assisted recent national events in blunting

"the discriminating powers of the mind, and unfitting it for all voluntary exertion to reduce it to a state of almost savage torpor"
(*PrW* 1:128). De Quincey's account of himself as an effect of bad
reading slyly extends the logic of Wordsworthian cause and effect.
The trajectory he traces in himself, more explicit than the one
the "Preface" imagines, reveals the conventional aspect of
Wordsworth's reasoning and suggests an unsettling corollary: if
people are what they read, then a poetics grounded on rural illiteracy may just replace one set of fictional types by hypothesized
counterparts. How, in other words, are dissipated readers to recognize the "language really spoken by men," and how will it
change them if they do? De Quincey offers one answer to this question, but only by twisting a polemic on the nature and function of
poetic language into a romance of compulsive mimesis – addiction
and repetition.

The "gross and violent stimulants" of Wordsworth's "Preface"
become a "stimulating class of desires" in De Quincey's more
seductive narrative. The phrase echoes in passages of the
Confessions describing his early opium debauches, but the language of intoxication predates its most famous referent.[7] Always
already intoxicated, De Quincey addicted himself to addiction
before he began his long affair with laudanum. Addiction for him
is first a condition of reading and only secondarily a physiological
fact; it begins when readers identify themselves with figures in
books. According to Wordsworth, genre fiction encourages
boundless desire, a "degrading thirst after outrageous stimulation"
(*PrW* 1:130). De Quincey's gothic spin on this idea suggests that a
sense of intoxicating boundlessness may inhere in the experience
of reading. For De Quincey, this suspension ("dreams of meditation") translates into a limitless absorption of literary models.
Addiction, in other words, is mimesis in reverse, life endlessly imitating art. With the apprehension of his own textual origins, De
Quincey converts a cultural phenomenon into a personal theme.
His confession carries a virulent strain of narcissism endemic to his
reading habits: the coy articulation of his mania makes loss of
control available as a rhetorical effect. Insinuating himself into
literary history by emulating gothic villains, he draws a portrait of
the artist as young parasite, feeding on delirious texts. His adaptation of the "Preface" neatly substitutes an autobiographical subject
for Wordsworth's abstract one. This maneuver, finally, gains a ret

rospective plausibility from the way it recapitulates both the themes and the obscurity of Wordsworth's poetic experiments before *Lyrical Ballads*. Gothic De Quincey, the "Dark Interpreter" of the "Preface" (*C* 156), emerges from the underside of Wordsworthian theory.[8]

Wordsworth's speculations about the mental costs of constant stimulation assume a pattern in De Quincey. Fall prepares the way for redemption; mimetic debauch leads ineluctably to Wordsworthian restoration. "Admidst [*sic*] all these feverish & turbulent dreams of meditation," De Quincey continues,

it was not possible that I, maintained from my infancy in the Love of Nature, should not, at times relent & resign myself to a confused feeling of purer & more permanent pleasure flowing from other sources – therefore during my long & lonely rambles through many beautiful scenes sometimes in the stillness & silence of surrounding nature, & sometimes in her merest sights & sounds I felt her mild reproach, and so, gradually prepared for being weaned from my temporary frenzy, I looked round for some guide who might assist to develope & to tutor my new feelings, & then it was that from a recollection of the deep impression made on me by the short poem I have mentioned I knew where to seek that guidance, & where I sought, I found it. (*J* 37)

For Wordsworth, love of nature leads to love of mankind. For De Quincey, love of nature leads to love of "We Are Seven." "We Are Seven" then turns De Quincey toward a cure for his frenzied gothicism. On first glance, his redemption consists simply of exchanging a pernicious model for a benignly strenuous one. "The recovery of a healthier tone," he later stated of Wordsworth's "maturer taste," "presuppose[s] a difficult process of weaning, and an effort of discipline for reorganizing the whole internal economy of the sensibilities, that is both painful and mortifying" (*R* 172). But what does De Quincey find, when he begins his *sortes Wordsworthianae*?[9] The supplicant's half-quotations and allusions follow a more labyrinthine path than the narrative line suggests.

Thus, the first part of this passage suggests an uncomplicated appropriation of themes developed in the "Preface" and "Tintern Abbey": the ethical influence of Nature; its permanence and purity compared to the "din/ Of towns and cities" (*PW* 164:25–26); its role as a nurse to the developing mind. In "Tintern Abbey," the child's unthinking closeness to nature is described as gradually modulating into dialectical awareness. For De Quincey, the "reproach" of Nature lacks the authority to cause moral change: it prepares him to be weaned, but does not actually break his habit. Nature's reproach leads him to seek "some guide" analogous to Wordsworth's Dorothy, who appears just as magically near the conclusion of "Tintern Abbey." De Quincey's guide, however, is neither nature nor another person, but a poem; or rather, the *recollection* of its "deep impression" tells De Quincey "where to *seek*." His equivocation on this point refers the role of guide to three implied objects: "We Are Seven," the short poem; *Lyrical Ballads*, the book it comes from; and Wordsworth, the poet who wrote the book. On the one hand, "We Are Seven" is elevated into synecdoche; on the other, the image of a human companion disappears, to be replaced by a string of metrically arranged words. The intricate syntax personifies "We Are Seven" and textualizes Wordsworth.

More significant than these parallels is the way De Quincey reconceives the structure of memory that organizes "Tintern Abbey." Both the poem and his letter are generated by the notion of reactivating a previous experience, so that the interval between the original event and its repetition divides an unthinking or merely potential self from the chastened perspective of the present speaker. Wordsworth revisits a landscape, while De Quincey recollects a poem he once saw. Just as Wordsworth's speaker values the scene for its later transmutation into a "picture of the mind," so De Quincey's "deep impression" acquires depth retroactively, when abetted by reproachful Nature. This deferred action advertises De Quincey's complex grasp of Wordsworthian subjectivity. The same principle helps De Quincey to explain how "We Are Seven" could affect him so singularly at so young an age, an idea the poem itself – with its emphasis upon the child's "inability to admit" verbal distinctions (*PrW* 1:126) – apparently contradicts. How could one text both initiate the child into consciousness and also culminate the evolving consciousness that arose through the love of Nature? Describing his return to "We Are Seven," De Quincey outlines a bookish variation on "Tintern Abbey," one more readily assimilable to the reflexive temporality of Freudian *nachträglichkeit*.[10] A poem once seen becomes meaningful – and scenic – by means of an interpretive schema acquired after the fact. De Quincey calls this schema Nature, but, as his long digression on influence suggests, his Nature comes straight out of literature. This account of development, and of interpretation, situates the genesis of the subject in revisionary reading. "We Are Seven" assumes the place-saving function held by the locale in "Tintern Abbey."

The perversity of this exchange consists in the attribution of a moral, a developmental model, and an epistemology derived from a poem "written in the highest" to one "in the humblest style" (*BL* 1:70), as Coleridge would have seen it. "Tintern Abbey" is never even mentioned, acting instead as the neutral ground for a poetic figure. De Quincey's suppression elicits particular scrutiny of the different ways the two poems represent relations between a poet-figure and his "second self." While it is conceivable that De Quincey was unaware of his own confusion, the contestatory scenario of "We Are Seven" also makes it more vulnerable than "Tintern Abbey" to antithetical manipulation, as well as more susceptible to ventriloquistic self-inscription. The first half of his letter clearly indicates De Quincey's intention to find a niche in the Wordsworth circle; and the Wordsworth circle (or triangle) is, as he well knows, a textual construct. To enter it he must rewrite the script, but some scripts are easier to crack than others. Coleridge's "Ode to the Rain," for example – which De Quincey probably read in the *Morning Post* of October 7, 1802 – represents the poets and their "sister dear" as private to the point of hermeticism:

> We three dear friends! in truth, we groan
> Impatiently to be alone.
> We three, you mark! and not one more!
>
> (*CPW* 384:45–47)

By contrast with this poem and with "Tintern Abbey," the numerical argument of "We Are Seven" concedes both the possibility of "one more" and the social causes and consequences of variant interpretations.

Though formally and tonally dissimilar, "Tintern Abbey" and "We Are Seven" raise related questions about how to accommodate loss and the passage of time within consciousness. Both also explore the extent to which one person can resolve these issues for another. Both poems, that is, dramatize models of tutelage: each speaker assumes the authority of greater experience over the character being addressed, an authority secured by the other's obedient memory or correct response. The speaker attempts the task of reforming the other's sense of completeness; in each case, he imagines a relationship between a developing self and its missing parts, figured as dead siblings.

If this sounds too lofty or abstract to count as a description of "We Are Seven," that is at least partly because the poem's resolution parodies the sentiments of more meditative and less ironized Wordsworthian voices, such as the voice of "Tintern Abbey." In "Tintern Abbey," the positing of a tutelary bond between the poet and his auditor hinges on a muted appeal to violence. For the speaker to assume his proper place in his companion's mind, he must project her fall into "solitude, or fear, or pain, or grief" (*LB* 117:144); to need a guide, she must become needy. The poet's reliance on his listener's suffering is veiled by his professions of love for her; and the erotic scenario these declarations suggest is in turn cancelled by the names he uses: "friend" and "sister." The coerciveness of "We Are Seven"'s speaker is unrestrained by any comparable affective bond. Equally inflexible, the haunted little girl in the churchyard literalizes the conceit of the mind as "a mansion for all lovely forms" (*LB* 117:141). She evidently shocked Coleridge, who saw her fidelity as the expression of a "horrid . . . belief" in live burial (*BL* 2:141).[11] The poem's sexual charge has attracted less comment than its gothic undertones, perhaps because readers have accepted the terms of its pedagogical dilemma: what should "a simple child . . . know of death?" (*LB* 66:1–4).

The frankness of the sexuality in "We Are Seven" is best appreciated by reference to Coleridge's efforts at masking it. In the first stanza, which he wrote after Wordsworth had completed the rest, Coleridge frames a delicate encounter between an ungendered infant and a speaker whose "dear brother Jim" (66:1) suggests an analogy between child and adult. But Wordsworth's heroine is no disembodied voice, nor is she presented as typical of all children. Instead, she has been closely, if partially, observed:

> Her hair was thick with many a curl
> That cluster'd round her head.

> She had a rustic, woodland air,
> And she was wildly clad;
> Her eyes were fair, and very fair,
> – Her beauty made me glad.   (*LB* 66:7–12)

This abbreviation of the courtly blazon, recalling the "shooting lights/ Of thy wild eyes" in "Tintern Abbey," invests the pastoral scene of instruction with certain peculiar allures.[12] The man instructs the little maid first by seeking particular responses, and then by editing and parcelling out the words she produces. The lesson to be learned is about subtraction: the girl, who persists in believing that her dead siblings count as family, should be brought to identify the personal pronoun with less than seven referents. To tame her wild will, the man must make her recognize a gap in her own consciousness. In one sense he attempts the opposite of the "Tintern Abbey" speaker – to shatter a familial identity, rather than to nurture it. For both, however, the condition of being civilized is defined in terms of a felt loss, and each designates himself as guide to the knowledge beyond nature. And in each poem, the formation of a mind takes place across gender boundaries and is hedged by language traditionally reserved for courtship.

Both the continuities and the discrepancies between "We Are Seven" and "Tintern Abbey" hinge on their representations of the feminine figure. If only because "Tintern Abbey" is an internalized "conversation" while "We Are Seven" recounts a dialogue, the poems' interlocutors necessarily perform different structural roles. For De Quincey, these characters embody the relative attractions of one poem over the other. The position of the "dear, dear friend" in "Tintern Abbey" is both close to the poet (whose likeness she is) and representative of a universalized developmental stage and mode of perception. She is invoked late in a poem that until that point had seemed to be addressed either to the poet's own consciousness or to an anonymous public, and she looks on nature with a quick and joyful but untutored eye, one that has not yet learned to hear the sad music of humanity in the landscape it sees. She is, in short, a stand-in for the reader, learning to read like Wordsworth. The situation of the child in "We Are Seven" precludes this naturalization of apostrophe. Particular in her appearance, but nameless except for the tautological assertion that "we are seven," she is represented as refusing the admission that would catapult her into recognizably modern (in Coleridge's term, "Christian") and individual identity. Less a reader's surrogate than is the poet's sister, the cottage girl more closely resembles a personification, clad in the rustic remnants of allegorical romance.[13] A pre-subjective creature meeting her caricatured opposite, she knows no time when she was not as now. Of all Wordsworth's poems, then, "We Are Seven" seems among the least likely to replace "Tintern Abbey" as the locus of a reader's identification. It is to the very impossibility of the child's position, however – her appearance of intransigent and creaturely victimage – that De Quincey responds.

At the end of "We Are Seven," the speaker's best efforts have not budged the "little Maid" from her claim that "we" are indeed seven. The speaker calls this tenacity willfulness, with the implication that a more tractable child would submit to the teachings of her elders. In its portrayal of cross purposes, the poem invites adjudication by readers who may side with one character over the other, or reconcile their competing claims.[14] De Quincey does neither, and both. In the last paragraph of his letter he adopts a new persona and family of tropes, as literary as those he borrowed from German Drama. The turn to the eschatological is announced by a Gospel reminiscence: "where I sought, I found it."

And now dr Sir at this day I – once so bewildered & wretched find myself delivered from much undue influence or rather bondage, & many wrong tendencies of passion which involved in themselves the needs of infinite misery. I feel every principle of good within me purified & uplifted – & above all I have such visions of future happiness opened to me as, in my deepest fits of gloom are sufficient continually to sustain & cheer me for since that time I have prayed for the hour when I shall become my own Master, as that in which I shall assert my perfect freedom, & I look forward, after some years travelling to no less happiness (for higher surely cannot be) than to live with those of my Brothers & Sisters who still remain to me, in solitary converse with Nature. (*J* 37–38)

De Quincey surrenders little of his gothic glamour in this renunciation, the "wrong tendencies of passion" lingering as a reminder of the various genres being superimposed. This melancholy flair nearly obscures the affinity between his "solitary converse" and the "We Are Seven" girl's converse with the dead. Like the cottage girl deferentially addressing her "Master" or "Sir," De Quincey is a minor (only eighteen), the coeval of living and dead siblings rather than a head of household. But unlike that *simple* child, he understands that the dead brothers and sisters are lost, and only proposes to cohabit with the living. Thus, without ever positing a direct correspondence ("once I was a gothic despot, but now I am an innocent child"), De Quincey adopts the vocabulary of a fictional character while modifying that character's emblematic stance. As opposed to his explicit identification with characters of ancient story, his echo of "We Are Seven" intimates a suspended identification and subtle play of differences.[15] This rhetorical maneuver, entailing the transfer of qualities from an allegorical figure to a reader, derives its pathos from the way it inverts the workings of personification. In his reflexive turn on the imaginary, the childlike De Quinceyan reader appears fragile, abstract and permeable. Considered as strategy, however, De Quincey's play of abstraction and sympathetic absorption makes audible a voice – however contingent – he represents as his own. By animating this "nature sprite"[16] rather than a pseudo-subject like Dorothy, De Quincey obtains the pleasure of supplementing Wordsworth's "company of flesh and blood" (*PrW* 1:130).

Crucial to this strategy is his glancing reference to a depleted roster. In contrast with the child of "We Are Seven," De Quincey has learned his subtraction lesson; he has, as it were, been cured. Cure figured as originary loss further disqualifies his remaining siblings, a broken set, from participation in his "solitary" reverie. De Quincey projects his rebirth into humanized consciousness as the moment when he tabulates his human "additions" and still finds himself incomplete: his subjectivity is simultaneous with its own fracture. Both moments also coincide with De Quincey's "weaning" from narcissistic frenzy and his gesture of submission to the author of his being. To abstract a reader, then, is also to subjectify a personification. De Quincey is born when a figure falls into reflection; when an abstraction sheds human tears; when the father's word is made flesh.

The transition seems inevitable rather than outrageous because De Quincey rewrites Wordsworth's mediated dialogue as a dramatic script for two parts. This device initially clarifies the roles of the seeker and his guide, a guide no longer envisioned as text but instead, less ambiguously, as an authoritative older man. The script also conjures a scenic backdrop: "visions of future happiness" that counterpoint a present state of aestheticized gloom. Sustained in "fits" of unpleasure by these pleasing images, De Quincey enacts a masochistic reading of "We Are Seven." The rubric of masochism links an attraction to victimage with an inversion of gender; to ventriloquize the child means to adopt the feminine role as the poem articulates it. De Quincey's transference is therefore characteristic of masochism, defined as a marked convergence of sexuality and representation.

Adela Pinch suggests in an essay on *Lyrical Ballads* that any "transaction between subject and representation" may be regarded as a "masochistic relation to a representation" because it recapitulates the simultaneous emergence of fantasy, the unconscious, and sexuality in a "turning round upon the subject."[17] The structure of masochism, in which masculine subjects "transfer themselves into the part of a woman," mediates the confrontation with paternal law through a theatrical understanding of identification (*SE* 17:197). As performed, however, the masochistic scenario troubles the very poles (active and passive, "freedom" and "bondage," even master and pupil) upon which its thematic inflection relies. Sadomasochism raises the problem of subjective autonomy in an especially acute form because, by definition, two subjectivities are implicated in its structure. De Quincey's masochism, acting on Wordsworthian tropes, threatens the integrity of Wordsworth's corpus as well as disfiguring his own. If De Quincey's dark interpretation of the "Preface" cast himself as the poet's gothic unconscious, here tropic drift between text and intertext gives rise to an eerily familiar voice: De Quincey confronts Wordsworth as the very personification of the uncanny.[18] By the last paragraph of his letter, it is uncertain whether Wordsworth is correcting De Quincey, or the reverse; or whether indeed both identities have dissolved into merely characteristic textual effects.

The unfolding of subjectivity as *textual* character, as convention, is as characteristically De Quinceyan as it is characteristically poststructuralist. De Quincey is never more at home than in the discovery that he has previously "been contemplated in types," has even "been reading a legend concerning [him]self": inverting the Lacanian imaginary, he "literally reproduce[s] in [him]self" the protagonist of some "mere fiction" (*C* 135).[19] His uncanny repetition seductively intimates an unconscious not thematic but more fundamentally linguistic, a movement that transports his rhetoric out of the domain of individual consciousness. Alluring as such an insight may be, however, the conclusion that subjective boundaries between Wordsworth and De Quincey are simply not stable risks defusing the further recognition that erasure of these boundaries is part of the De Quinceyan – or analytical – project.

The critical temptation to invoke pairs like consciousness and the unconscious arises partly in response to De Quincey's thematic emphasis on passivity, coupled with his lack of anxiety about literary priority.[20] De Quincey generally pictures himself as either the victim or the beneficiary of "undue influence," whether recalling how he "was shewn" "We Are Seven" or imagining future bliss. Even his plan to "assert . . . perfect freedom" suggests nothing so much as the freedom to prostrate himself. But what takes the place of any agonistic self-definition is a startling claim of election – "where *I sought, I found*" – that breaks with his otherwise passive persona. The sudden shift in register indicates a strategic aspect of his transference, and the alternation of active and passive voices once again recalls Laplanche's account of masochism, in which submission becomes indistinguishable from its opposite. The positions of sadist and masochist originate in the same moment of reflexivity; the sadist identifies with the masochist; the masochist begins as an aggressor.[21] The masochist, subject of self-abnegation, orients himself theatrically through and against another subject, defined retroactively as the more powerful of the two. Thus De Quincey's testimonial performs the corrective swerve that he, like Harold Bloom, calls *clinamen* – with the difference, however, that he proves his precursor both more right, and less "knowing," than the hapless speaker of "We Are Seven" could have guessed.[22] In his weak concession of influence, then, De Quincey occupies the *strong* position of an "unconscious" his testimonial has *produced.* The masochistic stance, in this sense, serves his interest, while also magnifying the (critical) interest of Wordsworth's text. For De Quincey, then, textual drift converts to a mode of persuasion, while the revelation of the unconscious is also a seduction.[23]

De Quincey, that is, conceives his transmission of a poetic effect as the inducement to a counter-transference. "As the consumation [*sic*] of all earthly good," and to supplement the company of his siblings, he hopes "to enjoy if not an intimate connexion yet perhaps (if it is your good pleasure)" (*J* 38) – but here the letter breaks off, censored or merely set aside by its copyist, Dorothy Wordsworth.[24] Though it would not be difficult for any reader of De Quincey's early letters to fill in a plausible conclusion, this one ends suspended in mid-sentence, a token of the distance between what has been discarded (psychological "intimacy," a variant on friendship) and other conceivable connections. Framed as a boon, wholly within Wordsworth's power to grant or to refuse, De

Quincey's interpretive desire is, like a Freudian dream-wish, already fulfilled in its own displaced articulation. Unnamed or even unnameable, this "connexion" can be figured as the inheritance that descends to the poet's future representative.

The strategic figure of passivity is also a rhetorician, at pains to earn the title he has written for himself. To penetrate the charmed (and closed) "circle of human beings in whom half my love, & all my admiration are centred" (*J* 36), De Quincey presents himself as the figure of lyrical childhood, chastened and subdued. Wordsworth's subject in two senses, the incarnation of language as "incarnation," he is thus also father of the poet's posterity. The circle opens out into a family in need of heirs. Yet as chastened *daughter* rather than sister, brother, or son, De Quincey exemplifies poetic influence as the reticulated family-romance (superimposing "the sexual appetite" for "similitude in dissimilitude" [*PrW* 1:149] upon generational discontinuity) that is repressed by the Bloomian ideal of "strength." If "Tintern Abbey," finally, envisions the House of Fame as a "dwelling-place" for pious "exhortations," De Quincey represents transmission as a violent and faintly ridiculous courtship: a willing assumption of "contumely and ridicule" (*R* 33), a subjection by force rather than example. The pedagogical imaginary of "Tintern Abbey" figures the impression of mind upon mind as physical and psychological likeness:

> . . . in thy voice I catch
> The language of my former heart, and read
> My former pleasures in the shooting lights
> Of thy wild eyes. Oh! yet a little while
> May I behold in thee what I was once,
> My dear, dear Sister!   (*LB* 117:117–22)

De Quinceyan or *minor* transmission, by contrast, speaks the strange language of the Other, or the rhetoric of temporality. To be the true child of Wordsworth (knowing his work better than he himself does) is to be subject to this linguistic effect, binding oneself to the father by the force of figures that are his own and not his own. De Quincey's acquaintance with Wordsworth entails the postulate of a fall into gothic emulation so that he can be restored by the suspended identification, or personification, that places him both within and without the poet's control. In this letter, so influential in shaping that acquaintance, De Quincey offers himself as a creature made in the image of poetry, "your's for ever" (*J*31). Wordsworth, like Frankenstein, must either accept the offering or repudiate his own creation.

"THE SUBJECT IS INDEED IMPORTANT!"

In fact, as Marcel Mauss observes, "one does not have the right to refuse a gift," particularly the radicalized kind in which "a man gives himself."[25] The correspondence between Wordsworth and his epigone had already assumed the characteristics of gift-exchange, to judge by the two long, appreciative, and unusually confiding letters the poet sent De Quincey even before he received this more specialized tribute. On this occasion he reiterated how "much pleasure it gave" him

> to learn that my Poems had been of such eminent service to you as you describe. May God grant that you may persevere in all good habits, desires, and resolutions.
>
> Such facts as you have communicated to me are an abundant recompense for all the labour and pains which the profession of Poetry requires, and without which nothing permanent or good can be produced. (*EY* 458)

The echo of "Tintern Abbey" attests to Wordsworth's perception that like the "gift" he claimed in that poem, De Quincey offers the "abundant recompence" of a second self who will preserve his writings on the mind (*LB* 116:89; *Prelude* 6:218). By having Dorothy transcribe the letter into his commonplace book – an honor he had accorded neither to De Quincey's earlier testimonials nor to his first devotee, John Wilson – the poet delegated one surrogate to induct another.[26] In De Quincey's peculiar epistle, Wordsworth found an apostle: the original member of what Coleridge described as a "school of imitators, a company of almost *religious* admirers . . . among young men of ardent minds, liberal education and not 'with academic laurels unbestowed'" (*BL* 1:75).

De Quincey later proudly recalled "the prophetic eye and the intrepidity" that distinguished himself and Wilson from his Oxford classmates, ignorant as they were of "their own domestic literature" and of Wordsworth above all (*R* 114–18). In the immediacy and intensity of his admiration De Quincey resembled Coleridge himself, who, when "during the last year of [his] residence at Cambridge" he "became acquainted with Mr. Wordsworth's first publication," had felt that "seldom, if ever, was the emergence of an original poetic genius above the literary horizon more evidently announced" (*BL* 1:77). But De Quincey, having unlike Coleridge no independent reputation as an author, represented for the Wordsworths an unimpeachable test of the poet's empirical effectiveness. As Dorothy remarked in a letter to Lady Beaumont,

I think of this young man [De Quincey] with extraordinary pleasure, as he is a remarkable instance of the power of my Brother's poems, over a lonely and contemplative mind, unwarped by any established laws of taste . . . a pure and innocent mind! (*MY* 1:180)

The iterability of the "We Are Seven" syndrome is legible in Dorothy's rapturous portrayal of a *tabula rasa* newly inscribed by her brother. Ignoring the gothic interval that frames De Quincey's account of his conversion, Dorothy relocates terroristic influence in the "power" of Wordsworth's poetry to restore primary impulses. "Except ye be converted and become as little children," there can be no attaining the kingdom of poetry; for "have ye never read, Out of the mouths of babes and sucklings thou hast perfected praise?" (Matthew 18:3, 21:16).[27]

Self-destined "worshipper" or pliant "example," De Quincey is to be valued as the sagacious child of the Gospels. Wordsworth's precepts on "good habits, desires and resolutions" thus enlist both correspondents in the Pauline narrative evoked by his disciple's repudiation of "lawless pleasure" and evil "influence."[28] "I do not mean to preach," the poet implausibly concludes after expressing his hope

that you have not been seduced into unworthy pleasures or pursuits . . . I need not say to you that there is no true dignity but in virtue and temperance, and let me add, chastity; and that the best safeguard of all these is the cultivation of pure pleasures, namely, those of the intellect and affections. (*EY* 453–54)

Whatever their spontaneous motivations in feeling, these injunctions also obey the law of their genre. Paul's epistles to Timothy, his "son in the faith," similarly counsel against "partak[ing] of other men's sins." "Keep thyself pure," Paul advises, while prescribing "a little wine for thy stomach's sake and thine often infirmities" (1 Timothy 5:22–23).

Wordsworth's adoption of the Pauline persona does not so much indicate a project of "temporal redemption" as it illustrates the magnetism of narrative clarity: his discovery of vocation is contemporaneous and correlative with De Quincey's.[29] The subtext that will orient Wordsworth toward an increasingly explicit prophetic role (in the *Prelude*'s Book Thirteenth, for example) gives the disciple a more contingent and equivocal part to play. To be converted is to shed the "bondage" of childhood without quite emerging from minority, as Paul explains in Galatians 3:26–4:7.

For ye are all the children of God by faith in Christ Jesus. . . . And if ye be Christ's, then are ye Abraham's seed, and heirs according to the promise. Now I say, That the heir, as long as he is a child, differeth nothing from a servant, though he be lord of all; But is under tutors and governors until the time appointed of the father. Even so we, when we were children, were in bondage under the elements of the world: But when the fulness of the time was come, God sent forth his Son, made of a woman, made under the law, To redeem them that were under the law, that we might receive the adoption of sons. And because ye are sons, God hath sent forth the Spirit of his Son into your hearts, crying, Abba, Father. Wherefore thou art no more a servant, but a son; and if a son, then an heir of God through Christ.[30]

Having resolved that by his "seventeenth birth-day" he "would no longer be numbered among school-boys" (*C* 8), De Quincey has indeed liberated himself from the five "tutors and governors" who had managed his upbringing since his father's death. Taking Providence and Wordsworth as his guides, he carries "a favourite English poet in one pocket; and a small 12mo. volume, containing about nine plays of Euripides, in the other" (*C* 11). This promotion from "servant" to Wordsworthian "heir" does not constitute maturity, however; De Quincey dismisses as chimerical any "precise era" at which an individual has "ceased to be a boy, and" has "attained his inauguration as a man," even claiming that "as regards the moral development . . . hardly any of our species ever attain manhood" (*M* 1:317–18). To "receive the adoption of" Wordsworthian disciple is to embrace what De Quincey would call a "reversionary" identity, attenuating the transition from child-hood to adulthood into a passage both already accomplished and evermore about to be.

De Quincey's "Primal Scene of Instruction," to adapt a trope from Bloom's scriptural reading of literary history, consummates a love supposedly "unconditioned in its giving, but wholly condi-tioned to passivity in its receiving."[31] As Coleridge paints such a

disciple

scene in "To William Wordsworth," the disciple listens "in silence," "passive," "like a devout child," "driven as in surges" by "thoughts bec[o]me/ A bodily tumult" (*CPW* 406–08). Arrested at the moment of conversion, De Quincey *cathects* this "spasmodically potent . . . state of suffering and disquiet," recurring again and again to the "anguish of revival" sustained in such "cases of suspended animation" (*R* 173). "A primitive Christian amongst a nation of Pagans," he carries "his devotion about with him as the profoundest of secrets," like "a lover" sheltering "the name of his beloved" from "the coarse license of a Bacchanalian party" (*M* 3:42; *R* 33–34). Unlike St. Augustine he is not turned from "rhetoric" toward proselytism, but from one private textual pleasure to another. His "almost . . . blamable adoration" (*R* 123) perverts evangelical teleology into a whirligig of reactive subjectivity.

Whereas for Wordsworth, the evangelical narrative offers a career trajectory, to De Quincey it suggests a language for consciousness as such. Wordsworth's "revolutionary principles" "had to struggle," De Quincey asserts,

against sympathies long trained in an opposite direction . . . for – and that is worthy of deep attention – the misgivings of any vicious or unhealthy state; the impulses and suspicious gleams of the truth struggling with cherished error; the instincts of light conflicting with darkness – these are the real causes of that hatred and intolerant scorn which is ever awakened by the first dawnings of new and important systems of truth. Therefore it is that Christianity was so much more hated than any mere novel variety of error. Therefore are the first feeble struggles of nature towards a sounder state of health, always harsh and discordant; for the false system which this change for the better disturbs, had, at least, this soothing advantage – that it was self-consistent. Therefore, also, was the Wordsworthian restoration of elementary power, and of a higher or transcendent truth of nature . . . received at first with such malignant disgust. For there was a galvanic awakening in the shock of power, as it jarred against the ancient system of prejudices, which inevitably revealed so much of truth as made the mind jealous that all was not right, and just so far affected as to be dissatisfied with its existing creed, but not at all raised up to the level of the new creed; enlightened enough to descry its own wanderings, but not enough to recover the right road. (*R* 172–73)

The overlay of physiology upon theology identifies the corporate body of the literate public with the eroticized body of the De Quinceyan convert. De Quincey thus reads his own "recovery of a healthier tone" as the synecdoche of a revolution at the epistemic level, entailing a "transformation" in "the whole economy of . . . thoughts" (*R* 174). Its ultimate cause extends beyond even the prophetic poet to the French Revolution, which gave to Wordsworth "a sense of the awful *realities* which surround the mind; by comparison with which the previous literary tastes seemed . . . fanciful and trivial." Poets at this juncture, writes De Quincey with another bow to St. Paul, "everywhere felt themselves to be putting away childish things, and . . . entering upon the dignity and the sincere thinking of mature manhood" (*R* 174–75). Here De Quincey diagnoses the metahistorical "shift from the self as static . . . and inherited to the rounded, psychological and self-made subject" that Clifford Siskin christens "a new *developing* self."[32] The disciple's personal cure intimates a collective translation into a new "stage of life" (*C* 107), a consensual picture of human nature characterized by the mastery of change as organic maturation.

However self-dramatizing, De Quincey's allegorical reading of *Lyrical Ballads* and its reception constitutes a plausible line of response to the more messianic strains of Wordsworth's "Preface." Invoking "revolutions, not of literature alone, but likewise of society itself," the "Preface" erects its famous case for poetry on the need to reform "moral relations" (*PrW* 1:121, 158). Its didacticism grows most conspicuous when Wordsworth explains the "general importance of the [poetic] subject" for counteracting "depraved" mental processes (*PrW* 1:128).

The subject is indeed important! For the human mind is capable of excitement without the application of gross and violent stimulants; and he must have a very faint perception of its beauty and dignity who does not know this, and who does not further know that one being is elevated above another in proportion as he possesses this capability. It has therefore appeared to me that to endeavour to produce or enlarge this capability is one of the best services in which . . . a Writer can be engaged. (*PrW* 1:128)

According to Wordsworth, poetry should not merely exalt the taste, but should also enlighten the understanding and ameliorate the affections of its readers (*PrW* 1:126); it both demands and cultivates a populace capable of increasingly refined ethical discriminations. Or, as he more succinctly phrased the problem with the help of Coleridge, "every author, as far as he is great and at the same time *original*, has had the task of *creating* the taste by which

he is to be enjoyed" (*PrW* 3:80, 102). The ethical purpose "hails,"
to use Althusser's term, a reconfigured "subject," stopped in his
lawless tracks by a blinding light and a disembodied voice.[33] In
1817, Coleridge would describe in like fashion the "sudden effect
produced on [his] mind" by Wordsworth's recitation of "Salisbury
Plain," which he experienced as an "awaken[ing]" to a "freshness
of sensation which is the constant accompaniment of mental, no
less than of bodily, convalescence" (*BL* 1:78–81). For De Quincey,
as for Coleridge, Wordsworth is the good physician of human
nature. But whereas Coleridge, Wordsworth's theorist and impresario, "no sooner felt, than [he] sought to understand" (*BL* 1:82),
De Quincey simply presents himself to Wordsworth as the creation
that vindicates the poet's originality. The first "pupil" of
Wordsworth's "new school," he redeems Francis Jeffrey's ridicule
by giving it substance.[34]

Wordsworth's second epistle to De Quincey offers his own "life"
as precedent for the embryonic subject he has engendered. The
letter was so important to him that, believing it lost, he instructed
his disciple to apply for it at the Dead Letter Office (*EY* 457–58).
Appropriating the Augustinian *tolle e lege*, he confesses "writing a
Poem on my own earlier life" which

it would give me great pleasure to read . . . to you at this time. As I am
sure, from the interest you have taken in the L.B. that it would please you,
and might also be of service to you. This Poem will not be published these
many years, and never during my lifetime, till I have finished a larger and
more important work to which it is tributary . . . I have taken the liberty
of saying this much of my own concerns to you, not doubting that it would
interest you. You have as yet have [*sic*] had little knowledge of me but as
a Poet; but I hope, if we live, we shall be still more nearly united. (*EY* 454)

In Wordsworth's secret ministry, the "service" of redemption
extends a series of correspondences, from Paul, Antony and
Augustine down to Wordsworth's "residence at the University" and
De Quincey's emulation. Wordsworth's spiritual autobiography
prescribes De Quincey's behavior at Oxford, to keep him free from
"diseases of the mind" until the son in the faith shall be "more
nearly united" with his master.[35]

The discrepancy between Wordsworth's relentless, but orthodox, narrative of self-replication and De Quincey's masochistic
turn on "We Are Seven" suggests the strain exerted upon their
shared model by the jurisdictional ambitions to which it gives

shape.[36] De Quincey's belated response to Wordsworth's pastoral letter (which had crossed with his own confession) underlines its apocalyptic threat while amplifying its internal dissonance. "To the world at large," De Quincey concedes, the poet's "greater work" (the projected *Recluse*) must be "more extensively useful." But against these dutiful petitions "for [his] country's sake" he balances his more wayward "individual gratification." "Any person, who is not a perfect stranger to you, must wish most earnestly to see that work completed which you . . . call the least important of the three," he stipulates, adding that

the poem on your own life is the one which I should most anxiously wish to see finished; and I do indeed look with great expectation for the advent of that day, on which I may hear you read it, as the happiest I shall see. (*J* 39)

The life itself here stands enfranchised of what the "world at large" calls "works." If, however, De Quincey discerns the poet's true jurisdiction, the growth of an individual mind, he also intuits the finality of Wordsworth's return on his *own* gift. Here is a stroke that cannot be parried: the promise of a "face to face" encounter with his maker. "The very image of Wordsworth," De Quincey later claimed, "crushed my faculties as before Elijah or St Paul" (*R* 122). Committed by this scriptural analogy to an idealization of presence, he defers his meeting with Wordsworth – "that man whom, of all the men from the beginning of time, I most fervently desired to see" (*R* 127) – for more than four years, until he can bring it off through an orchestrated accident.

The "interval" or "advent" that must precede this climactic day represents a temporizing strategy rather than a term of self-perfection. De Quincey's epistolary exchange with Wordsworth is governed not by successful, but by *missed*, correspondence: pastoral letters gone astray, "transforming forced delay into strategic deferment."[37] Generic exigencies dictated the mirroring of pastor and disciple, but only its corruption by errors of timing allowed this exchange to continue. De Quincey "addressed" his first letter to Wordsworth in 1802, sent it in 1803, and received his answer "at the very moment when" he had "ceased to expect it"; virtually all his letters thereafter begin with apologies for their belatedness (*R* 116; *J* 32). Bad timing sustains epistolary desire in spite of its impossible premise. This attenuation saves the "mimetic lure" of pastoral correspondence from its own legitimizing fiction; for while the spirit giveth life, the letter killeth. De Quincey can only begin his career, scripting his minor conversion, in the absence of his "absolute Other," Wordsworth's epistle on the *Prelude*. If, as Lacan claims, "a letter always arrives at its destination," this is because it has already "been diverted from its path."[38]

In the guise of errant apostle, De Quincey fulfills Wordsworth's desire for an iterable testimonial – the type of a repeatable cure. Not in fact a prophet, Wordsworth requires some "recompense for all the labour and pains which the profession of poetry requires." Evangelism supplies one vocabulary for this reward: a credential of professional competence in that most abstract of domains, the human heart. "A man speaking to men" (*LB* 255) in the voice "of classes to which [he] did not [himself] belong," Wordsworth extrapolates the need for his services from the retroactive confirmation that a constituency had gone unspoken for.[39] By attesting to his Wordsworthian cure, De Quincey marks the efficacy of a new form of social power, which both parties mistake for "apostolic fervour of holy zealotry" (*R* 181). The nature of this *méconnaissance*, and the way it structured the reciprocal desires of agent and patient, would not lack consequences in their later meetings and misunderstandings. It is one paradox of professionalism that, as a creed without a scripture, it disseminates through error and scandal (lest a chronic jurisdiction be simply eradicated); the price of an apostle is apostasy.

De Quincey's answer to Wordsworth's call exploits the inherent tension in professionalist ideology between egalitarian rhetoric and the drive toward acceptance as a class by the dominant class. A ventriloquist of infantine simplicity, the Oxford scholar embodies democratic "reception" both despite and because of his class disparity with the real men Wordsworth claims to represent.[40] In his very singularity, De Quincey exposes the theoretical fissure between the collective, rural objects of Wordsworth's expertise and the poet's requirement, as an individual practitioner, for a specific, voluntary and self-conscious client. The subject of Wordsworthian discourse is a split subject, corresponding neither to the laborers that populate his poems nor to the literacracy he addresses in his "Preface." Wordsworth's subject, in short, is imaginary; the personification of De Quincey gives this phantom its empirical presence.

PERSONAL ACCOUNTS

The sustaining contradiction of the minor's discipleship – the representation of ethical growth as psychic regression – suggests both a plausible extension and an eccentric variant on the "behavioral truth" of development with which, Siskin argues, Romantic historiography "naturalize[d] the destabilizing experience of social and literary change."[41] On the one hand, De Quincey's insistence that "children have a specific power of contemplating the truth, which departs as they enter the world" (*C* 127) elaborates on the theme of the child prominent in Coleridge's conversation poems, Wordsworth's Intimations Ode, and the *Prelude*. Under the rubric of education ("whatsoever *educes* or *developes*") De Quincey offers his life to illustrate "a necessity of all children" (*C* 147, 113). In *Suspiria de Profundis*, for example, he shapes the "deep, mysterious identity between himself, as adult and as infant," into Keatsian dialectic:

though a child's feelings are spoken of, it is not the child who speaks. *I* decipher what the child only felt in cipher . . . Whatsoever in a man's mind blossoms and expands to his own consciousness in mature life, must have pre-existed in germ during his infancy. I, for instance, did not, as a child, *consciously* read in my own deep feelings these ideas. No, not at all; nor was it possible for a child to do so. I the child had the feelings, I the man decipher them. In the child lay the handwriting mysterious to *him*; in me the interpretation and the comment. (*C* 92, 113)

The elderly commentator translates the strange language of childhood, bridging temporal discontinuity in the manner of the *Prelude*'s "two consciousnesses" (*Prelude* 2:32). But if the developmental model predicates the man's mind on the child's latency, elsewhere De Quincey complicates this teleology in a way that anticipates a later normative adjustment of the Romantic thesis. A paragraph from De Quincey's *Autobiography* supplies his own antithesis:

"*The child*," says Wordsworth, "*is father of the man*"; thus calling into conscious notice the fact, else faintly or not at all perceived, that whatsoever is seen in the maturest adult, blossoming and bearing fruit, must have pre-existed by way of germ in the infant. Yes; all that is now broadly emblazoned in the man, once was latent – seen or not seen – as a vernal bud in the child. But not, therefore, is it true inversely – that all which pre-exists in the child finds its development in the man. Rudiments and tendencies, which *might* have found, sometimes by accidental [*sic*], *do* not find, sometimes under the killing frost of counter forces *cannot* find, their natural evolution. . . . Most of what he has, the grown-up man inherits from his infant self; but it does not follow that he always enters upon the whole of his natural inheritance. (*M* 1:121)

Here De Quincey imagines the adult as a less capacious version of his "father," eking out a stinted mental life on a traumatically reduced "inheritance." Freud concurs, with the compensatory addition that the "suppressed or . . . diverted" "germs . . . which are contained in the undifferentiated sexual disposition of the child" will nonetheless "provide the energy for a great number of our cultural achievements" (*SE* 7:50). Still, De Quincey's picture of psychic dwarfism coexists oddly with his frequent boasts about the "premature expansion" (*C* 107) of his own intellect, rather as though he were acknowledging that early growth had accelerated his decay. The notion echoes such unsympathetic judgments as that of the *Eclectic Review*, which found that the hero of the *Confessions* "begins his career as a run-a-way school boy" and ends "a premature dotard at the age of thirty-six."[42] One is tempted, as well, to adduce "the oddness" registered by De Quincey's acquaintances "at the sight of so very little a Man." Dorothy Wordsworth described the five-foot De Quincey as "*unfortunately* diminutive," while Robert Southey "wish[ed] he were not so little" (*MY* 1:283; *J* 23). In his textual life, De Quincey was if not a child then perhaps the "monster birth" that Wordsworth satirizes in the *Prelude*: "a dwarf man . . . / The noontide shadow of a man complete" (5:292–97). Even his essay subjects and formal strategies turn on "the long *regressus*"; *Suspiria de Profundis*, the "sequel" to the *Confessions*, begins at a chronologically prior point to shed a light "backwards into the shades of infancy, [like] the light perhaps which wrapt the destined apostle on his road to Damascus" (*C* 143–45).

If Romanticism's canonical narrative idealizes childhood as prelude or paradox, the De Quinceyan version never outgrows its premise. More explicitly than the first-generation poets, De Quincey treats infancy as "a distinct peninsula" (*M* 1:121) on the map of human consciousness, a sub-jurisdiction in which, prefiguring the birth of psychoanalysis, he claims a special expertise. In this "limited privilege" he represents, and often represents himself as, the aberration that defines normative structures of thought. Such claims typically crystallize around his many citations and revisions of "We Are Seven," one subtext of the "deep deep tragedies" (*C* 146) he revisits in *Suspiria.* De Quincey's appropriation poses itself against Coleridge's attack on the Intimations Ode, where the "little poem of 'We are Seven'" stands in for "the assertion, that a *child* . . . has no other notion of death than that of lying in a dark, cold place" (*BL* 2:140–41). In preference to this "absurdity" Coleridge chooses the "bald truism" that "'he is not dead, but sleepeth.'" If this be the child's belief, however, it "does [not] differ from that of his father and mother, or any other adult and instructed person": "To form an idea of a thing's becoming nothing; or of nothing becoming a thing; is impossible to all finite beings alike, of whatever age, and however educated or uneducated" (*BL* 2:141). The "splendid paradox" dwindles to the irreducibility of metaphor; however literal a fact death may be, there can be no idea of absence that does away with figures.

What Coleridge poses as antinomy, though, De Quincey presents as developmental passage or narrative pivot. For Coleridge, the "best philosopher" of the Intimations Ode can be only "conscious being" or rhetorical vehicle – "*ego contemplans*," the "personal identity," or "*ego contemplatus*," the "external image . . . by which the mind" symbolizes "its individuality" (*BL* 2:138–40; 1:72–73). De Quincey negotiates these alternatives in the logically scandalous form of the "bull," "*I was a fine child, but they changed me,*" which incongruously subjects the unity of the "I" to internal difference (*BL* 1:72). In an appendix to the *Confessions* he introduces "the little Carnarvonshire child in 'We are Seven'" as an instance of "life in its earliest stage," poised against "an adventitious and secondary voice consequent upon an earthly experience" (*M* 3:461–62). Unlike Coleridge, he does not ask whether or what kind of truth she speaks, but how she *prefigures* the reflexive turn philosophy calls "consciousness." Oddly, the most fraught and fretted aspect of this question concerns the trivial detail of her age: "she *said*" that "she was eight years old" (*LB* 66:6, my emphasis), "but this might be an ambitious exaggeration, such as aspiring female children are generally disposed to practice." "Naturally," he adds,

we must not exact from Wordsworth any pedantic rigour of accuracy in such a case: but assuredly we have a right to presume that his principle, if tenable at all, must apply to all children below the age of *five.* However, I will say *four.* (*M* 3:462)

At what point or by what means, De Quincey wonders, does the "earliest stage" modulate into the "secondary voice" chastened by "the reflex shadows of the grave" (*M* 11:301)? Offering an experiential rather than a logical solution, he invokes a "memorandum . . . drawn up by myself" for an anecdote that "impeach[es]" the doctrine of Wordsworth's poem (*M* 3:462). The citation identifies his biography as the standard of reality by which to judge the *Lyrical Ballads*. Thus it elevates anecdote to the level of "philosophical truth," a gesture authorized by Wordsworth's promise of ethnographic rigor. "I have at all times endeavoured to look steadily at my subject," the poet soberly declares in his "Preface" (*PrW* 1:132). The tension between such claims for documentary realism and the self-authorizing "principles" that Wordsworth deduces, like Kant and the economist Ricardo, "*a priori*, from the understanding itself" (*C* 65), invests even slight empirical adjustments with disproportionate prestige. If, on the other hand, the "perplexity and obscurity" that attends the "We Are Seven" girl's "notion of death" is to count as psychological verisimilitude rather than as personified virtue or vice, it must evoke corresponding "facts" of "personal observation" from Wordsworth's readers (*PrW* 1:126, 117). In this sense, De Quincey's soft impeachment dialectically *confirms*, by adjusting, the poet's mimetic skill in "tracing . . . the primary laws of our nature" (*PrW* 1:122).

It is this interplay that generates the plot of *Suspiria*, which both retroactively avouches Wordsworth's profundity (for the poet could not have known he was telling De Quincey's story), and asserts the epistemological priority of the reader's memoir. Writing in 1845 of his very early childhood, De Quincey premises that he "could, at that time, have had no experience whatever" of death.

This, however, I was speedily to acquire. My two eldest sisters – eldest of three *then* living, and also elder than myself – were summoned to an early death. The first who died was Jane – about a year older than myself. She was three and a half, I two and a half, *plus* or *minus* some trifle that I do not recollect. But death was then scarcely intelligible to me, and I could not so properly be said to suffer sorrow as a sad perplexity. (*C* 97)

That the age of the "We Are Seven" girl should even arise as a question depends evidently on De Quincey's "experience" of failing to register experience, which marks the utmost verge of (subjectively) conscious and (objectively) pre-conscious being. The girl's report that "the first [who] died was little Jane" shows, he elsewhere remarks, that as a merely incipient consciousness she "is unable to admit the thought of death, though, in compliance with custom, she uses the word" (*LB* 68:49; *M* 3:461). Deciphering the hieroglyphics of Wordsworthian *naïveté*, he recalls knowing

little more of mortality than that Jane had disappeared. She had gone away; but, perhaps, she would come back . . . I was sad for Jane's absence. But still in my heart I trusted that she would come again. Summer and winter came again – crocuses and roses; why not little Jane? (*C* 99)

For baby Thomas, as for the poem's heroine, Jane's absence and the possibility of her return link with the revolving cycles of white snow and green grass. This "ignorance" possesses the strength of St. Paul's conviction that "the dead rise," just as "that which thou sowest is not quickened, except it die" (I Corinthians 15:29–36).

While at two-and-a-half De Quincey feels only perplexity, when he reaches "little above six years of age" a formally identical event inflicts "the sorrow for which there is no consolation" (*C* 101–02). The next (and only other) sibling he mentions in *Suspiria* is, like the named siblings of "We Are Seven," a graven memory rather than an empirical presence:

Thus easily was healed, then, the first wound in my infant heart. Not so the second. For thou, dear, noble Elizabeth . . . thou next, but after an interval of happy years, thou also wert summoned away from our nursery; and the night which, for me, gathered upon that event, ran after my steps far into life; and perhaps at this day I resemble little for good or for ill that which else I should have been. (*C* 99–100)

The Carnarvonshire girl could surely not have been as old as eight, because the merely four- or five-year "interval" that divided Thomas's first loss from his second has left him "changed . . . from what [he] was" (*LB* 115:67) – as though "We Are Seven" represented not a counterpart but the prehistory of "Tintern Abbey." The effect of this contrast is to reify the Wordsworthian distinction between "primary" animal gladness and "secondary" reflection, while displacing it to an earlier chronological moment. De Quincey takes as his particular subject this *threshold* of consciousness, the approximation of a turn or conversion "in itself."

Perhaps it is the elusiveness of such a project that motivates De Quincey's countervailing insistence on concrete particulars in the revision of *Suspiria* for his 1853 *Autobiographic Sketches*. Appended to the record of his affliction is a footnote in which, merely for the purposes of intelligibility, . . . I here record the entire list of my brothers and sisters, according to their order of succession; and Miltonically I include myself; having surely as much logical right to count myself in the series of my own brothers as Milton could have to pronounce Adam the goodliest of his own sons. (*M* 1:29)

To clarify the record of a "passage" marked by periodic disappearances, he correlates a series of deaths with the set of all Quincey children. This, however, does not mend matters. By including himself "Miltonically" in what he nonetheless calls a "series," De Quincey, like the "We Are Seven" girl, "conflate[s] possession with existence, *having* sisters and brothers with *being* sisters and brothers."[43] His list recalls Lacan's allegory for the "formation of the subject . . . who thinks" and "who situates himself in it." As an antecedent to *ego contemplans*, Lacan cites

the level at which there is counting, things are counted, and in this counting he who counts is already included. It is only later that the subject has to recognize himself as such, recognize himself as he who counts. Remember the naive failure of the simpleton's delighted attempt to grasp the little fellow who declares – *I have three brothers, Paul, Ernest and me*. But it is quite natural – first the three brothers, Paul, Ernest and I are counted, and then there is I at the level at which I am to reflect the first I, that is to say, the I who counts.[44]

The little boy who commits a more obvious version of the Coleridgean bull is also himself that hypothetical "fine child," the self before subjectivity. Yet if identification with the set connotes simplicity, De Quincey's list *mimes* such a state by superimposing several formal systems to suggest their mutual incoherence – an effect he associates with the egoism of the literary.

Evoking the logical "knot which constitutes the subject," "something which is at the same time one or two," De Quincey instances the bull as the cardinal absurdity of autobiography.[45] Narrative begins with the acknowledgment of the discrepancy between series and tally. To the question "how many may you be?" (*LB* 66:14), De Quincey gives two answers:

First and last, we counted as eight children – viz., four brothers and four sisters, though never counting more than six living at once – viz., 1. *William*, older than myself by more than five years; 2. *Elizabeth*; 3. *Jane*, who died in her 4th year; 4. *Mary*; 5. myself, certainly not the goodliest man of men since born my brothers; 6. *Richard*, known to us all by the household name of *Pink*, who in his after years tilted up and down what might then be called his Britannic Majesty's Oceans (viz., the Atlantic and Pacific) in the quality of midshipman, until Waterloo in one day put an extinguisher on that whole generation of midshipmen, by extinguishing all further call for their services; 7. a second *Jane*; 8. *Henry*, a posthumous child, who belonged to Brasenose College, Oxford, and died about his 26th year. (*M* 1:29)

Are we eight or are we six? Neither, and both at once. Obsessive recounter, De Quincey extrapolates from the series to a purely hypothetical set, producing the figure eight by a formal operation masquerading as empiricism.[46] The coexistence of both counts forces a reconciliation of the argument in "We Are Seven," though the result is less a synthesis than a version of the fantasy "time loop" in which "the subject *qua* pure gaze . . . precedes itself and witnesses its own origin."[47] Its instability generates a supplement, in the form of miniature biographies attached to the itemized names.

In no way does the Miltonic list elucidate the phenomenal experience of the child, for at no point in childhood could Thomas have given an answer like De Quincey's. The narrator who composes this list can, however, claim with some plausibility that he "saw from afar and from before what [he] was to see from behind" (*C* 160). That is to say, De Quincey's account combines chronological seriality with formal closure, as though the end of each numbered life were not only latent but legible in the "germ" of infancy. If the childish, like the satanic, state consists in knowing no time but the present, the Miltonic perspective requires foreknowledge absolute. Narrative views "the past . . . not *as* the past, but by a spectator who steps back . . . deeper into the rear, in order that he may regard it as a future" (*C* 174). It also implies a "memory" of one's own precursors, like De Quincey's account of numbers one through four. So at least hints the Dark Interpreter, who illustrates the relation between seriality and finitude with a version of Zeno's paradox.

Look here: put into a Roman clepsydra one hundred drops of water; let these run out as the sands in an hourglass; every drop measuring the hundredth part of a second, so that each shall represent but the three-hundred-and-sixty-thousandth part of an hour. Now, count the drops as they race along; and, when the fiftieth of the hundred is passing, behold! forty-nine are not, because already they have perished; and fifty are not, because they are yet to come. You see, therefore, how narrow, how incalculably narrow, is the true and actual present . . . The time which *is*, contracts into a mathematic point; and even that point perishes a thousand times before we can utter its birth. All is finite in the present; and even that finite is infinite in its velocity of flight towards death. (*C* 158–59)

The enumeration of points only serves to approximate the true irrepresentability of time, which like De Quincey's siblings has either already "perished" or "not [been] born." From this infinite finitude of the passing moment, the Dark Interpreter infers that "for God there can be no present" (*C* 159). But if God "sacrifices" human time to the future, memory sacrifices the finite past to the infinite present of the text. Narrative comprises just such a doubled vision, insisting both on the sequentiality of events (like drops running out of a clepsydra) and on their deformation by a determinate closure. De Quincey's list of his siblings, in other words, constitutes a miniature paradigm of autobiographical form, "forc[ing] the infinite into the chambers of a human brain" (*C* 88).

The Interpreter construes God's purposes from the silence of nurseries "where the children were all asleep, and *had* been asleep through five generations" (*C* 158) – time's mortality gauged by the deaths of the newly born. De Quincey ticks off the vanishings of autobiographical time with the intervals that divide literal death from figurative resurrection. Thus it is not merely his immaturity that blinds him to the loss of Jane. Jane's death does not count to him because, in another sense, she counts twice: two items in his list have identical names. Because the names cannot perform their usual role of deixis, they must be linked with ordinal numbers ("succession") to produce an intelligible set.[48]

Counting was, indeed, more than usually difficult for De Quincey; the 1822 Appendix to his *Confessions* tabulates in egregious detail the fluctuations in his descent from 8000 drops of laudanum per day to the relatively small dose of 160 to 300 drops (*M* 3:466–72). The twofold name, however, complicates his reportedly naive "trust" that Jane would "come again." In a way, she did; it depends how the relation between a dead three-year-old and her namesake is conceptualized. St. Paul seems to authorize their conflation when, in the verses that form part of the English burial service, he asks "what . . . they [shall] do which are baptized for the dead, if the dead rise not at all? why are they then baptized for the dead?" (I Corinthians 15:29). Multiples of the same Christian name were fairly commonplace in English families, down through

the late eighteenth century when "for the first time," Lawrence
Stone argues, "parents were beginning to recognize that each
child, even if it lived for a few hours or days, had its own unique
individuality."[49] For the Quinceys during the 1780s, it was still possible to express grief by reviving the lost child's identity in the next
to be born. The two Janes were to occupy a single place in the set,
perhaps because the first died *infans* – before reaching the age of
knowledge, the traditional threshold of personhood. Thus, while
a positivist account of De Quincey's "intimate response" (*OE* 31)
to "We Are Seven" might assume that the poem helped reconcile
him to his several losses, the infant's recollected innocence is
conditioned by a future in which contingency has been rewritten
as narrative form. Thomas's "immunity" from grief is the internal-
ization, as psychological prehistory, of the second Jane, who is
stricken from the memoir in order that he may be instructed to
count correctly.[50]

"We Are Seven" formalizes Thomas's accident into the narrator's developmental phase. It is worth noticing, then, the pains De
Quincey took to represent this first death as prototype. His
enumeration notwithstanding, both Janes were born *after* himself,
the second before Elizabeth grew ill; he was approaching five when
his three-year-old sister died.[51] Only by tampering with this
sequence can he insert a significant (Wordsworthian) period
between infantile ignorance and premature bereavement.
Elizabeth dies as Thomas turns seven, completing one "stage of
life" and about to be "translated . . . into a new creature" (*C* 107).
Her death does not *originate* this transformation, though, except
in the sense that a repetition stamps the character of a biographical "event." Freud's term for such a disclosure is *nachträglichkeit*; as
Lacan makes the point, "the *two* is here to grant existence to the
first *one*": "it is necessary that this two constitute the first integer
which is not yet born as a number before the two appears." For De
Quincey, Elizabeth's death marks the thematic appropriation of a
temporality "structured as a language."[52]

This redoubling, the "first mark," institutes "the status of the
thing." Lacan contends that "this insistence in repetition . . . neces-
sitates the 'fading,' the obliteration, of the first foundation of the
subject." Jane's death recedes into an endless series, each iteration
reducible to the template "there was a girl, named — , and she
died." Names in these stories work much like number, sub-

ordinated to the mark that binds them into sequence. In the *Confessions*, De Quincey loses Ann of Oxford-street because, like the elderly Wordsworth in quest of the Carnarvonshire girl, he has no name to distinguish her: "she had either never told me, or (as a matter of no great interest) I had forgotten, her surname," for "girls of humble rank in her unhappy condition" generally "style themselves . . . simply by their Christian names, *Mary, Jane, Frances,* &c." (*C* 27). Lacan's analogy for this "trait of the sameness" comes from mathematics, which generates natural numbers by the formula "*n* plus 1." If narrative perpetuates the Lacanian or Coleridgean "one more," however, "the subject is the introduction of a *loss* in reality" representable as $n - 1$; "the two does not complete the one to make two, but must repeat the one to permit the one to exist." The end of a perfect love "between two children," for example, marks De Quincey as a "solitary child" (*C* 106–07). The integer "is not an empirical fact," at least in the sense that it derives from, rather than founds, the extension of the series.[53]

De Quincey's tales of loss compensate isolation with precocity: his solitude is also his singularity. The same principle supplies the germ of his rebuttal to Coleridge. No "finite being," Coleridge asserts, can "form an idea of a thing's becoming nothing." In other words, zero is not a natural number. The mathematician's response is, on Frances Ferguson's account, a formalist one, in which the consistency of a system (like 1, 0 precipitates from the addition of 1) supplements pure cognition.[54] "Nothing" may be represented if not intuited, somewhat as Freud infers the primal scene from its permutations in fantasy. The "loss in reality" corresponds to a *reflexive* turn that Lacan dubs variously the "inverted eight," "the essential inscription at the origin," or "the knot which constitutes the subject." Like $n + 1$, the subject "repeat[s]" or doubles itself, which is to say that the "thing" that "changed me" – for example, a first death – lives on as the "phantasm" of the finite being. The De Quinceyan answer to Coleridge's idealist dilemma also, therefore, implies a vindication of the bull, for *ego contemplatus* can only be found *within* the "I," as the personified trace of the other. There can be no undoing this knot: Thomas was a fine child, but always already changed.

To phrase the issue in these terms is to mark a return to the purview of "We Are Seven," whether the poem's conflict is understood in ontological terms or as a disagreement on the nature and limits of representation.[55] "We Are Seven" poses the question of Wordsworth's "Preface" – "what is a subject?" – in the less ideologically charged form, "what is a person," or simply, "who counts?" The narrator's equivocal pleasantry, "how many may you be," tilts the exchange toward a Lacanian impasse which he then tries to resolve through a series of arguments grounded on the girl's perceived failure to "tell the figural from the proper." She represents for him an embodiment of the allegorical child who, in eighteenth-century epistemology, exposes the logical solecisms of tautology (in defining simple ideas like death) and disguised metaphor (in evoking complex ones like persons). Wordsworth's speaker overlooks the possibility that he might share the same predicament.[56] On the girl's claiming two relations who "lie,/ Beneath the church-yard tree," as if that were an address like Conway or a ship, he objects: "You run about, my little maid,/ Your limbs they are alive" (*LB* 67:31–34). While an obvious enough point, this is a strategic mistake, for its power as an empirical statement depends on an unacknowledged personification of parts of the body. One appeal to ocular proof simply yields another; she responds that "their graves . . . may be seen" – and touched, for they lie just a few paces away. As De Quincey notes, "she reiterates her assertion of their graves as lying in the churchyard, in order to prove that they were *living*" (*M* 3:461).

To the man, this gesture of pointing betrays a psychotic conflation of signs and what they signify; yet such a fine disregard for incongruity is apparently endorsed by Lacan:

> In my day we used to teach children that they must not add, for instance, microphones with dictionaries; but this is absolutely absurd, because we would not have addition if we were not able to add microphones with dictionaries or as Lewis Carroll says, cabbages with kings. The sameness is not in *things* but in the *mark* which makes it possible to add things with no consideration as to their differences.[57]

The man himself sees nothing odd, after all, in a plural pronoun whose other referents are as physically distant as "the sea." His beleaguered empiricism loses its remaining credibility when he suggests that the disputed two "are in Heaven," a far harder place to localize but one where, as he unwittingly concedes, "spirits" may be said to live (*LB* 68:62–66). His alternating accounts of identity as body *or* soul are incommensurate but also, of course, complementary; buried in the logical contradiction is a fissure in the concept of the person. The moral can be phrased several ways. Wordsworth might comment that "where the Poet speaks through the mouths of his characters," his language "must necessarily be ... *alive* with metaphors and figures" (*PrW* 1:137, my emphasis). For Coleridge, such language exemplifies the inescapable figurality of absence *and* existence. The Lacanian twist on this insight is simply to remark how the poem's signifiers of personhood supplement without completing each other.

De Quincey learns from "We Are Seven" that not only Jane and John, but the little girl and the poetic speaker as well, should be understood as personifications supported by language, rather than as integral (autonomously self-evident) beings.[58] For while their debate apparently revolves around whether the dead still count as people, this question is finally ancillary to the indirect claims lodged by the two characters. If the speaker's omission of the formality "what's your name" indicates one condition of subjectivity, the mere ability to produce a name is not enough to constitute an individual. De Quincey, that is, reads the girl's miniature biographies of Jane and John – who lay moaning, were released from pain, and are now solaced by her songs and companionship – as chapters of her own story. Yet if her tale of being "made up of many beings" through "the internal annexation of others"[59] conveys both "philosophical truth" and a certain moral heroism, De Quincey's genesis of a mind "populous with solemn imagery" (*C* 87) more disturbingly suggests an antithetical relation between the chronicler and the lives retold.

The eeriness of "We Are Seven" consists less in the girl's attachment to her dead sister and brother than in the implication that they possess a more vivid reality for her than the living but unstoried siblings she mentioned earlier. De Quincey extends this insight into the narrative origins of identity toward an account of himself as the "resurrection" of "mysterious handwritings of grief" (*C* 145). Thus, he borrows the girl's proclivity toward memorial stasis, while acknowledging the man's contention that dead children retain only a figurative presence in the world. This lesson comes to him from St. Paul, whose "sublime chapter" on "the grave and resurrection" (*C* 108, 132) corrects superstitious faith in reincarnation with the assurance that "we shall be *changed*" hereafter (I Corinthians 15:52, quoted in *C* 109). The text of the autobiographer is itself the "spiritual body" of the lost objects, "revive[d] in strength. They are not dead, but sleeping" (*C* 145). De Quincey has a word for the psychic prolongation that Freud calls "mourning": it is "*palingenesis* (or restorative resurrection)," a "visionary" faculty (*M* 11:303).[60] But do the recursions of a textual afterlife deal the *coup de grace* to the sacrificial object? De Quincey remarks of Elizabeth that "the lesser star could not rise, before the greater would submit to eclipse" (*C* 105).[61] The younger brother purchases his expansion at the cost of the other's disappearance.

Putting the case this way has as one of its consequences a challenge to the empirical status of biography. To represent the "inscription at the origin" as a (sublimated) death, De Quincey must, for example, elide the second Jane, whose resurrection may appear all too literal. Perhaps his brief lives do more – or less – than flesh out the bare bones of statistical data; perhaps "even a biographical 'event' like birth could be considered . . . as a discursive occurrence," subject to the exigencies of narrative form.[62] Dead siblings are the *only* ones who count to De Quincey, for their change objectifies the "gap" of subjectivity, the "nothing" that "contains everything."[63] It follows that De Quincey himself should be included among the "impersonations" (*C* 148) that haunt his dreams. Consoled in his "separate experience" by three Sisters of Sorrow (*C* 91, 148), he indemnifies reality's loss with multiplied abstractions.[64] Thus he finally *personifies*, rather than empirically *illustrates*, "the effect upon the reader" that he notices in "We Are Seven":

> she whose fulness of life could not brook the gloomy faith in a grave, is yet . . . brought into connexion with the reflex shadows of the grave . . . and through this very child, the gloom of that contemplation obliquely irradiated, [i]s raised in relief upon his imagination even by *her*. That same infant, which subjectively could not tolerate death, being by the reader contemplated objectively, flashes upon us the tenderest images of death. Death and its sunny antipole are forced into connexion. (*M* 11:301–02)

The variant on the bull he admires in this essay "On Wordsworth's Poetry" finds a correlative in the "sad retrospect of life in its closing stage" which for him "shed its dews . . . upon the fountains of life" (*C* 160). Dialectical scandal rewritten as catachresis, his own involution partakes of the "antagonism" (*C* 103) that defines his aesthetic. Under the guise of etiology, De Quincey instead *diagrams* melancholia, tracing a formal pattern of subjectivity that will soon be enshrined by psychoanalysis.[65]

With each of his losses, finally, De Quincey remarks the "infinite declensions" (*C* 159) of the subject into the stages of countable units. Death arrests the minor's "threshold" of self-difference at its very "moment of birth," just as "if the moment were as punctually marked as physical birth is marked" (*C* 161). Returning to his reading of the Intimations Ode, De Quincey concludes that:

Man is doubtless *one* by some subtle *nexus* that we cannot perceive, extending from the newborn infant to the superannuated dotard: but as regards many affections and passions incident to his nature at different stages, he is *not* one; the unity of man in this respect is coextensive only with the particular stage to which the passion belongs. (*C* 107)

Only the life of narrative can order "those successive themes . . . which by pure accident have consecutively occupied the roll" into "parts of a coexistence" or, more exactly, measures of a cadenced self-serialization (*C* 144–45). In some sense these recursions naturalize the static Ages of Man, those seven units of seven years by which an older, though still legally pertinent, cultural narrative had affirmed that "we are seven."[66] Yet as De Quincey warns, his is less an account of progressive "evolution" than of "primary convulsions" that "come round again and again by reverberating shocks," and of a "system" that perpetually "wheels back into its earliest elementary stage" (*C* 129, 146). Beginning amidst the revolutions of "this year 1845," De Quincey concludes his *Suspiria* with the hypothesis of a conscious summons to "face the hour of birth" (*C* 87, 181).

"Originally a mere reflex" of the profundities he reverences, De Quincey acts out the "secret consciousness" of development, its fractures, failures, and incoherences (*C* 156; *M* 5:351). Thus the minor's relation to Romantic truth may be *figured*, I have been suggesting, both as its "iteration" and as its "repressed." Adapting these terms to the scale of national trauma, my next chapter will argue that De Quincey figures in Romantic historiography as the repressed *of iteration*. Entering upon his novitiate at a moment of constitutive historical recurrence, De Quincey comes to embody, for the revolution's self-appointed spokesman, the *minority* of its second coming: its status as belated echo and also, paradoxically, as negation. While the birth of a Romantic subject may be said to institute the progenitor's originality, the reenactment of the 1790s will mark this second generation – and Wordsworth's own later career – as a falling-off from the first.

More immediately, and regarded at the level of genre history, De Quincey's involutions suggest why and how his experiments in "impassioned prose" will be consigned to *literary* minority. Having extended the project of formal isolation as far, in the dimension of memory, as it can go, the *Suspiria* present this "fragmentary exigency" as sheer *reductio*.[67] De Quincey is the born autobiographer who, realizing Romantic tendency, continually reproduces the structural equivocation of its origin. Yet he who "chequer[s] his life with solitude" attains for his sequestration a "power" of insight denied to the "vast . . . majority" (*C* 87–88). If Wordsworth divined the facts of his biography in the *Lyrical Ballads*, De Quincey's confessions turn and return this gift, writing a life whose intertextual relations supplement the primacy of social experience. And like all tributes, De Quincey's allusions enfold the germ of unforeseen ends. The last chapter of this book, therefore, will recur in De Quinceyan fashion to its beginnings. In his periodical *Reminiscences*, De Quincey tells the story of his origin as the prefiguration of Wordsworth's end, reclaiming the poet's life because Wordsworth wrote, or underwrote, his own.

CHAPTER 2

Transmissions: composing
The Convention of Cintra

TIDINGS

De Quincey attended Oxford during the middle years of the Napoleonic Wars, "at [the] height," as he recalls, of "the superstition in respect to the French military prowess . . . so dishonouring" (*M* 3:107) to his compatriots. He was himself at the height of his infatuation with Wordsworth, having briefly visited Grasmere in 1807. Keeping the minimal "short term" at Worcester College, he spent most of his university career in transit; in the fall of 1808 he finally fled, just on the eve of his baccalaureate examinations. Much later, in "The English Mail-Coach" (1849), he was to evoke this period in terms that connected his frequent travel with the "awful political mission" then occupying the country.

The mail-coaches it was that distributed over the face of the land, like the opening of apocalyptic vials, the heart-shaking news of Trafalgar, of Salamanca, of Vittoria, of Waterloo . . . The victories of England in this stupendous contest rose of themselves as natural *Te Deums* to heaven; and it was felt by the thoughtful that such victories, at such a crisis of general prostration, were not more beneficial to ourselves than finally to France, and to the nations of western and central Europe, through whose pusillanimity it was that the French dominion had prospered.

The mail-coach, as the national organ for publishing these mighty events, became itself a spiritualised and glorified object to an impassioned heart; and naturally, in the Oxford of that day, all hearts were awakened. (*C* 184)

In fact, all but the first of these famous battles occurred well after De Quincey left Oxford. He marked his own political awakening by the coincidence of these transitions with "the commencement of [his] *literary life*," which he "date[d] from . . . leaving Oxford" (*NLS* MS. 1670) and taking up residence with Wordsworth and Coleridge at Allan Bank. Thus it happened that from a state of confessed indifference to "public affairs" he became intimately familiar with the "organ[s] for publishing" them, galvanized by the "strong impulse the opening of the Peninsular War communicated to our current literature" (*M* 10:37). "Not having been old enough, at the first outbreak of the French Revolution, to participate . . . in the golden hopes of its early dawn" or the "vast stimulation to the meditative faculties of man" that it engendered, De Quincey's genesis as political subject came in the Revolution's *second* dawn: a late consequence that he understood as an original repetition (*R* 225; *M* 10:195). Along the way he immersed himself in the praxis of textual production and, indeed, began himself to write for print. These developments arose in connection with his involvement in *The Convention of Cintra* – Wordsworth's first published political tract, and the exclusive focus of his attention throughout the winter of 1808–09.

De Quincey arrived at Allan Bank to encounter "a heaving and a fermentation" (*CL* 3:137) of political agitation and literary labor. Coleridge was ensconced as a permanent guest and busy advertising, writing and arranging to distribute *The Friend*; he planned an inaugural number for January 1809. He was also helping Wordsworth compose a series of essays for the *Courier* on a subject that had provoked their mutual rage and fascination: the agreement recently concluded between the British forces commanded by Arthur Wellesley (later Duke of Wellington), and Napoleon's representative General Junot, for the French army's evacuation from Portugal. The Convention of Cintra, as the agreement became known, followed the first British victory in the Peninsular War, which had begun in May 1808 with a popular revolt in Spain against the French invasion. After joining forces with the Peninsular armies in August, Wellesley's forces defeated the French at the battle of Vimiero. The Convention of Cintra arranged for Junot's army to leave the Peninsula in exchange for safe passage and the retention of movable property, including the spoils of the campaign.

Because it succeeded a dramatic victory, and because it appeared to consult the rights of a defeated and detested army over the Portuguese on whose behalf the battle was supposedly fought, the armistice was condemned as a "treason against all moral feeling" when the news reached England.[1] Three years later, this rebuke resonated in the contempt of Byron's "Childe," at the

start of his four-canto career, for the "dwarfish demon styl'd"
Convention: "Britannia sickens, Cintra! at thy name."[2] "Never,"
Robert Southey claimed, "was any public feeling so unanimously
and instantaneously manifested."[3] While debatable as empirical
description, his remark accurately characterizes the premise upon
which Wordsworth began the "vindication" of the "People of Great
Britain" (*MY* 1:278) that gradually expanded into a two-hundred-
page disquisition published in June of the following year. "The
tidings of this event," recapitulating the "shocks" of the French
Revolution, spread, Wordsworth wrote, "like an earthquake which
rocks the ground under our feet." "Year follows year, the tide
returns again,/ Day follows day, all things have second birth;/ The
earthquake is not satisfied at once": history is not merely doomed
to repeat itself, but must happen twice before it happens at all
(*PrW* 1:224; *Prelude* 9:182, 10:72–74). The Convention of Cintra,
second coming of his generation's "turn of sentiment," became for
Wordsworth the occasion to consider the role of repetition in historical consciousness.[4]

   The Convention of Cintra is in several respects a transitional text
for Wordsworth's career, however the linked terms are described.
Often situated on the cusp of his "apostasy" from early radicalism
to reactionary Toryism, the tract also marks a return to the explicit
topical polemics foregrounded in his early work but relatively
muted in his poetic "great decade."[5] Wordsworth's enthusiastic
endorsement of the Peninsular War exemplifies a widespread phenomenon among British intellectuals who had sympathized with
the early phases of the French Revolution, but whom subsequent
events in England and in France had variously chastened or
subdued. The "new-born spirit of resistance" (*PrW* 1:228) that
manifested itself in the Spanish Revolution combined the populist
appeal of an anti-aristocratic uprising with a rebuke to Napoleon's
territorial ambitions, providing an uncontroversial opportunity to
rejoin nationalist and republican rhetoric. Writing for the *Courier*
in December 1809, Coleridge described "the noble efforts of
Spanish patriotism" as a prompt that "restored us, without distinction of party, to our characteristic enthusiasm for *liberty*."[6] Thus the
Peninsular War represented, as Peter J. Manning observes, "a purified repetition of the [1789] revolution . . . in which Wordsworth's
patriotism was renewed and aligned with his countrymen."[7] Yet
like the internal "revolution" felt by "all ingenuous youth" when,

in 1793, Britain declared war on the new French republic (*Prelude* 10:232–37), Wordsworth's conversion to "active citizen" marks not a generalized optimism but his sense of its betrayal.

That, finally, the uprising was motivated in large part by anti-enlightenment Catholic and monarchist sentiment was a historical irony which, in being misrecognized or discounted by British sympathizers, contributed to the hardening of liberal and conservative identifications in the Parliamentary politics of the 1820s. Therefore the Spanish campaign, and its "long succession of victories" (*C* 202) until 1815, also figures a turn in English political and intellectual history whose subsidiary phenomena include the division of "first generation" Romantic writers from the Byronically jaded "second generation."

So far was Wordsworth in 1809 from considering his support of the Peninsular cause to be motivated by conservatism that he even feared his pamphlet would be condemned as subversive. Southey, too, still viewed himself as "a Jacobine,"[8] and his dialogues with Wordsworth, in which sentiments were expressed "which seemed absolutely disloyal" and even "hostile to . . . a monarchical form of government," shocked De Quincey as coming from men he so admired (*R* 226). *The Convention of Cintra* unsettles the standard account of Wordsworth's political trajectory with a text in which Rousseauian and Girondist tropes mingle with phrases echoing Burke's attacks on Jacobinism. Neither radical nor reactionary, Whig nor Tory, *Cintra* – like the war itself – only found its partisan meaning in retrospect. Thus, its argument suggests how the interpretation of a charged historical moment may superimpose the codes and objectives of competing political discourses. In denouncing the Convention, Wordsworth found common cause not only with Coleridge, now writing for the moderate Tory *Courier*, with Southey, soon to be a mainstay of the hardline *Quarterly Review*, and with De Quincey, "bred up in a frenzied horror of Jacobinism" (*R* 225), but also with Crabb Robinson, a progressive Whig, and the reformist Francis Wrangham.[9] The origins and tendencies of political representation – its conditions of production, its efficacy as action, the purity of its intentions, and its responsibilities to constituents – are, correspondingly, the tract's primary concerns. Its complex and imperfectly coherent thesis is also mirrored in the perplexed and over-systematic circumstances in which it was composed.

The idea for a formal condemnation of the Convention apparently began with a plan for a public meeting jointly concocted by Southey, Coleridge and Wordsworth. The meeting was suppressed by Lord Lonsdale on the grounds of suspected anti-ministerial leanings, and, as Southey wrote, "Wordsworth – who left me when he found the business hopeless – went home to ease his heart in a pamphlet."[10] That Wordsworth, rather than Southey, should have undertaken this task represents the first of its many deflections; Wordsworth had no experience with pamphleteering except for the manuscript "Letter to the Bishop of Llandaff," while Southey was not only a prolific prose writer, but also a specialist on Spanish and Portuguese literature and history. He had even been to Cintra.[11] If in this sense it was penned by the wrong hand, the pamphlet's later evolution shows a similar divagation of accident from design. It was first envisioned as a series of articles or "letters"; two installments were published in December and January, but the text so "increased in size" (*CL* 3:160) that the serial format was quickly abandoned. At this stage, Wordsworth and Coleridge worked together, aided by one or two modest contributions from De Quincey.[12]

Coleridge represented his own part as collaboration and "re-compos[ition]," writing to Daniel Stuart that "we have been hard at work" and to Thomas Poole that "the two Columns of the second [essay], excepting the concluding Paragraph, were written all but a few sentences by me" (*CL* 3:164, 160, 174). "They did not think of authorship *meum* and *tuum* then," Henry Nelson Coleridge later claimed.[13] *Cintra* was the last project undertaken in the name of Wordsworth or Coleridge to which this egalitarian model of textual genesis might apply. When, at the end of February, De Quincey volunteered to oversee the printing of the pamphlet in London, the composition of *Cintra* took on the spatial character of a political delegation, with Grasmere at the center of authority and De Quincey serving as the author's agent in London. From a brief interlude of literary democracy, with its fiction of proportional representation, textual production took on an increasingly territorial and authoritarian cast. Hence the material conditions in which *Cintra* was written, transcribed, printed, and published recapitulate the problems of interpreting, representing, and responding to a series of political and military changes taking place in another country. The dynamics of intertextuality, for which De Quincey's early letters suggest psychoanalytic models, may be reformulated for the *Cintra* period in terms of the political theory Wordsworth imposes on events in the Peninsula. In the sections that follow, I outline a reading of *Cintra*'s argument and its reverberations in De Quincey's later work, arguing that, where historical consciousness is concerned, what goes around, comes around — even a residual "Jacobinism" in the high-Tory De Quincey. I then discuss some problems of representation, transmission and timing raised by Wordsworth's call to action; and, thirdly, show how these political and rhetorical problems were played out in the author's transactions with his footsoldier De Quincey. The rhetoric of confession, I lastly suggest, emerges as a historical response to the inevitable failure of Romanticism's ideal first-generation alliance.   *confession*

JACOBIN CONVENTIONS

When Wordsworth predicted that the tract he was about to publish would "call forth the old yell of Jacobinism" (*MY* 1:312), he may have mystified readers more critical than he of Canning's foreign policy. That *The Convention of Cintra* might be thought subversive or anti-ministerial is certainly eccentric as regards explicit policy recommendations; far from condemning military involvement in the Peninsula, as some of the Whig opposition had done, Wordsworth advocated greater commitment to it.[14] Nor, in championing Spanish resistance, did he emphasize positive liberty or legal equality, the cornerstones of French Revolutionary propaganda.[15] *Cintra*'s "Jacobinism" is an abstraction, but the term carries descriptive force both as a rubric for Wordsworth's idealist premises and as a figure for a historical accommodation that became thinkable with the virtuous model for "unanimous" political action that presented itself in the Spanish revolt, more than fifteen years after the events Wordsworth had witnessed in France. In defending both the injured Spanish and Portuguese and their right-thinking sympathizers in Britain, Wordsworth espoused a purified "Jacobinism" in which, as Coleridge defines it, "every man feels his interest as a *Citizen* predominating over his individual interests," and "all the inhabitants without distinction of property are roused to the exertion of a public spirit" (*CW* 3[1]:75). Free from "visionary speculations of *natural* rights" (*CW* 3[2]:38), this

"Jacobin state" is founded in an epochal reassertion of the monolithic popular will.

What Wordsworth and Coleridge found promising in British
sympathy for the Spanish and Portuguese was an object that could
evoke nonpartisan agreement, registering by doubling the galvanic effect of the Peninsula's "birth" as a desiring consciousness.
Universal sympathy consolidates social atomism and incoherence
into what De Quincey calls "presence of mind" (*C* 219). Coleridge
writes of "the *People* of England, not the *Populace* – apud *populum,*
non *plebum,*" that

> there is a heaving and a fermentation, as different from the vulgar sedi-
> tions of corresponding Societies and Manchester clubs, as A. Sidney from
> Horn Took[e] –. Never were a nation more uniform in their content-
> ment with, and gratitude for, their glorious Constitution. (December
> 1808; *CL* 3:137)

Coleridge's partition of *populum* from *plebum* distinguishes his
corporation of feeling from the deluded mob of radical democracy. At the same time, it recalls François Furet's account of how
the "tangible 'people' . . . who attended revolutionary meetings . . .
provided visible evidence for" the French Revolution's legitimating "abstraction called 'the people.'"[16] Still, Coleridge's picture
suggests a degree of class stratification incompatible with
Wordsworth's "spirit of the people." For Wordsworth, populace
converts into *populum* when an "authentic voice" (*PrW* 1:227) is
uttered – as it were, by all levels of society at once – in response to
perceived injury from without. This voice may be heard in the
immediate popular condemnation of the Convention of Cintra, "a
whole nation crying," as it cried in 1790, "with one voice" (*Prelude*
10:212). It is yet more clearly audible in the manifestos of the
revolutionary Juntas, which bespeak

> that unanimity which nothing but the light of truth spread over the
> inmost concerns of human nature can create . . . that simultaneousness
> which has led Philosophers upon like occasions to assert, that the voice
> of the people is the voice of God. (*PrW* 1:247)

Possessed by common feeling, "these millions of suffering people
have risen almost like one man," reincarnating the French of
1791, who then seemed "a people risen up,/ Fresh as the morning
star" (*PrW* 1:247; *Prelude* 9:391–92). Sincerity is attested by
punctuality: the synchronization of psychic and historical time

that, like the French Revolutionary calendar, represents its new-born subjects "standing on the top of golden hours" (*Prelude* 6:353).

Wordsworth's figure of society fused into single agent with a single object presents an evangelical restatement of French Revolutionary ideology. As Furet observes, Jacobinism posits a unitary will shared by the entire "people," who are

defined by their aspirations, and as an indistinct aggregate of individual "right" wills. By that expedient . . . the revolutionary consciousness was able to reconstruct an imaginary social cohesion in the name and on the basis of right wills.

The people, "a collective, unanimous, and vigilant protagonist," comes into existence with the concept of politics as a means of restoring lost rights.[17] "Politics" here denotes subjective cohesion rather than the articulation of group interests, and the action taken by the "people" mainly signifies, for Wordsworth, the capacity to "embody [their] deep sense" and "give it outwardly a shape" (*Prelude* 9:408–09). This picture of the mind is uninflected by peculiar circumstance; "large bodies of men," Wordsworth claims, "are nothing but aggregates of individuals" (*PrW* 1:267). To give this in the language of the Revolution's icon, Rousseau, the "act of association creates an artificial and collective body" with "a common *ego* . . . life and . . . will."[18]

Despite its reliance on the authenticity of "low and rustic" (*PrW* 1:124) peasant revolt, Wordsworth's version of *idéologie* elides rather than honors the marks of class and occupation; his is emphatically not the revolution of economic or social history. Indeed, the "Jacobin" rhetoric of universality, with its stress on aural reciprocation, uncomfortably resembles De Quincey's nostalgic and frankly jingoistic recollection of the "great national sentiment [that] surmount[ed] and quell[ed] all sense of ordinary distinctions" in the wake of Peninsular victories.

One heart, one pride, one glory, connects every man by the transcendant bond of his English blood. The spectators, who are numerous beyond precedent, express their sympathies with these fervent feelings by continual hurrahs . . . what redoubling peals of brotherly congratulation, connecting the name of the particular mail – "Liverpool for ever!" – with the name of the particular victory – "Badajoz for ever!" or "Salamanca for ever!" (*C* 203–04)[19]

"Imaginary social cohesion" is achieved, as De Quincey suggests, by the suspension of material differences ("washerwomen and char-women" are promoted to "daughters of England") in the name of opposition to "the adverse faction" (*C* 192, 206). Jacobinism, in Furet's account, conceives of only two historical agents: the "people" and its "common enemy," the impersonal force that once usurped the people's rights and now constantly plots to subvert its will.[20] The "people" excludes all deviations from the punctuality of revolutionary consciousness. For Wordsworth, the difference between the revolutionary *populum* and its Napoleonic adversary distinguishes "the constitution of human nature" from the "combinations of malevolence" found in "reprobate spirits" (*PrW* 1:226, 241). The French, "zealots of abstract principles" sprung from "the laboratory of unfeeling philosophists," are merely an old opponent "under a different shape" (1:226–29). Opposed to Wordsworth's collective, vigilant and unanimous protagonist is an aggregate personification of abstract ideas. The conflict between these two agents dramatizes the essential but ineffable difference between "flesh and blood" and bloodless abstraction: the presence or absence of feeling.[21]

This "feeling" cannot be derived from loyalty to concepts like liberty and equality – or, in fact, from *ideas* at all. Yet feeling should be governed by "principle," a category occupying the place in Wordsworth's epistemology held by popular "opinion" in revolutionary discourse.[22] Deriving from "habit," principle supposedly cures Jacobinism's theoretical dependence on the unity of action and cognition, a general and an individual will both completely enlightened. In this sense, Wordsworth's prescription for national unity may be described as a Burkean ideology against "*idéologie*."[23] This phrase also points up the definitional problem in his appeal to principle without abstraction. Concerned to vindicate imagination over "unfeeling philosophists," Wordsworth can nevertheless only *identify* feeling in moments of righteous reaction. To find a voice that is not spurious or merely selfish – Rousseau's "alien, partial will ... prone to error"[24] – the people must be moved, prior to any conscious volition, by some object "adequate ... to the utmost demands of the human spirit" (*PrW* 1:338).

Such an object presents itself in the evil of the French invasion, which is redeemable as a stimulus to "reduce men, in all ranks of society, under the supremacy of their common nature; to impress upon them one belief; to infuse into them one spirit" (*PrW* 1:288). Wordsworth's recuperation of gross and violent stimulants under the Manichean rubric of a common enemy indexes the difference between the intersubjectivity of the *Lyrical Ballads* and the internationalism of *The Convention of Cintra*. The rhetorical determinations of consciousness allegorized in the poems, but repudiated in the "Preface," are here both acknowledged and distanced, by locating the source of pressure in an *in*human attack. Again, De Quincey's "English Mail-Coach" vividly conveys the tenor of Wordsworth's prescription. Spontaneous overflows of unanimous feeling may be provoked in either of two ways. On the one hand, the class-divided occupants of a mail-coach are unified by their trumpeted "derision" for the "treason" threatened when a mere "Brummagem coach" attempts to "usurp" their "imperial precedency" on the road (*C* 190–92). Alternatively, as in "The Vision of Sudden Death," the "all-conquering" vehicle may, by trespassing to the "wrong side of the road" and striking a blow to a smaller gig, release the "chaunt[ed]" "tidings ... of a grandeur that measured itself against centuries" (*C* 219–29). If the first scenario enacts a playful miniature of the "race" between two rival powers, the second more somberly illustrates the impact of an "over-towering" empire's surprise-attack upon a backward and torpid lesser entity.[25]

The impact of this aggression deflects into the *performance* of nationhood. As the locus of political will or belief, however, Wordsworth's notion of voice raises as many representational difficulties as it solves, thus recapitulating a major dilemma of the French Revolution. A successful performance requires that voices be "re-echoed," repeated and answered by some appropriate "participant."[26] Thus, "the devout hymn that was chaunted" by the Spanish and Portuguese is activated by "the responses, with which our country bore a part in the solemn service" (*PrW* 1:288). English response is at once original to itself ("from her soul") and an echo of alien consciousness, the contradiction that guarantees authenticity. At this point the vocal model of representation breaks down; for the "stirring and heaving" of concrete individuals to be consolidated into the "voice of the people," they must be embodied in writing (*CL* 3:129).[27]

Such a text, however, is only admissible as a surrogate body, or "incarnation."[28] Describing the relation between his text and the sentiment it articulates, Wordsworth claims: "I have drawn out to open day the truth from its recesses in the minds of my country-men. – Something more perhaps may have been done: a shape hath perhaps been given to that which was before a stirring spirit" (*PrW* 1:292). De Quincey imagines this representative shape as the mail-coach, which is not merely "the vehicle that transports the post" but also "a 'vehicle' in the rhetorical sense of a figure signi-fying the tenor 'language.'"[29] The mail-coach transports "the idiom of our language, the mother tongue" in its cargo, and is itself an unambiguously legible spectacle: "young and old under-stand the language of our victorious symbols – and rolling volleys of sympathising cheers run along behind and before our course" (*M* 10:142; *C* 205). Wordsworth, following the example of Robespierre, presents *himself* as such an incarnation, staking his authority on the infinitely delicate task of embodying, without muting, both the Rousseauist "general will" and the principle of its mobility.

The questions raised in *Cintra* about how to substantiate the popular spirit rehearse the tension in French Revolutionary ide-ology between the "absolutist" claims of direct democracy and the political necessity of representation.[30] Democracy by proportional representation posits a dialectic of individual and class or party platforms, but the concepts of "minority" interest and mediation are antithetical to radical Jacobin politics. Rousseau flatly asserts that "the sovereign, which is simply a collective being, cannot be represented by anyone but itself – power may be delegated, but the will cannot be."[31] Thus, as Furet observes, competition among Revolutionary leaders and factions posed "the insoluble problem of what forms the Revolution should take, and of who was speak-ing in its name."[32] Lynn Hunt adds that Revolutionary politicians were "concerned with authority, audience, and the correct inter-pretation of revolutionary history," because "the authorship of the revolutionary text . . . was uncertain."[33] Wordsworth's ideal of governmental action as "an image of" the people's "under-standings," or mirror for "the sense of their hearts" (*PrW* 1:280), participates in the Jacobin imaginary. Reiterating his wish to "defend my countrymen," he concludes that "if their feelings deserve reverence, if there be any stirrings of wisdom in the motions of their souls, my task is accomplished" (1:289). The champion of the people is a personified tautology: defender of what, were it worthy of defense, need not be defended.

The symptom of tautology is a turn to allegory. "When the people speaks loudly," Wordsworth insists,

it is from being strongly possessed either by the Godhead or the Demon; and he, who cannot discover the true spirit from the false, hath no ear for profitable communion. But in all that regarded the destinies of Spain, and her own as connected with them, the voice of Britain had the unquestionable sound of inspiration. If the gentle passions of pity, love, and gratitude, be porches of the temple; if the sentiments of admiration and rivalry be pillars upon which the structure is sustained; if, lastly, hatred, and anger, and vengeance, be steps which, by a mystery of nature, lead to the House of Sanctity; – then it was manifest to what power the edifice was consecrated; and that the voice within was of Holiness and Truth. (*PrW* 1:290)

Wordsworth invokes Spenserian or Bunyanesque language at every point where ideological categories are called for: to circumscribe the domain of "the people" (or "Man"), and to invalidate competing interpretations.[34] In its explicit anachronism, and in its typological rigidity, the "oracle" bespeaks Jacobinism even as, in Burkean fashion, it differentiates the passional language really spoken by the people from the conceptual language spoken by zealots of abstract principle.[35] Revolutionary consciousness "tends," Furet writes, "to promote a Manichean explanation and to personify social phenomena."[36]

That difference should be so crucial, yet so hard to define, is both common to binary thinking in general and particular to the contradiction involved in "Jacobin" rhetoric directed against former Jacobins. Napoleon, for example, is both antithesis and reincarnation of the early Revolutionists; in *The Friend*, Coleridge blames the *philosophes* for "harangu[ing] without ceasing of the *Volonté générale*" and thereby clearing the way for "military despotism, for the satanic Government of Horror under the Jacobins, and of Terror under the Corsican." Like Robespierre, the current "Jacobin of France" maintains his "truly satanic Government" through "animal terror" (*CW* 4[1]:173, 194; 4[2]:215).[37] De Quincey rings several changes on the paradox of Jacobin Anti-Jacobinism when he describes the "revolution in the republic of letters" (*C* 189) effected by Oxford students on the mail-coach. His "aristocratic" fellow-students trade places with the "raffs" when they decide that, tradition notwithstanding, they prefer the outside of the coach to the inside. Their "treason" against respectability, mimetically reversing that "personal Jacobinism . . . which is native to the heart of man," constitutes "a perfect French revolution; and we had good reason to say, *Ca ira.* In fact, it soon became too popular" (*M* 1:70; *C* 188). Yet far from allying themselves with the "public," the students resolve "that the box was the imperial place." Similarly, all passengers are united against the "jacobinical" "thing from Birmingham," with its "air of sedition"; but De Quincey, "represent[ing] the conscience and moral sensibilities of the mail," fulfills his role "in words too celebrated in those days from the false echoes of Marengo," adapting a speech attributed to Napoleon. The continual "reverses of the French revolution" (*PrW* 1:229), with "reactions" like the Thermidor coup posited as "returns" to the people's true will, instill the suspicion that to displace "traitors" (even in the name of the republic) is to assume, at least "constructively," the voice of empire (*C* 185–92).[38]

Wordsworth's House of Sanctity prefigures a version of this conundrum at the level of figural incoherence. Voice is described as both identical with the edifice of passion and interior to it; the oracle speaks of nothing more than what it is. Indeed, in De Quincey's revision of this figure – the "mighty minster" through which he gallops in the "Dream Fugue" – the choristers literally sing Wordsworth, a "dreadful *sanctus*" borrowed from the sonnet "Siege of Vienna Raised by John Sobrieski": "'Chaunt the deliverer's praise in every tongue,' . . . 'such as once in heaven and earth were sung'" (*C* 229–31; cf. *PW*, 259). The expression of "feeling" lapses into quotation; voice is mystified, or loses its *transparence*, when Wordsworth "transfer[s] language" from St. Paul to the "new-born spirit of resistance" (*PrW* 1:227–28). Thus a theoretical crux yields a metacritical figure for the aporia of ideology: insofar as the revolutionary speaks *language* (and not merely Wordsworth's "cry"), he speaks false.

The House of Sanctity, then, speaks as "incarnation" speaks, echolalically. In his exegesis of the House of Sanctity, Wordsworth reads the transformation of isolated protests into "imaginary absolute power," a symbolic function modeled on the relentless codification of national "opinion" in eighteenth-century France.[39] The very architecture of Wordsworth's edifice reveals its ideological foundation: Sanctity dwells in the neoclassical temple of Revolutionary thought. Its porches and pillars mark out the "shape [of] political culture itself" – or the shape of that culture's unofficial institutions, the clubs and societies which, devoid of executive power and electoral responsibilities, were imagined by their members as pure instruments of popular response.[40] Wordsworth claims an analogous role when he argues, again tautologically, that "nothing, but a knowledge of human nature directing the operations of our government, can give it a right to an intimate association with a cause which is that of human nature" (*PrW* 1:304). "That specific knowledge," however, is by definition inaccessible to professional administrators and politicians. Conversely, "men of comprehensive sensibility and tutored genius" who do understand "the instincts of natural and social man" can only maintain the independence of their "Empire" by renouncing any "formal profession" to serve the public (*PrW* 1:305–06).[41] *Cintra*, then, could be described as a statesman's manual in the sense that the *philosophes* were politicians: representative men instructing governors in the meaning of the *volonté générale*.[42] Yet by sharpening this contradiction, Wordsworth also radicalizes the critique of liberalism inscribed in the Revolution itself. If the role of public citizen requires the abnegation of empirical identity ("interest" or "profession"), it follows that no *individual*, as such, may represent "human nature," or indeed be representative "for himself."[43] Hence the otherness of abstract zealotry may infect the logic of representation, though in the form of its apparent opposite – the imperfectly "associated" subject.[44]

By nominating himself as spokesman for human nature, Wordsworth articulates his relation to the Spanish insurgents as that of an emptied or formalized representative (the citizen without interests, or professional citizen) to a purified subjectivity (the "voice" without representation). If, however, his own analysis suggests that never the twain shall meet, the ambition of his tract is to accomplish just such a union. Hence his politics are thoroughly Jacobinical, but neither egalitarian nor, in the sense in which the term applies to modern politics, democratic. *Cintra* aspires to transcend indirect or representative democracy by restoring the people's presence to itself, "reviv[ing] in the memory those words and facts, which first carried the conviction to our hearts: that . . . we may see as we then saw, and feel as we then felt"

(*PrW* 1:230). This is, of course, a version of the phonocentric dream, but one that could only arise in response to a historical experiment that permanently destabilized accepted truths about the origins of political authority and the various media through which "opinion" might be registered.

De Quincey was later to propose the telegraph as an imperfect answer to his wish for "a state of communication between the centre and the extremities of a great people, kept up with a uniformity of reciprocation" such that action and opinion should be linked with "absolute certainty,"

> whether in the way of support or of resistance. Action and re-action from every point of the compass being thus perfect and instantaneous, we should then first begin to understand, in a practical sense, what is meant by the unity of a political body, and we should approach to a more adequate appreciation of the powers which are latent in organisation. (*M* 1:270–71)

The telegraph, as De Quincey imagines it, realizes a performative utopia, making each citizen's voice his ballot on any "public act." The resulting "unity," however, is bought at the price of a straitened sense of participation, with sound emanating from "every point of the compass" reduced to the poles of "support" and "resistance." In relation to the monolith of "national will," contingency can only register a *yea* or a *nay*. Wordsworth's version of this utopia is even more absolutist, since power and language must either coincide with the general feeling or betray it.

Yet Wordsworth turns Jacobinism back in on itself by refusing to give voice any content beyond its plainly legible architecture. If Spain, as subject, possesses only "feeling," the representative is vindicated by his approximation to pure spirit, or "the inward disavowal of any tribunal higher and more dreaded than the mind's own judgment upon its own act" (*PrW* 1:256). Far from ceding the luxury of private conscience to his nation's delegates, Wordworth *internalizes* the relation between subject and citizen in "the mind's" reflexivity. De Quincey's "inviolable sanctuary" of selfhood reproduces the House of Sanctity in miniature, while reinstating the division Wordsworth attempts to heal. "Housed within himself," the would-be representative may find "some horrid alien nature" occupying a "separate chamber in his brain." To purge equivocation from this sanctuary will require the "alienation" marked by sacrifice; the "traitor," says Rousseau, "must either be banished into exile . . . or be put to death as a public enemy."[45]

Turned inward, the oscillation of spokesman and revolutionary subject produces a version of doubling as dissension: "the alien nature contradicts his own, fights with it, perplexes, and confounds it" (*C* 201). Turned outward, as when Wordsworth designates himself citizen for the Peninsula, the representation of "the people" collapses into representing mind. In urging military support for the Peninsular cause, Wordsworth advocates not an alliance between autonomous powers but an occasion for acts that bypass the contingencies of expression.

It was not for the soil, or for the cities and forts, that Portugal was valued, but for the human feeling which was there; for the rights of human nature which might be there conspicuously asserted; for a triumph over injustice and oppression there to be atchieved, which could neither be concealed nor disguised, and which should penetrate the darkest corner of the dark Continent of Europe by its splendour. We combated for victory in the empire of reason, for strong-holds in the imagination. Lisbon and Portugal, as city and soil, were chiefly prized by us as a *language*; but our Generals mistook the counters of the game for the stake played for. (*PrW* 1:261–62)

From the perspective of abstract "human nature," the Peninsular subject recedes into what De Quincey calls an "original notice" (*R* 162) for liberal hegemony. *The Convention of Cintra* is at once reflexive and terroristic, vigorously emptying out the historical field it surveys. Like the campaign of terror which, Furet argues, was intrinsic to the Jacobin experiment with radical democracy, the casualties of war serve Wordsworth's need for symbolism by materializing the abstraction of popular voice.[46] The "language" of "human feeling" is spelled out in the "counters" of military casualties. Death is indeed "a displaced name for a linguistic predicament," but only its reality makes it tell.[47] "Head after head, and never heads enough/ For those who bade them fall" (*Prelude* 10:335–36): when can representation conclude its armistice with the people?

Wordsworth's translation of the Peninsular battlefields into "strongholds of the imagination" suggests as well that this sanguinary call to action betrays a wish to purge ambiguity from the interpretation of world events. The empire of reason can only be won through the erasure of ~~local inflection. As~~ Coleridge observed, Wordsworth's Peninsula is "somewhat too much *ideal-*

ized" (*CL* 3:216) to count as political agent; Southey noted that the poet "looks at the principle, abstractedly, [while] I take into view the circumstances."[48] Thus the stage of Portugal enacts a historical drama that, by recapitulating the French tragedy, purifies revolutionary strength of feeling of both its theoretical weakness and its contemporaneity. The human feeling Wordsworth finds in the Peninsula underwrites such allegorical strongholds of English imagination as the House of Sanctity, whose Jacobinical exclusion of difference suggests that *The Convention of Cintra* is less a historical event than a pretext, or post-text, for picturing the triumph of a mind without historical grounding.[49]

ON THE STRETCH

The claim that Lisbon and Portugal were valued "as a language" has the dual effect of unmasking a humanitarian plea and deconstructing the expressive premise of national identity. The equation of language and soil reveals the reactive or echoic conception of voice as a ruse for imperial assimilation, in which the immediate expressions of one "people's" struggle are annexed as the ground for a *trans*national ethos. To put the problem this way is to re-echo De Quincey's *Lake Reminiscences* of life during wartime, which both query the demand for timely utterance and prefigure a "conditional and derivative" (*R* 162) relation toward the politics of unanimous belief. De Quincey takes his cue from Wordsworth's phonic myth of sympathetic transmission, with its appeal to a static-cleansing interval between Spanish call and British response:

here were no factions to blind; no dissolution of established authorities to confound; no ferments to distemper; no narrow selfish interests to delude. The object was at a distance; and it rebounded upon us, as with force collected from a mighty distance; we were calm till the very moment of transition; and all the people were moved – and felt as with one heart, and spake as with one voice. (*PrW* 1:289)

The politics of sublimity are founded on a scenario of tense expectation, amid the pauses of factional strife, for a sound amplified by its long journey from the Continent. Pure subjectivity now reified as "object," sound acts as a "force" to produce the mobility that, Celeste Langan suggests, is Wordsworth's language for freedom.[50] Also sublimated, though, is the rhetorical and *material* question of history, which may be defined as the lag between call and response. De Quincey reopens this issue when he recalls Wordsworth's insatiable appetite for news from abroad during the early months of the Peninsular War.

Often and often it would happen that, in the deadly impatience for earlier intelligence, Wordsworth and I would walk off . . . about midnight, to a distance of three or four miles. Upon one of these occasions, when some great crisis in Spain was daily apprehended, we had waited for an hour or more, sitting upon one of the many huge blocks of stone which lie scattered over that narrow field of battle on the desolate frontier of Cumberland and Westmoreland, where King Dun Mail, with all his peerage, fell, more than a thousand years ago. The time had arrived, at length, that all hope for that night had left us: no sound came up through the winding valleys that stretched to the north; and the few cottage lights, gleaming, at wide distances, from recesses amidst the rocky hills, had long been extinct. At intervals, Wordsworth had stretched himself at length on the high road, applying his ear to the ground, so as to catch any sound of wheels that might be groaning along at a distance. (*R* 159–60)

Ears pricked for distant groans, Wordsworth literalizes his own idealist conceit, as though by listening hard enough he might catch the faint noise of uplifted voices from across the water – or, at least, hear the "tidings, fitted to convulse all nations," that were first announced by the mail-coach trumpet "screaming on the wind, and advancing through the darkness" (*C* 194). But the "crisis" Wordsworth so avidly awaits fails to answer his call. The "rapid transmission of intelligence" promised by the mails, "like fire racing along a train of gunpowder" (*C* 202–04), lapses into its parodic opposite, "this procrastinating mail," a vehicle delayed by its very freight of meaning: "there is a large extra accumulation of foreign mails this night, owing to irregularities caused by war" (*C* 216). The weightier the "content," the slower it travels. Wordsworth's anxiety for "earlier intelligence" was, it seems, rarely gratified: first the *Courier* made its way from London to Keswick on the mail-coach; then, after Coleridge and Southey had finished reading it, the newspaper came to Wordsworth "by the slow conveyance of a carrier" who was often compelled "to stop on his route well short of Grasmere" (*R* 159). This unpredictable schedule must have been galling to the revolutionary spokesman who urged "prompt decisions of the public voice" so that irresponsible agents might "be condemned the moment they are known" (*PrW* 1:274–75).

Rambling over the lonely fells at evening, Wordsworth "had a natural resemblance to Mrs. Ratcliffe's Schedoni and other assassins roaming through prose and verse," writes De Quincey, who nonetheless felt little danger "that [he] should be murdered for speaking freely" (*M* 8:291). In his mood of "deadly impatience" with the vehicles of public authority, Wordsworth also resembles his dramatic character Oswald (or Rivers), the terrorist of the French Revolutionary allegory *The Borderers*. The play's tragic action turns on Oswald's obscurely motivated efforts to persuade his dupe, Marmaduke, to kill the aged Baron Herbert: "something shall be done," Oswald vows, "which Memory/ May touch," creating a monument to the transforming power of "belief" (*PW* 46:1147, 1173–74). Marmaduke is easily convinced by the revolutionary narrative of Herbert's injustice, but finds himself paralyzed when, on the brink of murder,

> Upwards I cast my eyes, and, through a crevice,
> Beheld a star twinkling above my head,
> And, by the living God, I could not do it.
>
> (*PW* 43:988–90)

The unexpected vision of the star introduces a moment of hesitation or skepticism into the simultaneity of language, belief, and action; or, as Marmaduke puts it, "a creed, built in the heart of things," is "dissolve[d] before a twinkling atom" (*PW* 47:1219–20). Thus Marmaduke's failure of will represents a passive resistance to the power of Oswald's "swelling phrases," and to his absolutist fantasy of making the younger man "mine for ever" (*PW* 37:563, 565). If Oswald may be thought to promote a frictionless equivalence of private and public will, the twinkling atom suggests the material resistance to their conversion.

Wordsworth's less lurid fantasy of simultaneous communication between Britain and the Peninsula defuses with the gentling shock prefigured in *The Borderers*.[51] When finally he lifted his ear from the ground, Wordsworth's "eye caught a bright star" and "he gazed upon it for a minute or so." He then remarked

that, if under any circumstances, the attention is energetically braced up to an act of steady observation, or of steady expectation, then, if this intense condition of vigilance should suddenly relax, at that moment any beautiful, any impressive visual object, or collection of objects, falling upon the eye, is carried to the heart with a power not known under other circumstances. Just now, my ear was placed upon the stretch, in order to catch any sound of wheels . . . at the very instant when I raised my head from the ground, in final abandonment of hope for this night, at the very instant when the organs of attention were all at once relaxing from their tension, the bright star hanging in the air above those outlines of massy blackness fell suddenly upon my eye, and penetrated my capacity of apprehension with a pathos and a sense of the infinite, that would not have arrested me under other circumstances. (*R* 160)

In emphasizing the vigilance, energetic observation, and intensity of expectation that precede his "arrest," Wordsworth translates revolutionary virtues into the register of psychology. Like De Quincey, who, on another silent night during the wars, rode the mail-coach through "a veil of equable transparency," Wordsworth falls from erect attention into "profound" Rousseauian "reverie" (*C* 218). But the sequel casts doubt on whether his condition of epistemological vigilance, achieved by reducing the world to a stretch of rumbling earth, indeed attunes him to the experience of the real. The access of imaginative power consequent on Wordsworth's abandonment of this attitude implicitly critiques his dogmatic faith that he could compel the ground to tell him what news he needed to hear. Further, the association between this moment and the deflected murder in *The Borderers* links his expectation of auditory intelligence to violence, literal or figural: the deadliness of Wordsworth's mood consists in its indifference to the coercions of meaning to which his own poems character- istically attend.[52]

In its undercurrent of threat, the *Lake Reminiscences* anecdote recalls Rousseau's "Second Walk," in which "the flow of my rever- ies was suddenly interrupted" by "a Great Dane rushing at full tilt towards me, followed by a carriage." Rousseau was struck and lost consciousness; when he awakened,

Night was coming on. I saw the sky, some stars, and a few leaves. This first sensation was a moment of delight. I was conscious of nothing else. In this instant I was being born again, and it seemed as if all I perceived was filled with my frail existence. Entirely taken up by the present, I could remember nothing; I had no distinct notion of myself as a person, nor had I the least idea of what had just happened to me. I did not know who I was, nor where I was; I felt neither pain, fear, nor anxiety. I watched my blood flowing as I might have watched a stream, without even thinking that the blood had anything to do with me. I felt throughout my whole being such a wonderful calm, that whenever I recall this feeling I can find nothing to compare with it in all the pleasures that stir our lives.[53]

"Born again" into the *absolute* subjectivity Wordsworth imagines for Spain, Rousseau allegorizes the perfect *transparence*, or reciprocity, of individual desire and *volonté générale* he describes in the *Social Contract.* Conscious of no identity but a nature "filled with my frail [*légère*] existence," he submits himself to the act of "incorporation" in which "each one of us puts into the community his person and all his powers under the supreme direction of the general will."[54] The name for this exchange, though, is not "contract" but "conversion," whereby the mark of historical sacrifice is sublimated into the "flow" of purified language (*un rouisseau,* or river).[55]

Wordsworth's impatience, associated with the speeding carriage and the gunpowder mail, is providentially deprived of its object by a star whose function as trace suspends the teleology of "transition." However hard he had listened, the sound in his prophetic ear could only have forecast the arrival of King Mail, bringing news congealed into print and chilled by a delay of several days. No site of contention, the "narrow field of battle" at Dunmail Raise anachronistically retells the loss of an ancient kingdom; the epitaphic "blocks of stone" are all that remain of soldiers "stretched . . . upon one bloody aceldama" (*C* 208).[56] There can be little possibility of instantaneous response for a spokesman at this "great distance from London" (*PrW* 1:357). Nor should there be, as De Quincey shows *pace* Wordsworth, who "went on to illustrate the same psychological principle from another instance," the "exquisite poem" describing "a mountain boy . . . provoking the owls to a contest with himself, by 'mimic hootings' blown through his hands." "The poem," De Quincey adds,

goes on to describe the boy as waiting, amidst "the pauses of his skill," for the answer of the birds – waiting with intensity of expectation – and then, at length, when, after waiting to no purpose, his attention began to relax – that is, in other words, under the giving way of one exclusive direction of his senses, began suddenly to allow an admission to other objects – then, in that instant, the scene actually before him, the visible scene, would enter unawares –

"With all its solemn imagery" –

This complex scenery was – What?

> "Was carried *far* into his heart,
> With all its pomp, and that uncertain heav'n received
> Into the bosom of the steady lake."

This very expression, "far," by which space and its infinities are attributed to the human heart, and to its capacities of re-echoing the sublimities of nature, has always struck me as with a flash of sublime revelation. (*R* 160–61)

The shock that carries the visible scene "unawares into his mind" transfigures the boy into the stricken Rousseau experiencing his "moment of delight." The deflection of the senses from mimic sound to figurative vision is De Quincey's contribution, which he emphasizes by omitting the lines on "the voice/ Of mountain-torrents" that Wordsworth's boy heard "in that silence, while he hung/ Listening" (*PW* 145:18–21). De Quincey's pause mocks Wordsworth's diplomatic skill: in the persona of revolutionary spokesman, the poet has "been hoaxed" like his own most obtuse critic "into entering upon a sentimental correspondence of love or friendship – almost regularly 'duplying,' 'replying,' and 'quadru-plying'" an imagined commonality with the Spanish "original theme" (*R* 161–62).[57]

This is Jacobinism at its most naive; Rousseau and the Winander boy know better. As De Quincey explains,

The very object of the poem is not the first or initial stage of the boy's history – the exercise of skill which led him, as an occasion, into a rigid and tense effort of attention – not this, but the second stage, the conse-quence of that attention. Even the attention was an effect, a derivative state; but the second stage, upon which the poet fixes his object, is an effect of that effect; and it is clear that the original notice of the boy's talent is introduced only as a *conditio sine qua non* – a notice without which a particular result (namely, the tense attention of expectation) could not have been made intelligible; as, again, without this result being noticed, the reaction of that action could quite as little have been made intellig-ible. (*R* 162)

Extending Rousseau's critique of social "incorporation," the poem reverses his experience of a full universe into the boy's apprehen-sion of the infinity within. Of particular interest to De Quincey, though, is how Wordsworth figures both the materiality (as rhetoric) and the asymmetry of this conversion, in the speaker's inexplicable "trance of reverie" over the grave of fraternal corre-spondence. Poem and poet elude both Lord Jeffrey's peremptory challenge and "some reader's" insistence that "a poem ought to explain itself" (*R* 161–62). In refusing to yield up the content of the reverie, the poem exemplifies the kind of resistance to contractual meaning that Marx describes as the excess of content beyond phrase.[58] The "memorable effects produced by poets" cannot "be even imperfectly explained" without "jolting" and "retard[ing]" the "fluent motion" of narrative (*R* 162–63; *M* 10:193).

In "The Vision of Sudden Death," De Quincey returns these issues to the historical field by assuming unapologetically what is intimated in Rousseau and implicit in Wordsworth: that social contract and *convention* – whether between Arthur Wellesley and the Portuguese insurgents, between the imperial mail-coach and private subjects, or, indeed, between the liberal British citizen and his suffering Peninsular correspondents – always carries a trace of coercion that figures, in extremity, as violence. The mail-coach has been linked throughout De Quincey's essay not merely to speed but to punctuality, in all its revolutionary glamour and danger. As De Quincey wrote in an 1818 editorial for the *Westmoreland Gazette,* "when the mad driver Democracy sits upon the dickey, an overturn must soon follow."[59] If "we, the collective mail," collided with the "traitors" "usurping" the road,

we had not even time to laugh over them. Tied to post-office time, with an allowance in some cases of fifty minutes for eleven miles, could the royal mail pretend to undertake the offices of sympathy and condolence? . . . If even it seemed to trample on humanity, it did so, I contended, in discharge of its own more peremptory duties. (*C* 190–91)

Inevitably, the state tramples on some in the triumphant progress of its "mighty renovation." "I feel/ An impulse to precipitate my verse": "'Come now, ye golden times,'" Wordsworth prays to the "open sands" as in post-Revolutionary frenzy he considers "when and how/ The madding factions might be tranquillized" (*Prelude* 9:9–10; 10:541–54). Wordsworth's sympathy with power accelerates into De Quincey's uncheckable "storm-flight" of horses' feet "running on a sandy margin," while he experiences the reverie that, as in Wordsworth and Rousseau, conflates "equable transparency" with its opposite, resistance. His reverie is broken by "a sullen sound" announcing a "ruin" which, "being foreseen, was not the less inevitable" (*C* 218–23). Knowing that "the signal is flying for *action*," De Quincey can summon no "pres-

ence of mind," for he is already committed to a political "action"
– the mobility of the mail-coach – that has overtaken his consent.[60]
Yet his very incapacity exonerates him from the charge of Jacobin
ruthlessness; "men of genius," Coleridge notes of the Gironde
leader Brissot, "are rarely either prompt in action or consistent in
general conduct" (*CW* 4[1]:328).

The sound De Quincey hears, like the rumble Wordsworth
anticipated, threatens not the listener but the "light," "frail" (*C*
219) obstacle in his way. The coach has traversed its proper
bounds. Unable to match his thought to its pace, De Quincey
experiences his historicity as lag or *a*synchrony, a dilemma his solution thematizes.

> Strange it is, and to a mere auditor of the tale, might seem laughable, that
> I should need a suggestion from the *Iliad* to prompt the sole recourse that
> remained. But so it was. Suddenly I remembered the shout of Achilles,
> and its effect. (*C* 221)

Even the radicalized utterance of a shout must echo some other.
De Quincey shouts, and his own failure is redeemed by the gig
driver's "sudden answer to the call. He saw, he heard, he comprehended" (*C* 222). Bettering Rousseau, who comically imagines
"leap[ing] into the air at precisely the right moment to allow the
dog to pass underneath me," the young man emulates the self-
command of Caesar, taking the timely action of the subject who
"works."[61]

Swept by circumstance into the role of invading army, De
Quincey attempts to rewrite history by mitigating its consequences. The shout of Achilles, which announced the end of his
rage against Agamemnon, recoups aggression as alliance, just as,
according to Wordsworth,

> the British and Spanish Nations, with an impulse like that of two ancient
> heroes throwing down their weapons and reconciled in the field, cast off
> at once their aversions and enmities, and mutually embraced each other
> – to solemnize this conversion of love, not by the festivities of peace, but
> by combating side by side through danger and under affliction in the
> devotedness of perfect brotherhood. (*PrW* 1:228)

Wordsworth does not mention that Achilles and Agamemnon
reunite in revenge for the death of Patroklos.[62] Achilles's grief over
the body of his friend prefigures, but cannot prevent,
Wordsworth's similar vigil by the grave of the Winander boy. Thus
Wordsworth's program, in *The Convention of Cintra*, for a corrective

repetition of historical trauma mutates, for De Quincey, into *uncontrollable* repetition, as the Revolution reenacts itself in the 1810s, in 1830, and again in the 1840s.[63] Consciousness is always belated *vis-à-vis* contingency; language necessarily articulates the future as anterior, the response to a voice from the past (*C* 223). All that remains of De Quincey's collision with history are the "averted signs" (*C* 225) reminding him that no mimetic shout can make the present moment answer to the record. "Presence of mind" is a chimera; at best, history – the deferred action of reconstructed causes – suggests a *language* for transition.

It may be objected that this account indicates an unwarranted capitulation to De Quinceyan pathos. In another sense, De Quincey's anachronism does represent a successful performance: the gig moves, catastrophe is averted, and the shock of impact merely causes a "pivot" in the position of the carriage. No one dies, and perhaps the young people rise sadder and wiser the morrow morn. The pause of deep silence that follows his warning might then be said to intimate the future as "bias" or "torsion" (*C* 222–24) from the text of history. That innovation known as the Reform Bill, for example, was "built on a mere reverberation of one petulant word, dropped in a moment of irritation by the Duke of Wellington."[64] The performativity of language, in this view, is part and parcel of its failure to meet circumstances head on. The analysis of ideology measures the angle of refraction between an intentional utterance and its belated reverberations. History is the agent of that refraction, the resistant material of the subjectively unforeseen.

The notion of resistance, finally, returns the De Quinceyan text to the political context from which it swerves. Implicitly endorsing the sublime indifference of the mail-coach, Wordsworth excoriates the Convention-makers of Cintra for the venality of their aims:

Riddance, mere riddance – safety, mere safety – are objects far too defined, too inert and passive in their own nature, to have ability either to rouze or to sustain. They win not the mind by any attraction of grandeur or sublime delight, either in effort or in endurance: for the mind gains consciousness of its strength to undergo only by exercise among materials which admit the impression of its power, – which grow under it, which bend under it, – which resist, – which change under its influence, – which alter either through its might or in its presence, by it or before it. These, during times of tranquillity, are the objects with which, in the studious walks of sequestered life, Genius most loves to hold intercourse; by which it is reared and supported. (*PrW* 1:291)

Wordsworth's disdain for "mere safety" evokes the antithetical logic of Robespierre's Public Safety, whose reach expanded when "beset with foes on every side" (*Prelude* 10:215, 311). Resistance to the expansive power is a dialectical necessity of the imperial project itself; as Wordsworth argues in letter of 1811, "if a nation have nothing to oppose or to fear without, it cannot escape decay and concussion within . . . My prayer, as a Patriot, is that we may always have . . . enemies capable of resisting us" (*MY* 1:480). The explicit pretext for such a sentiment comes from Napoleon, the man of "*commanding* Genius" who, in contrast to the "self-sufficing . . . absolute *Genius*," must "impress [his] preconceptions on the world without, in order to present them back to [his] own view" (*BL* 1:31–32).

To theorize the necessity of resistance, however, is not to foresee its form or its direction. *Cintra* posits opposition as material facticity to be sublated: by countering imperial France, the Peninsular rebels would provide the historical friction that tests and consolidates universal "mind." But Wordsworth mistook the kind of history he was writing, which turned out not to be *The Phenomenology of Spirit* but the story of his textual production. If the mind's progress (or even "the march of a Poem") suggests to him the readiest analogy for "mov[ing] the Continent" (*MY* 1:482, 484), De Quincey reverses tenor and vehicle, while deflating allegory to the level of *literary* history, or biography. His resistance turns on the letter. Disregarding abstract principles, De Quincey presents himself in the *Lake Reminiscences* as the material impressed by Wordsworth: "struck" by his expressions, bending to his will, holding intercourse with him in his walks, and changing under his influence to an ardent supporter of Spain.[65] Thus he exactly fulfills Wordsworth's prophesy, but only by shifting registers. Indeed, the idea of resistance includes an element of surprise: the proof that an "inert" object has been roused into life comes in its *clinamen* from the path of Genius. Swerving from mechanical exemplum to conditional and derivative narration, De Quincey both vindicates the citizen's conversion and suggests its material disfigurement. Wordsworth's genius is attested by the paradoxical result that all minds do *not* resemble his.[66]

The turn from the grand historical stage to the biographical anecdote is both an apostasy from politics as such and strong in its resistance to totalization.[67] Rather than a picture of the mind, De Quincey offers a fragment from the past, belatedly reminding Wordsworth of the lack of fit between transitory action, its super-imposed slogans, and the historical field in which it will have transpired. De Quincey's difference from the author of *The Convention of Cintra* lies in his confession that he lives out of time: his numbered hours carry "the dreadful legend of TOO LATE" (*C* 198–99). Far from unharnessing referential traces, though, asynchrony manifests itself in such material effects as the expulsion of resistance to Wordsworth's transcendental ambition. In De Quincey's cast of *The Borderers*, Wordsworth plays both Oswald and Marmaduke in the scene at Dunmail Raise, but De Quincey would re-echo the younger man's fate when, a few months later, he left Grasmere for London. "Your pupil," says Marmaduke to Oswald, "is, you see, an apt proficient" (*PW* 61:2287). Prefiguring a more lasting estrangement, De Quincey took the role of time itself in the drama of *Cintra*'s composition. The "huge blocks of stone which lie scattered over . . . the desolate frontier," stand like "monuments" "on the dreary waste" of the imaginary collaboration he left behind (*R* 160; *PW* 61:2326).

LONDON CORRESPONDENT

During the Peninsular War, De Quincey remembers, "the motions of the British armies were accompanied by a corresponding activity among British compositors" (*M* 10:37). Wordsworth's compositors, however, failed to keep pace with his own march. Scarcely had he begun work on his tract before its timeliness in relation to British public opinion and the latest continental developments became a major concern. In particular, his distance from London presented considerable difficulties at the level of news-gathering and manuscript transmission for a project couched in the ephemeral form of a prose pamphlet. News of the Convention had reached England in September 1808. By November 25, Wordsworth mentioned being at work on a response, adding that "as I hope that what I am writing may be of some use to the Public, no time ought to be lost" (*MY* 1:274). Southey wrote one day later that he "daily expect[ed] to hear" of the pamphlet's completion,[68] and Coleridge assured Stuart on December 6 that "Wordsworth has nearly finished a series of most masterly Essays" (*CL* 3:134). Nevertheless, the first essay did not appear in the *Courier* until December 27; the second was delayed by revision and a postal accident until over two weeks later. Wordsworth then abandoned the serial format he had initially adopted "for the sake of immediate and wide circulation," and, motivated partly by "a wish to possess additional documents and facts," determined to put off further publication until the work could be embodied in a separate shape (*MY* 1:278; *PrW* 1:223). His rationale suggests how the ethic of timely utterance combines conflicting requirements for immediacy and inclusiveness. To this technical dilemma of *print* impression, De Quincey would propose himself as solution – becoming, thereby, its embodiment.[69]

Wordsworth composed more slowly and at much greater length than he had projected in November, and though with the help of Dorothy and Mary as well as Sara Hutchinson he was regularly able to send off packets of manuscript to the London printer, he was still at work on the body of the pamphlet by mid-February. As its prefatory "Advertisement" suggests, he blamed his slow progress on the isolation he otherwise prized: even discounting the delay of "intelligence," the labor of proofreading would be compounded by the interval needed to transmit the sheets to and from the press. "Nothing can be more unfortunate for a work of this kind," Wordsworth later concluded, "than a residence so far from London and so unfavorable to communication with the post" (*MY* 1:354). His frustration represented an opportunity for De Quincey, who volunteered to serve as press agent, staying in London from late February until the pamphlet should be complete. Time would be saved if the proofs could be corrected on location, and Wordsworth would be assured of all that zealous supervision could do to hasten along the compositors. De Quincey also envisioned making a diacritical impression by taking over the tract's punctuation; curiously, he seems to have convinced Wordsworth that his own method lacked "proportion and symmetry" (*J* 123). Punctuality and punctuation are related by their joint concern with the synchronization of tenor and vehicle; as "The English Mail-Coach" suggests, rhetorical performance demands both "*timing* and periodical interruption" (*C* 197). Working for Wordsworth in London, De Quincey could portray himself as "the good and faithful servant" who "organizes the hours, and gives them a soul": his days and months, like those of Coleridge's methodical man, "the stops and punctual marks in the records of duties performed" (*The Friend, CW* 4[1]:450).

Thus he gave up the relative camaraderie of the midnight rambles to assume a role that he magnified into "editing a pamphlet" (*J* 199), but which Wordsworth described in terms of pure dispatch. The impossible position he had brought upon himself kept him in London for four lonely months, during which his cordial relation with Wordsworth deteriorated into an exchange of impatient directives and increasingly tedious self-justifications. "Deputed" to the office of circumventing the mail and eliminating "press errors" (*MY* 1:320; *PrW* 1:357), De Quincey nonetheless came to personify the hazards of print, as alienation and as deferral. This result was not only psychologically foreordained; it was allegorized in the text he undertook to purify and perfect.

The Armistice and Convention between Generals Wellesley and Junot represented, for Wordsworth, a sinister parody of the French National Convention and, hence, a usurpation in the guise of a contract. Considered as text, the treaty became vulnerable to a detailed close reading that focuses on questions of authority and intentionality. The Convention, Wordsworth alleges, was corrupt in its very premises; the British generals had no right to act on behalf of the Portuguese government, and indeed wielded no political powers at all. "In their readiness to flourish with the pen," he charges, they "overlooked the sword, the symbol of their power, and the appropriate instrument of their success and glory" (*PrW* 1:260). Their job was not to write but to kill. (Byron likewise derides the "diadem hight foolscap" worn by the "fiend" who "foil'd the knights in Marialva's dome.")[70] Elevated into signatories, the generals exceeded their authority as agents of British sovereignty, deludedly fancying "themselves and their army to be *the British government*" (*PrW* 1:274).[71] This idea perverts the relation between a people and its representative: rather than being "carried forward" by a voice that spoke through them, the generals exaggerated their individuality, each "writ[ing] down with his own hand, *I am the man*" (*PrW* 1:263). Wellesley's infatuation with the "shews and forms" of "sounding titles and phrases, come from what quarter they might" suggests an attempt to "magnif[y] himself and his atchievements" through the artificial diction and stale conventions characteristic of both bad rulers and bad poets (1:234, 251).

Not only did the generals arrogate representative powers to themselves; they failed to "call . . . forth" any response that might vindicate them (1:267). Therefore, Wordsworth concludes, "the contract was self-destroyed from the beginning"; it was, indeed, "not a shattering of the edifice of justice, but a subversion of its foundations" (1:281). At the moment when the people of the Peninsula

> were in a stage of their journey which could not be accomplished without the spirit which was then prevalent in them . . . the heads of the British army and nation . . . stepped in with their forms, their impediments, their rotten customs and precedents, their narrow desires, their busy and purblind fears; and called out to these aspiring travellers to halt – "For ye are in a dream"; confounded them (for it was the voice of a seeming friend that spoke); and spell-bound them . . . by an instrument framed "in the eclipse" and sealed "with curses dark" . . . We had power to give a brotherly aid to our allies in supporting the mighty world which their shoulders had undertaken to uphold; and, while they were expecting from us this aid, we undermined . . . the ground upon which they stood. (*PrW* 1:300)

Compacts between nations, if they "do not uphold, and feed, and leave in quiet," become counter-plots, "unremittingly and noiselessly at work to derange, to subvert, to lay waste, to vitiate, and to dissolve" (*PrW* 2:85). Any delay to the "journey" of the people's voice translates into a conspiracy against the revolutionary subject. "What!" De Quincey exclaims, "shall it be within benefit of clergy, to . . . interrupt the great respirations, ebb or flood, of the national intercourse – to endanger the safety of tidings running day and night between all nations . . . ?" (*C* 190). The Convention of Cintra, an obtrusion of precedent, artifice and "private will" into a situation that demanded a bloody enactment of the people's voice, realizes the worst-case scenario for language that Wordsworth would theorize a few months later in his "Essays Upon Epitaphs." The Jacobinical tension between embodiment and representation is predictably displaced into a betrayal of voice by writing.

The Convention displays the specialized, hermetic features that Wordsworth criticizes, in the "Preface" to *Lyrical Ballads,* as symptomatic of an attempt to widen the distance between print culture and real language. *Cintra* rehearses this theme in the idiom of revolutionary paranoia. Wordsworth's earlier horror at the "ephemeral monsters" countenanced by the Republic (*Prelude* 10:36) is now turned back on the anti-Jacobins Wellesley and Dalrymple, who allowed "the sovereign of this horde of devastators" to say "that his army of Portugal had 'DICTATED THE TERMS OF ITS GLORIOUS RETREAT'" (*PrW* 1:289). The English generals have become collaborationists, "chang[ing] all things into their contraries" and "revers[ing] every thing" (1:252). But the treaty itself is the real evil, a "*lusus naturae* in the moral world – a solitary straggler out of the circumference of nature's law – a monster which could not propagate, and had no birthright in futurity" (1:281). At once dispassionately mechanical and malign in its effects, counter-revolutionary representation is the man-made enemy of gothic fiction.[72]

It is therefore the citizen's duty to "pass sentence upon" "the remote and immediate authors" of the Convention, lest it appear "no longer as the forlorn monster which I have described," but "put on another shape, and [be] endued with a more formidable life – with the power to generate and transmit after its kind" (1:248–49, 282). Like the authors and executors of the French Constitution, Wordsworth slays counter-spirits to contain the errancy of the letter, somewhat as the decapitation of Louis XVI "*imprinted* a grand character on the National Convention."[73] Wellesley and Dalrymple, authors of monstrosity, must be branded with "unremovable contempt and hatred" to prove that they acted alone (*J* 152).[74] Sentencing takes the form of a rival poetics: incorporating, analyzing, and rebutting the text of the Peninsular Convention, Wordsworth invalidates the contract by fiat of the poet–legislator.[75]

Wordsworth's loathing for agents turned authors should have forewarned his press agent. Chary indeed of posing as the poet's surrogate, De Quincey began his self-appointed duties on a small scale, diligently proofreading, describing the London political climate, and forwarding international news to the "Grasmere Secretary for foreign affairs" (*J* 111).[76] Upon his arrival he assured the poet that "the Convention of Cintra is [not] at all out of date"; if published by mid-April, the pamphlet would "come out under greater advantages – in point of time – than it could have done, if published *at any other time whatsoever*" (*J* 96, 131). "With respect to the printing," he added, "nothing can be more correct." (*J* 107). But even these early dispatches betray the ironies and contradic-

tions of De Quincey's role: delegated to reconcile authorial intention and printed text, he created the distance he was assigned to
broach. The most mechanical editorial tasks rapidly developed
interpretive dimensions. While punctuating the first two packets
of manuscript from Grasmere, for example, he discovered "a
lacuna"; observing that "no man, short of an Oedipus, can tell how
it shall be supplied," he anxiously solicited a decision from
Wordsworth, who, he was sure, "would not wish one single invalid
to delay the march of the army" (*J* 97).[77] From the beginning, he
was caught between the equally untenable alternatives of delaying
progress by deferring to Wordsworth, or second-guessing the
author's "will" by assuming local authority.

Given a choice between two evils, De Quincey incurred the consequences of both. On the one hand, he dutifully reported every
"slightest alteration" made on his "own discretion" (*J* 110–11), so
that these could be canceled if Wordsworth disapproved. On the
other, his exaggerated diligence as a proofreader, along with his
pedantic rigor in enforcing a "logical equilibration of sentences"
and a "learned and *ineffable* orthography" (*J* 124, 138) had the
paradoxical result of eliciting faulty proofs in place of the immac-
ulate typesetting he had praised on his arrival. Within three weeks
he was finding such "monstrous errors (whole passages left out –
and words substituted which leave a *kind* of meaning &c.)" that he
was demanding a second proof before the sheets were struck off;
a few days later he was up to three, and "the compositor thinks that
I shall soon after want a dozen" (*J* 116–19). Errors mutated into
inversions, as the compositor took his revenge by "introduc[ing] a
not in the followg. place – 'Done and concluded *not* the year and
day above-mentioned'" (*J* 166). The uncanniness of print was to
be a motif of De Quincey's career; to William Tait, publisher of the
Lake Reminiscences, he complained of an "unknown persecutor"
who followed "in . . . [his] steps doing secretly whatever mischief
he can" to his corrected proofs (*NLS* MS. 10998).

Throughout March and April De Quincey worked in ostenta-
tious haste, encouraging Wordsworth to believe that the pamphlet
might be published by early spring even though new manuscript
was still arriving at least through the end of March (*J* 77). The
danger of "very serious delay" for "a pamphlet adverting perpetually to passing occurrences" (*J* 117) also justified his single
abortive ploy for representation in the text. Between the composi-

tion and the typesetting of Wordsworth's apostrophe to Saragossa (*PrW* 1:296), that city had been attacked for a second time, and finally defeated. De Quincey took the occasion to insert a florid note "as from a friend of the author's employed to correct the press errors," praising the city's "glorious martyrdom" and declaring that "all which had been here prophesied of her she had faithfully ratified" (*J* 117). Wordsworth retorted implacably, "it will . . . be necessary to *cancel* the . . . footnote" (*MY* 1:298), condemning it as both redundant and *un*faithful. Implying a private and proprietary relation to voice – "I am the friend" – it mimicked Wellesley's officious posturing (*PrW* 1:263). Perhaps it even threatened to usurp a poetic subject; a sonnet beginning "Hail, Zaragoza!" appears in Wordsworth's 1815 collection *Poems Dedicated to National Independence and Liberty* (*PW* 215).

De Quincey declared himself "miserable in making any discretional alterations since the canceled note," and even more miserable in being accused of "such an opinion as . . . I am supposed to have held and expressed about Saragossa" (*J* 136, 133). Trivial as was the occasion, the suspicion of a difference in perspective had serious repercussions in such a totalitarian climate. Just as typographical inaccuracies became "monstrous errors" – and attempts to correct these hydra-headed errors only multiplied them – any lapse in the perfect *transparence* of the remote author and his agent raised the specter of things "changed . . . into their contraries" (*PrW* 1:252). De Quincey felt obliged to insist that his "note said the very *contrary* (not *rhetorically* the contrary, but *logically*) of what Mr. Wordsworth has supposed it to say" (*J* 133). This was no palliation: Wordsworth "had learned from Mrs. C[oleridge] – a vulgar phrase for all attempts at reciprocal explanations – he called them contemptuously *'fending and proving'*" (*R* 376). De Quincey's older brother (another William!) similarly accused him of "quibbling" and "pettifogulising" during their childhood war-games with the factory "Jacobins"; the charges arose from De Quincey's sensitivity to

flaws of language, not from pedantic exaction of superfluous accuracy, but, on the contrary, from too conscientious a wish to escape the mistakes which language not rigorous is apt to occasion . . . most unwillingly I found, in almost everybody's words, an unintentional opening left for double interpretations. (*M* 1:77)

His concern to avoid *double entendres* had, of course, precisely the opposite effect: "I was continually falling into treason, without knowing exactly how I got into it" (*M* 1:78).

De Quincey's editorial scrupulousness led to a contretemps over the pamphlet's motto, an excerpt from Bacon's "Advertisement Touching the Controversies of the Church of England" abjuring "politic" language ("ideology," rendered ideologically) for the voice of "a feeling Christian" whose words spring from "hate or love" (quoted in *PrW* 1:222). Distrusting Wordsworth's scholarship, De Quincey unwisely consulted several editions of Bacon's works to check the reading, which he corrected to "a character of *zeal* or love" (*J* 192–96). Wordsworth quickly labelled this an "exceedingly" important mistake, adding that he was "sadly grieved about that error in the Press in the Mottoe, *zeal* for *hate*, as it utterly destroys the sole reason for presenting the passage so conspicuously to notice" (*MY* 1:341, 347).[78] His excessive response turns on the distinction, basic to *Cintra*, between the righteous hatred of a "people with imagination" and the "unfeeling" agency of the "zealots of abstract principle" (*PrW* 1:332, 229). The concept of zeal, a passion without affect, brings powerful feeling into uncomfortable proximity with abstraction. But however damaging to Wordsworth's argument, the "character of Zeal" nicely summarizes Coleridge's portrait of De Quincey: "anxious yet dilatory, confused from over-accuracy . . . at once systematic and labyrinthine," his efforts amplified "by his zeal & fear of not discharging his Trust" (*CL* 3:205).

The greater the zeal of the deputy, the worse-placed the trust; though Wordsworth found few other press errors to lament, he had a ready grievance in the pamphlet's late publication date, June 9, 1809. "What a pity that it did not come out sooner!" Dorothy lamented; "it would have been then much plainer to all Readers (very few of whom will bear in mind *the time* at which the Tract was written) what a true prophet [William] has been" (*MY* 1:356–57). A text whose success is gauged solely in terms of prophecy may be doomed by any other measure.[79] Accounting in advance for this outcome, Wordsworth claimed that "my hands . . . have been completely tied." The occasion of the delay he naturally assigned to De Quincey, who was "so scrupulous with the Compositor, in having his own plan rigorously followed to an iota, that the Man took the

Pet, and whole weeks elapsed without the Book's advancing a step." "That [De Quincey] has failed is too clear," he concluded, "and not without great blame on his own part" (*MY* 1:352, 350–51). For Wordsworth, De Quincey personified the return of a repressed historical materiality, both in the sense of postponement and in the way he called to light the invisible hand of labor, that refractory agency of print impression.

Not only was De Quincey blamed for halting progress; he was even assigned the burden of the pamphlet's ponderous style. Having volunteered to punctuate Wordsworth's prose, he associated himself with the "mechanology" of style, the "representation of the logical divisions – and . . . gamut of the proportions and symmetry of the different members – of each sentence" (*J* 123). Punctuation, "the product of typography," is, he later wrote, "an artificial machinery for maintaining the integrity of the sense against all mistakes of the writer," and withdraws "the energy of men's anxieties from the natural machinery [*sic*], which [lies] in just and careful arrangement." As he learned, machinery can take on a life of its own:

All punctuation narrows the path, which is else unlimited; and (*by* narrowing it) may chance to guide the reader into the right groove amongst several that are *not* right. But also punctuation has the effect very often (and almost always has the power) of biassing and predetermining the reader to an erroneous choice of meaning. Better, therefore, no guide at all than one which is likely enough to lead astray, and which must always be suspected and mistrusted. (*M* 10:164–65).

Southey believed De Quincey had indeed made Wordsworth's sentences "more obscure by an unusual system of punctuation" (quoted in *J* 83–84).[80] To Coleridge, it was a case of mechanology supplanting organology; "Mr De Quincey's strange & most mistaken System of punctuation . . . perplexed" both sentence structure and "the understandings of common readers." "Never," he roundly declared, "was a stranger whim than the notion that , ; : and . could be made logical symbols expressing all the diversities of logical connection" (*CL* 3:214). A minor strain of "pestilential philosophism," "system" oddly enough conduces to a "depth of Feeling . . . so incorporated with depth of Thought, that the Attention is kept throughout at it's utmost Strain & Stretch" (*PrW* 1:332; *CL* 3:214). Over-fastidiousness as to logic does not mute the "note . . . of the Instrument," but augments it to a point of (inaud-

ible) excess. In short, Coleridge puns inscrutably, "the apple pie
. . . is made all of Quinces" (*CL* 3:214).[81] Despite regarding his
labor as intellectually negligible, Coleridge attributes to De
Quincey all the static that would prevent Wordsworth's voice from
reaching its audience.[82]

Wordsworth's undersecretary has become, at length, the personification of *material* resistance to the philosophic mind. De
Quincey's zealous attention to detail looked to Wordsworth like so
much rotten custom and precedent, a busy and purblind display
of impedimenta. His every attempt to rephrase the manuscript or
to assert editorial prerogative was regarded by the poet as an irruption of noisy subjectivity into the impersonal current of pure
feeling. "Overvalu[ing] the message," as Michel Serres puts it,
Wordsworth "undervalues the noise . . . [of] the functioning of the
system. He represses the parasites in order to send or receive
communications better and to make them circulate in a . . . work-
able fashion."[83] De Quincey's labor correspondingly exemplifies
the delay, distortion, and subversion of any intelligence conceived
as ontologically prior to expression.

Given a polemical division of unanimous voice from counter-
plotting representation, it was inevitable that the agent "who corrects the press errors" (*PrW* 1:357) should come to signify the
resistant matter of print, or even "error" itself. To say so is both to
reiterate an article of deconstructive materialism and to insist
upon its historical consequences. When Wordsworth found his
scapegoat for "the dreadful knell of *too late*" (*C* 211), he also found
his rationale for the pamphlet's failure to embody national voice.
"I have no hopes of the thing making any *impression*," he wrote to
Daniel Stuart, echoing his own trope for historical causality; "the
style of thinking and feeling is so little in the Spirit of the age" (*MY*
1:296; my emphasis). But he had forgotten this admission when,
complaining of his agent's behavior two months later, he brooded
that "if I were superstitious, I should deem that there was a fatality
attending this, my first essay in politics" (*MY* 1:350). De Quincey,
that attendant fatality, made visible the unbreachable gap between
an ideal "people" and the empirical "populace" whom
Wordsworth mystified as the Spirit of the Age.[84] As the convenient
figure for *Cintra's* failure to shape public policy, De Quincey
embodied history's revenge on idealism.

De Quincey never again presumed to collaborate on a project

of Wordsworth's. Not content with the "inert" role of amanuensis, and preempted by Coleridge from the position of *The Friend,* he could only be construed as desperate or impertinent when he made any impression at all. The diffuse efforts that produced a published pamphlet – titled *The Convention of Cintra* and attested by "Wordsworth" – proved irreconcilable with the text's governing trope, for the claims of "voice" to absolute inclusivity rest upon its denial of all circumstantial mitigations. Committed, however, to the *ideal* of representation as embodied universal, Wordsworth would go on in *The Excursion* to attempt the poetic consolidation of national identity. But before Wordsworth and his London agent parted professional ways, De Quincey had achieved a small incursion into the militantly homogeneous body of the pamphlet.

The main text of *The Convention of Cintra* is followed by five appendices, as well as reprints of the "Suspension of Arms" and "Definitive Convention" signed by Wellesley, Junot, *et al.* After these, and occupying ten dense pages of Wordsworth's *Prose Works,* comes a "Postscript on Sir John Moore's Letters," attributed to "the friend, who corrects the press errors" and absolving "the Author" from responsibility "for any thing which follows" (*PrW* 1:357). This apparently is the "long note on Spanish affairs" which De Quincey later claimed to have written while "superintend[ing] the publication of" Wordsworth's tract, and on which he prided himself for expressing early confidence in the Spanish and "contempt" for the French (*M* 3:106–07). Authorship for this parasitical coda is nonetheless difficult to assign conclusively. Wordsworth's editors include it on the principle that its ideas are substantially his, but decline "to attempt a complete critical apparatus" for a text he did not write. A manuscript draft of the note has the inscription: "Convention of Cintra/ All in confusion/ Is this Wordsworths/ hand or my Fathers" (*PrW* 1:410, 370).[85]

The problem of the note's authorship again doubles its argument, which attempts to acquit the Spanish Resistance of Sir John Moore's recently-published accusations without reflecting negatively on the general himself. Wordsworth, observing that Moore's letters "had made a great impression" on public opinion, delegated to De Quincey the sensitive task of erasing this impression while honoring a military hero whose death had, in his contemporaries' "tender estimations, *cannonized*" him (*MY* 1:306–07). To adjust a canonical narrative without impugning its general premise is to engage in the exercise of what De Quincey calls "casuistry," a "supplement to the main system" of "moral principles; – the latter supplying the *major* (or normal) proposition; the former supplying the *minor* proposition, which brings the special case under the rule" (*M* 10:30; my emphasis).

> *Casuistry!* the very word *casuistry* expresses the science which deals with such *cases*; for, as a case in the declension of a noun means a falling away or a deflection from the upright nominative (*rectus*), so a case in ethics implies some falling off or deflection from the high road of catholic morality. (*M* 3:165)

The distinction would become a hobbyhorse with De Quincey, who ultimately claims "the immense superiority of this supplementary section to the main body of the system" of ethics (*M* 3:164). These fallings-off, he is at pains to argue, constitute neither apostasy nor treason; casuistry, the ineluctable deviation of principle into minute particulars, tempers moral absolutes in the flame of historical circumstance.

In the Postscript, De Quincey accordingly focuses on Moore's delicate position as the leader of a poorly planned campaign, reporting "to the very persons who had imposed this dilemma upon him" (*PrW* 1:358). Spinning out the parallel between military and literary instruments, De Quincey ventriloquizes his subject:

> Somewhere there must be blame: but where? with himself he knew that there was none: the English Government (with whom he must have seen that at least a part of the blame lay – for sending him so late, and with a force so lamentably incommensurate to the demands of the service) it was not for him – holding the situation that he did – openly to accuse (though, by implication, he often does accuse them); and therefore it became his business to look to the Spaniards; and, in their conduct, to search for palliations of that inefficiency on his part – which else the persons, to whom he was writing, would understand as charged upon themselves. (*PrW* 1:358)

Moore, like De Quincey, was deputed too late to a task that was always already fraught with contradictions. "Writing with such a purpose," then, and hampered by "anxious forebodings of calamity or dishonour; and . . . the pain he must have felt at not being free to censure those with whom . . . the embarrassments of his situation had, at least in part, originated," he could not but translate a problem of "relative circumstances" (*PrW* 1:358) into one of faulty national character. Potentially a scapegoat himself, he found another convenient to hand. De Quincey exculpates both: if Moore points to the contradictory "demands of his service," the Spanish represent a form of "resistance" easily mistaken for apathy or procrastination (*PrW* 1:360–61). De Quincey's reading of Moore introduces what Serres calls a "shift" in the system of Wordsworth's argument: the "noise" of petty contingency has become a "message" of self-justification.[86]

Wordsworth, perhaps alert to this shift, judged De Quincey's rebuttal all too gentle for the purpose (*MY* 1:347). But by then the Postscript had been struck off and printed, and De Quincey had made his point: "I did . . . as well as, under the circumstances, I could" (*J* 175). "Doubts of casuistry" (*C* 2) thus return the merely subjective to the domain of the political, contaminating the purity of Wordsworth's principles but also articulating a rationale for biography as something both more and less than representative "incarnation." In "assign[ing] the value" (*PrW* 1:358) of Moore's testimony, De Quincey prefigured his own "exposure of . . . errors and infirmities," a case of self-indulgence itself "open to doubts of casuistry." The *Confessions*, his "breach of the general rule," would affirm his "religious zeal" in "resistance" to an imputed offense. "Infirmity and misery do not, of necessity, imply guilt": rather, they mark the deflection from idealism into idiosyncrasy, from language into history, and from transparent embodiment to the fallible private body (*C* 1–2).

In their resistance to representative status, and in their thematization of eccentricity, De Quincey's confessions constitute themselves as "minor propositions," or special cases of protestant morality. But viewed in connection with the "majority" articulated in *The Convention of Cintra*, their exceptionalism seems less a consequence of psychic predisposition than the trace of a *generational* turn: that is to say, historical. Further, I have been arguing, the minority of this history consists in its manifestation as accident and interruption, matter and *technē*. If De Quincey's literary debut may be considered as anything other than a "typical aberration" – the expression of his own, or his culture's, pathology[87] – it is because, as I will suggest in the next chapter, it does *represent*, or trope, the conditions of its own production, beginning with the mere mechanics of punctuation and orthography, letters and numbers. In this materialist sense, De Quincey's *Confessions* recuperate, though they do not redeem, the negative dialectics of his novitiate. Prized "as a language" for the casualty of Romantic idealism, his failure made him the agent of a transition he could not voice.

CHAPTER 3

Impersonations: the magazinist as minor author

THE CALAMITIES OF MY NOVICIATE IN *LONDON*

Distanced from the Wordsworth circle in the aftermath of the *Cintra* débâcle, De Quincey spent several quiet years confirming his opium habit, reading German philosophy, depleting his modest fortune buying books, and gradually articulating the recondite intellectual and artistic themes that turned his subjective isolation to account. Though he may have written some fragments – perhaps even beginning the "one single work," *De emendatione humani intellectûs,* of his magniloquent ambition (*C* 64) – he published nothing for a decade. As he later wrote, "it had never once occurred to me to think of literary labours as a source of profit. No mode sufficiently speedy of obtaining money had ever occurred to me, but that of borrowing it on the strength of my future claims and expectations" (*C* 24). But by 1818, recently married and with two young children, he was finally reduced to the point of seeking paid work, and, after publishing an anonymous political pamphlet titled *Close Comments Upon a Straggling Speech,* secured with Wordsworth's help the editorship of the *Westmoreland Gazette.* He kept this post for just over a year, supplying almost all the paper's original copy; afterward, in late 1820, he was briefly "engaged" to write for *Blackwood's Magazine,* the spectacular and salacious monthly edited by his friend John Wilson. His work for the *Gazette* reads as a virtual *précis* of his later career: editorials; reports of especially lurid rape and murder trials; articles on political economy, "Kant and Herder," and "The Danish Origin of the Lake Country Dialect"; and proposals for "translations from the best parts of German Literature, and . . . Philosophy" as well as critical and biographical studies of the great English poets.[1] De Quincey's *Friend*-like plans for the *Gazette* were, in other words, no less ambitious in scope than the miscellaneous journalism by which he later eked out his precarious living. For *Blackwood's,* he produced a translation from Schiller and promised an "Opium Article" to compensate for his "silence" on other subjects.[2] Having, though, alienated both Blackwood and Wilson with a combination of arrogance and non-performance, he severed the *Blackwood's* connection in early 1821. Later that year, once again through the auspices of Wordsworth, he obtained an introduction to John Taylor and J. A. Hessey, owners of the relatively new *London Magazine,* and there *The Confessions of an English Opium-Eater* appeared anonymously in the "numbers" of September and October 1821 (*OE* 225–45).

By no means De Quincey's first publication, the *Confessions* nonetheless founded his literary career and the persona of the "Opium-Eater" by which he was known for most of his writing life.[3] The *Confessions* narrate the professional debut of a minor writer, reinscribing the "long minority of over fourteen years" (*M* 3:277) that prefaced De Quincey's capitulation to the periodical market in which his career took form.[4] Purportedly a reminiscence of his fugitive winter in 1802, the work "solicits," to use De Quincey's term (*C* 23), an allegorical reading as the turn in his personal history from experience to representation, and from scholarly intake to journalistic output. In 1802, after absconding from school and guardians, De Quincey for the first time found himself in need of money. On "August 15, 1821, . . . [his 36th] birth-day" (*C* 19), in straits so desperate that he could beg for the return of a £300 "loan" made anonymously to Coleridge in 1807, he revisited Brunell's house on Greek Street, the scene of his early tribulations – under cover of night, to elude irate creditors (*OE* 246). The parallel suggests a facile translation from former to present self: the grown man converts the exigencies of his youth into the profit of literature.[5] Indeed, from this point forward De Quincey will write rather than live; in the more than fourteen volumes of prose, much of it explicitly autobiographical, that he composed over thirty-five years, he virtually never alludes to any personal experience after 1821. Dividing his boyhood from his expectations, the *Confessions* figure his career as the gradual depletion of a meager inheritance that, whether defined genetically or economically, has already been exhausted.[6]

Whatever he may have thought at age seventeen, then, by 1821 *later*

De Quincey could *only* conceive of literary labor as a source of cash. The idea of magazine writing as a job was relatively new in the early 1820s, having been introduced in 1802 with the *Edinburgh Review*'s policy of compulsory compensation for its editors and contributors. Payment, though, is not the same as profit: *London* contributors, like their counterparts at *Blackwood's* and the *Edinburgh Review*, wrote on a fee-for-work basis, being paid from ten to (occasionally) twenty guineas per "sheet" of sixteen printed pages. De Quincey claimed to have received forty guineas for the forty-six-page *Confessions*, making him about equal with Hazlitt, though less valued than Lamb, "the pride of *our* Magazine" and its highest-paid writer (*LM* 3:69).[7] The *profit* or surplus value from this enterprise belonged to the publishers, Taylor and Hessey, as De Quincey insinuated when, in a *London* essay on political economy, he protested that "not any abstract consideration of credit, but the abstract idea of a credi*tor*. . . has for some time past been the animating principle of my labours" (*M* 9:25). Yet if the disavowal of credit suggests a relinquishment of fame as well as riches, the form of De Quincey's literary debut indicates that his scheme of "borrowing on . . . [his] future claims and expectations" still remains in force. The *Confessions* serve as his letter of security, to guarantee his "coming of age" (*C* 26) as an author of reputation.

The *London*'s rates may initially have seemed "ultra-munificent" (quoted in *OE* 245) to De Quincey, but for writers who – unlike Lamb, a clerk with the East India House – depended on the magazine for their main income, ten guineas a sheet represented a slender and uncertain middle-class living.[8] On the one hand, *London* contributors had no guaranteed salary: Lindop observes that "there is no evidence that De Quincey ever signed a contract with Taylor"; even Lamb's essays were occasionally turned down; and anyway, the publishers would "only take so much material by one author" (*OE* 251, 262). On the other hand, with a very few exceptions like Hazlitt, writers were expected not to submit their work elsewhere. Just before his split with Blackwood, De Quincey promised to "send you *my bond* . . . selling myself soul and body to the service of the Magazine for two years" (quoted in *OE* 243). More closely resembling the system of factory wage-labor than the lawyer's discretionary fee, this bond classified textual production as, for De Quincey at least, an oppressively *physical* rather than disembodied activity: bewailing "the load of labour under which I groan," he told Wordsworth in 1824 that "when . . . not utterly exhausted," he was always "writing, and all is too little" (quoted in *OE* 268). Later he recalled of his *London* years,

very often it turned out that all my labours were barely sufficient (sometimes not sufficient) to meet the current expenses of my residence in London. Three months' literary toil terminated, at times, in a result = 0; the whole *plus* being just equal to the *minus* created by two separate establishments, and one of them in the most expensive city of the world. (*M* 3:171)

By this account, the periodical essayist fits Marx's definition of the producer as one who "offer[s] for sale as a commodity that very labour-power, which exists only in his living self" and who is accordingly paid "a sum of the means of subsistence" exactly equal to "his reproduction of himself [and] his maintenance."[9] The point is by no means to suggest any nascent solidarity on De Quincey's part with the Manchester textile-workers who shared his opium habit (*C* 3), but to indicate a site of disequilibrium between what Bourdieu calls the class *habitus* – "a system of lasting, transposable dispositions which, integrating past experiences, functions . . . as a *matrix of perceptions, appreciations, and actions*" without being mastered as consciousness – and the "objective structure" of remuneration that both reproduces and *represents* those "internalized structures."[10] Lavishly endowed with "cultural capital," as the title of "scholar" (*C* 51) suggests, the free-lancer is barred from material accumulation and the signs of status that it would purchase in turn.

"There is not a more helpless or more despised animal than a mere author, without any extrinsic advantages . . . to set him off," writes Hazlitt: "the real ore of talents or learning must be stamped before it will pass current" (*H* 8:210). This is to say that as a new social entity, the magazine writer occupies not only an alien work "environment" but a defamiliarized body. His disproportion of cultural capital and circulating capital gives rise to that cluster of anxieties about prestige, continuity, and the legibility of identity that may collectively be called professional. Hazlitt's "ragged regiment of genius suing at the corners of streets" illustrates the "misery of pretensions beyond your station, and which are not backed by any external symbols of rank, intelligible to all mankind!" (*H* 8:211, 284). Intricately related to the problem of canonicity, these writerly discontents are addressed at the level of representation, through the construction of "persona" and "style." The publisher's control of the means of *reproducing* language (the fixed capital of the printing press) must, then, be sharply distinguished from the (imaginary) ownership of language itself that characterizes the possession of cultural capital.

The nature and value of the writers' work was, indeed, a recurrent topic in the pages of the *London*. While great poets may "spurn our pay," as the magazine's first editor, John Scott, lamented,

> our prose contributors have other notions altogether, – corresponding to the difference between prose and poetry: *they* reckon with us pretty closely, and occasionally *strike*, as it is called, finding the rate per sheet too low. (*LM* 2:627)

One essayist, satirically proposing that an "automaton writer" might take the place of paid contributors, cautioned punningly that "as in all cases where *manual* labour is to be superseded by machinery – a great number of hands will be flung out of employ, by enabling *publishers* to manufacture their own *stuffs*. A literary Ludditism may be apprehended" (*LM* 6:25). The writer's demotion to paid "hand" threatens the reduction of scriptoral "hand" to mere stenography. Magazine writing is both less ethereal and less lucrative than the creations of the book-market poet who can donate a lyric "in charity" and then "turn from us to walk into Mr. Murray's shop," where his copyrights will fetch a handsome sum (*LM* 2:627).

Prestige and market value are depicted here not as antithetical, but as coterminous, in marked contrast to Wordsworth's contention that "the value" of "most works in the higher departments" must be gauged in inverse proportion to their contemporary sales (*PrW* 3:67). "W. H." [Hazlitt] concurs with his editor on the importance of "reckoning":

> Punctuality is "the immediate jewel of our souls." We leave it to others to be shrewd, ingenious, witty and wise; to think deeply, and write finely; it is enough for us to be exactly dull. The categories of *number* and *quantity* are what we chiefly delight in; for on these depend (by arithmetical computation) the pounds, shillings, and pence. We suspect that those writers only trouble their heads about fame, who cannot get any thing more substantial for what they write. (*LM* 2:685 [*H* 18:367])

In Hazlitt's wittily self-canceling account, fame is a ghost, a mystification; the periodical writer measures both self and literary value arithmetically, content to be reduced to a sequence of pages in each number, or issue. Not having yet learned to repress his participation in commodity production, he embraces the "substantial" terms of "pecuniary emolument" (*C* 23). "Elia" [Lamb] similarly apologizes for the compromise of his "literary dignity" by the role that "it is [his] humour" to play from morning till afternoon. Magazine text, he suggests, begins not with leisured interiority, but with the physical work of compositors, proof-readers, "[printer's] devils and runners of the press" (*C* 24; *M* 14:138–39). No clerk can overlook the materiality of the signifier, for

> your outside sheets, and waste wrappers of foolscap, do receive into them, most kindly and naturally, the impression of sonnets, epigrams, *essays* – so that the very parings of a counting-house are, in some sort, the settings up of an author. The enfranchised quill, that has plodded all the morning among the cart-rucks of figures and cyphers, frisks and curvets so at its ease over the flowery carpet-ground of a midnight dissertation. – It feels its promotion. (*LM* 2:365 [*E* 9])

The copyist or accountant "promoted" to magazine writer has risen one rung on the company ladder; alternatively, he has employed his private time in pursuit of a hobby; but in either case, authorship differs in degree rather than kind from his day job. He thus prosaically converts his indignity – the objective lack of freedom represented by wage labor – into liberation from the burdens of autonomous imagination. Prepared by the counting-house for his "punctual accuracy" (*C* 24) in numbers, he reworks his "figures and cyphers" into the "flowery carpet-ground" of figuration.

The cipher also figures the writer's literal invisibility: unlike the book-market, where anonymous authorship presented an exception rather than the rule, periodicals were typically composed of numerous brief "articles" printed without attribution. A response to vigorous libel prosecutions and increasingly stringent protection of book-market literary properties, this practice was institutionalized by the major reviews, the *Edinburgh Review* and the *Quarterly Review*, where critical essays were generally not only unsigned but couched in a magisterial "we" that "carried the implication of a symposium" while "sinking [the writer's] identity in that of the journal."[11] Allowing critics to vilify their subjects with personal impunity, the "unimaginable plurality in unity, wherewithal Editors, Reviewers, and, at present, pretty commonly

Authors, clothe themselves" (*LM* 1:286) implicitly cast the writer as social superior rather than laborer, while simultaneously reducing him to one faceless corporate worker among the other clerks in the counting-house.

De Quincey alludes to this problem in the more piquant analogy of the "peripatetic philosopher," "a Catholic creature" who, "standing in equal relation to high and low," falls in "with those female peripatetics who are technically called Street-walkers" (*C* 20). The well-born boy negotiating "the mighty labyrinths" of working-class London (*C* 34) acknowledges the identification of writing and prostitution that became increasingly commonplace during the nineteenth century. Writers for periodicals, especially, were "prostituted" by the double indignity of producing anonymous work on speculation.[12] The prostitute also ironizes the *London Magazine*'s personification of the metropolis whose "vast pulsations circulate life, strength, and spirits, throughout this great empire" (*LM* 1:iv), and even evokes the burgeoning and "promiscuous" (*BL* 2:142) readership collectively represented by the magazine. Lacking a surname, De Quincey's prostitute-heroine Ann is effectively anonymous, so that her Christian name comes to resemble a pun or abbreviation like the *London*'s "Noemon" or "L'Anonyme Litteraire."[13] Ann's association with "numbers" and serial encounters suggests the threat to "high" literary ambitions by their submersion in the "low" medium of "what could only appear to be an essentially authorless text."[14] If text cannot be "found," how may it be valued? As Foucault observes of the eighteenth-century transformation of the literary market,

"literary" discourse was acceptable only if it carried an author's name; every text of poetry or fiction was obliged to state its author and the date, place, and circumstance of its writing. The meaning and value attributed to the text depended on this information. If by accident or design a text was presented anonymously, every effort was made to locate its author.[15]

The Opium-Eater's unavailing scansion of "many, many myriads of female faces, in the hope of meeting" his lost friend, poses the "literal and unrhetorical" (*C* 34) correlative of a professional dilemma: how can anonymous "articles" and standardized "characters" be imprinted with a traceable identity?

Contributors to the *London*, a few of whom, like Lamb and

Hazlitt, already commanded some degree of book-market recognition, developed strategies for promoting their literary dignity while conforming to editorial policy, often appending random initials or an obviously invented name to their submissions. These tags did not establish a one-to-one correspondence between text and producer in the manner typical of a properly named "author-function," however. Initials and signatures were used selectively and irregularly, partly so writers could submit to more than one department without appearing to dominate the magazine. A copious producer thus maintained some approximation of a gentleman's income without violating his "bond." Hazlitt, for example, wrote the Drama column throughout 1820, variously subscribing the letters "L. M.," "L.," "T.," or "W. H."; at the same time he contributed occasional book reviews and Fine Arts criticisms, often with no signature at all, and began his monthly feature, "Table Talk," as the alliterative "T." A single review essay received the full "T. William Hazlitt." The break with book-market conventions occasioned ironic reflection on signature and context. "E. B." complained of

those confounded initials, "of blackest midnight born," whose very birth and essence are mystery . . . In letters which make up a name . . . there is something tangible; – some groundwork, as it were, for eulogy, which one vainly seeks in the meagreness of A.B. or Q. or XYZ. (*LM* 1:657)

The bulk of a two-part name simulates the tangibility of a body, but initials suggest a "denaturation of the proper" that redefines "identity as the abstract moment of the concept."[16] While the tag at least implies an identifiable producer who may be eulogized, its attenuation makes economic subsistence – the multiplication of numbers – seem inconsistent with substantial personal presence.

The thematic urgency attached to matters of attribution was generated in part by *Blackwood's Magazine*, the *London*'s model and closest competitor, whose writers parodied the editorial policies of established journals like the *Edinburgh Review* by propagating aliases – "Peter Morris," "Z.," "William Wastle," "Timothy Tickler," "Christopher North" – which often functioned as personae but which could not be linked securely to individual writers. For one thing, many articles were written collaboratively, so that the signature simply consolidated piece-work. But much more strangely, the personae combined the qualities of pseudonyms (false names for real people) with the qualities of fictional characters. Several names associated with the magazine debuted in the satirical *Peter's Letters to His Kinfolk* of 1819; others began as signatures appended to purportedly unsolicited letters, and then gradually acquired "characters" with "pet topics or favorite interests."[17] Many names appeared chronically as by-lines, but most *Blackwood's* writers used several, and some by-lines had more than one possible referent. Certain characters were pure inventions, and others carried the names of real people who had never, *in propria persona*, written a line. "The net effect," Peter T. Murphy argues, "is that the fictional characters poach reality from the real ones. The characters speak with constancy and regularity and represent, often, the real voices (the real styles) of actual people."[18] No reader unacquainted with the principals could have told the difference, and in some cases the distinction between pseudonymy and invention remains technically undecidable; the published poet James Hogg, for example, was credited as "Hogg" and as "The Ettrick Shepherd" with, "in addition to his own genuine compositions," "numberless performances, both in prose and verse, which he had never beheld till they appeared under his name in the pages of the Magazine," John Wilson's daughter later claimed.[19]

This conspicuous blurring of ethical identities and juridical realities made *Blackwood's* both notorious and a notable commercial success. The *London* thematized anonymity in a more ambivalent, less flamboyant way. The newer magazine had its own cast of characters, many of them invented by T. G. Wainewright, who stole the first issue with a letter from "Egomet Bonmot" and went on from there to perpetrate "Cornelius Van Vinkbooms," "Dr. Tobias Ruddicombe," "Jonas Wagtail," "A Roue," and, in the figure Lamb found most "characteristic" of the magazine as a whole, "Janus Weathercock." Other *London* contributors followed suit with by-lines of a word or phrase, less often the classical "Vitruvius" or "Veteranus" of eighteenth-century periodical correspondents than puns and cryptograms like "One of the Fancy," "An Idler," "Pomarius," "Incog," or, most memorably, "Elia." Frequent contributors treated attribution as an inside joke, alluding to colleagues as "invisibilities" and hinting at "matters of occult significance . . . disguised in open simplicity" (*LM* 1:23, 5:468). Bonmot, for example, satirized both *Blackwood's* and his own magazine when he proposed to his "reader" that wert thou admitted, for a moment, within the veil of mystery, among the puppets of a magazine, thou would'st learn, that it is not an *unknown* thing for authors to criticise *their own works*; wherefore I, Egomet Bonmot, Esq. do agnise, as the offspring of mine own proper quill, every atom . . . which thou hast been reading with so much delight. (*LM* 1:661)

Like *Blackwood's*, the *London* elicits curiosity about its own production, which it represents as the real subject of the magazine. Invention tropes necessity, as the objective condition of facelessness is rewritten into a self-reflexive literary game. Genuine anonymity, where the text cannot be appropriated to an interpretive "body" of formal and biographical coherence, is antithetical to the disciplinary notion of literature Foucault describes. Construed as a puzzle, however, unsigned or pseudonymous writing becomes a mode of sophistication, all the more expressive for its apparent inauthenticity. Magazine writing asserted its claim to artistic status by converting the "loss of the proper" into a pseudo-dialectic of transgression and discovery. "There is a Freemasonry in all things," "T." observes; "you can only speak to be understood, but this you cannot be, except by those who are in the secret" (*LM* 2:256). To this extent, the periodical essayists participate in the larger project of Romanticism: to create its own readership by inscribing the terms of its interpretation.

From secrecy, it is a short step to disguise. "These are the days of authors in masquerade," the *London* announced in its first number; "and we do not pretend to be able to say, in every instance, *je vous connais, beau masque. Mystification* is now added to the other allurements of popular writers" (*LM* 1:85). This lure comprised both sly allusions and "prurient solicitations to the libidinous imagination, through blanks, seasonably interspersed," as when the *Confessions* identified its author as "the second son of —" and appealed for solidarity to "Lord —" (*M* 3:176; *C* 3, 25). Described as a "veil of mystery," the blank space in the text signifies not the uniformity and interchangeability of mass-market writing, but, rather, an intending, calculating (if sexually ambiguous) subject, *self*-withdrawn into the wondrous depth of his unreadable countenance. This effect is abetted in the *Confessions* by the motifs of gothic fiction: the flight from oppression; the pursuit "into the central darkness"; the tenancy of a "large unoccupied house," with its "Blue-beard room" full of law parchments (*C* 16–18, 22). More generally, the magazine form *gothically* conflates interpretation (a surplus of "meaning") with empirical decoding (the "answer" to an implied question). Regardless of genre, the individual articles of the magazine take part in the metafiction of its writing.

THE GREAT UNKNOWN, AND THE LESSER

The generic name for such fictions is "The Author of Waverley," mentor of *Blackwood's* and subject of the *London's* inaugural issue. Through the vehicle of his popular fictions, "THE GREAT UNKNOWN" (*LM* 7:160) Scotch Novelist converted objective relations of production into a signature, or character of serial legibility. "After the author of *Waverley* had for a considerable succession of years delighted the world with one or two novels annually," De Quincey recalls, "the demand for Waverley novels came to be felt as a periodical craving all over Europe" (*M* 14:132). Serial production, the temporalization of textual space through "plays upon variations and differences," induces the "craving" supplied by periodicals.[20] Scott's son-in-law, J. G. Lockhart, memorably depicted the prolific novelist's ploddingly seductive character in an anecdote of *Waverley's* composition:

> I observed that a shade had come over the aspect of my friend, who happened to be placed immediately opposite to myself, and said something that intimated a fear of his being unwell. "No," said he, "I shall be well enough presently, if you will only let me sit where you are, and take my chair; for there is a confounded hand in sight of me here, which has often bothered me before, and now it won't let me fill my glass with a good will."
> I rose to change places with him accordingly, and he pointed out to me this hand which, like the writing on Belshazzer's wall, disturbed his hour of hilarity. "Since we sat down," he said, "I have been watching it – it fascinates my eye – it never stops – page after page is finished and thrown on that heap of MS., and still it goes on unwearied – and so it will be till candles are brought in, and God knows how long after that. It is the same every night – I can't stand a sight of it when I am not at my books." – "Some stupid, dogged, engrossing clerk, probably," exclaimed myself, or some other giddy youth in our society. "No, boys," said our host, "I well know what hand it is – 'tis Walter Scott's." This was the hand that, in the evenings of three summer weeks, wrote the last two volumes of Waverley.[21]

Not in the least enfranchised by its "promotion" to fiction-writing, this living hand moves with the automatism of an accountant's, bound to laborious accumulation. This doggedness ought to be contemptible, but it isn't; as Baudrillard paradoxically discovers, "*Subjectivity triumphs in the mechanical repetition of itself.*"[22] Scott's productivity bypasses the register of the merely tedious to triumph as the uncanny. Miming the substantial labor of writing, the *function* of Scott's authorship, defined in terms of style – or what the *London* calls an "infinite variety" of "repetitions" – converts the factory hand into the inimitable hand, or "character," of "the living author whom we would [most] wish to be" (*LM* 1:11, 17). Scott's professionalism is the reflexive reappropriation, as subjectivity, of a de*class*ified and disarticulated body that wavers uneasily between the discourses of *plebum* and aristocracy.

The Scotch Novelist's career, periodically reevaluated in the reviews of *Ivanhoe*, *The Monastery*, *The Abbot*, and *Kenilworth* that appeared in the *London* during 1820–21, shadowed the magazine's attempts to define a corporate identity and served as the equivocal brand of a fame that need not, or will not, speak its name. A humorous verse printed in the fifth issue pointed to the Author of Waverley as head of a "new school" whose

> only aim's to queer and to confound us:
> Some how or other every body knows
> Its fellows – though to be unknown's their pride –
> I mean to be *unnamed*; – they but affect to hide.
>
> (*LM* 1:543)

Purporting to criticize *Blackwood's* and its ilk, this designation of a "new school" also performs as self-advertisement, implying that "unnamed" *London* stalwarts like "Elia" and "The Author of Table-Talk" command a degree of reader-recognition comparable to Scott's. Lamb and Hazlitt took every occasion to support this view; both "Table-Talk" and the "Elia" essays cite "L." and "Mr. Lamb's 'Works'" (*LM* 2:483); "T." alludes to opinions published under the name of Hazlitt; both writers hint broadly of their acquaintance with Coleridge. The *London's* readers were thereby encouraged to believe that they were catching the essayist in revelation, as though his "vigorous personal identity" (*LM* 1:286) were simply too singular to suppress. The *Confessions* imagine this singularity as the anachronistic spectacle of a vagrant boy "challenged . . . upon the strength of [his] family likeness" (*C* 23). So to challenge a magazine writer would be to recapitulate the eyewitness testimonial to *Waverley's* authorship: "I know well what hand it is."

The book-market Author of Waverley represents the ideal limit of self-evidence for writers working in the very different publishing context of the magazines. Jon P. Klancher observes of this "intricate nexus" that

> knowing readers might infer the identity of the writer by his "style," but playing this game of authorship meant that what is at stake is not the author of the discourse, but the position it occupies on a diverse discursive landscape. One can determine authorship only by the text it secretes. The importance "style" itself assumes in the nineteenth century owes partly to this impersonality of the public text. Style becomes a sign, a marker of the (always inferred) relation of the audience to the writer hidden behind the corporate text.[23]

In print, of course, there are no hands, in the forensic sense; only a uniform typeface. The reification of style rescues profundity from the textual surface, sublimating the more overt quizzes on authorship characteristic of *Blackwood's*. But the shade of difference implied in *hiding* behind the public facade suggests the potential dishonor personified, along with chivalry itself, in the Scotch Novelist. Pseudonyms and aliases may, John Scott (!) allows, "sometimes be innocently employed, to give variety, infuse life, and create interest in a periodical work," but only when untainted by "moral deception," in other words, "when the object is *entirely literary*, and has no reference whatever to personal considerations" (*LM* 2:513; my emphasis). Such, presumably, is the object meditated by his *London* writers. But since the point of an alias would indeed seem to be the evasion of "personal considerations" – or, more precisely, the reinscription of the personal under the heading of style – the caveat poses an oddly clumsy contradiction.

The seepage of ethical concerns into the domain of the professedly literary crystallizes in the market strategy of the best-selling and highest-paid living writer. "Amongst the many sterling claims to public attention, and legitimate means of exciting public interest, which Sir Walter Scott possesses," the *London* editorialized in November, 1820,

> he is pleased (supposing him to be the author of the Scotch Novels), to employ one of a less valid kind – namely mystery as to the authorship. The question remains a perpetual puzzle; and in some respects it may be said to become more puzzling, in proportion as it seems more certain who the writer really is. (*LM* 2:516)

This puzzle concerns motive, not identity; or rather, it is over-determined, a puzzle about puzzling that weighs down the gauze-thin, sheerly formal veil of anonymity. Yet to pose the issue this way is of course to presume the solution, whereas the charm of Constable's secret lies in the way it *produces* an authoring selfhood through "*mystification* . . . for the authorship of the works is keenly discussed" (*LM* 2:517). As the gothic novel teaches, any disguise, however thin, will serve to induce narrative desire. The periodical installments on the identity of the Great Unknown convert indi-vidual novels into a tale of commercial saturation. How much longer can he "carry further the series . . . without reducing his present popularity, and . . . the value of his copyrights" (*LM* 2:428)? Scott's refusal to be named, John Scott continues, "now *appears* quite unaccountable, except by alleging motives which we should be sorry to believe occupied a paramount place in so gifted a mind" (*LM* 2:517). The discomfiting feature of anonymous publication resides in the fissure it introduces into the literary as such – not only because Scott's motives seem imperfectly disinter-ested, or free from financial considerations, but also because liter-ary "interest" begins to seem extrinsic to the literary "work": "the book itself scarcely excites so much curiosity as the question who is the author?" (*LM* 2:517). By voicing these concerns, John Scott attempts to reinstate the ontological security of the estimable "body of work" *in itself.*

Inferring motives, whether honorable or dishonorable, John Scott unwittingly reinforces Walter Scott's author-effect; this "strategem of a trader in books" (*LM* 2:516) aims at just such cod-ifications and reflections. As Baudrillard remarks, "it is through this ambiguous conjunction of a subjective series (authenticity) and an objective series (code, social consensus, commercial value) . . . that the system of consumption can operate."[24] Once credited with secret intent, the producer of *Waverley* becomes a subjectivity and not simply a fortuitous conjunction of nostalgia, ethnography, and good timing. In the 1829 "General Preface" to his collected novels, Walter Scott correspondingly defended his choice "to remain anonymous" by

saying with Shylock, that such was my humour . . . The knowledge that I had the public approbation, was like having the property of a hidden treasure, not less gratifying to the owner than if all the world knew that it was his own. Another advantage was connected with the secrecy which

I observed. I could appear, or retreat from the stage at pleasure ... In my own person also, as a successful author in another department of literature, I might have been charged with too frequent intrusions on the public patience; but the Author of Waverley was in this respect as impassible to the critic as the Ghost of Hamlet to the partisan of Marcellus. Perhaps the curiosity of the public, irritated by the existence of a secret, and kept afloat by the discussions which took place on the subject from time to time, went a good way to maintain an unabated interest in these frequent publications. There was a mystery concerning the author, which each new novel was expected to assist in unravelling, although it might in other respects rank lower than its predecessors.[25]

The trivial desire for a non-fictional solution, Scott admits, kept the public reading and buying his novels even when their value *qua* literature was negligible. The author's substantial identity, then, resembles the seductive fallacy entertained by novel readers who imagine that the end will reveal what "really" happened. Completing the gothic dematerialization of labor that Lockhart's anecdote began, Scott figures mechanical (plot) interest as a ghost, freeing the anonymous author not only from the appurtenances of quotidian identity but from embodiment altogether. "Public approbation" (equivalently, aesthetic esteem and material reward) functions as a form of reserve or excess, seemingly a *consequence* of secrecy rather than something circumstantially obscured.

Symptomatic both of *Waverley*'s ascendancy and of a countervailing professionalist tension is John Scott's attempt to pierce the curtain. The *London* editor concluded his laudatory inaugural essay on the "inimitable" Scotch Novelist by calling him out. Alleging that "we hear a cry of '*name! name!*'", he invokes the authority of unwritten consensus: "we should be very much mortified, were it afterwards to turn out, that these fine works have been improperly attributed by the public voice to – WALTER SCOTT" (*LM* 1:21–22).[26] This ambivalent gesture prefigures his fateful quarrel over the "scandalous juggling of signatures and characters" (*LM* 2:513) practiced at *Blackwood's*, which the *London* denounced in a series of editorials beginning later that year. Whatever it may have owed to his indignation on behalf of the "Cockneys," John Scott's indictment of "the INFAMOUS SCOTCH HOAX" (*LM* 2:666) turns thematically on the uses and abuses of naming. On the one hand, *Blackwood's* writers conceal their own identities; on the other, they "have calculated on [authorial] *names*" – in other words, "libel" – "as the surest means of getting off their numbers" (*LM* 2:673–77). Ostensibly, the charge of libel refers to the magazine's notorious practice of spicing critical reviews with "personalities," or biographical invective; more radically, it evokes the subversion of empirical personality that the *Blackwood's* mode of pseudonymy implies. The resulting conundrum bespeaks the mutual imbrication of literary and juridical criteria in determining what Foucault calls "the name of an author."

An alias does not, in itself, present any challenge to a coherent taxonomy of careers: witness the examples of "Mark Twain" and "Lewis Carroll." But contributors to *Blackwood's* violated the principle of characterological consistency. The "ingenious manner in which names and characters can be varied, without any corresponding change of persons," means that the same critic might exalt an author in one number and excoriate him in the next. "Double capacity" becomes synonymous with duplicity, as expressed in a proliferation of signatures: "Peter Morris . . . and Christopher North . . . are but varieties of the same personage" (*LM* 2:510–14). When one personage espouses opposite views, it ceases to perform the authorial role of nullifying contradictions. If "personage" seems a peculiar synonym for "true identity," then, it also suggests how the author-function is propped on the conventions of literary realism. For John Scott, "personage" means the chameleonic J. G. Lockhart, and in this he commits an understandable, even necessary, factual error. "Morris" was one of Lockhart's characters, but "Christopher North" was (usually) written by John Wilson, by then "the *real impersonation* of Blackwood's 'veiled editor.'"[27] Scott's mistaken ascription demonstrates how *Blackwood's* circumvents the contractual definition of signature as a guarantee of bodily presence. The content of its reviews produces the reverse effect, "an infusion of bitter personality" (*LM* 2:512) into an ideally impersonal medium. The critics "drag forth *real names*, without authority," and subject those names (especially "Wordsworth" and "Coleridge") to abuse, making "the defects of the author. . .the ground of slander against the man" and "gratifying the paltry and nefarious curiosity which hovers round the enclosures of private life" (*LM* 2:511–17, 3:3). *Blackwood's* treats real names with the freedom of fictional creations – as though their only referents were literary.[28] "The Ettrick Shepherd," an epithet synonymous with "James Hogg," suffers this disappropriation most acutely. It was, Hogg later commented, "using too much freedom with any author to print his name in full to poems, letters, and essays which he himself never saw," especially when these putative "credits" were undermined by the absence of a corresponding fee: Hogg was, of course, not paid for the ghosted productions, nor for the use of poems, published elsewhere and "sung" in the *Noctes*.[29] Worse, as the "Shepherd," Hogg was made to voice sentiments he did not personally endorse, and even, John Scott charged, to utter empirical falsehoods (*LM* 2:668).

Should the published essays, poems and pronouncements of the "Ettrick Shepherd" be included among James Hogg's "Works"? The question suggests how *Blackwood's* radicalized the "oscillat[ion] between the poles of description and designation" that determines authorship. The author's name, Foucault writes, "is not a function of a man's civil status, nor is it fictional; it is situated in the breach, among the discontinuities."[30] Peter Morris and Christopher North make these discontinuities all too visible, wielding the referentiality of names with real effects (or even deadly ones, as was later claimed for Keats), but themselves evading referential criteria. Legally, Christopher North does not exist. When, as happened on several occasions, the owners of traduced names sued *Blackwood's* for libel, it was William Blackwood, the magazine's owner, who paid – willingly incurring this small price for the excellent profits his writers brought him.

The *London* editor characterizes their immunity as a "moral" outrage, denying the pressures that might fuel a mere "squabble between rival magazines . . . an appeal to posterity, Baldwin *versus* Blackwood; – Europe adjured by *Weathercock* against *Wastle*!" (*LM* 2:509). De Quincey, committed at this point to *Blackwood's* and writing to John Wilson, dismisses Scott's polemic as "a case of one professional man endeavoring to supplant another: a Magazine attacking a Magazine!! and a Mag. not in sale attacking one having a large sale!" Declining to acknowledge any categorical difference between one anonymous periodical essayist and another, De Quincey notes that the *London*, too, has calculated upon "real names." As to "private attacks," he concludes, "produce me from one end of Blackwood to the other a fouler intrusion into the privacies of life than that about '*the fortunate youth at Abbotsford*'" (*NLS* MS. 9819, f. 85).[31] This curious rebuttal – for John Scott's only breach of respect toward Walter Scott (that fortunate youth) has been, literally, to name him – calls attention to the jurisdictional conflicts that attend the codification of practices; to criticism's imbrication in both fictional and referential conventions; to its blurring of ethical and commercial judgments; and to the delicacy of the magazine text's negotiations between the book market and the periodical market, the cultural capital of established names and the ambiguous freedom of namelessness. Experimenting with the limits of textual identity, *Blackwood's* constructs its own market identity as a speculation, having "made it's way," De Quincey later notes, "as a foundling or an adventurer would, by . . . absolute weight of power" (*NLS* Acc. 8578).

De Quincey's sheer "speculation" represents for John Scott the extreme case of authorship's *constitutive* fictionality, which, precisely because it cannot be legally distinguished (libel suits notwithstanding) from his own practice, impels him toward the lapsed code of honor. "An article such as this is a *branding* one," he avows in his first blast. Figured as bodily writing, publication supposedly ensures that "all men will now know" the men who have been "dragged forth to infamy by a powerful hand" (*LM* 2:521, 3:7a). Calling upon Lockhart, by name, to "avow or deny" his "*pecuniary* interest" in *Blackwood's*, John Scott sets aside "his public capacity" to speak in *his* real name about "the distinction between the *dealer* in scandal and the man of honour." The one has "been actively and secretly engaged, as a paid writer, in . . . anonymous outrages on truth and character"; the other, with a "quick and fine sense of honour, which would shudder at wearing a vizor," "stand[s] frankly, in his own proper person" (*LM* 3:3a-7a). Scott's confusion of orthographic and gestural hands suggests energetic repression, but however delusory this feudal rhetoric of embodiment, its effects were material enough. To condense the ensuing story, Lockhart answered the wound to his honor (as both coward and mercenary) by setting in motion a duel with Scott, who lost his life defending the notion that written allegations must, like physical actions, be "openly committed in [a gentleman's] own name, and palpably in his own person" (*LM* 3:3).[32]

John Scott's violent end punctuates the theoretical death of the author that gave birth to literary minority. The *London's* most successful contributors would henceforward represent the improprieties of their position in terms of aberrant corporeal agency.

The author of "New Year's Eve" and "Recollections of the South Sea House" protects himself against imputations of "sickly idiosyncrasy" by "retir[ing], impenetrable to ridicule, under the phantom cloud of Elia" (*LM* 3:6 [*E* 33]). The author of the *Confessions*, admitting that "the greater part of *our* confessions . . . proceed from demireps, adventurers, or swindlers" – including the "Formosan" impostor George Psalmanazar, and the Shakespeare forger William Henry Ireland – protests that he would not "willingly, in [his] own person," join their ranks (*C* 1–2).[33] But as "T." comments on "this trade of authorship," even "the most sterling reputation is, after all, but a species of imposture" (*LM* 1:647, 653). The "Preliminary Confessions" accordingly relate the boy's resentment at being classed with "English swindlers" and his literary impersonations of young women in love (*C* 13–15). In *London*, the second son of — discovers that the corporate text is a "speculative zone" where proper names do not signify.[34]

More exactly, names produce excess of one kind, paucity of another. "It was strange to me," he recalls of his application to the money-lenders, "to find my own self, *materialiter* considered (so I expressed it, for I doated on logical accuracy of distinctions), accused, or at least suspected, of counterfeiting my own self, *formaliter* considered" (*C* 25). This self-simulation is not, however, the exception he then thinks it, but the condition of the periodical career. The revised *Confessions* of 1856 backdate the hero's fall into ciphers by delivering him a letter bearing "this address in a foreign handwriting – *A Monsieur Monsieur de Quincy*" (*M* 3:285). "Translated by a touch of the pen not only into a *Monsieur*, but even into a self-multiplied *Monsieur*, or, speaking algebraically, into the square of Monsieur," with the further threat "at some future day of being perhaps cubed," the boy knows that the letter *cannot* be his, for it contains a monetary sum he can only redeem through "forgery" (*M* 3:286, 303). To profit on a name is to be guilty *ipso facto* of counterfeiting, and to witness, simultaneously, the dispersion of being into numbers. The boy's naive belief that he "might be too well known" (*C* 25) as himself suggests a faulty syllogism, recapitulating the argument of "We Are Seven," De Quincey's touchstone for ontology. Personhood can never be assumed or even proven, only conceded. As Susan Stewart observes, "the modes of suspending being that literary writing came to pose throughout the eighteenth century . . . depended

suspending being

upon separating literary form from the contingencies of its temporal moment and spatial position."[35] Since the textual economy
both requires the fiction of identity and forecloses it, the body
posited as the ground of "character" and "style" must be regarded
instead as their more or less persuasive material imitation. The
Confessions earn the "credit" of periodical reproduction by eliciting "some previous interest of a personal sort in the confessing
subject" (*C* 4). John Scott's "brand" has become the essayist's
brand-name.

The point may be illustrated by a brief account of De Quincey's
entanglement, during his *London* years, in the authorship of
Waverley. In 1824, Scott's hitherto constant production faltered,
precipitating a crisis in both the English and the Continental
book-markets. Rather than face a season without Waverley, the
German bookseller Herbig commissioned a forgery under the
pretext of "translation." In plot and coloring a pastiche of the
Waverley series, *Walladmor*'s formal weaknesses were dictated by the
"occult law of the Constable press, which compel[led] it into" the
material shibboleth of "three-headed births," for as De Quincey
observed, "a Constable novel in *two* volumes . . . would have been
detected as a hoax *in limine*."[36] Scott's "peculiar gifts" (*LM* 1:17),
De Quincey recognizes, go hand in hand with canny marketing:
"we are three." Having obtained a copy of the "German pseudo-
Waverley novel" for review, a task he completed without actually
reading it, De Quincey later agreed to produce an English version.
Extracts and translations from foreign journals were standard
periodical filler, and among De Quincey's reliable sources of easy
copy. But in this case, finding the book a hodgepodge of "atrocious
absurdities," he was reduced to

forging new materials, in pure despair of mending the old; and recon-
structing very nearly the whole edifice from the foundation upwards.
And hence arose this singular result, – that, without any original intention to do so, I had been gradually led by circumstances to build upon
this German hoax a second and equally complete English hoax. (*M*
14:138)

The "mystery as to [*Waverley*'s] authorship" did not only, as John
Scott charged, encourage "a fashion of hoaxing and masquerade"
(*LM* 2:516–17) among magazine writers; it also made the Scotch
Novelist himself vulnerable to counterfeiters, since prosecution
would of course require publicly stating his name. The rapid

sequence of the novels, all bearing the "inimitable" stamp of their author's hand, also raised peculiarly pointed questions of originality and imitation; "it had been much agitated in Germany," De Quincey claims,

whether – if a translation were made of a Waverley novel into a foreign language, and afterwards that translation . . . were translated back into English by a person who had never seen the original, and who consequently would give a sufficient colouring of difference to the style . . . that retranslation might not be lawfully introduced into England. (*M* 14:134)

Proving this hypothesis, the imitation of the imitation deviates into "forgery" (that is to say, an original) from the mere pressure of making book, or adhering to the ossified material conventions of volume and chapter. Thus, De Quincey translates his hero into the identical twin of his Byronic antagonist, surrounds him with impersonators, has him accused of forging his "papers," and while he is incarcerated, pictures him reading "the *first* volume of *Walladmor*, a novel, 2 vols . . . the second being not then finished," in Borgesian reinscription of periodical desire.[37]

   The *Walladmor* incident was an embarrassment to De Quincey, but not because the result fell below the qualitative level of his other *London* work. Rather, the hoax presents a *reductio ad absurdum* of periodical imposture. In his "Preface" and "Postscript" to *Walladmor*, De Quincey dilates on the proverbial tale of the darned silk stockings:

a question arose amongst the metaphysicians, whether Sir John's stockings retained . . . their personal identity. The moralists again were anxious to know whether Sir John's stockings could be considered the same "accountable" stockings from first to last. The lawyers put the same question in another shape, by demanding whether any felony which Sir John's stockings could be supposed to have committed in youth might legally be the subject of indictment against the same stockings when superannuated . . . Some such questions will arise, I apprehend, upon your German *Walladmor*, as darned by myself.

Flouting in turn the discourses of metaphysics, ethics, and the law, the foundling text affiliates itself with Scott in the "absolute" literariness of its fictionalized production. De Quincey even challenges the German novelist to retranslate the English version, and vice-versa, until "Professor Kant . . . [should] confess himself more thoroughly puzzled and confounded, as to the matter of personal identity, by the final *Walladmor*, than even he had been by the Cutlerian stockings."[38] By this point it is the mere idea of textual "identity," rather than the particular hoax, that seems the better jest.

De Quincey resolves the question by appealing to "'a friend of mine' (as we all say when we are looking out for a masque under which to praise ourselves," who concluded his *London* review of *Walladmor* by quoting *The Fairie Queene* on the "false Florimel"'s trial by fashion-show: "' . . . natheless to her, as her dew right,/ It yielded was by them that judged it' . . . Spenser is here prophetic, and means the Reviewers."[39] "Florimel" may be a counterfeit, but she "seem'd to passe"; readers "buy" her. Indeed, if Spenser is to be trusted here, they "thought that [Scott] was not so faire as shee": "so forged things do fairest shew."[40] The criteria have shifted from authenticity to seduction. Identity, retroactively conferred by the amorous reader, becomes less a statement of ontological confidence than a charter to commit the crime once more. The reader's investment repays the confessor's gambit of "plac[ing] myself at a distance of fifteen or twenty years ahead of this time, and . . . writing to those who will be interested about me hereafter" (*C* 62).

"The strength of future expectations" takes the form, in the *Confessions*, of what Lacan calls "a trap for the gaze."[41] Beginning with the hypothetical "spectacle of a human being obtruding on our notice his moral ulcers or scars, and tearing away [his] 'decent drapery,'" the Opium-Eater completes his strip-tease by inviting readers to "paint me . . . according to your own fancy" (*C* 1, 61). The *British Critic* responds by designating him "the great unknown," a lower-case version of Scott's alias that, whatever its ironic intention, concedes the essential point.[42] The reader of the *Confessions* "cannot be supposed capable of resisting those spells of attraction" that De Quincey had imagined in the *Gazette*.[43] The *London's* false Florimell and prostituted daughter, rhetorically exposing the "lack" beneath her seven veils of illusion, courts recognition on the commercial terms John Scott's ethical panic strove to deny.[44]

In the flimsiness of the author's "personality," the *Confessions* recall the "burlesque on the Fichtean Egoismus" cited by Coleridge in his *Biographia Literaria.*[45]

> Self-construed, I all other moods decline:
> Imperative, from nothing we derive us;
> Yet as a super-postulate of mine,
> Unconstrued antecedence I assign
> To X, Y, Z, the God infinitivus!   (*BL* 1:160)

The edge of this joke is honed on the Derridean grapheme. "I" construe "myself" insofar as substance accrues from the printed "repetition in the finite [number] of the eternal act of creation in the infinite I AM" (*BL* 1:304). "The solution of" the ontological riddle "must be sought," De Quincey writes, "in the letter" (*M* 3:287). Hence, the "super-postulate" of the *Confessions* need be no more than the string of "confounded initials" that fill the empty space in the essay's second installment: "in popular estimation," the narrator avers, "I am X. Y. Z., esquire" (*C* 51).[46] When these initials reappear at the end of a December 1821 "letter" to the *London*'s (corporate) editor, typography has become *literary* character. There the author of the *Confessions* offers his thanks for "the disproportionate result . . . of a personal nature" produced by his two "short and inconsiderable" papers, and promises to regard them as "a fund of pleasant remembrances" for the future. In return, he pledges

a Third Part of my Confessions: drawn up with such assistance from fuller memoranda, and the recollections of my only companion during those years, as I shall be able to command . . . I do not venture to hope that it will realize the whole of what is felt to be wanting: but it is fit that I should make the effort, if it were only to meet the expressions of interest in my previous papers which have reached me from all quarters. (*LM* 34:585–86; *M* 3:465–66)

If the opium itself is the "centre on which the interest revolves" (*C* 78), the surplus generated by its "fascinating power" supplies the personal ground for eulogy telegraphically represented as "X. Y. Z." "Personal interest" and its corresponding signature – alluring in its very announcement of artifice – both arise at the point $n + 1$, the foundation of a *Confessional* series. "What is felt to be wanting" refers to the periodical craving of readers, henceforth to be fed by the *London*'s "Notes from the Pocket-Book of a Late Opium-Eater" and any number of longer articles signed "X. Y. Z." This personality is, at best, "*merely* a man of letters," the specter Coleridge dreads (*BL* 1:229). Yet this abstract, meager, and attenuated signature soon becomes, for his colleagues, "that thrice-double demoniac the oeconomical Opium-eater," monopolist of the *London* (quoted in *OE*, 268).[47] Scandalous magazine cousin of the Wordsworthian Wanderer or Byronic Childe, he is the real impersonation of the materiality from which they spring.

THE BODY OF THIS DEATH

Ambiguously signature, fiction, and autobiographical subject, the Opium-Eater may stand as a paradigm for the figuration of periodical writing, most subtly elaborated by essayists in the *London*, that approaches the name-status of "The Author of Waverley" as a *virtual* author-function. *Blackwood's*, it is true, won both the skirmish with John Scott and the lion's share of the market: while the *London* ceased publishing by 1829, its competitor maintained its sales and its position of eminence throughout much of the century. Nevertheless, it was the *London* that articulated the more coherent literary "personality," while "the masked battery of Blackwood's Magazine" (*H* 8:222) devolved into the eccentric, highly topical, critical fiction *Noctes Ambrosianae*. The Shepherd's apothegms did *not* become Hogg's "Works." Suspending juridical identity as did *Blackwood's*, the *London* subordinated the convulsive enactment of contradictions to a reflexive analysis of the literary "sociolect" and its persistence in a devalued genre. Like other periodicals of its time, the *London* represented a point of intersection between book writers and "general readers" in the larger cultural project which Klancher dubs "the making of English reading audiences." By taking the process of transmission as an explicit *literary* subject, and by simulating this process in the formal elaboration of its numbers, the *London* gave rise to authors who "transcended" the magazine format, albeit in minor ways.

The *London*'s corporate personality inheres partly in the dense "tissue of obsolete expressions," Spenserian archaisms, and self-conscious allusions that counterfeit its own prehistory.[48] Elia is merely the most famous *London* practitioner of this "singular but traditional mode of conveyance" (*H* 8:245). As one writer diagnoses his colleagues' penchant for quotation, "the beauty of this essential part of fine writing consists mainly in quoting from the older English poets, and a few of those of our day who are pretty generally unread" (*LM* 6:24). The *London*'s egregiously "literary language," to borrow a term from John Guillory, verges on becoming a persona in itself, represented by Elia's seventeenth-century folios, the Opium-Eater's study, "populous" with "about five thousand" books (the "only. . .property in which I am richer than my neighbours"), and T.'s "character of a scholar," with his "old-fashioned" "air of books about him" (*C* 60; *LM* 2:261).[49] Counterpoised against these depictions of literary capital are reports of conversation; as "W. H." comments, "we not only say good things ourselves, but are the cause of them in others" (*LM* 2:686). As it happens, "W. H." is "Table-Talk" under another name, the title of the series reflecting his contention that

to write a genuine familiar or truly English style, is to write as anyone would speak in common conversation, who had a thorough command and choice of words, or who could discourse with ease, force, and perspicuity, setting aside all pedantic and oratorical flourishes (*H* 8:242).

T.'s ideal prefigures Bakhtin's circular definition of literary language as the sociolect having "as its area of activity the conversational language of a literarily educated circle." Indeed, much of "Table-Talk" revolves around "The Conversation of Authors"; the trope neatly epitomizes "the interface between the language of preserved literary texts and the context-bound speech that continually escapes total regulation and hence *changes*" – in other words, the social threshold of "general literariness" as such.[50] Writing continually of books, book-talk, and writing, the *London*'s "familiar" essayists (who double as conventional reviewers) not only establish their elite credentials but also foreground the question of the literary as chiefly a *relation* to language, or "purity of expression" (*H* 8:242). For De Quincey, the domain of "style" is bounded by the "picturesque" idiomatic speech of women, at one end, and "the whole artificial dialect of books," as disseminated by newspapers, at the other. The properly literary, therefore, is to be distinguished above all from the mere "novelties of diction" and "lazy indifference" in construction employed by the "dangerous class" of "professional authors." "Most classes" of writers, he avers, "stand between the pressure of two extremes: of coarseness, or carelessness, of imperfect art, on the one hand; of spurious refinement and fantastic ambition on the other" (*M* 10:141–49). Both poles, tellingly, are redeemed in the works of Elia, noted by De Quincey for a "diction . . . natural and idiomatic, even to carelessness" and by "Phil-Elia" for affecting a "self-pleasing quaintness" (*M* 5:217; *E* 171).

The co-presence of contrary errors defines the style of the "parvenu," as De Quincey calls Janus Weathercock (*M* 5:247). The epithet suggests that the periodical's relation to literary culture participates in a heightened rhetoric of social discrimination – in the vulgar sense, as well as in the mediated sense described by Guillory. As Hazlitt observes,

To be at all looked upon as an author, a man must be something more or less than an author . . . Unless an author has an establishment of his own, or is entered on that of some other person, he will hardly be allowed to write English or to spell his own name. To be well-spoken of, he must enlist under some standard; he must belong to some *coterie*. (*H* 8:210–11)

Such a coterie, or set of connections, is simulated in the *London* itself, where the contemporary book market, conflated with anti-quarian learning and high-prestige literary genres, underwrites the essayists' sometimes humorously blatant self-promotions.[51] In the first number, Bonmot proffers his services by claiming with "the Lakiest of bards" that "beneath the plain and simple sincerity of the foregone observations, there lies a moral far too deep for the fathom-lines of uninformed minds" (*LM* 1:23). The *London* writers' "conversations" personify this kind of familiarity as speaking acquaintance, mystifying conditions of production as the tokens of social exchange. Coleridge – Elia's "*inspired charity-boy*" (*LM* 2:489 [*E* 25]), all talk, no achievement – is the touchstone here. The figure of Coleridge in "Christ's Hospital Five and Thirty Years Ago" prompts "W. H.," in his final Drama Column, to ventriloquize "Mr. Coleridge's better genius" under the pretext that "our flimsy discourse" had run aground. "Thus we hear him talk" (*LM* 2:687 [*H* 18:379]). The Opium-Eater commences his fantasia of reproduction the same way: "Many years ago, when I was looking over Piranesi's Antiquities of Rome, Mr Coleridge, who was standing by, described to me a set of plates by that artist" (*C* 70). The exchange can also be reversed; according to T., "L." "has furnished many a text for C — to preach upon" (*LM* 2:257). These references even extend to invoking "C —"'s blessing for the *London*; when asked "why he did not like Gold's 'London' as well as ours," he allegedly answered, "*Because there is no* WEATHER-COCK, *And that's the reason why*" (*LM* 5:536). In conversation, the boundary between the weightiness of books and the ephemerality of periodicals dissolves, and "learning," elsewhere reified into originals and copies, appears instead as (Hazlitt's) "transferable property" (*H* 8:208).

Unlike print, talk cannot be copyrighted; as conversation, then, writing develops the "notion of literary system as a matter of intertextuality, allusion, notation, and reference" that Stewart associates with the rise of scholarship, rather than claiming the "unbearable originality" of those "impeccable writers . . . who never wrote" (*H* 8:206). Periodical writing typically and explicitly "emphasize[s] the secondary or staged quality of literary discourse."[52] In "On the Conversation of Authors," Hazlitt proposes a theory of literary production that notably eschews expressivism:

> From reading, too, we learn to write. If we have had the pleasure of studying the highest models of perfection in their kind, and can hope to leave any thing ourselves, however slight, to be looked upon as a model, or even a good copy in its way, we may think ourselves pretty well off. (*LM* 2:252 [*H* 12:28])

This states less invidiously the thesis of "On Magazine Writers," which complained that the periodical essayist "looks upon a library as his domain, and the works of all who have preceded him as his fair property," reading only to "glean from the toils of others all that may spare [him] the expense of thought" (*LM* 6:25–26). Writing about books and writers, one might infer, scarcely counts as writing at all. Rather than contest this view, Elia makes it his boast, "at the hazard of losing some credit on th[e] head" of "originality": "I love to lose myself in other men's minds. . .Books think for me" (*LM* 6:33 [*E* 195]). This admission, as Peter J. Manning has noticed, converts the imbalance in prestige between books and magazines into an argument for the inwardness of the reader-*cum*-writer; "though dependent on prior writing," reading "is free of the taint of commodity production, and suggests an act performed by a subject."[53] Magazine production *dialectically* negates book-market discourses of authenticity.

The *London's* public bows to Coleridge's orality may be said, then, to prefigure the emergence from the "commonwealth of letters" of an author who will "win for himself . . . a name which become[s] the property of his country" (*LM* 6:27). Out of the "myriads" of unowned words comes the "plurality of egos" which characterizes authorial discourse.[54] "General literariness" is a necessary but insufficient condition for canonicity; writers for the *London* not only represent the magazine as "the scene of hetero-glossia," not only promote the essay as the genre "paradigmatic for a socially differentiated *speech*," but continually reenact "the simu-lacrum of a personal history" as a figure for readerly identifica-tion."[55] Thus if written "style" is, in the last instance, the *lingua franca* of sublimated quotation – as Hazlitt's essays come close to asserting – nonetheless it becomes the project of the *London* to anchor this floating style in narrative.

Literary style must, to acquire symbolic value, be owned, and much of the playful business of the *London* concerns the distribu-tion and adjudication of specialties and characterological quirks among potential owners. One persona might take another as subject: Wainewright's "Bonmot" complains of Wainewright's "Janus"; Janus critiques other contributors and suggests topics to them; "Mr. Drama" [Hazlitt] answers "our friend and coadjutor, of the whimsical name, – that Bucolical Juvenile, the Sir Piercie Shafton of the London Magazine" (*LM* 2:88 [*H* 18:344]). Such reflections then furnish sources for other signature pieces. "Oxford in the Vacation" echoes T.'s portrait of "L —" in "On the Conversation of Authors," while "Poor Relations" adopts a topical suggestion by Janus: "I have not time to point out all the variety of intelligence which is combined in [Stephanoff's] little picture; but I think that our *Elia* would manage it beautifully" (*LM* 5:75).[56]

The term "symbiosis" does not adequately describe the confla-tion of originality and plagiarism in this corporate culture, for it implies a mutually advantageous arrangement between two *sub-jects*, whereas personae work to consolidate subjectivities from the *abîme* of magazine text and intertext. Lamb alludes to this process – misidentifying it, however, with a Keatsian negative capability – when "Phil-Elia" counters his predecessor's "egotistical" reputa-tion with the remark

that what he tells us, as of himself, was often true only (historically) of another; as in his Fourth Essay (to save many instances) – where under the *first person* (his favourite figure) he shadows forth the forlorn estate of a country-boy placed at a London school, far from his friends and connections – in direct opposition to his own early history. – If it be egotism to imply and twine with his own identity the griefs and affections of another – making himself many, or reducing many unto himself – then is the skilful novelist, who all along brings in his hero, or heroine, speaking of themselves, the greatest egotist of all; who yet has never, therefore, been accused of that narrowness. (*LM* 7:20 [*E* 171–72])

Elia would have his figure and embody it too: but there can be no distinguishing the composite figure from the factitious memories that "imply and twine with" the authorial "I." Pluralities like Elia and Janus Weathercock (with his alter-egos "like Cerberus, three gentlemen at once!" [*LM* 5:470]) literalize the immunity from unilateral reference, the "unimaginable plurality in unity," that is assumed as the privilege of literary writing.

Paradoxically, this very unreliability of pronominal "shifters" conduces to identifiable character. Well before Elia declared the first person his favourite figure, T. G. Wainewright composed a humorous indictment of "Egomet Bonmot" titled "Much Ado About Nothing." Bonmot, "nothing" but a string of outrageous claims and inconsistent demands,

does afford *one* specimen of immutability, in that perfectly semper-identical display of idiosyncratic egotism which runs throughout and leavens his varieties . . . *unus est BONMOT, si non sit BONMOT, mutus crit.* and we are much mistaken if this system of self-centering does not speedily throw every rival of the same stock into the shade. (*LM* 1:657)

The moral charge of egotism ironizes the slenderness of the tautology on which it rests: the principle of immutability consists merely in using the singular "I" rather than the orthodox "we," as Bonmot's editor confirms when he threatens "rendering him impersonal for the rest of his life" (*LM* 1:628). Lamb's version of this point obscures its commercialism by taking the part of the literary consumer. "A series of Miscellaneous Essays," he observes in an unpublished review of Hazlitt's *Table Talk*, "if it have not some pervading character to give a unity to it, is ordinarily as tormenting to get through as a set of aphorisms, or a jest-book." "Egotism" is "the charm which binds us" to the series; without such "a perpetual self-reference," essays present only a "heterogeneous mass," "hanging together with very slender principles of bond or union."[57] "Series" and "character" substitute here for "Egomet" and "egotism" or "self" and "similarity": just as the repetition of a cratylic pseudonym confers seriality upon textual space, so too "it is seriality that constitutes character" as the protagonist of the implied narrative.[58]

Only thus can a coherent volume of *Table Talk* be collected from numbers of periodical essays destined for obsolescence by the end of each month. "This," Baudrillard argues,

is the phenomenon of the series – or, in other words, of two or of *n* identical objects. The relation between them is not that of the original to its counterfeit, or its analogue, or its reflection; it is a relationship of equivalence, of indifference. In the series, objects are transformed indefinitely into simulacra of one another and, with objects, so are the people who produce them. Only the extinction of original reference permits the generalized law of equivalence, which is to say, the *very possibility of production*.[59]

"He who writes his own biography. . .is pretty sure to write a work which will be acceptable to all classes of readers," John Scott mused of the "magical charm" that pleased his own "innate curiosity" (*LM* 2:129). Scott cited "Saint Augustin and . . . Rousseau" as exemplars. But the charm of perpetual *self*-reference depends upon the very extinction of *original* reference that mass publication effected, that Scott deplored in *Blackwood's*, and that his own death dramatized. If the "assumption of a character" turns *Table Talk* into "a piece of autobiography," – or, in other words, if each essay converts into a simulacrum of the last, and if the law of equivalence called "style" makes of "fourteen ample Essays" a continuous "piece" or "bold confession" – the formal unity of the work is the obverse of its essential anonymity.[60] Selves, or "the people who produce them," writes Baudrillard *contra* De Quincey, "would not have to be *counterfeited*" because, since the expansion of the print market, "they were being *produced* on such a gigantic scale."[61] "Themes" generate "affiliation to the model," not vice-versa. "Family resemblance" is the effect of a certain *staging* of commodity fetishism, in which "something slips, passes, is transmitted, from stage to stage, and is always to some degree eluded."[62]

"Casting a preparatory glance at the bottom of this article . . . methinks I hear you exclaim, Reader, *Who is Elia?*" wrote the author of "Recollections of the South Sea House" in his second essay for the *London*. His ambiguous syntax positions the writer as his own reader, "as if a man should suddenly encounter his own duplicate!" (*LM* 2:365, 368 [*E* 8, 13]). The question is answered with another essay, which temporarily extenuates the desire it sustains through epistemological suspension or "solemn mockery." "Shadows of fact," the Elia essays convey "verisimilitudes, not verities . . . sitting but upon the remote edges and outskirts of history";

"be satisfied," Elia adjures the inquirer, "that something answering to them has had a being" (*LM* 2:146, 4:284 [*E* 8, 103]). Even the seemingly more forthright T. asks that an apparent confession be considered "merely as a specimen of the mock-heroic style, and as having nothing to do with any real facts or feelings" (*H* 8:238). The author's subjectivity comes into existence as the noumenous horizon of the fragment, equated with its resistance to stable generic classification. In place of the juridical person who might "answer to" the reader's summons, the narrative supplies the materiality of commodified appurtenances: "Janus Weathercock" withdraws to allow inspection of his "boudoir" full of curios, books and prints; Elia invites readers into his "little back study in Bloomsbury" to show off his folios; and the Opium-Eater calls on a painter to depict his library, "populous with books" and a glass container of opium "as much like a wine-decanter as possible. Into this you may put a quart of ruby-coloured laudanum: that, and a book of German metaphysics placed by its side, will sufficiently attest my being in the neighbourhood" (*LM* 4:655; 2:624; *C* 60–61). Allured by familiar places and objects (the South Sea House, Oxford-Street, Christ's Hospital) the reader's gaze is arrested just short of full identification by a refusal of contractual presence: "as to myself, there I demur," writes the Opium-Eater, while conceding that "naturally, I ought to occupy the foreground of the picture; that being the hero of the piece, or (if you choose) the criminal at the bar, my body should be had into court" (*C* 61).[63]

The author has his existence in the domain of the reader's transference, as one of those phantoms that Freud aptly calls "new editions or facsimiles" of a "stereotype plate" imprinted in early life (*SE* 7:116, 12:100). Inferred from the textual materials and aesthetic objects that he recycles for his next production, the "person" of the magazinist is ascribed to a consensual "delusion – pleasing both to the public and to" the writer (*C* 61). The Opium-Eater posits an *imaginary* resemblance between the production and consumption of literary commodities, whereby the library collections of the writer become interchangeable with the magazine subscriptions of the reader. Like the "trick" effect of surplus value, the impersonation of cultural capital appears greater than the "simple addition of existing values," figuring its charm as displaced affect.[64] The *London's* most successful and most imitated writers each gradually acquire an "*ideal character*," affiliated with the concept of organic form, that exists over and above the repetitions of which it is composed.[65]

Thus Elia elicits correspondence, real or fictional, which he "answers" in the magazine's editorial column. Empirical "church-warden critics," for example, are put off with the warning that "he hath not so fixed his nativity (like a rusty vane) to one dull spot, but . . . if he seeth occasion, or the argument shall demand it, he will be born again, in future papers" (*LM* 4:466). In the March 1821 number he rebuffs "a writer, whose real name, it seems, is *Boldero*, but who has been entertaining the town for the last twelve months . . . under the assumed signature of *Leigh Hunt*." This Hunt ("clearly a fictitious appellation; for if we admit the latter of these names to be in a manner English, what is *Leigh*? Christian nomenclature knows no such") has

> thought fit to insinuate, that I *Elia* do not write the little sketches which bear my signature, in this Magazine; but that the true author of them is a Mr. L — b . . . I must needs lie writhing and tossing, under the cruel imputation of non-entity. Good heavens! that a plain man must not be allowed *to be* –
> They call this the age of personality: but surely this spirit of anti-personality (if I may so express it) is something worse.
> Take away my moral reputation – I may live to discredit that calumny.
> Injure my literary fame, – I may write that up again –
> But when a gentleman is robbed of his identity, where is he?
> Other murderers stab but at our existence, a frail and perishing trifle at the best. But here is an assassin, who aims at our very essence; who not only forbids us *to be* any longer, but *to have been* at all. (*LM* 3:266)

Elia's witticism on the impropriety of names went to press just as John Scott, another would-be "assassin," lay dying. Playing on the two antithetical senses of "personality," Elia depicts Hunt, another linguistic naif, as a libelist aiming to strip him of literary mystique. X. Y. Z. defends against the opposite "scruple on the question of authenticity" – that his narrative might describe "a fictitious case as respected the incidents" – when he assures James Montgomery of the *Sheffield Iris* that the *Confessions* describe his "own experience . . . drawn up with entire simplicity and fidelity to the facts," though he may not have told "the *whole* truth" (*LM* 4:585). Later he declined to write his meditated *Confessions of a Murderer* on the grounds that "if I begin to write imaginary Confessions, I shall seem to many as no better than a pseudo-confessor in my own too real confessions" (quoted in *OE* 258). The issue is not "veracity," however, but the delicate equivocation between the registers of the empirical and the fictional that guarantees the personal as reserve.

"It would be as false to seek the author in relation to the actual writer as to the fictional narrator," observes Foucault Eliacally; "the 'author-function' arises out of their scission – in the division and distance of the two."[66] Elia's choice of "essence" over "existence" suggests that Romantic authorship extends character not only beyond the elements of the series, but beyond the purview of the juridical individual. The fantasmatic equivalence between producers and consumers, articulated in the premise that "thou art a lean annuitant like myself" (*LM* 2:142 [*E* 1]) begets new writers whose essences preserve the stamp of their simulacral originals. A *London* reviewer of Hazlitt's *Lectures on the Literature of the Age of Elizabeth*, for example, praises the critic's "personal allusion to himself," citing Gibbon's tribute to Longinus as his precedent: "He tells me his own feelings upon reading it; and tells them with such energy that he communicates them. I almost doubt which is more sublime" (*LM* 1:187–88). By implication, Hazlitt's sublime responsiveness emulates his literary original; and so, perhaps, this new reviewer becomes "a Hazlitt." Familiar criticism is a mode of autobiography. And if, as Barbara Johnson writes, "the desire for resemblance, the desire to create a being like oneself . . . is the autobiographical desire par excellence," the critic not only "hails" his readers but sheds some of his superabundant value on them too.[67] The transference of reading canonizes serial character as the adjective that modifies another signature.

Finally, then, Elia's retort to Boldero critiques the expressivism that would limit his "confessions" (*LM* 3:264) to the essays actually written by Lamb. Like Janus Weathercock, implored by other contributors to "write again, – and again" (*LM* 6:360), Elia can only *be* insofar as he is reflected in readers' letters, editorial notices, and gratuitous allusions. He "authors" any number of imitations as well: in the September 1820 issue of the *London*, for instance, a reviewer praises "that most beautiful Paper . . . in our last number, on the 'ledger-men,' of the South Sea House." The October issue features both the second "Elia" essay ("Oxford in the Vacation") and another called "The Cider Cellar" that begins, "I read with much pleasure, in THE LONDON MAGAZINE, a delightful paper entitled, *Recollections of the South Sea House*" (*LM* 2:317; 2:384). It is debatable which of the two October essays more closely resembles the "original," and which is more instrumental in consolidating the Elia-effect. Character and style comprise, then, both the individuality that Hazlitt appreciates in his friend and its contradiction, iterability. As Hazlitt knows, one cost of reputation is the necessity of hearing admirers "pick out something not yours, and say, they are sure no one else could write it" (*H* 8:284–5).

Not the origin of Elia's psyche, Lamb is its material impersonation. "Charles Lamb" is the simplest, but not necessarily the most nuanced or honorific, answer to the question, "Who is Elia?" *Materialis* and *formalis* aspects of identity are not only destabilized, but reversed, by the relation between producers and constituted authors. The problem recalls the semantic difficulties Marx experiences in describing the worker and his work: on the one hand, the empirical laborer appears as "the *impersonation* of . . . labour-power"; on the other, his potential "must be *embodied* in a use-value of some kind."[68] Which is most material, the body of the writer or the concrete value he produces? The *London* writers make much of the body's "pleasures" and "pains," from roast pig and rackets to drunkenness and starvation. But as Murphy comments of the "overwhelming, unbelievable carnality" depicted in *Noctes*, this represented "physicality . . . is made possible by the immateriality of the scene."[69] The issue of materiality is further complicated by the way literary artifacts trope the body, particularly when the "frail and perishing" magazine format is rectified by the gravity of the book.

January 1823 witnessed two significant events in the career of Elia: his death – mimicked in the "literary decease" of Janus Weathercock – and the publication of *Elia; Essays Which Have Appeared under that Signature in the London Magazine.* Lamb submitted an essay for the *London* that month signed "Elia's Ghost," as well as "A Character of the Late Elia, By a Friend," signed "Phil-Elia"; Wainewright's final contribution, "Janus Weatherbound; Or, the Weathercock Steadfast for Lack of Oil. A Grave Epistle," took the occasion of his own "counterfeit death" to review the magazine's progress and offer a valediction on *his* friend Elia (*LM* 7:19–52). Elia's decease was well-timed, wrote "Phil-Elia"; "he just lived long enough (it was what he wished) to see his papers collected into a volume. The pages of the LONDON MAGAZINE will henceforth know him no more" (*LM* 7:19). Conferring closure on the series, death allegorizes the translation from one medium into another. The book, poor earthly casket of the "body of work," or *corpus,* now counts *materialiter,* while the mortal body decays into mere formality. Thomas Hood capitalizes on these metaphysical enigmas by assuring readers that "Elia's ghost . . . cannot sleep in its grave, for it has been constantly with us since his death, and vows it must still write for its peace of mind"; indeed "his *ghostship* has promised us very *material* assistance in our future Numbers" (*LM* 7:3–4; original emphasis).

The collective edition represents both the material reward for a *succès d'estime* and the weighty basis for a more lasting fame. It also marks Elia's devolution from equivocal persona to fictional character. Phil-Elia elegizes:

> Well, Elia is gone . . . and these poor traces of his pen are all we have to show for it. How little survives of the wordiest authors! Of all they said or did in their life-time, a few glittering words only! His Essays found some favourers, as they appeared separately; they shuffled their way in the crowd well enough singly; how they will *read,* now they are brought together, is a question for the publishers, who have thus ventured to draw out into one piece his "weaved-up follies." (*LM* 7:21)

The magazine writer's singularity is a paradoxical effect of over-crowding, or the market's saturation with words. His afterlife in *Elia* constitutes a form of reification, the traces of a disposable culture embodied in the durable and "detached" shape of a volume that may be fondled and lovingly bound in its "winding-sheet" of Russia or Morocco leather – unlike "a set of Magazines," which Elia himself would never "dress . . . in full suit" (*LM* 2:366, 6:33 [*E* 11, 196]). The volume retroactively affirms the presence that has accrued to Elia, precisely through the omissions that define the Eliacal as against those productions judged too trivial or context-ridden for bookish transcendence.

In a "letter declaring Elia's existence" published two months later, the author returned to claim his property "in his own hand-writing." Revivified for a second series later to be collected as his *Last Essays,* Elia thanked

> the facetious Janus Weathercock, who . . . took advantage of [Elia's] absence to plot a sham account of his death; and to impose upon the town a posthumous Essay, signed by his Ghost – which, how like it is to any of the undoubted Essays of the author, may be seen by comparing it

with his volume just published. One or two former papers, with his signature, which are not re-printed in the volume, he has reason to believe
were pleasant forgeries by the same ingenious hand. (*LM* 7:243)

The protest resonates with multiple ironies. "Rejoicings upon the
New Year's Coming of Age," signed "Elia's Ghost," is as certainly by
Lamb as any of the essays in *Elia* (it was eventually published in *Last
Essays*), though it barely resembles the more *characteristic* first-
person meditations. Several other undoubted essays, including
"Detached Thoughts on Books and Reading" and "Confessions of
a Drunkard" – also omitted from *Elia* – are dismissed as "forgeries"
by the "ingenious hand" of Wainewright, who, never again to write
for the *London*, years later pled guilty to a charge of bank forgery
rather than be tried for murder. There can be little question that
Lamb wrote the "former papers, with his signature," that Elia dis-
avows here, but it is equally clear that Eliacal essays could be forged
successfully; not only were convincing simulacra like "The Cider
Cellar" and "Death – Posthumous Essays – Children" printed in
the *London*, but an unauthorized American edition of *Elia: Second
Series* (1828) contained three essays not written by Lamb.

   The appearance of a collective edition – and of piracies – completes the cycle of production, consumption, reproduction, and
canonical inscription that is simulated in the self-referential pages
of the magazine. Guillory observes that "the conditions of [liter-
ary] production and reception" must be conceived "as an indivis-
ible complex" of reading turned writing. As readers of the *London*
become writers, their models acquire the status of originality.[70]
Once the series materializes into a book, for instance, it is recycled
in periodical reviews (the *Confessions* attracted fifteen; *Table Talk*
was puffed in the *London* itself). Earlier, the Opium-Eater had
received the subtler tribute of imitation. Lamb reprinted his 1813
"Confessions of a Drunkard," by "a poor nameless egotist," in the
August 1822 issue of the *London*; the next month brought "The
Memoir of a Hypochondriac," which purportedly originated in
admiration for the "too eloquent, too interesting" confessions of
"your 'Opium Eater.'" Affecting to criticize the way he "dresses up
his pleasures and his pains in" "gorgeous and alluring" diction, B.
W. Procter (also Elia's imitator) is so "struck by the coincidence
between the writer's sensations and my own" that he must produce
a formally identical two-part essay, including a version of De

Quincey's architectural dreams and a pastiche of the quoted
Excursion passage (*LM* 6:249–50, 256–57). Emulation proceeds
under the guise of infection, fulfilling the perhaps wishful remark
in "On Magazine Writers" that "there is no scribbler so mean" as
to lack "some meaner one in his *suite,* and so on down to an infinite littleness" (*LM* 6:26).[71] Even the Opium-Eater, subject of
textuality, found his lilliputian impersonators: Wainewright once
claimed to have written the *Confessions* himself,[72] and in 1829
Edward Quillinan told the Wordsworths "of a 'person here calling
himself *De Quincey Mee*' and introducing himself as the author of
the *Opium-Eater*" (*J* 300–301).

Confessions of an English Opium-Eater *was issued as a book in
December 1822, just before the publication of *Elia.* De Quincey
could expect little financial benefit, having in effect already disposed of his copyright, though Taylor and Hessey made him the
modest present of twenty pounds on the occasion (*OE* 248). Still,
X. Y. Z. honored the decision of "the Proprietors of this little work"
to reprint it "in a separate Volume" with a minutely argued excuse,
in that month's *London,* for "the non-appearance of a Third Part"
promised one year earlier (*LM* 6:512 [*M* 3:466]). As though compensating for his dereliction, he concluded by surrendering the
spectacle he had withheld from earlier readers. "*Fiut experimentum
in corpore vile*" completes the proleptic self-burial of the narrator
who "hesitated about the propriety" of bringing his sufferings
"before the public eye, until after my death" (*C* 1). The body of this
death, in one volume octavo, prompts the writer to "bequeath his
wretched structure" to the College of Surgeons, should "any
benefit . . . redound to their science from inspecting the body of an
Opium-eater" (*LM* 6:513, 517 [M 3:467, 472]). Offered as textual
guarantee and annihilated in the same gesture, the "person" dies
into the *canonized* author. Hogg would rehearse this trope two years
later when, in the "authentic letter" to *Blackwood's* that prefaced the
appearance of his *Private Memoirs and Confessions of a Justified Sinner,*
he announced the discovery of a corpse (slain by "his own erring
hand"), shortly to be exhumed with an autobiographical *corpus* "in
small bad print, and the remainder in manuscript."[73]

Ten months after publishing his testament, De Quincey rein-
voked the Eliacal equation of book and fame in a rebuke to J. A.
Hessey.

I could never understand on what principle you thought the Opium-Eater's Conf. a *temporary* work – or more belonging to one year than another, – or why according to its value it should not as well belong to the *literature* as Elia or any other work whatever: *accordg. to its' value,* I say: meaning, that simply in the *subject* I see nothing transitory or less suited to the next year or century than to this. – Now that I am right in this, appears from the fact of my having had scarcely one day's interval since my return without callers from amongst the Lakers, bringing letters of Introd. to me *as* the Op.-Eater. (*NLS* MS. 15973, f. 15)

Having transcended the "mere medical subject of the opium" (*C* 94), the *Confessions* migrate, with *Elia,* into "the literature"; the empirical De Quincey, meanwhile, has become "The Author of Confessions," or simply, "the Opium-Eater." The alias sticks, though an open secret: Crabb Robinson, for example, was visiting Glasgow in September 1821 when he read "a strange article, *Confessions of an Opium Taker* [*sic*] in *London Magazine,* which must be by De Quincey" (*HCR* 267).

Two concluding notices of the *Confessions* limn the vicissitudes of personality in the phantom world of literary fame. In the October 1823 installment of *Noctes Ambrosianae,* Christopher North, the Ettrick Shepherd and Timothy Tickler meet the English Opium-Eater, an early prefiguration of the talk-show "personality." This guest appearance signals the expansion of the confessor's celebrity beyond London literary circles, while marking the Opium-Eater as an appropriable *character*; De Quincey probably had no part in composing the dialogue, and certainly would have received no fees for "Laudanum"'s remarks. The Opium-Eater's contributions recognizably parody the ornate prose of "our eloquent friend's 'Confessions,'" but the introductory dialogue is almost pure advertisement. The Shepherd sets the tone of comically exaggerated admiration:

> THE SHEPHERD. ...hech, sirs, yon bit Opium Tract's a desperate inter-
> esting confession . . . I tried the experiment mysel, after reading the
> wee wud wicked wark, wi' five hunner draps . . . but how could I
> CONFESS? for the sounds and sights were baith shadows; and whare
> are the words for expressing the distractions o' the immaterial soul
> drowning in matter? . . . Mr. Opium-Eater, I used aye to admire you,
> years sin syne; and never doubted you wad come out wi' some wark,
> ae day or ither, that wad gar the Gawpus glower.
> THE OPIUM-EATER. Gar the Gapus glower! – Pray, who is the Gapus?

THE SHEPHERD. The public, sir; the public is the Gawpus. But what for are you sae metapheesical, man? There's just nae sense ava in metapheesics; they're a' clean nonsense. But how's Wudsworth?[74]

As the Gawpus personifies the "public" of periodical subscribers solicited by *Blackwood's*, *homo opiatus* personifies the exemplary exception to the anonymous rule, giving an honorific name to the *author's* "immaterial soul" of sensation and prodigious intellectualism. The *Confessions* straddle the domains of popular success and peer review, demanding from their readership both aesthetic sensitivity (which the rustic Shepherd possesses) and formal erudition (which he does not). Like "Coleridge's Ancient Mariner" and "Wordsworth's Ruth," the Opium-Eater's productions lack "common sense"; "therefore," North asserts, "dolts and dullards despise them – and will do to the end of time."

The Shepherd's response, indeed, exemplifies a reductivism the others derogate:

NORTH. Pray, is it true, my dear Laudanum, that your "Confessions" have caused about fifty unintentional suicides?
THE OPIUM-EATER. I should think not. I have read of six only; and they rested on no solid foundation.
TICKLER. What if fifty foolish fellows have been buried in consequence of that delightful little Tractate on Education? Even then it would be cheap. It only shows the danger that dunces run into, when they imitate men of genius.

The Shepherd, who reacts to laudanum by collapsing into "ae snore frae Monday night till Friday morning," has failed to experience the "apocalypse of the world within" that follows from opium's excitation of the system (*C* 38, 44).[75] He fails because he is not a genius; because he confuses literary consumption with literal consumption; or, because he cannot see opium as the material *figure* for the transvalued "PURSU [it of] LITERATURE AS A TRADE." In his "exhortation to the youthful literati," Coleridge had warned that

money, and immediate reputation form only an arbitrary and accidental end of literary labor. The *hope* of increasing them by any given exertion will often prove a stimulant to industry; but the *necessity* of acquiring them will in all works of genius convert the stimulant into a *narcotic*. (*BL* 1:223–24)

The Opium-Eater, having begun his career in just the circumstances Coleridge deplores, transcends by allegorizing the narcosis of materiality. Like Wordsworth, his affiliated genius, he may (and must) be mimicked, but he cannot be reproduced.[76]

In the *Noctes*, where materialism can be no more than a figure, the relation between authorial persona and empirical writer undergoes strange inversions. The Opium-Eater expresses several emphatic opinions during his appearance, some of which, like the assertion that "all the magazines of the day are deficient; first, in classical literature, secondly, in political economy, and thirdly, in psychology," might readily be inferred from De Quincey's published work for the *London*. When the conversation shifts to speculation over the editorship of the *Quarterly Review*, however, the Opium-Eater unleashes a kind of fierce invective that signals his generic mutation.

> THE OPIUM-EATER. Mr. Coleridge is the last man in Europe to conduct a periodical work. His genius none will dispute; but I have traced him through German literature, poetry, and philosophy; and he is, sir, not only a plagiary, but, sir, a thief, a *bona fide* most unconscientious thief . . . except as a poet, he is not original; and if he ever become Editor of the Quarterly . . . then will I examine his pretensions, and show him up as an impostor . . . Coleridge has stolen from a whole host of his fellow-creatures, most of them poorer than himself; and I pledge myself I am bound over to appear against him.[77]

Unsupported as this is by any examples, it is without a doubt libelous. The surprise is neither that this claim would be made in *Blackwood's* – Wilson had been singled out by the *London* for his betrayal of Wordsworth, his "*intimate friend*" (*LM* 2:673) – nor that De Quincey, whose later political writings are full of personal vituperation, could say such a thing. In fact, he was to make the same accusation, albeit more gently worded, in his memorial essays on Coleridge a decade later (*R* 36–41). But he had published no such hints in 1823. It is certainly possible that De Quincey mentioned his suspicions to his friend, and that Wilson simply reassigned them to the Opium-Eater rather than further besmirch Christopher North. Still, the deferred echo implies that the real writer acts out a fictional agenda, prescribed for him by his periodical double.[78] Would De Quincey have maligned Coleridge in 1834 had the Opium-Eater not already done so? Undecidable in itself, this question suggests how the empirical writer's career precipitates from the anonymous imaginative work.

The Opium-Eater's appearance in *Blackwood's* exemplifies the mode of authorship as "personality" that was inculcated by the magazine culture of the 1820s; fittingly, the other kind of personality reached De Quincey by the same route. In a malicious reenactment of Elia's "assassination" by Leigh Hunt, the June 1824 number of *John Bull Magazine* printed a satire on "The Opium-Eater," whom it identified for the first time as "Thomas De Quincey" and then proceeded to arraign:

Conceive an animal about five feet high, propped on two trapsticks, which have the size but not the delicate proportions of rolling pins, with a comical sort of indescribable body, and a head of most portentous magnitude, which puts one in mind of those queer big-headed caricatures that you see occasionally from whimsical pencils . . . There is something excessively disgusting in being obliged to look into any man's private life, but when we have it tossed into our faces, we must now and then do so. (quoted in *OE* 270)

Echoing X. Y. Z.'s disparagement of his "despicable human system," the libelist substitutes for the "public"'s pleasing delusion a mere pencil caricature (*C* 61; *LM* 6:513). Points of personal honor are also cited; in particular, he charges De Quincey with bedding his "servant-maid," and insinuates (accurately) that his first child was born out of wedlock. These "biographical researches" yoke the speculative textual identity to a "proper" (social) name, to a punishable body, and to a set of falsifiable data. The effect is to demote the *Confessions* from a "spontaneous and extra-judicial" (*C* 1) literary venture to the referential discourse of the lie.

De Quincey later learned that the "brutal libel" was by William Maginn, a *Blackwood's* contributor known as "O'Doherty" in *Noctes*, whose information must have come – once again – from John Wilson. His motive, De Quincey concluded, was simple "jealousy . . . a little book of mine had made its way into the drawing-rooms, where some book of his had not been heard of" (*M* 3:176). De Quincey briefly considered challenging his libeler to a duel; but unlike John Scott, he finally allowed the uncanny, unhandy logic of print reputation to take its own course (*M* 3:177). To be traduced by a writer of personalities was after all to join the company of Wordsworth and Coleridge, the "Cockney" poets Hunt and Keats, and his *London* colleague Hazlitt. In a sense, the libel just cements the social concession of identity that is the dialectical counterpart of fiction: the character-assassin ends neither by killing his victim nor by terminating his career, but by adding to the fund of biographical anecdotes incorporated into authorial presence. Maginn does little more than mirror the Opium-Eater's attack on Coleridge, reiterating the contradiction between "literary license" and scandal-mongering exposure that characterizes magazine *ressentiment.*

The virulence of magazine personalities symptomatizes both the subversion of proper identity and the commodification of fame as (sheer) personality that became increasingly exaggerated in the world of periodical print. The hallucinatory materiality of the libelous personality indicates the magazine writer's distance from the formal presence urged, for example, in Wordsworth's meticulous rearrangements of his poems for collective editions. The historical permutation of authorship I have called the Eliacal or the minor is necessarily also a symptom, but one that profits from the reflexivity it achieves by encoding an account of its own production. My next chapter will discuss how De Quincey's essays on political economy *theorize* his magazine writing as a medium of cultural transmission. Representing at once a materialist critique of aesthetics and a meditation on "labor" and "value," *The Logic of Political Economy* articulates for professional aesthetes, like the *London* writers, the role of middlemen *vis-à-vis* cultural capital. In this way De Quincey both asserts the structural dependence of canonical majority upon its disreputable minor practitioners, and – by converting a functional discourse into a minor work of literature – further consolidates the stylistic signature he had ventured in the *London.*

By construing their objective alienation as subjective impropriety, the *London* writers accrued a simulation of "surplus value," or symbolic capital, that elevated the ontologically elusive persona into taxonomic authorship. To this extent, their ironies on the subject of labor and payment no doubt constitute a form of denial, or resistance to material determination. Yet if the ghosts of Elia and the Opium-Eater ultimately fill in for the single selfhood associated with Romanticism, they also pose its critique, in the form of a counter-discourse of the readerly, the spectral, the mechanical, the inauthentic. Lamb cajoles his reader not to "be frightened at the hard words, imposition, imposture"; to "*give, and ask no questions*"; Hazlitt retorts that "there is not a more deliberate piece of grave imposture going" than the book-market Aristocracy of Letters (*LM* 5:536 [E 137]; *H* 8:206). Reducible neither to copyrights nor to spontaneous overflow, the materiality of language complicates the mystique of both book-market success and its Wordsworthian inversion. Allegorical impersonation of his serialized letters, the minor hints that the essentialist canon is but the more brilliant fraud.

CHAPTER 4

Reproductions: opium, prostitution, and poetry

THE COLOR OF PURPOSE AND THE FORM OF CONTINGENCY

In the *Noctes*, the Shepherd blunders by mistaking laudanum for the raw material of published *Confessions*, as though it were only necessary to lubricate the automaton of "On Magazine Writers" with "five hunner draps" to produce a saleable commodity. This is at least a plausible error, given De Quincey's earlier prediction that "this same opium" might enable him "to send [Blackwood] an article not unserviceable to [his] magazine."[1] In his less sublime moments, De Quincey often characterized opium as fuel or as the figure for alienated labor; "without opium I can't get on with my work," he claimed, while apologizing for the "stains of laudanum" that obscured his manuscripts and deploring the drug's influence on his writing.[2] Clearly, though, opium is not grist for the writer in the sense that paper, a dictionary of quotations, or even a topic might be; rather, opium frees the Kantian "faculty of presenting *aesthetical ideas*," those "representation[s] of the imagination" which occasion "much thought, without however any definite thought, i.e. any *concept*, being . . . adequate to" them (*K* 157). The *Confessions* aestheticize a substance that itself promotes aesthetic contemplation: for example, "that particular mode of [the mind's] activity by which we are able to construct out of the raw material of organic sound an elaborate intellectual pleasure," music (*C* 45). Opium not only heightens sensitivity to form, but even spiritualizes marketplace exchange (*C* 47) and, finally, brings about a purified aesthetic experience (dreaming) that persists in the absence of any external object at all. Opium is thus a commodity whose paradoxical "use" is its stimulus to the human activity most exempt from what Kant calls "industry," and whose products are "not to be imitated (for then that which in it is genius and constitutes the spirit of the work would be lost)" (*K* 162).

In the hands of "dunces," opium reverts from genial inspiration to standard item of consumption, "rather dear" at "three guineas a pound," "dusky brown in colour," a vice among factory-workers, and dangerous to the over-indulgent: "if you eat a good deal of it, most probably you must – do what is particularly disagreeable to any man of regular habits, viz. die" (*C* 39–40). Its dual ontology as animating "spirit" and material commodity bespeaks its amphibious relation to the two discourses seemingly most remote from one another in the early nineteenth century: political economy, the analytic of production, and aesthetics, the analytic of "taste," or cultural reception. Both subjects were specialties with De Quincey, who saluted his patron saint of political economy, David Ricardo, in the *Confessions* and who introduced Kantian terminology to English readers in essays for the *London Magazine*. His combined expertise, anomalous among English Romantic writers, gains historical resonance from Guillory's account of the "separation at birth of aesthetics and political economy" in eighteenth-century moral philosophy.[3] More pointedly, this context suggests that what is at stake in the ontology of a substance which, like opium, troubles either discourse separately, is a prefiguration of their reunion in current social theory, particularly the work of Jean Baudrillard and Pierre Bourdieu.

Opium, then – or the topos of the drug more generally – offers a point of entry to the questions of purpose and valuation that, in very different guises, link political economy and aesthetics, while it symptomatizes what De Quincey would call their mutual "interrepellence" (see *M* 9:133). De Quincey's deviations from orthodoxy on both subjects can thus be understood as the efflorescence of their constitutive omissions. In particular, his 1844 *Logic of Political Economy* insists on "the *ornamental* or *pleasurable*" (*M* 9:120) as a factor in economic "use," and as the site of his own intervention. Hence a problem which, from the perspective of political economy, can only seem minor or exceptional supplies the rationale for the Opium-Eater's *economic* identity, the professional "amateur" or dilettante. Without synthesizing the divorced disciplines, the *Logic* articulates a (pre-)materialist account of aesthetic value that is allegorized in the *Confessions*, as the last part of this chapter will demonstrate. Thus, De Quincey theorizes the "aesthetic disposition" he shared with other *London* writers as the means of *re*production for the literary commodity. The *Confessions* imagine, and the *Logic* defends, the economic genesis of the Opium-Eater's "diviner part" (*C* 41) as well as its earthly reward in what Bourdieu calls cultural capital.[4]

The *Confessions* turn on an economic transformation figured developmentally as a regression: the exchange of a liquid diet for the wholesome food of a "good man's table" (*C* 31), and of speculative subsistence for patrilineal expectations. The hero's conversion from the nature of "animal economy" (*M* 3:224) to the culture of aestheticism is framed as a *pietà*, with the famished boy "leaning [his] head" against the prostitute Ann's "bosom," when "all at once [he] sank from her arms and fell backwards." At that moment, he

> felt an inner conviction of the liveliest kind that without some powerful and reviving stimulus, I should either have died on the spot – or should at least have sunk to a point of exhaustion from which all reäscent . . . would soon have become hopeless.

Ann runs off and returns with a glass of port wine and spices that, he believes, saved his life, acting on him "with an instantaneous power of restoration" at a time when his stomach "would have rejected all solid food" (*C* 21–22). Ann's gift of wine, miming the mother's gift of milk to her child, confirms the posture of helpless infancy into which the boy falls before he is reborn. The moment of induction into the economy is "propped," in Jean Laplanche's sense, on the association between breast-feeding ("patten") and natural value that supplied one of De Quincey's favorite anecdotes.[5] This weaning from one food to another thus also prefigures the "revulsion" and "upheaving" that announce opium's "apocalypse of the world within" (*C* 38).

The thematic resonance of this scene calls attention to a certain incongruity of tenor and vehicle: Ann's simulation of mothers' milk is predicated upon her exclusion, as a sexual professional, from the domain of nature. Not an agent of salvation, she is instead the harbinger of addiction – a profane parody of the maternal icon. Indeed, the Opium-Eater explicitly distances himself from Ann as a figure of sexual reproduction before he will accept the fortified wine, a substance that, unlike milk, is neither wholesome nor naturally abundant. On the contrary: it is a luxury.

"For this glass the generous girl without a murmur paid out of her own humble purse," he recalls,

at a time – be it remembered! – when she had scarcely wherewithal to purchase the bare necessaries of life, and when she could have no reason to expect that I should ever be able to reimburse her. (*C* 22)

The Opium-Eater, Ann's "debtor for life" (*C* 27), will never eat a square meal again. "I had no appetite. I had, however, unfortunately at all times a craving for wine . . . and on all occasions when I had an opportunity, I never failed to drink wine – which I worshipped then as I have since worshipped opium" (*C* 32).[6] Late in life De Quincey would still decline any "luxurious standard" of diet, being "a mere anchorite as to such enjoyments" (*M* 9:209). With the aesthete's perverse asceticism, he starves the corpus to feed a habit of distinction. "Pure" taste, Bourdieu suggests, may originate in "visceral" disgust: the nausea the boy feels when he tastes bread or contemplates "impure" relations with his companion.[7] Spiced wine is a more ethereal, sublimated pleasure, an alcoholic solution of exotic "tinctures" that resembles the "ruby-coloured" "*laudanum negus, warm, and without sugar*" (*C* 44, 61) that later replaces it. Thus intoxication supplants nourishment; a taste for colored water subverts biological necessity.[8] To the "connoisseur," mere bodily health "look[s] pale by the deep crimson of" the "majestic intellect" (*C* 82, 41).

The motifs of sacrifice and luxury necessarily invoke the context of economics and its central problem, the nature of value. Breastmilk, a substance that provides maximum nourishment for minimal (indeed, invisible) cost, ideally exemplifies what Adam Smith calls "value in use," or usefulness in the ethical sense.[9] Wordsworth has this kind of value in mind when, positing reading as a biological impulse like hunger, he affirms his "faith that He,/ Who fills the mother's breasts with innocent milk/ Doth also for our nobler part provide,/ . . . As innocent instincts, and as innocent food" (*Prelude* 5:271–75). The supplementation of milk by wine, an article of less obvious utility, recalls Smith's founding antithesis between use value and "value in exchange," or "the power of purchasing other goods." "The things which have the greatest value in use," Smith observes in *The Wealth of Nations,*

have frequently little or no value in exchange; and, on the contrary, those which have the greatest value in exchange have frequently little or no value in use. Nothing is more useful than water: but it will purchase scarce any thing; scarce any thing can be had in exchange for it. A diamond, on the contrary, has scarce any value in use; but a very great quantity of other goods may frequently be had in exchange for it.[10]

The wine for which Ann forgoes "the bare necessaries" appears, like a gemstone, to be priced inversely to its value in supporting life. The apparent purposelessness of luxury is belied in this instance, though: wine revives the starveling boy as *real* food could not have done. Use value and exchange value must, then, be linked by another and a finer connection than that of contrast. It is possible, as the *Confessions* argue and as Baudrillard reasserts, for the categories of need and desire to be reversed; in fact, it is precisely this reversal that characterizes market psychology.[11]

The idea that any commodity (wine, milk, diamonds, or what have you) could command a price in excess of its utility is repeatedly disputed in *The Logic of Political Economy* ("Ricardo made Easy"). The opening chapter cites the example of wine, which admittedly meets "a necessity already provided for by nature in the the gratuitous article of water," to redefine Smith's

distinction . . . between the things useful to man which are too multiplied and diffused to be raised into property and the things useful to man which are *not* so multiplied and diffused, but which, being hard to obtain, support the owner in demanding a price for them. (*M* 9:124)

No exchange, De Quincey argues, can occur in the absence of a use. Rather than being opposed to use value, exchange value ranks as one *mode* of use value – the other mode being "wealth," or natural resources.[12] The distinction is not inevitable, but coincides with the advent of society. Exchange value derives from an imposition of force: the "power (howsoever gained) to command an equivalent" (*M* 9:126). The economic recipe for wine thus calls for "the original element, value in use," *plus* the power that stains the water clear (*M* 9:127).

The Christological conversion of water into wine vividly allegorizes the birth of exchange value, making wine, for De Quincey, the primal commodity. The same substance, however, is problematic for Ricardo, whose 1817 *Principles of Political Economy and Taxation* was the agent of redemption for the torpid Opium-Eater and remains his guide in all matters economic (*C* 64–65). Ricardo begins his first chapter, "On Value," with a strategic limitation:

There are some commodities, the value of which is determined by their scarcity alone. No labour can increase the quantity of such goods, and therefore their value cannot be lowered by an increased supply. Some rare statues and pictures, scarce books and coins, *wines of a peculiar quality*, which can be made only from grapes grown on a particular soil, of which there is a very limited quantity, are all of this description. Their value is wholly independent of the quantity of labour originally necessary to produce them, and varies with the varying wealth and inclinations of those who are desirous to possess them. . . In speaking, then, of commodities . . . we mean always such commodities only as can be increased in quantity by the exertion of human industry, and on the production of which competition operates without restraint.[13]

Wine is an anomalous commodity, sharing with certain collectibles the quality of reflecting the "inclination" of the buyer – not the amount of productive labor, the index of commodities as such. The power of such articles to command a return does not, in other words, seem commensurate with the labor-power they embody. Founded upon the "labor theory of value," political economy excludes from consideration items that appear to be priced subjectively, or according to "the caprice of taste." Thus it also excludes any conception of power inassimilable to a hydraulic or Newtonian model.[14]

Ricardo's brief list of exceptions provides the germ of De Quincey's *Logic*, which corrects the master by proposing a theory of "affirmative" value, or price founded "upon the intrinsic worth of the article in your individual estimate for your individual purposes" (*M* 9:138). Affirmative value stands in a complementary relation to "negative" or "resistance" value – i.e. labor value – as its condition of possibility, as its upper limit, and as one modality of market price. It is only their high affirmative value, for example, that could justify the labor-cost of diamonds. Indeed, the true utility of an article can only be gauged when, as in the case of diamonds, exchange value approaches its affirmative limit. Affirmative value is, then, none other than use value, reflexively redefined as "the simple power of ministering to a purpose" (*M* 9:179) contemplated by a user. The concept may be understood as De Quincey's attempt to reintegrate the pole of consumption into a science that had, since *The Wealth of Nations*, concerned itself solely with production.[15] Affirmative value – *power* in a more absolute sense than Ricardian labor-power – amounts to the repressed of political economy, maintaining a secret commerce with "the real unfreedom of wage-labor, its coercion," as well as with the vicissitudes of desire; affirmative value, in a word, communicates with violence.[16]

While De Quincey concedes that pure examples of affirmative price are rare, he is at pains to demonstrate both that they do exist and that they may be subsumed under economic laws. A long section of the *Logic* describes commodities that have been, are sometimes, or are always valued affirmatively; these range from the very novel or very scarce (rhinoceroses, rare books) to items prized for their "excess of beauty" (large gemstones, Arabian horses) (*M* 9:164). Mediating between examples like these and more conventional commodities are cases of luxury taste, which De Quincey illustrates with the example of salmon: though many people's "intrinsic esteem for salmon," along with demand for culinary variety, or "one luxury *amongst* others," would doubtless support a higher price than the delicacy generally bears, still "a limit is soon reached at which it would always be pulled up suddenly by some other commodity of the same class" (*M* 9:169). The great bulk of commodities, then – even those which, like fine wines, depend on unknown variables – are ultimately calibrated on the same scale: that is, by their representation in money. The principle of commensuration resurfaces at the level of competition among otherwise dissimilar articles. "Everything in every case," De Quincey asserts, "is known to be isodynamic with some fraction, some multiple, or some certain proportion, of everything else" (*M* 9:154). There is no escaping the laws of the market, even for objects like poems, paintings, and statues, which – contradictorily – derive their value from a claim to transcend commodity status.

It is the rupture between commodity pricing and *aesthetic* evaluation that De Quincey attempts to repair with his notion of affirmative value. The relation between negative and affirmative value might then be redefined, with the early Adam Smith, as "a distinction internal to the commodity itself . . . between its being as means (its 'beauty') and its being as end (its use)."[17] Some primitive aesthetic lurks even in the humblest article of daily consumption. And while the divorce of aesthetics and economics presumes irreconcilable differences between artistic value and exchange value, De Quincey suggests that when affirmative value is submitted to the pressure of monopoly, aesthetic "esteem" will indeed be embodied in price:

where a *pretium affectionis* ["fancy price"] is not without a general counter-sign from society, we do not find that it fluctuates at all. The great ITALIAN MASTERPIECES OF PAINTING have long borne an affirmative value (*i.e.* a value founded on *their* pre-eminence, not on the cost of producing); and that value pushed to the excess of a monopoly, continually growing more intense. It would be useless now to ask after the resistance price; because, if that could be ascertained, it would be a mere inoperative curiosity. Very possible it is that Leonardo da Vinci may have spent not more than £150 in producing his fresco of the Last Supper. But, were it possible to detach it from the walls of the convent refectory which it emblazons, the picture would command in London a king's ransom; and the Sistine Chapel embellishments of Michael Angelo probably two such ransoms within a week. Such jewels are now absolutely unique – they are secure from repetition; notorious copies would not for a moment enter into competition. It is very doubtful if artists of power so gigantic will reappear for many centuries; and the sole deduction from their increasing value is the ultimate frailty of their materials. (*M* 9:168)

The value of an artistic masterpiece is to be understood as a price founded upon "the feelings or opinions of the individual" where ratified by a "general countersign from society." Strictly subjective, it is nonetheless *underwritten*, or guaranteed, by historical consensus. De Quincey's account of aesthetic value thus amounts to an economic translation of the "title to subjective universality" that Kant attributes to sensations of the beautiful in his *Critique of Judgment* (*K* 46). The purchaser of Da Vinci's "Last Supper" can be regarded as an investor in judgment whose speculations are protected by a tacit pledge from society.

The Kantian subtext of De Quincey's argument becomes more explicit when the example of great paintings is recast in terms of the *purposiveness* of art. "From the Greek word for a purpose (or final cause)," De Quincey writes,

we have the word *teleologic*; to denote that quality in any subject by which it tends toward a purpose, or is referred to a purpose. Thus the beauty of a kitchen-garden, of a machine, of a systematic theory, or of a demonstration, is said to be teleologic; as first of all perceived upon referring it to the purposes which it professes to answer. On the same principle all affirmative value, or value in use, is teleologic value – value derived from the purpose which the article contemplates. (*M* 9:190)

For Kant, the teleological "beauty of a kitchen-garden" cannot be equated with the pure judgment of taste, a subject's perception of purposiveness *without* any thought of objective purpose. De

Quincey, however, elides the Kantian qualitative distinction in order to argue that

a genuine picture of Da Vinci's or Raphael's sells *always* on the principle of value in use, or teleologic value. An enlightened sensibility to the finest effects of art – this constitutes the purpose or teleologic function to which the appreciation is referred . . . It is right, therefore, to say that the picture sells for its use, *i.e.* its capacity of being used and enjoyed; and that this price cannot now be intercepted (as so generally the affirmative of prices of articles *are*) by a price founded upon cost of reproducing. (*M* 9:192)

Against Smith and Ricardo, De Quincey contends that use value should be understood as a positive "power," isodynamic with – but not reducible to – the labor embodied in mass-produced objects. (Kant: "only that which a man, even if he knows it completely, may not therefore have the skill to accomplish belongs to art" [*K* 146].) Against Kant, De Quincey suggests that the work of art is indeed a commodity and that it does conform to an objective purpose: to please the discriminating consumer. The subjective, non-cognitive basis of aesthetic judgment does not differentiate it from the judgment involved in any affirmative valuation, which always has its grounds in the individual's "own contingent appreciation" (*M* 9:143) of an article's adaptation to his private desires – even the nebulous desire for aesthetic gratification. "Taste," then, rather than being opposed to "rational" maximization, is subordinated to economic activity as one of its modes.

De Quincey's attempt to integrate aesthetic and economic value is weakened, nonetheless, by his difficulty in adducing factual cases of equivalence between price and ideal esteem: the "Last Supper" will after all never be detached from its refectory wall. The chasm between the affirmative value attributed to a work of art and its actual market price is especially broad where literary artifacts are concerned, as De Quincey reluctantly shows in the case of *Paradise Lost*:

Were you (walking with a foreigner in London) to purchase for eighteenpence a new copy of this poem, suppose your foreign friend to sting your national pride by saying – "Really it pains me to see the English putting so slight a value upon their great poet as to rate his greatest work no higher than eighteenpence" – how would you answer? Perhaps thus: – "My friend, you mistake the matter. The price does not represent the *affirmative* value – the value derived from the *power* of the poem to please or exalt; *that* would be valued by some as infinite, irrepresentable by money; and yet the *resistance* to its reproduction might be less than the price of a breakfast." (*M* 9:165–66)

Regarded as an article of consumption, *Paradise Lost* ranks among the cheapest and most readily available; its value, or its *power*, must be postulated as "irrepresentable by money," a notion that apparently compromises De Quincey's effort to square the "double system" (*M* 9:155) of values. This dichotomy is, however, embodied in the double ontology of the literary work, which – as unique artifact (the object of copyright) and mass-produced commodity; as the creation of an autonomous author, and the product of alienated labor – materializes the internal contradictions of *both* aesthetic and economic discourse as statues and paintings do not.

Thus, in *Paradise Lost*, the sting of the rupture between quantifiable and "infinite" values comes to signify the "violence to the imagination" committed by the sublime (*K* 97, 83). "The feeling of the sublime," Kant summarizes, is "a feeling of pain arising from the want of accordance between the aesthetical estimation of magnitude formed by the imagination" – De Quincey's "affirmative" value – "and the estimation of the same formed by reason" (*K* 96) – De Quincey's labor-power or "resistance." If the beauty of horses or gemstones can be approximated in money, sublimity is the incapacity to reconcile two measurements: here, the great number of reproductions, signifying imaginative esteem or "power," and the low price of each copy. The book's only measurable difference from another commodity is its "opposition to the interest of sense" (*K* 107), which De Quincey emphasizes by posing an imaginary choice between a book and a breakfast. The literary work emerges as both symptom and symbolic resolution of the tension between empirical and transcendental representations that De Quincey has attempted to resolve in the *Logic*.[18] The violence of this tension even finds thematic expression in *Paradise Lost*, where Milton "enriche[s]" the primal scene of Abel's murder with the "warm, sanguinary colouring" of laudanum negus or wine (*M* 13:17).[19]

That enrichment, like the wine-dark hue of exchange value, serves as a reminder of compulsion, or "work, i.e. [an] occupation which is unpleasant (a trouble) in itself and which is only attractive on account of its effect (e.g. the wage)" (*K* 146). Even the creation of a work of art (be it an oratorio, *Paradise Lost*, or the "Last Supper") entails "something compulsory or, as it is called, mechanism, without which the spirit, which must be free in art and which

alone inspires the work, would have no body" (*K* 147). If red is, as
Kant would have it, the color of the sublime – or the disproportion
between production and consumption – at the same time it signifies the impossibility that any work of art could shuffle off its
commodity status.[20] The transcendent is also ineluctably the
material. In the experience of the sublime, the object's trace of
compulsion is borne not by the maker but by the appreciator,
whose pained pleasure reveals how "the imagination is depriving
itself of its freedom . . . it *feels* the sacrifice or the deprivation and,
at the same time, the cause to which it is subjected" (*K* 109). Great
art, in a word, is difficult; *someone* has to work. The "resistance to
its reproduction" ordinarily signified by price is incorporated into
the great poem as its prestige, or its aura of erudition. In
Wordsworth's version of this claim, "the ease and gracefulness with
which the Poet manages his numbers" produce aesthetic surplus,
or "an overbalance of pleasure," a quantity measured by the fact
that "the verse will be read a hundred times where the prose is read
once" (*PrW* 1:151). Disequilibrium is posited as the cause of a consumer (the taste by which the poet is enjoyed) who not only
grounds the notion of poetic power but whose reciprocal "effort,
. . . exertion, and *action*" (*PrW* 3:81) supplement the work's inadequate market price.[21] But as De Quincey discovers when, as a boy,
he orders a multi-volume work from a bookseller, "here there
might be supplements to supplements – the work might positively
never end" (*C* 133). The commodities market *materializes* aesthetic
overbalance: "having purchased some numbers, and obtained
others on credit," the new-born consumer "contract[s] an engagement to take all the rest, though they should stretch to the crack
of doom" (*C* 133). The labor of appreciation is indeed an endless
work; no one ever wished *Paradise Lost* any longer, and anyone who
calls it "amusing" is simply, De Quincey declares, a liar (see *M*
10:47–48).

The taint of barbarism that clings to *Paradise Lost* is more pronounced in its symmetrical opposite, the "powerful drug" that De
Quincey proposes as exemplar of *pretium affectionis* to resolve the
impasse he encounters in his discussion of works of art. He recurs
to this example three times in the *Logic*, having first posed a hypothetical case in which the "prodigiously greater powers" of some
new compound could enact a "violent revolution" in "the
consciousness of the individual appreciator" (*M* 9:142–43): the

revolutionary consciousness, that is, of how very much he is willing to *pay* for this substance. "Drug" names the sublime even more precisely than "*Paradise Lost*," exposing the loophole in Kant's insistence that "true sublimity must be sought only in the mind of the [subject] judging, not in the *natural* object" (*K* 95; my emphasis). An *unnatural* object, the drug further strains the notion of "teleology" that De Quincey attributes to paintings and kitchen-gardens alike. Narratives of its uses run the gamut from stark functionalism to baroque reflexivity. Whereas, for example, "a glassful of water, taken out of a brook in England to quench a momentary thirst, has only a use value . . . a glass of *medicinal* water" – *pace* Smith – possesses value in exchange (*M* 9:187; my emphasis). A "subtle elixir" such as the "drastic medicine" croton oil acquires the mystique of "an amulet, a charm," when viewed in connection with the "oriental reward" it might command from a desperate and wealthy patient (*M* 9:170–71). Its high cost invests it with a quasi-aesthetic dimension, like that of the "powerful musical snuff-box" which "you are vehemently desirous to purchase" at the extortionate price of sixty guineas (see *M* 9:138). This imbalance, the empirical mode of the sublime,

calls up from the prehistory of political economy the analogy of the work of art, as an example of the object's capacity to produce a need in the consumer that did not exist before . . . political economy cannot give a systemic account of the system of production-exchange-consumption even in its own terms, without reluctantly attributing to the commodity what it *actually* possesses, an "aesthetic" aspect.[22]

"Like Aeschylus or Milton in poetry, like Michael Angelo in painting," or like the great murderer Williams, the oriental drug achieves a "colossal sublimity, and, as Mr. Wordsworth observes, has in a manner 'created the taste by which [it] is to be enjoyed'" (*M* 13:12).[23] As affirmative value approaches infinity, usefulness shades into the ineffable, the drug's alleged excess of means over ends registering as a new "need for itself" in the consumer whose "seven-fold chain" of "servile" captivity literalizes the imagination's loss of freedom in the contemplation of the sublime (*C* 4).[24] The drug demands of its worshipper what is less obviously true of the poetry-fancier: that is to say, while any given dose might be had for less than the price of a breakfast, the amateur must pay again and again for (different incarnations of) the same object.

At this point aesthetic judgment is decisively severed from the ethical sense of utility that governs "Adamic" political economy and covertly supports Kantian aesthetics as well.[25] "It is not meant that by possessing value in use a thing is useful – is valuable – *quoad commodum* or *quoad utilitatem*," De Quincey reiterates, "but valuable *ad utendum, utendi gratia*, with a view to being used; not that it accomplishes some salutary or laudable purpose [Smith's mistake], but that it accomplishes a purpose – however monstrous, pernicious, or even destructive to the user" (*M* 9:189–90). The salutary exertion and laudable refinement that Wordsworth finds in poetic reception have no corollary in De Quincey's materialist account. Where the economy is concerned, it is literally the case that one man's meat is another man's poison:

It is clear that political economy neither has resources nor any motive for distinguishing between the useful and the noxious; it is clear that political economy has quite as little of either for distinguishing between the truly useful and the spuriously useful. No man has paid for an article less or more because it is fascinating and ruinous; no man has paid for an article, either less or more, because it is dull and useful. (*M* 9:190–91)

Thus "diamonds have the use value of water"; thus a painting by Da Vinci sells "on the principle of value in use"; and

So, again, the phial of prussic acid which you buy in a remote Australian colony, accidentally drained of its supplies, at a price exorbitantly beyond its ordinary cost, must be classed as a price founded on value in use, notwithstanding that I will assume it to have been bought with a view to self-destruction. It would argue great levity of heart to view in the light of a useful thing any agency whatever that had terminated in so sorrowful a result as suicide. Usefulness there was not in the prussic acid, as any power sufficient to affect or alter the price; but a purpose there was, however gloomy a purpose, a teleologic use attached to the acid, under the circumstances supposed. (*M* 9:192)

The agency of a poison in effecting the user's self-destruction – the obverse of the croton oil's powers of resurrection – luridly exemplifies the reflexivity both of use value and of its Kantian equivalent, "purpose." The acid's "teleologic use," or intentionality, must be supposed to be "attached" to it by the consumer, since a substance manufactured for the express purpose of abetting suicide would presumably be a contradiction in terms. Like the beautiful in nature, prussic acid has a purpose in the subjective sense that it "can be explained and conceived by us only so far as we assume for its ground a causality according to purposes" (*K* 55).

Not purpose*ful*, prussic acid is construed as purpos*ive* by those who regard its "gloomy" aura as a hint to "do it beautifully." De Quincey's treatment of suicide, in other words, pursues Kant's account of aesthetic response to its logical and macabre conclusion.

Derrida observes that "there are no drugs 'in nature.' There may be natural poisons and indeed naturally lethal poisons, but they are not as such 'drugs.'"[26] The drug's aesthetic dimension unfolds precisely "in the mind of the subject judging," and it finally bears no necessary connection to the objective (e.g., anaesthetic) purpose of the substance. If *Paradise Lost* represents the pleasure of reading as a kind of pain, the drug instantiates the possibility of experiencing pain as pleasure; De Quincey was indeed criticized for "so manag[ing] the second narrative" of his *Confessions* "as to leave an overbalance on the side of the *pleasures* of opium"; "the very horrors themselves," reviewers complained, "do not pass the limit of pleasure" (*M* 3:465). Thus, as Kant puts it, "the apprehension of [this] otherwise formless and unpurposive object gives merely the occasion through which we become conscious of" our own satisfaction; "the object is . . . *employed* as subjectively purposive, but is not judged as such *in itself* and on account of its form (it is, as it were, a *species finalis accepta, non data*)" (*K* 121). The example of prussic acid reveals, then, how aesthetic appreciation usurps both labor value and any residual authority of the natural object. While for Kant the sublime wreaks violence on the imagination, De Quincey's illustration further suggests the violence *to the object* inflicted by a consumerist theory of value. It is one thing to grant purposiveness to "nature"; another for subjectivity to override a maker's intentions and wishes. If suicide – the deliberate misuse of a classified substance – constitutes the ultimate expression of the aesthetic disposition, radically distinguishing objective from subjective purposes, it also subverts any notion of the commodity as given (*data*). The anecdote has less to do with cultural relativism than with a materialism of *reception*, or consumption as production.

Either to call the charms of prussic acid "commodity fetishism" or to derogate the stung pride of the Miltonist as "ideology" is to miss the point here. Aesthetic value is not simply a misrecognition of labor value, nor is it free of empirical determinants. Whether the commodity is priced too high, like the prussic acid, or too low, like the great poem, the *question* of the aesthetic may be said to arise at the moment of exchange, resting "latent" till awakened by a revolution in consciousness. Thus, De Quincey recalls his first *purchase* of opium, eulogizing "the beatific vision of an immortal druggist, sent down to earth on a special mission to myself," who nonetheless returned "real copper halfpence" in change for a shilling (*C* 38). At the moment of changing hands, the object mutates from essence to contingency, from the use value of water to the specious or "colorable" pleasure of wine.[27] Understood as a matter of tincture, the equivocation at the commodity's heart infects philosophy as well as economics; Ricardo's reluctant admission of "caprice" is echoed in Kant's treatment of color as both incidental "charm," hence merely sensory, and as a component of aesthetic form (*K* 46–47, 58–62, 144–45). Tincture, De Quincey's trope of exchange, colors the representation of exchange itself as trope: the customer is less its arbiter than its personification.

The loss of the empirical object does not only complicate labor theory. The ontology of artistic productions is threatened as well, for aestheticism mounts the tacit claim that artistic works are determined by the mode of their consumption rather than by the maker's label. The aesthetic consumer may half create a work of art in imaginative perception, but he may also downgrade statues, poems and paintings to the condition of ordinary commodities. The structural disequilibrium of production and reception manifests itself indifferently as Francis Jeffrey's "perverted taste for simplicity," as the "fascinating, but absurd" habit of opium-eating, and in the use of a sculpture for the commission of a murder.[28] As the "aesthetic disposition," the phenomenon is familiar in the collection, which invests a "found" object – an anonymous peasant ballad, for example – with formal closure. As "commodification," it appears in the failure of "the elaborated taste for the most refined objects" to divest itself of "the elementary taste for the flavours of food."[29] Wordsworth, for example, derides readers who "converse with us as gravely about a *taste* for Poetry . . . as if it were a thing as indifferent as a taste for rope-dancing, or Frontiniac or Sherry" (*PrW* 1:139), in the fantastic hope that the economy of poetry might bypass commodity production altogether. That the same item, wine, can be classed by Ricardo with artistic productions and by Wordsworth with mass-cultural ephemera merely suggests how permeable is the boundary between consumption and reception, commodity and work of art. De Quincey's attempt to treat all works of art as commodities thus represents both the apogee and the perversion of Kantianism, in its suggestion that even "disinterested" judgment will always be modeled on market exchange.

The work of art resembles the narcotic in the precise sense that both are defined by the incorporation of response into the being of the thing consumed. (Thus, *Paradise Lost* becomes a treatise on opium, which "must already have existed in Eden," where "it was used medicinally by an archangel" to fortify Adam's "mental sight" against the vision of his original crime [*M* 5:211].)[30] This does not mean that the work is simply reducible to individual perceptions, or even that, urn-like, it contains all its possible readings.[31] More radically, both drug and poem illustrate the suspension of objecthood, an itinerary of perpetual deviation that is dictated by the structure of the market. The aesthetic object is constituted by a paradoxical turn away from its own essence that De Quincey calls a "determinate tendency or *clinamen*, eventually decisive of its pretensions" (*M* 9:129).

In being consumed, an object is not what it is. "The word *literature*," for example, "is a perpetual source of confusion, because it is used in two senses, and those senses liable to be confounded with each other." In one sense it means "the total books of a language," including those "in which the matter to be communicated is paramount to the manner or form of its communication ('ornari res ipsa negat, contenta doceri')." In the other, it signifies "the direct . . . antithesis" of the first meaning, "a fine art – the supreme fine art," in which latter case "it is difficult to construct [its] idea . . . with severe accuracy" (*M* 10:46–47). Indeed, literature in this autogenetic sense can only be known as effect:

All that is literature seeks to communicate power; all that is not literature, to communicate knowledge. Now, if it be asked what is meant by communicating power, I, in my turn, would ask by what name a man would designate the case in which I should be made to feel vividly, and with a vital consciousness, emotions which ordinary life rarely or never supplies occasions for exciting, and which had previously lain unwakened, and hardly within the dawn of consciousness – as myriads of modes of feeling are at this moment in every human mind for want of a poet to organize them? I say, when these inert and sleeping forms *are* organized, when these possibilities *are* actualized, is this conscious and living possession of mine *power*, or what is it? . . . when I am thus suddenly startled into a feeling of the infinity of the world within me, is this power, or what may I call it? (*M* 10:48–49)

Books of knowledge have Adamic use-value; they may be used, and so used up. Literature is defined, first, by a different telos, the actualization of a "power" that at last displaces the "knowledge" of Ricardian labor-power. In so doing, however, power migrates from the gigantic maker to the reading subject, or, more exactly, "turns round upon" that subject in a moment of constitutive (productive and *self*-productive) revelation. In *Paradise Lost*, for example, Milton "peopl[es]" the "lifeless form" or geometrical "postulate" of abstract space "with Titanic shadows, forms that sat at the eldest counsels of the infant world . . . so that, from being a thing to inscribe with diagrams, it has become under his hands a vital agent on the human mind" (*M* 10:49). "Communicating power," the great poem tautologically heightens the reader's awareness of inner space, a "possession" he already possessed, albeit unconsciously. The pain of studious application is compensated by a subjective power that *infinitely* exceeds the "power of purchasing other goods" which he exchanged for it. The pains expended by the producing poet thus translate into the reader's limitlessly renewable resource; the prospect of unending reproduction redresses the poem's initial low price. This fall from essentialist accounts of poetic greatness is, then, no demystification but a theoretical defense of the possession we know as cultural capital. De Quincey's "power" may be redefined, with only slight anachronism, as professional authority: a material effect of the economy's sublimation into the "potent rhetoric" of "eloquent opium" (*C* 49). The literature of power finds its use as an agency of *cultural* reproduction, fueling the aesthetic machine in which passive consumption becomes its own genial commodity.

CULTURAL CAPITALIST

De Quincey's rendition of the sublime as power covertly reintroduces conventional teleology into the experience of aesthetic grandeur, not only by converting Miltonic space into an agency of (his own) mind, but by *communicating* Milton's communication through a rhetorical question to a certain "Young Man Whose Education Has Been Neglected." While imagined as a private

transfer of power between the literary commodity and its consumer, appreciation expresses itself in another linguistic artifact –
becoming, thereby, an experience *for* something or someone else.
The idealization of aesthetic response commonly called reception
is therefore better understood as transmission, with all the
complications this entails both for the bipolar model of political
economy and for transcendental philosophy. Because reception
must itself be represented, it produces a material *excess* of
purposiveness, implicitly available for reinscription as mere
purpose. Kant intimates such a possibility when he remarks that
the contemplative imagination is not simply "reproductive [i.e.,
photographic] but "productive and spontaneous"; it is "the author
of arbitrary forms of possible intuition," and even of "*fiction*[*s*]" (*K*
77, 81; original emphasis). The supervention of form verges even
here on the disingenuous, suggesting an interest in disinterested-
ness, or imaginative "agenda," that materializes in the De
Quinceyan rhetorician.

Lest the medium of transmission be mistaken for transparency,
De Quincey allies the appreciation of literary power with the real-
ization of advances in economic theory. Because Ricardo wrote for
"the *clerus*, not the *populus*," like Milton he "needs a commentary"
from "the professional body who seek to teach" (*M* 9:117).[32] While
Ricardo belongs among "the *labourers of the Mine*," De Quincey
takes his place with the "*labourers of the Mint*" who "work up the
metal for current use" (*M* 9:50–51). The minter's "changes in terminology" and "improvements of classification" – like the opposition between "power" and "knowledge" – impart

> a *value* which could be adequately expressed only by . . . the completion
> of a galvanic circle, where previously it had been interrupted. Not merely
> an addition of new power, but the ratification of all the previous powers
> yet inchoate, had been the result. It was impossible to use adequately the
> initial powers of the science until others had been added which distrib-
> uted the force through the entire cycle of resistances. (*M* 9:147–48; my
> emphasis)

Conceived in these performative terms, language participates in
the system the economist describes: conductivity is a mode of production as well as reception.[33] To profess Ricardo is to *supplement*,
whether by introducing technical refinements or through an
admixture of literary pleasure. Hence it is transmission, rather
than either the "affirmative" or "negative" poles in themselves, that

activates whatever latent power slumbers in the original work. De Quincey's analogy between linguistic media and physical machinery emphasizes the role of discourse in generating value – a role considered neither by classical economics nor by Kantian aesthetics.[34]

The laborer of the mint, then, resembles not the artisan but the capitalist middleman, who "appropriat[es]" and reissues "superfluous words" that would else merely extend the "waste fertility of language" (*M* 10:72–73). Converting wealth to exchange value, the conductor forms gratuitous expressions into "new shades and combinations of thought" (*M* 10:72). In this he is "forestalled. . . and guided by the tendency of language itself"; transmission represents itself as the belated awareness of distinctions already manifested in popular use. Thus, to "remint" the superfluity of language is *both* to produce value *and* simply to find it. Like "a golden coin," rhetoric ought, De Quincey argues, to "be as florid as it can," for in both currencies symbolic value outweighs the neutral standard.[35] Profiting from this disequilibrium, just as the capitalist "personifie[s] capital," the professional or linguistic middleman personifies "the insensible *clinamen*" – the curvature or *différence* – that characterizes both language and market exchange (*M* 10:72–73).[36]

If even money, the abstraction of economic purpose, owes its power to a superfluity of form, it should be no surprise to find that the profits of linguistic mediation are marked in De Quincey's *Logic* by a dispute over the monetary representation of a "beauty." The *Logic* begins with an anecdote from Plautus's *Asinaria* intended, De Quincey claims, to illustrate the fundamental opposition between water and wine, use and exchange. It depicts what seems, in outline, a straightforward transaction between characters representing "negative" and "affirmative" value: physical labor and consumer desire. The laborer in question never appears in the scene, however, because like Ricardo she is spoken *for* by a "professional character" – in this instance, a *lena*, or madame (*M* 9:122). Rather than exemplify the predictable reaction of "two elements," then, the scene dramatizes the inadequacy of both labor theory and reception theory to account for the genesis of value. In this sense it may be read, in line with Foucault's view of the relation between discourse and thought, as an allegory of the repressed knowledge of Ricardian economics.[37] At the same time, it exaggerates what is most problematic in Kant's analytic of the beautiful: the question of interest that arises in connection with *human* form.

As De Quincey recounts the dialogue, Argyrippus, "a young man . . . occupied in sowing wild-oats," negotiates with Caelereta, "a prudent woman settled in business on her own account," for the hire of a "young beauty." "The question which arises between the parties" concerns whether and how much Argyrippus should pay. It is the role of the *lena* to demonstrate that "under an apparent unity of meaning" – that is, "value" – "there lurk[s] a real dualism" (*M* 10:72). She must, as De Quincey exhorts readers of the *Logic*, "so . . . use a sameness as to make it do the office of a difference" (*M* 9:136).[38] Like De Quincey, Caelereta is in the business of Coleridgean desynonymy (*BL* 1:82–84).[39] Her *professionalism* consists in the slippage between the semantic distinction she asserts and the material effects thereby to be achieved. "The following," De Quincey alleges, "is the particular passage which concerns the present distinction between *value in use* and *value in exchange:*"

ARG. What has become of those sums which in times past I gave you?
CAEL. All spent, sir – all consumed; for, believe me, if those moneys still survived, the young woman should be despatched to your house without another word: once paid in full, I'm not the woman that would trouble you for a shilling. Look here: – *The successions of day and night, water, sunlight, moonlight – all these things I purchase freely without money; but that heap of things beside which my establishment requires, those I pay for on the old terms of Grecian credit. When I send for a loaf to the baker's, for wine to the vintner's, certainly the articles are delivered; but when? Why, as soon as those people have touched the cash.* Now, that same practice is what I in my turn apply to others. My hands have still eyes at their finger-ends: their faith is strong in all money which actually they see. For "caution," as you call it – for guarantees – they are nothing: security be d – d; and that's an old saying.

The latter part of the speech wanders off into the difference between the system of prompt payment on the one hand and of credit on the other. But the part in italics confines itself to the difference between value in use and value in exchange. (*M* 9:123–24)

Both the characters and the motifs recall the scene of the Opium-Eater's conversion: there is the impoverished youth applying for credit; a prostitute to whom he is in debt; a question about "the propriety of the household economy"; and, finally, the selection of wine to represent value in exchange. The expanded context suggests, however, that the commonsensical contrast between freely obtainable water and expensive wine displaces the more delicate issue of how to describe the anonymous beauty. The problem has less to do with propriety than with property, that is, the profits of ontological discriminations.

Caelereta accuses Argyrippus of mistaking her employee for a "gratuitous article" like water or sunlight. This notion, in its specious plausibility (for it is well known that the best things in life are free), she rejects as a scandal to the economy – the purely hypothetical "wealth" that De Quincey calls a "regulative" idea (*M* 9:129). The doubleness "lurking . . . under the elliptical term *'value'*" (*M* 9:126) perpetually threatens to resurface as duplicity or coercion: "waste fertility" trumped up as magical charms, or aversive labor dismissed as natural inclination. The sociological problem apparently reduces to a linguistic one; by figuring the "imperfection" that troubles economic discourse, the woman becomes chargeable with "the prostitution of language."[40] A personified "verbal *equivoque*" (*M* 9:125), her very being is a matter of representation. Caelereta's analogical distinction between free sex and paid sex mimes the Coleridgean proof that "two conceptions perfectly distinct" – like negative value and affirmative value, knowledge and power, commodity and work of art – "are confused under one and the same word" (*BL* 1:83–84). By this account, exchange value precipitates from the intrinsic imbalance of language. The alleged deficit of words in relation to concepts registers as a surplus of meaning (or exchange) over designation (or use).

To make the point in what Derrida would call this "classical" way is, however, to ignore the *imposition* of the letter. The *lena's* fierce rebuttal, proof of De Quincey's claim that "verbal" disputes "set in violently towards things" (*M* 9:146), proves as well that desynonymy may produce effects quite remote from the apparent discrimination. In shifting the ground of the debate to domestic economy, Caelereta substitutes obvious contrast for an argument whose premise is shared by the two disputants. Argyrippus never denies that pleasure must be paid for; he and Caelereta concur on the propriety of his asking, in a variant of the "We Are Seven" question, "how many may she be?" They merely disagree about how the units should be tabulated. Argyrippus believes he has *already* paid, or that his past "sums" add up to a property. The *lena* counters by insisting that "those sums are dead." The dispute turns on an untheorized distinction between product and service that enables Argyrippus to conflate a renewable "contract" with barter, and Caelereta to describe circulating capital (money used to maintain a business establishment) in terms of household consumption.[41] Does a "left-handed marriage" give Argyrippus a property in the woman's body, or has he only purchased individual performances? Putting the question differently, is her body a commodity or is it capital?

When Caelereta assures Argyrippus that his sums have "all [been] spent," she presumes the second alternative, as surely she must if she is to keep collecting her percentage. Compared to bread or wine, the prostitute's body represents fixed capital, but considered as capital it is not her own: its value belongs to the professional doyenne of a service economy. "One of that unhappy class who subsist upon the wages of prostitution" (*C* 20), the young beauty sells her labor *as* herself – and sells both twice, first to her madame and then to her customer. So long as customers return for her, she is worth more as a laborer than she could fetch in the commodities market. Her identity as exchange value, in other words, cloaks her production of *surplus* value, the symptom or remainder of De Quincey's *Logic*.

"Surplus value" is not, of course, a term in the Ricardian vocabulary, though De Quincey coins the neologism "surplussage" to describe the value of rhetorical adroitness like Caelereta's.[42] That is to say that the De Quinceyan name for surplus is quite simply beauty, or aesthetic pleasure more generally. The very incongruity of this notion suggests a crux in Kant's analysis that corresponds with the Ricardian disregard for aesthetic pleasure. To Kant, human beauty remains caught between the empiricism of sensible charms – in other words, desire – and the conceptual idealism of moral *purpose*, because "the only being which has the purpose of its existence in itself is *man*" (*K* 69). It is impossible for the imagination to construe sheer purposiveness where intentionality must always already be: impossible, that is, without its seeming reprehensibly oblivious to the person's existence. Persons, in other words, cannot be beautiful for themselves, so that even purified aesthetic pleasure becomes a kind of expropriation. If, to Argyrippus, the young beauty is all sensual charms, Caelereta's property in her suggests the unthinkability of a *disinterestedly* aesthetic perception of another person.

De Quincey's story "The Household Wreck" takes this dilemma as its main theme. No sooner has the narrator's innocent wife entered a shop as a purchaser than she is transformed into an object of consumption, eliciting "ardent expressions about 'the lady's beauty'" (*M* 12:173, 187). "To consume" becomes synonymous with "to represent," as the narrator indicates when he laments the "description of my wife's person, as would inevitably summon to the next exhibition of her misery . . . the hardened amateur in spectacles of woe" (*M* 12:188). Representation, finally, consigns the woman to membership in a "class," when in a "vast calendar of guilt and misery, amidst the *aliases* or cant designations of ruffians, prostitutes, felons," the narrator finds "the description, at full length . . . of my Agnes" (*M* 12:188).[43] Like the Plautian squabble over an invisible woman, the plight of Agnes confirms and ironically extends Kant's thesis that beauty must be sought in "the representation by which an object is *given* to us" (*K* 56). The market's "harm to some other person" produces an aesthetic overbalance indistinguishable from the "capacity of being used or enjoyed" (*M* 9:192).

In short, beauty figures in the *Logic*'s primal scene less as the ground of affirmative value than as its "alibi." That beauty is use, use beauty, may be seen in the way Caelereta confuses her wares with objects of daily consumption, rewriting Argyrippus's desire as physiological need. The consequent redundance of "fitness" over functionalism, according to *The Theory of Moral Sentiments*, propels circulation by inducing refinements of consumer desire. The topos of excess registers as a compulsion to repeat; not any girl will do for Argyrippus, though others could provide similar services. In Caelereta's account, then, use value does not (like "a glassful of water, taken out of a brook in England") stand "opposed as a *collateral*" or "*sisterly*" idea to value in exchange, but instead (like "a glass of medicinal water") assumes its rank "*under* exchange value" as a "*filial*" idea (*M* 9:187; De Quincey's emphasis). Beauty is the dutiful *daughter* of exchange, even when she prostitutes herself. Each subsequent recognition promises a return on the *lena*'s capital, the surplus of *aesthetic* value which constitutes the professional character.

For De Quincey, the beauties of literature both share this feminine vulnerability and color the medium of exchange. (Thus, in "The Household Wreck," Agnes personifies the "divine beauty" of a passage in *Paradise Lost* [*M* 12:184–85]). If beauty is a woman in the marketplace, marketplace language is a madame. De Quincey expands Kantian imagination into an *office*, occupied by an alchemist who, simulating "the entire cycle of resistances," produces beauty as the absent cause of economic circulation. Caelereta personifies representation and dramatizes its activity as rhetorical, hence both diverting and potentially fraudulent. Pursuing her interests "through a maze of inversions, evolutions, and harlequin changes" (*M* 10:97), she converts the form of beauty into the color of money.[44]

The wine adduced as a "striking" instance of exchange value may now be seen in its true colors as the aesthetic trace of a completed exchange: both token and tonic for the economic wound. The prescription is an ancient one. In the same letter in which, railing against the "foolish and hurtful lusts" incurred through the "love of money," St. Paul urges contentment with domestic "food and raiment," he makes a small exception for his disciple Timothy: "Drink no longer water, but use a little wine for thy stomach's sake and thine often infirmities" (I Timothy 6:8–10, 5:23). The symptom of the economy's reinscription as need, Paul's advice recalls Freud's etiology of "conversions" in the "domestic economy of the mind": "the current flows along these paths from the new source of excitation to the old point of discharge – pouring into the symptom, in the words of the Gospel, like new wine into an old bottle" (*SE* 7:43, 54). Or, as De Quincey puts it, "the same hydraulic machinery has distributed, through the same marble fountains, water, milk, or wine," as animal economy converts to the desire for reproduction (*C* 142).

When the prostitute Ann administers her medicinal glass to the future Opium-Eater, she indeed renders him a service greater than he can ever repay, for she thereby initiates another consumer into the economy of desire. If, as he wryly observes of his youthful relations with street-walkers, *sine cerere et libero friget Venus* ("without bread and wine love freezes"), her gift of surplussage provides the "powerful and reviving stimulus" (*C* 20–22) to his pleasure in the forms of exchange. As if in compensation for "the existing state of my purse," which forbade any "impure" connection, the Opium-Eater mediates aesthetically between "high and low . . . educated and uneducated . . . guilty and . . . innocent." It may harm the natural man, but Ann's gift physics the Opium-Eater *formaliter* considered, permitting him not only to resume "the purpose which had allured me up to London, and which I had been (to use a forensic word) *soliciting* from the first day of my arrival," but also to contemplate soliciting "on [Ann's] behalf" (*C* 23, 21). (The *clinamen* of representation *is* sexuality.) The gain on one side of the ledger is gauged by the loss of the referent: the natural woman, or absent cause.

As a reflection on professionalism, De Quincey's submerged analogy between sexual profiteering and aesthetic appreciation suggests that the discourse of "free beauty" (*K* 65) symptomatically reproduces the surplus value it can neither theorize nor do without. Professionalism capitalizes, through desynonymy, on the Kantian (and Ricardian) relegation of the *Ding an sich* to an otherness inaccessible except as representation; but the figure of the prostitute haunts its rhetoric as the abject reminder of some unitary value-in-itself. Less oblique in this regard than Coleridge or his clerisy, De Quincey conflates the disinterested professional with the unrepentant whore in a figure we may call the cultural capitalist. Vulgar and grasping as she is, Caelereta nonetheless prefigures the mode of aesthetic exchange Bourdieu calls a "'sense' for sound cultural investment," the

internalized form of the objective relationship between the site of acquisition and the "centre of cultural values" . . . the sense of investment secures profits which do not need to be pursued as profits; and so it brings to those who have legitimate culture as a second nature the supplementary profit of being seen (and seeing themselves) as perfectly disinterested, unblemished by any cynical or mercenary use of culture. This means that the term "investment," for example, must be understood in the dual sense of economic investment – which it objectively always is, though misrecognized – and the sense of affective investment which it has in psychoanalysis.[45]

Bourdieu cautions against any inference that the professional's behavior "is guided by rational calculation of maximum profit, as the ordinary usage of [economic] concepts . . . implies." The investment has, by this point, been *sublimated*, a process De Quincey allegorizes when, near the end of the *Logic*, he briefly adopts a macroeconomic perspective to consider "how . . . profits [are] kept down to the average level" – how, in other words, we can know that manufacturers do not reap in profits more than they sow in wages and materials. He finds the answer in circulation itself, or the fact that "capital moves with velocity where the capitalist cannot move."

If our human vision were fitted for detecting agencies so impalpable . . . we might sometimes behold vast arches of electric matter continually passing and repassing between either pole and the equatorial regions. Accordingly as the equilibrium were disturbed suddenly or redressed, would be the phenomena of tropical hurricanes, or of auroral lights. Somewhat in the same silent arches of continual transition, ebbing and flowing like tides, do the re-agencies of the capital accumulated in London modify, without sound or echo, much commerce in all parts of the kingdom. Faithful to the monetary symptoms, and the fluctuations this way or that eternally perceptible in the condition of every trade, the great monied capitalist, standing at the centre of this enormous web, throws over his arch of capital or withdraws it, with the precision of a fireman directing columns of water from an engine upon the remotest quarter of a conflagration . . . the true operation goes on as silently as the growth of light . . . Not a man has been shifted from his station; possibly not a man has been intruded; yet power and virtue have been thrown into vast laboratories of trade, like shells into a city. But all has been accomplished in one night by the inaudible agency of the post-office, co-operating with the equally inaudible agencies of capital moving through banks and through national debts, funded or unfunded. Such is the perfection of our civilisation. By the simple pressure of a finger upon the centre of so vast an organisation, a breath of life is hurried along the tubes – a pulse is enlivened or depressed – a circulation is precipitated or checked . . . enormous changes may be effected, and continually *are* effected, without noise or tumult, through the exquisite resources of artificial action first made possible by the great social development of England. (*M* 9:272–74)

Ultimately, value is *no more* than conduction, as Ricardo the stockbroker "almost *professionally* explains to us" (*M* 9:273). The machinery of the stock market violates the law of conservation of matter: sheer "transition" alchemically produces "power and virtue," just as disturbances of electrical "equilibrium" give rise to weather and colored light. Money itself becomes a principle of artificial action, effecting perpetual change in the nature of things – each *clinamen* a new source of excess.

Revising his earlier figure of the "galvanic circle" of verbal refinements, De Quincey now assimilates money with discourse in a universe of resistances: London is both financial center and hub of "the vast systematic machinery by which any elaborate work could disperse itself . . . could put questions and get answers" (*C* 134). If his depiction of the stock market seems to eddy about language rather than stock prices, then, it may be understood as a figure for language *as capital.* There can be no point in seeking for referential clarification; where light denotes mystery, its augmentation may just deepen the enigma. The stock exchange is "like" electricity, "like" tides; like a spider's web, a firehose, a chemical reaction, cannon-fire; the shower of similes drowns the "true operation" in exuberant *différence.* Language accumulates by implicit analogy with the "re-agencies of the capital accumulated in London," loading every rift of the dismal science with ore. De Quincey denies "even of Political Economy" that "'*Ornari res ipsa negat, contenta doceri*': for all things have their peculiar beauty and sources of ornament – determined by their ultimate ends, and by the process of the mind in pursuing them" (*M* 9:43). Its double determination by "ends" (purpose) and "the process of the mind" (formal purposiveness) enriches De Quinceyan political economy, the site where cultural capital intersects with technical expertise. The *Logic*'s alchemy completes the transformation of a subject considered by "most people . . . a sufficient opiate" (*C* 66) into a stimulant – a charm that produces a surplus of consumerist converts to Ricardian "doctrine."

If the use value of theory seems to get lost in this equation, England's "vast laboratories of trade" undergo a comparable *subreptio.* The human agency that Marx calls "labor" is virtually irrelevant to the artificial action of capital. "It is not," De Quincey emphasizes, "by looking out for new men qualified to enter an aspiring trade, or by withdrawing some of the old men from a decaying trade, that the equilibrium is recovered" (*M* 9:273). Instead, monetary movement simulates a banished organic referent: "a breath of life is hurried along the tubes – a pulse is enlivened or depressed – a circulation is precipitated or checked." Frankenstein's experiment with galvanism is realized as a colossal personification of commercial society, consumption as *re*production. The dwarf *homo opiatus* metamorphoses into the giant *homo economicus.*

Thus, in De Quincey as in Ricardo, the stock market redeems the economy's ineradicable trace of aestheticism. The capitalist, Ricardo observes, is "engaged in no trade, but live[s] on the interest of [his] money." His apparent unproductiveness, however, belies his "floating" power to "equalise the rate of profits" "arising from the *caprice of taste.*"[46] A reader and diagnostician of "monetary symptoms," the investor treats surplus and scarcity as semiotic phenomena, capitalizing on the "endless fluctuations and arbitrary associations" (*PrW* 3:82) that, Wordsworth fears, disturb the linguistic exchange between poetic producers and their readers. It is a regrettable fact for Wordsworth that language too often appears "incommensurate with" (*PrW* 1:149) the values it is charged to convey. The finger that manipulates this volatile medium belongs neither to the Adamic "invisible hand" nor to the writing hand of the poet, here demoted from cause to epiphenomenon of value-production. Instead, transformed from consumer into investor, the hapless reader acquires the regulatory agency of a physician's digit on a fluttering pulse. Not a maker, the capitalist is no Wordsworthian consumer either, signally failing to exhibit signs of effort, exertion, or action. But capital confounds the poles of idleness and industry; "we must," notes Ricardo, "confess that the principle which apportions capital to each trade . . . is more active than is generally supposed."[47]

To the investor, it is not merely inevitable but desirable that affirmative and negative value should so rarely coincide, for both the undervaluation of *Paradise Lost* and the scarcity of the powerful drug may pose the opportunity of a high return. Speculation resembles aesthetic contemplation in its indifference to use value; the investor judges "futures" on the grounds of an industry's purposiveness, or *formal* appearance of necessity. The homology between financial speculation and aesthetic investment is suggested by De Quincey's decision in "1805 or 1806" to buy up "all the remaining copies" of *An Evening Walk* and *Descriptive Sketches,* then lying entirely ignored, "as presents, and as *future* curiosities in literature to literary friends, whose interest in Wordsworth might assure one of a due value being put upon" them once the "*prestige* of a name in the author" had "give[n] them a season's currency" (*R* 173). De Quincey's strategy, in turn, makes Wordsworth's attempt to prophesy "the destiny of a new work" by its exemption from the immediate "admiration of the multitude" (*PrW* 3:62, 83) seem less a critique of commodification than a speculative refinement.

As great monied capitalist, then, the consumer not only "produces" the maker whom Wordsworth imagined as cause; he also produces himself, continually fathering new incarnations of the same artificial action. The fireman of capital is Wordsworth's reader writ large, a frail ephebe grown to the proportions of the young scholar Gargantua, who, to "buy [his] welcome" in Paris, offered a "*solatium*" composed of "some wine" he had previously enjoyed:

Then, with a smile, he undid his magnificent codpiece and, bringing out his john-thomas, pissed on them so fiercely that he drowned two hundred and sixty thousand, four hundred and eighteen persons, not counting the women and small children.[48]

The substance that originated in reception returns as sheer excess: the fluid expelled from the circulatory system, or "animal economy." Waste is not waste; it is recirculation. Gargantua compensates his hosts with a medicine so potent that, like opium, prussic acid, or the capitalist wage, it kills its recipients. A grossly disproportionate return of the aesthete's repressed corporeality, Gargantua drowns natural value in a golden shower of liquidity – the hydraulic power that makes exchange as such intelligible.[49]

Bourdieu's cultural speculator experiences his distinction as pure affirmative (or ethical) value, something "which will never win him a sou, any more than his courtesy, his courage or his goodness."[50] If De Quincey's giant may be read as a prolepsis of aesthetic investment, he has not yet succeeded in being misrecognized; rather, he programmatically converts his cultural competence to exchangeable form. No less aestheticizing or literary than Wordsworth's narrative of redemption, De Quincey's transmission theory of value takes account, as the poet does not, of the institutions that mediate the exchange between producer and consumer. These institutions materialize as discourse, understood in its specific Foucaultian sense as the matrix of theory.[51] Since, however, discourse is not only the field of representations "by which an object is given to us," but also produces commodities like *The Logic of Political Economy*, De Quincey's enrichment of Ricardo further suggests how imponderables of "style" contribute to the authority of evaluative judgments.[52] Neither a fine art nor a functional object, just as it antecedes the professional division of literature into "creativity" and reflective "criticism," the *Logic* exemplifies use value *as* aesthetic value. Like that "ruby-coloured elixir" valued for an "increased power" of "mental vision" (M 5:210–11), or judgment, the *clinamen* of transmission shades the sameness of language into professional distinction.

INSTITUTIONAL ARCHITECTURE

The refinement of distinctions, be they merely "verbal" or "true and substantial," constitutes both the praxis and the theory of "professional" value production in the *Logic* (M 9:146–47). Theory and practice converge when the analysis of economic value yields a figure of textual value: unsuspected richness and complexity beneath a blankly continuous surface. "Given a total identity," De Quincey commands, "you are to create a difference." He who "'do[es] the trick'" and removes the "obstacle which (whether observed or not observed) has so long thwarted" the progress of political economy, surely deserves the credit of the reader's entire absorption thereafter.

These considerations are calculated to stagger us; and at this precise stage of the discussion I request the reader's most vigilant attention. We have all read of secret doors in great cities so exquisitely dissembled by art that in what seemed a barren surface of dead wall, where even the eye forewarned could trace no vestige of a separation or of a line, simply by a simultaneous pressure upon two remote points, suddenly and silently an opening was exposed which revealed a long perspective of retiring columns – architecture the most elaborate, where all had passed for one blank continuity of dead wall. Not less barren in promise, not less abrupt in its transition, this speculation at the very vestibule of political economy, at the point where most it had appeared to allow of no further advance or passage, suddenly opens and expands before an artifice of logic which almost impresses the feelings as a trick of legerdemain. (M 9:134–35)

De Quincey's analogy both echoes and glosses the famous description of Piranesi's *Carceri d'Invenzione* in the *Confessions*, that speculation at the very vestibule of his literary career.[53] The passage from the *Logic*, in which a sublime vista is made to arise from a factitious logical quandary, suggests that resistance may function as the pedagogue's ruse – the occasion for a magical resolution that does not so much "overcome" difficulty as displace it. De Quincey's obstacle, in other words, presents an unusually diagrammatic example of the sublime "blockage" that fulfills "the scholar's *wish*" by "consolidat[ing] a reassuringly operative notion of the self."[54] Architecture elaborates the infinity of the world within both the text and its exegete. In his vision of Piranesi's architecture, the Opium-Eater pictures as "resistance overcome" the textual wealth that underwrites his career. He consolidates his professional authority by making sameness do the office of *différance*, or by generating surplus value from the secret differences of a poet and his impresario. At the same time, he implicitly deconstructs the idea of intrinsic value on which literary canonicity is predicated.

The description of Piranesi's engravings illustrates a discursive account of the temporal and spatial distortions introduced into De Quincey's dreams by opium. The picture is borrowed, like the "Gothic cathedral" of theorized Imagination that interrupts the *Biographia*'s chapter thirteen, "from a friend" – no less a friend than Coleridge, whose "superb intellect" and prodigious opium-consumption De Quincey had saluted in his "Preliminary Confessions" (*BL* 1:300–01; *C* 2–5). The reappearance of Coleridge's architectural trope suggests both how alert and how inapposite is Crabb Robinson's account of the *Confessions* as "a fragment of autobiography in imitation of Coleridge's diseased egotism" (*HCR* 267). De Quincey's Prisons of the Imagination constitute rather than imitate their origin, through the "repetition" or "echo" that "dissolves, diffuses, dissipates, in order to recreate" (*BL* 1:304).[55] "Many years ago," the Opium-Eater recalls,

when I was looking over Piranesi's Antiquities of Rome, Mr Coleridge, who was standing by, described to me a set of plates by that artist, called his *Dreams*, and which record the scenery of his own visions during the delirium of a fever. Some of them (I describe only from memory of Mr Coleridge's account) represented vast Gothic halls: on the floor of which stood all sorts of engines and machinery, wheels, cables, pulleys, levers, catapults, &c. &c. expressive of enormous power put forth, and resistance overcome. (*C* 70)

Transmuted into "dreams," Piranesi's dungeon presents a version of the absolute sublime or "creative state of the eye" (*C* 67), recalling Kant's analogy for the transcendent as "an abyss in which [the imagination] fears to lose itself" (*K* 97). If the title suggests an allegory of aesthetic perception, however, this is countered by the allusion to "power put forth, and resistance overcome," a formula for the "resistance to the reproduction" of a commodity. Indeed, with the possible exception of catapults, the "machinery" housed in these halls suggests factory production more than engines of torture; like the *London Magazine* more generally, the dream *gothicizes* the scene of labor.

The sequel problematizes both the idealist and the economic interpretations.

Creeping along the sides of the walls, you perceived a staircase; and upon it, groping his way upwards, was Piranesi himself: follow the stairs a little further, and you perceive it come to a sudden abrupt termination, without any balustrade, and allowing no step onwards to him who had reached the extremity, except into the depths below. Whatever is to become of poor Piranesi, you suppose, at least, that his labours must in some way terminate here. But raise your eyes, and behold a second flight of stairs still higher: on which again Piranesi is perceived, but this time standing on the very brink of the abyss. Again elevate your eye, and a still more aerial flight of stairs is beheld: and again is poor Piranesi busy on his aspiring labours: and so on, until the unfinished stairs and Piranesi both are lost in the upper gloom of the hall. – With the same power of endless growth and self-reproduction did my architecture proceed in dreams. (*C* 70)

De Quincey's "memory of Mr Coleridge's account" conflates the "series" of sixteen plates into one, collapses "numerous figures" into the "same person," and identifies this "figure . . . as the engraver himself, making the story into a parable of the artist."[56] If so, this artist has notably failed to achieve his Kantian "freedom"; "poor Piranesi" certainly seems to find his "occupation . . . unpleasant (a trouble) in itself" (*K* 146). It is significant to recall that gravure is a labor-intensive craft, used mainly for copying paintings and illustrating books, and so allied as well with the technology of print; as such it peremptorily demands "something compulsory or, as it is called, mechanism" (*K* 147).[57] Here, the machinery goes untended while the "labour[er]," Piranesi, toils continuously to make nothing at all. Rather than produce, he is himself reproduced: his appearance three times "and so on" betokens sheer iterability. The dream-workshop manufactures Piranesis, stamping out miniatures with all the implacability of the dark pedantic mills whose "mighty workmen of our later age/ . . . with a broad highway have overbridged/ The froward chaos of futurity" (*Prelude* 5:370–72, 382–83). Piranesi's labor, then, magically converts into self-fashioning, as the multiplied figure instantiates, for his recounter, the "hermeneutic or 'reader's' sublime."[58] "Self-reproduction" refers at once to the pains of the empirical laborer, to his transcendence by "resistance of a quite different kind" (*K* 100–01), and to the reproduction of both (contradictory) experiences in De Quincey's reader. Condensing the hermeneutic strategy of the *London*, the imaginary prison is an "*officina gentium*" (*C* 73), a factory where subjects are made.[59]

Serial reproduction – *by* "engines and machinery," *of* prints and their consumers – is thereby displaced into the psychological register of the compulsion to repeat. Piranesi's aspiring labours also redouble, at the level of visual motif, the echoic or transmitted quality of the anecdote. Repeated from Coleridge, it is imparted to the reader through increasingly pointed manipulations of person and tense: "you perceived," then "you perceive," then "you suppose." Beginning in the posture of Coleridge's student, De Quincey aligns himself with an imaginary viewer whose perspective is gradually maneuvered into the labyrinth ("raise your eyes"), while the tone shifts from disinterested contemplation to sympathetic concern – "whatever is to become of poor Piranesi"? "You" are now operating in Piranesian time, the readerly present tense of textual description. By the end of the passage, the reader has been absorbed into anxious pursuit of a retreating figure, while the narrator has evanesced into the "upper gloom of the hall."

The duplication of Piranesis corresponds to reiterated transmissions, from Coleridge to De Quincey, from De Quincey to his readers, and so on. Picturing a reading of Coleridge, foregrounding the process of interpretation (what the engravings "express"), and allegorizing transmission in the wheels and levers of infernal manufacture, the recursions of Piranesi's ascent both figure and enact a tortuous scene of instruction, with each repetition posited as a theoretical advance upon the last.[60] In this sense, De Quincey's narration exemplifies the reproductive or mimetic logic of writing *about* the sublime. If, meanwhile, the Opium-Eater's account of his "incapacity and feebleness" (*C* 66) suggests an identification with Piranesi, the narrative associates him instead with the interminably expanding structure. His self-reproducing architecture replaces the fragmentary work, *De emendatione humani intellectûs*, that, "like any Spanish bridge or aqueduct, begun upon too great a scale for the resources of the architect," was "never to support a superstructure" (*C* 64). In dreams, the "slow and elaborate toil" of writing detaches itself from voluntary exertion, so that "whatsoever things capable of being visually represented I did but think of in the darkness," were "like writings in sympathetic ink . . . drawn out . . . into insufferable splendour" (*C* 64–68). If writing were dreaming, the Opium-Eater could multiply his vaporous splendors without effort, uplifting more stately mansions from the depths of his literary mind. Opium supplies both materials and labor. As Coleridge wrote of a similar "psychological curiosity," "an anodyne had been prescribed, from the effects of which he fell asleep":

The Author continued for about three hours in a profound sleep, at least of the external senses, during which time he has the most vivid confidence, that he could not have composed less than from two to three hundred lines; if that indeed can be called composition in which all the images rose up before him as *things*, with a parallel production of the correspondent expressions, without any sensation or consciousness of effort. (*CPW* 295–96)

De Quincey's images further attenuate this consciousness of labor, for the pleasure-domes he sees were built by another. "In the early stages of my malady," he continues,

the splendours of my dreams were indeed chiefly architectural: and I beheld such pomp of cities and palaces as was never yet beheld by the waking eye, unless in the clouds. From a great modern poet I cite part of a passage which describes, as an appearance actually beheld in the clouds, what in many of its circumstances I saw frequently in sleep:

> The appearance, instantaneously disclosed,
> Was of a mighty city – boldly say
> A wilderness of building, sinking far
> And self-withdrawn into a wondrous depth,
> Far sinking into splendour – without end!
> Fabric it seemed of diamond, and of gold,
> With alabaster domes, and silver spires,
> And blazing terrace upon terrace, high
> Uplifted; here, serene pavilions bright
> In avenues disposed; there towers begirt
> With battlements that on their restless fronts
> Bore stars – illumination of all gems!
> By earthly nature had the effect been wrought
> Upon the dark materials of the storm
> Now pacified; on them, and on the coves,
> And mountain-steeps and summits, whereunto
> The vapours had receded, – taking there
> Their station under a cerulean sky. &c. &c.

The sublime circumstance – "battlements that on their *restless* fronts bore stars," – might have been copied from my architectural dreams, for it often occurred. – We hear it reported of Dryden, and of Fuseli in modern times, that they thought proper to eat raw meat for the sake of obtaining splendid dreams: how much better for such a purpose to have eaten opium. (*C* 71)

The dreamer's vision "rises up," repeating Coleridge's figure, from the abyss of objectified labor, "like water in a pump when released from the pressure of air" (*M* 9:139). "One gravity rises through another gravity," as De Quincey comments in his analysis of exchange value; "thus we find as the result, with the usual astonishing simplicity of nature, that the same machinery serves for sinking objects and for raising them" (*M* 9:136). The production of new images reduces to the juxtaposition of two "gravities," or the negative and positive sublime.

The reaction of a descent into the underworld, the celestial city bears few traces of "Piranesi's" "baffled efforts" (*C* 64); this version of sublimity dazzles rather than awes. Water condensed into gems – "alabaster domes" and "silver spires" tricked out in "fabric . . . of diamond, and of gold" – the apparition in the clouds may be said to embody the *idea* of affirmative value "in itself." The poem could almost have been written to illustrate De Quincey's contention that "water has the exchange value of diamonds, diamonds have the use value of water" (*M* 9:189). The bejeweled hallucination, a vision of grandeur tinged with vulgarity, exemplifies luxury taste or commodity fetishism while at the same time suggesting their very opposite: it is not, of course, materially transferable nor available to be bought at any price. Literally "irrepresentable by money," this private revelation is, like the "great Italian masterpieces of painting," a "jewel" "absolutely unique" and "secure from repetition" (*M* 9:168).[61] The aesthete's incommunicable pleasure posited as a delusion of inexhaustible wealth, the self-withdrawn city instances the reflexive teleology of the drug: its "*purpose*" of enhancing contemplation.

To recapitulate, then, while "Piranesi" projects the pole of resistance onto his consumer, "the great modern poet" offers a glimpse of the affirmative value for which the reader labors: that is, the "inspiriting satisfaction" of the mind in discovering "the proper sublimity of its destination" (*K* 101). This reward is emphasized by a kind of reverse *subreptio*, in which the quoted lines, the product of artistic intentionality, are imagined as copies "from [De Quincey's] architectural dreams." The production of commodified artifacts – a series of engraved plates, or of printed texts – is transformed by the reader's investment into aesthetic value-by-association. Not simply sublime set-pieces, the Opium-Eater's dreams offer exercises or lessons in the sublime; in other words, he converts the experience into an alienable property. The replicant Piranesis, then, personify the mass-produced taste by which the Opium-Eater is to be enjoyed. But if Kant finds in sublimity the expression of the mind's freedom, De Quincey's simulation coerces its results by obscuring its asymmetry: "by a certain subreption," we recall, the reader's experience of pain induces an exaggerated respect for the author, reproducing *half* of De Quincey's experience in reading *Paradise Lost*. De Quincey's aggrandizement, the commodified sublime, marks the birth of a disoriented, periodic, *poststructuralist* subjectivity.[62]

The chain of diminishing authenticity that descends from Piranesi down to the reader might seem to be restored by the immanence of nature in the clouds. For Kant, "nature . . . suppl[ies] constant food for taste" when even the most skillful artifice galls (*K* 80). For De Quincey, however, "the sublime circumstance" merely borrows legitimacy from a peculiarity of nature; "the appearance actually beheld in the clouds" – already a mediated image rather than a meteorological phenomenon – originated in the "theatre" that "opened . . . up within [his] brain" (*C* 67). Thus he apparently credits his self-culture for the purposiveness of the poetry, a gesture made possible by demoting the poetic fragment to the status of found object. Its anonymity gives it the luster of a precious secret. This pointed allusion to a great modern poet whom he refuses to name recalls Abraham and Torok's account of the melancholic "crypt" in which "reposes – alive, reconstituted from the memories of words, images, and feelings . . . a separate and secret life." The nature of this secret is dramatized by the melancholic through the "incorporation" of "a thing or an object," such as opium, "into the body."[63] The incorporated substance acts as the material trope of a "magic word" that may, in this case, be decoded precisely as "Words-*worth*." There remains, nonetheless, a mystery about how these particular words, quoted from Wordsworth's 1814 poem *The Excursion*, acquire their spatial quality as the cryptic locus of "separate" or specialized meaning.

The scene of Piranesi's travails situates this problem in the history of literary transmission, or, more specifically, in the relation of literature to criticism. Coleridge's "sudden abrupt termination" of his chapter on the Imagination is supplemented by a letter from an imaginary friend who, in turn, obligingly appeals to "a MS. poem of [Coleridge's] own in The FRIEND." This poem, earlier "applied to a work of Mr. Wordsworth's," is now applied to "the effect on [his] *feelings*" of Coleridge's "long treatise on ideal Realism" (*BL* 1:301–03). The (missing) exegesis of Imagination acquires the mystique of fiction, while its pretext, the original poem Coleridge had publicly admired, recedes further into the depths. This work, the *Prelude*, takes the position of an inaccessible first cause, known only by its "echo" in the Coleridgean representation. Coleridge further reminds his reader that, in *The Friend* – a text so obscure "that it had been well for the unfortunate author, if it had remained in manuscript" (*BL* 1:175) – he had excerpted a fragment he titled "Growth of Genius from the Influences of Natural Objects, on the Imagination in Boyhood, and Early Youth," part of "an unpublished Poem on the Growth and Revolutions of an Individual Mind, by WORDSWORTH" (*CW*4[1]:368). Coleridge's theoretical speculations are grounded upon, or underwritten by, this first extract of Wordsworth's poem, a token of treasure withheld. Quoted "with the author's permission" (*CW*4[1]:368), the avatar of the hidden *Prelude* was to be understood as an authorized preview, or a gift from the friend of *The Friend.*[64]

The critic mystifies his relation to the literary work as a symbolic exchange, reciprocated when Wordsworth, elaborating the architectural simile for *The Excursion*, mentions that the "ante-chapel" to the "gothic church" under construction is "addressed to a dear Friend . . . to whom the Author's Intellect is deeply indebted" (*PW* 589). Wordsworth writes the *Prelude* "to Coleridge," who uses this capital to establish himself in the business of reading Wordsworth. When the Opium-Eater re-echoes Coleridge by "repeat[ing] the lines" spoken by the Solitary in *The Excursion* (2:834–51), he *simulates* such an investment, picturing his own cultural capital in a passage that tropes the architectonics of creative and critical symbiosis. His incorporation of Wordsworth's vision – *as though* there were some secret about it, *as though* these lines were not available to anyone – serves as collateral on the Piranesian allegory of transmission.

Wordsworth is self-withdrawn from this picture, but a trace of agency remains in the "sublime circumstance" of its "*restless*" battle-

ments, as though, once again, the magic word had truly been
buried alive. The celestial city, that is, personifies "Wordsworth" as
given by "Coleridge" and regurgitated by "the Opium-Eater."
Beyond intimating De Quincey's acquaintance with the poet, the
excerpt from *The Excursion* depicts the living history, or institution,
of the canonical author. Indeed, Coleridge's thesis on the
Imagination (or Wordsworth) abstracts the original composition
into a complex synthesis of "philosophic" and "poetic" genius:

Grant me a nature having two contrary forces, the one of which tends to
expand infinitely, while the other strives to apprehend or *find* itself in this
infinity, and I will cause the world of intelligences with the whole system
of their representations to rise up before you . . . The counteraction then
of the two assumed forces . . . must be a tertium aliquid, or finite generation . . . Now this tertium aliquid can be no other than an inter-penetra-
tion of the counteracting forces, partaking of both. (*BL* 1:297–300)

The precursor to De Quincey's account of value, Coleridge's argument on the counteraction of opposites diagrams the relation
between the mighty city and Piranesi: the one tending "to expand
infinitely," the other striving "to apprehend or *find* itself in this
infinity." The interpenetration of these two elements – call them
"Wordsworth" and "Coleridge" – produces the "tertium aliquid,"
or third person, that might indifferently be named "De Quincey"
or "the crypt" or, as I have been suggesting, the institution of transmission. What Coleridge calls the "birth" of intelligence in dialectical synthesis coincides with the Opium-Eater's *incorporation* of
that exchange.

With the appearance of a third person, the calculus of dialectics
begins to resemble the calculus of the *universitate* or *corpora corpo-
rata*. "*Tres faciunt collegium*," writes Blackstone, was the principle of
Roman law: three make a "university," or corporation. The association of three empirical individuals in "an *artificial form*" and "under
a *special denomination*" is sufficient, in other words, to constitute "a
kind of legal immortality."[65] Such an artificial form, or institution,
may be glimpsed in the edifices that shape the literary prehistory
of Wordsworth and Coleridge, and that decree their own reproduction in the Opium-Eater's dreams. Legal immortality is exemplified for both Blackstone and De Quincey by "the general
corporate bodies of Oxford and Cambridge,"[66] dedicated to insur-
ing that the "unfailing fountain" of knowledge "shall be continually applied to the production and to the *tasting* of fresh labours in

endless succession" (*M* 2:18; original emphasis). A "collegiate incorporation," then, exists for the permanent preservation and dissemination of cultural capital, defined as the cultivation of taste. As such, it presumes no

> edifices of stone and marble; neither one nor the other presupposes any edifice at all built with human hands. A collegiate incorporation, the church militant of knowledge . . . is, in this respect, like the Church of Christ – that is, it is always and essentially invisible to the fleshly eye. The pillars of this church are human champions. (*M* 2:18)

Essentially incorporeal, the church of knowledge is of course dedicated to the refinement of mental sight, like the cultivated nature of the appearance beheld by Wordsworth's Solitary. Those restless battlements, anticipating the mirage of Jude Fawley's Christminster, limn the ideal outwardly manifested in the "vast systems of building, the palaces and towers" that compose the "pompous architectural monuments" of Oxford (*M* 2:17–20).

Hieroglyphs of the two poets "incorporated . . . under the name of the *Lake School*" (*R* 65), the Opium-Eater's monuments canonize poetry as a mode of sensuous perception, whereby the "matchless spectacle" of "an elaborate and pompous sunset," "originally mimicked by the poet from the sky, is here re-mimicked and rehearsed to the life" (*M* 3:301–02) by nature in the eyes of its exegete. Conceived as institution, taste acquires not only an imaginary presence in the world, but a power of self-reproduction.[67] Guillory argues of the "school," an apparatus for regulating "access to th[e] inheritable treasure" of literary tradition, that "institutions of reproduction succeed by taking as their first object . . . the reproduction of the institution itself." Or, as De Quincey less self-consciously remarks, the collegiate incorporation protects "rights of heirship" to accumulated knowledge by "converting a mere casual life-annuity into an estate of inheritance" (*M* 2:18). In this monumentalized form, the "textual tradition" seems "inexhaustible because it appears to reproduce itself – it is wealth never consumed by consumption."[68] Literature comes to resemble natural resources by being absorbed into the institution as its canon, an ideological task that is effectively complete when signature tropes can be envisioned as personal culture.

Like Derrida's "société à responsabilité limitée," an "anonymous company or corporation" of "self-made, auto-authorized heirs," the institution of the *Confessions* comprises "three + n authors,"[69] the formula of immortality. De Quincey affirmed the society's "dimension of *length*" (*M* 2:18) when, after Wordsworth's death, he reissued his *Confessions* under his own name and with the addition of an explanatory footnote on the *Excursion* passage.

What poet? It was Wordsworth; and why did I not formally name him? This throws a light backwards upon the strange history of Wordsworth's reputation. The year in which I wrote and published these Confessions was 1821; and at that time the name of Wordsworth, though beginning to emerge from the dark cloud of scorn and contumely which had hitherto overshadowed it, was yet most imperfectly established . . . I, therefore, as the very earliest (without one exception) of all who came forward, in the beginning of his career, to honour and welcome him, shrank with disgust from making any sentence of mine the occasion for an explosion of vulgar malice against him. But the grandeur of the passage here cited inevitably spoke for itself; and he that would have been most scornful on hearing the name of the poet coupled with this epithet of "great" could not but find his malice intercepted, and himself cheated into cordial admiration, by the splendour of the verses. (*M* 3:439)

This hazy picture notably distorts Wordsworth's critical reception, which by 1821 included the *Biographia,* John Wilson's eulogistic *Blackwood's* reviews, and the unstinting praise of the *London Magazine,* which maintained the editorial position "that no poetical power, equal to his, exists in the present day" (*LM* 1:284). No pretense of secrecy on De Quincey's part was likely to mislead a regular reader of the *London.* Rather, it upheld the poem's resistance value, simulating the imaginative *subreptio* that assigns grandeur to natural objects. In retrospect, however, the splendor that readers admired spoke not only "for itself," but for a career that outlived the juridical person. "The name of Wordsworth," a celestial body like the sun or moon, was rising in 1821, but had not yet emerged from its obscuring mist. With Wordsworth's greatness now "cheerfully and generally acknowledged," De Quincey can rewrite the "emblem of . . . the author's genius" Coleridge found in the "one dilated sun" that shone on the poet's dawning career (*BL* 1:77–78). "[The] original poetic genius" that appeared "above the literary horizon" ascends, in *The Excursion,* to the fully accomplished "gift of spreading the tone, the *atmosphere,* and with it the depth and height of the ideal world" over quotidian phenomena (*BL* 1:77, 80). And finally, having reached its meridian, the name emerges from its gothic self-withdrawal, emblazoning the *Confessions* with its reflected glory.

De Quincey's false teleology of reputation matches the self-aggrandizement of his claim to have been "the very earliest" to "welcome" a poet fifteen years his elder. The title of exclusive representation veils a shrewd investment, which has allowed him to participate in "that reversionary influence which awaits Wordsworth with posterity" (*M* 11:314). The speculator's capital reaps surplus value from readers "cheated" into admiration of the splendid verses to which he claims proximate title. This "cheat" refers, of course, to the sublime "trick" whereby the reader's "respect for the idea of humanity" is redirected into "respect for [De Quincey's] destination" (*K* 96). Perhaps, though, De Quincey also cheats by envisioning the "dark cloud" that obscured Wordsworth's fame as the "unfathered vapour" of Imagination in which the poet recognized his glory (*Prelude* 6:525–48). The *Excursion* passage and its echo in De Quincey also recall the "headlands, tongues, and promontory shapes" in the "silent sea of hoary mist" which Wordsworth denominates "the emblem of a mind/ That feeds upon infinity" (*Prelude* [1850] 14:42–71). By 1856, these echoes would reverberate for all readers of Wordsworth, though in 1821 they were presumably audible only to De Quincey and Coleridge.[70]

De Quincey's citation is thus belatedly enriched by its covert association with "something evermore about to be" (*Prelude* [1850] 6:608), a recognizably Wordsworthian telos for which *The Excursion* serves as synecdoche or signature-piece. Considered as a flash of the invisible *Prelude*, moreover, the passage has "a monopoly value" like the single unpublished work of Aristotle whose auction price of "a landed estate" illustrates the idea that a book might command its money's-weight of esteem (*M* 9:166). For Wordsworth, the value of poetry was guaranteed by a life-long habit of hoarding: always reluctant to exchange the gold of manuscript for the dross of printed paper, he withheld the meaning of his life as collateral on his poetic career. Like the owner of the manuscript Aristotle, "he would not suffer it to be copied. He knew the worth of the prize" (*M* 9:166).[71] The fantasy of glimpsing an infinitely precious manuscript – a jewel as yet uncheapened by reproduction – literalizes the mystique of privileged access, originary charter, monopoly patent, and institutional seal that underwrites both literary allusion and scholarly exegesis. But, Ricardo observes, "there can be no greater error than in supposing that capital is increased by non-consumption."[72] Or as De Quincey might put it, if security from repetition elicits the affirmative value of the commodity, the violation of the secret is the precondition of its acquiring any value at all.

The *Prelude*, literary paradigm of deferred action, *is* Wordsworth's fame, just as, in 1821, it was his unmined potential. There is no need to imagine, however, that De Quincey expected his first readers to recognize an occulted allusion to that poem, or even that such an allusion was "intended." Rather, it may be understood as a figure for speculative strategy. The sublime circumstance of the *Confessions* unfolds, at the end of the Opium-Eater's career, into deferred citationality, *the only kind there is*: "De Quincey" poses as "the Opium-Eater"'s ideal reader, imputing depths to a textual surface that establish its value within a system of notation and allusion. If the Opium-Eater, a *literary* birth, marks Wordsworth's canonization, De Quincey is the scholar of their mutual "debts." The speculation that pays off translates, *mutatis mutandis*, into the meaning latent from the beginning. Contrary to Benjamin's belief that "the aura of the work of art" "withers in the age of mechanical reproduction," authenticity is manufactured in a hall of literary mirrors; it is the ghost that animates the institutional machine.[73] Just as he could claim, in 1856, that he had "always fixed [his] eyes and . . . expectations upon a revolution in the social history of opium" (*M* 3:426), the disciple of the Lake School belatedly witnesses the conversion of his taste into a founding membership.

A final notice will return this strategy to the market in which the speculation was launched. In 1823 the *Monthly Review*, likening the Opium-Eater's "boldness" and "exactness of pencil" to "one or two prominent geniuses of our day," affiliated the unnamed writer with one of those geniuses, "the author of 'Christabel'" (a name to dream of, not to tell):

for that neither that gentleman nor Mr. C. Lambe [*sic*] is the real author of the present work, we have the best reasons for believing. Yet we are quite as well assured that the English Opium-Eater is partly identified, in genius and social habits, with those whom Lord Byron rather uncourteously calls the *Naturals*, we mean *the Lake-school*. That he chiefly resides among the hills, and is a favorite in many literary and private circles . . . we may state without unduly trespassing on the *incognito* character, or divulging the name of the author.

Neither Coleridge nor Lamb is the Opium-Eater's real incarnation; but the writer's partial identity with them both preserves him from acknowledging himself as his own author.[74] Authored by affiliation, the Opium-Eater is the "Natural" as cultural, his anonymity merely extending the field of reference that gives his habits their meaning. Poe reports, notwithstanding the *Monthly*'s disclaimer, that in America the *Confessions* were "universally attributed to Coleridge – though unjustly."[75] The Opium-Eater's visions of genius as "psychological curiosity" strip authorship of its ontological grounding, an uncannily reversible effect: the *Excursion* passage, never more than a hallucination of "value," may even have been plagiarized from his dreams. A prefigural allegory of criticism, the Piranesi effect marks De Quincey's incorporation into the Lake School, henceforth indelibly colored by this perverse vision of its future: "to my architecture succeeded dreams of lakes" (*C* 71).

Only in the guise of Wordsworth's "posterity" can De Quincey realize these dreams, collecting the full quotient of his reversion. Yet the poet's demise, inevitable as event, seems as well to fulfill the prognostications of De Quincey's *Logic*. "The birth of the reader," Barthes writes with militant optimism, "must be at the cost of the death of the Author."[76] This is not to suggest that the *Confessions* have overtaken or will supplant the *Prelude* in critical opinion, any more than De Quincey's materialist aesthetic demotes Wordsworthian ethics to sheer self-deception. On the contrary, the hollowness of De Quincey's position – loosely speaking, its *minority* – continues to offend even critics of avowedly postmodern sympathies.[77] This chapter has, however, attempted to theorize the mutual imbrication of authorial richness and scriptorial emptiness, and, more significantly, to suggest how the *critical* ideology of authenticity originates in a displacement and denial of the marketplace. The following chapter will discuss how De Quincey's *Lake Reminiscences* naturalize the contingency of his consumerist persona in terms of a generic mutation troped as family romance. Instituting the canonical antagonism of poet and scholar, the *Lake Reminiscences* erect the story of De Quincey's life upon the grave of the author whose death his *Confessions* had foretold.

CHAPTER 5

Appropriations: the counter-lives of the poet

HIS GHASTLY FACE

De Quincey's first sight of Wordsworth is the premature culmination of his *Lake Reminiscences,* a series of essays spun out from the early days and weeks of a years-long acquaintance. The episode is framed by a meditation on the double significance of his audacious attempt to "form personal ties which would forever connect" him to the poet. For years he had looked forward to this climactic day, picturing himself "as a phantom-self – a second identity projected from my own consciousness, and already living amongst" the Wordsworths (*R* 120). Before even meeting his idol, De Quincey predicated the doublets of autobiography upon physical proximity to the poet's body.[1] Yet the imagined "connexion" does not disguise an equally powerful contradiction, implied by De Quincey's long delay of the encounter. The conversion narrative that follows may be understood as an attempt to figure and refigure two mutually cancelling versions of this scenario: the biographical subject with his recording shadow, and the specular alignment of "face to face" (*R* 127) that consummates first-person narration. De Quincey's first sight of Wordsworth is staged as a confrontation between the demands of biographical recognition and the structure of the autobiographical "sketches" in which the encounter is embedded.[2] Just as the apparition of phantom-selfhood tropes autobiographical reflection, De Quincey's attempt to see the face of Wordsworth prefigures the necessity and the impossibility of biography, conceived as the portrait of a living author. Biography, that traditionally respectful and literarily unambitious corollary to the author's "canonization" – the transmigration of his spirit into the company of immortals – collides with the narrative demands of self-consciousness, teaching the unwelcome lesson that there can be neither spirit nor body enough to go around.

On his pilgrimage to Grasmere, while he "rehearsed and lived over, as it were in vision," the "chapters" of his own future life, De Quincey could only portray "the very image of Wordsworth" as the blinding gleam of divine immediacy (*R* 120–22). The quest after this unrepresentable countenance, with the concomitant crushing of his expectations, will eventually liberate De Quincey from the pictorial or iconographic tradition of biography. The trope of the trope's inadequacy justifies his oblique treatment of his subject, both more intense and less reverential than a Boswellian "filial devotion" (*R* 145).[3] In the Lake series, Wordsworth's face comes to be associated with the model of biography De Quincey forgoes, and with a conception of literary property which it is the project of the *Reminiscences* to subvert. These recollections of Wordsworth aim to substitute a dead body for a living face: De Quincey comes to bury Wordsworth, not to praise him.

He begins, though, as a diffident disciple and would-be foster child. De Quincey twice travelled to the neighborhood of Grasmere, once even coming within sight of Town End, without bringing himself actually to call on Wordsworth. When he finally accomplished his mission, it was under cover of escorting Mrs. Coleridge and her children to Keswick. Initially a surrogate for S. T. C., De Quincey quickly demoted himself from the head to the foot of a party that included Coleridge's "two surviving sons – Hartley, aged nine, the oldest; Derwent, about seven – her beautiful little daughter, about five; and, finally, myself" (*R* 125). Following Hartley through the gate of Dove Cottage, and so positioned as a miniature Coleridge, De Quincey awaited recognition as Wordsworth's prodigal son.

No sooner is this filial relation hazarded in the *Reminiscences* than De Quincey complicates it with an elaborate simile that reinvokes the gothicism of phantom-self autobiography. To bring home the magnitude of this meeting – he is, after all, about to see *in the flesh* the man whose poetry has so long dwelt in his thoughts – he imagines the supernatural inversion of such an encounter: seeing a ghost. Coleridge, De Quincey's model,

was of opinion that, if a man were really and *consciously* to see an apparition ... in such circumstances death would be the inevitable result; and, if so, the wish which we hear so commonly expressed for such experience is as thoughtless as that of Semele in the Grecian Mythology, so natural in a female, that her lover should visit her *en grande costume*, and "with his tail on" – presumptuous ambition, that unexpectedly wrought its own ruinous chastisement! Judged by Coleridge's test, my situation could not have been so terrific as *his* who anticipates a ghost – for, certainly, I survived this meeting. (*R* 127–28)

In the sickness of his impatience to see face to face, De Quincey has contracted "nympholepsy," the "delirious *possession*" of mortals who love "the beings whom it is not lawful to see and live" (*R* 119; *M* 7:219, 8:442). His desire for immediacy expresses itself as metonymic displacement; Wordsworth, of course, is neither apparition nor nymph. Coleridge's haunting speculation turns on a transfer of properties between the spirit and the living person, echoing the symmetry of Milton's sonnet on Shakespeare: "thou our fancy of itself bereaving/ Dost make us marble with too much conceiving."[4] Or, as De Quincey relates of a more commonplace superstition, to see your double means imminent death (*M* 8:440).

De Quincey's gloss on Coleridge rewrites the broken taboo in terms of pornography: the sin of blasphemy shades into the crime of solicitation. Semele presumptuously asked not only to *be* possessed, but to possess something, some secret knowledge, in return. For De Quincey, her wish to see the god incarnate amounts to courting rape; her death punishes, but also vindicates, her confusion of the penis and the phallus. In the overdetermined possibility of "sudden death," that "consummation of an earthly career most fervently to be desired" (*C* 209), lies the attraction of the fantasy. The violence of De Quincey's rebuke only underscores the parallel between Semele's crime and his own desire. Her "ruinous chastisement" shares the ambiguous syntax of "a child is being beaten," superimposing a masochistic identification with the woman "*whom I hate*" upon a sadistic pleasure in imagining that "*my father is beating*" her (*SE* 17:185; Freud's emphasis). The destruction of Semele (both nymph and nympholept) thus represents the "substitution of passivity for activity" that would allow De Quincey to be "*loved by* [*his*] *father*" "with his tail on" (*SE* 17:190, 198). Dismissing Coleridge's test, he distances his experience from "*his* who anticipates a ghost," aligning himself instead with *she* who solicits an omnipotent lover. Semele will suffer for his sins.[5]

The sequel confirms the sexual charge of De Quincey's fantasy, and, by defeating its aim, suggests the role it plays in the emergence of autobiography from the ashes of biographical representation.

> Never before or since can I reproach myself with having trembled at the approaching presence of any creature that is born of woman, excepting only, for once or twice in my life, woman herself; now, however, I *did* tremble; and I forgot, what in no other circumstances I could have forgotten, to stop for the coming up of the chaise, that I might be ready to hand Mrs Coleridge out. Had Charlemagne and all his Peerage been behind me, or Caesar and his equipage, or Death on his pale horse, I should have forgotten them at that moment of intense expectation, and of eyes fascinated to what lay before me, or what might in a moment appear. Through the little gate I pressed forward; ten steps beyond it lay the principal door of the house. To this, no longer clearly conscious of my own feelings, I passed on rapidly; I heard a step, a voice, and, like a flash of lightning, I saw the figure emerge of a tallish man, who held out his hand, and saluted me with the most cordial manner, and the warmest expression of friendly welcome that it is possible to imagine. (*R* 128)

De Quincey survives, as Coleridge might explain, because he cannot *consciously* see an apparition; or, to adapt the Pauline tropology of vision, what he finally sees is not a face, but a "flash," a "figure," and an "expression." When the moment comes for seeing face to face, he still labors for figures, his scriptural vocabulary yielding suddenly to the commonplaces of domestic fiction. The "catastrophe so long anticipated and so long postponed" seems to be over before it really happens, leaving De Quincey "stunned almost with [its] actual accomplishment" (*R* 128). The "actual" character of the event, the degree to which it registers cognitively, remains uncertain; is De Quincey "almost stunned" by his experience or stunned by its "almost accomplishment"? The narrative strains to accommodate a catastrophe so dubiously catastrophic.

The conceit on seeing ghosts turns out to be a reversed and inflated analogy for a more puzzling, elusive form of blindness. If De Quincey is unable to look Wordsworth in the face, that is not because Wordsworth is an apparition, but because he is real and alive. The face of imagination and the face of the living man cannot coexist in the same ontological space; it would be like seeing doubles. Or, shifting registers, Wordsworth's face is his own possession. "There needed no Roman nomenclator," De Quincey remarks, "to tell me that this *he*, the owner of this noble countenance, was Wordsworth" (*R* 128). An orthodox Lockean in such matters, Wordsworth blazons his assumption that "every man has a property in his own person; this nobody has any right to but himself."[6] The poet's remarkable control over his *corpus* begins with this exclusive right in his own embodiment.

De Quincey's fantasy of himself as Semele to Wordsworth's Zeus displaces these questions of perception, representation, and property into the intersubjective domain of sexual difference and conquest. He wanted not only to *see* Wordsworth but to be *possessed* by him, since passionate absorption implies some return from the beloved: as "the love-object of his *father*" (*SE* 19:250), De Quincey could bear the poet's second self. His knowledge of Wordsworth was to be a generative castration, reenacting the "feminine" Oedipal phase of the young Hume, "smit with" the "beautiful Representations" of ancient philosophy.[7] The family-romance of filiation sacrifices agency to the production of ravishing images patterned on De Quincey's touchstone of literary portraiture, the engraving of Milton that adorns Richardson's volume of notes on *Paradise Lost.*

This portrait, of all that was shewn to her, was the only one acknowledged, by Milton's last surviving daughter, to be a strong likeness of her father. And her involuntary gestures concurred with her deliberate words: – for, on seeing all the rest, she was silent and inanimate; but the very instant she beheld this . . . she burst out into a rapture of passionate recognition; exclaiming – "This is my father! this is my dear father!" (*R* 140)[8]

The daughter's rapture authenticates *strong* representation as not only the double, but the replacement, of its subject. In this way the biographer fulfills the wish to "nam[e] something first."[9] "Passionate recognition" domesticates a subtle shift from identity into ownership – the man becomes *my* father, the Milton I knew – by diverting authority from the subject of biography to his filial representative.

Yet for De Quincey it never quite comes to this. Wordsworth's figure dawns upon him "like a flash of lightning"; but just as he is ready to cry, "this is my Wordsworth!" the union devolves into mere conviviality. Wordsworth, as it appears, had emerged from the cottage not to embrace his disciple but to "receive Mrs Coleridge" (*R* 128), De Quincey's rival for the poet's affections. Even at his most cordial, the real Wordsworth is his own person, slightly beyond the reach of De Quincey's projections. What might be taken for mercy – choosing not to blast his young visitor –

conveys to De Quincey both personal frustration and the limits of his generic model. Though severe in his masculinity, Wordsworth, unlike the titans, does not smite. The fantasied castration fails reality on two counts: it mystifies Wordsworth's power as force, and it misrepresents communication with a contemporary as a solitary reading of the ancients. The Wordsworth thus negatively defined does not cause disease,[10] he cures "nervous complaints" (*R* 207); he represents the future, not the past; unlike the noble dead, he resists assimilation to the symbolic order of culture. De Quincey's bolt of phallic lightning reveals itself in retrospect as an attempt to resolve competing epistemological and rhetorical imperatives with an enlightenment figure for the giants of Greece and Rome.

Thwarted in his willing self-sacrifice to the godly poet, De Quincey discovers that his "more than filial devotion" elicits no corresponding ardor; Wordsworth never made "those returns of friendship and kindness" which De Quincey was "entitled to have challenged" (*R* 145). Incapable of "submitting his faculties to the humilities and devotion of courtship," neither indulging De Quincey's worship nor mirroring it, Wordsworth could not be "a lover . . . in any passionate sense of the word" (*R* 185). "Error, more or less . . . either on Wordsworth's in doing too little, or on mine in expecting too much," has carried De Quincey "far away from [his] early position"; his "fountain of love" has dried up (*R* 146). Having first adopted what Freud calls a "feminine attitude," he emerges with a stabilized gender and an ethos that absorbs Wordsworth's "separate narrative" into "connexion with [his] own life" (*R* 206). De Quincey's subjectivity originates in a mystified failure, the transcendental sign of Wordsworth's resistance to representation.

The collapse of the correspondence he had posited as the trope of biography deprives De Quincey of authority for reminiscences of a living author – a generic innovation of which Wordsworth had, in any case, firmly registered his disapproval.[11] In the canonical tradition of poets' biographies represented by Johnson's *Lives of the Poets* (1779–81) and Boswell's *Life of Johnson* (1791), the *Life* functions as a posthumous confirmation of literary standing, even if, like Boswell, the biographer had begun his work during the subject's existence. Such a *Life* transmutes frankly commercial considerations into matters of *literary* value: Johnson's prefaces were commissioned upon the decision of "the London Booksellers to print an elegant and accurate edition of all the English Poets of reputation," for which purpose "all the proprietors of copy-right in the various Poets [were] . . . summoned together . . . A committee was likewise appointed to engage the best engravers."[12] The engraved portrait, emblem of the Johnsonian "concise life of the poet . . . prefixed" to his poems (*PrW* 3:118), represented an acceptably modest and sublimated compromise with Wordsworth's distaste for the market in "personalities": biography should head the *corpus* of the author's completed works. Even so it approaches redundancy, for poems, Wordsworth claims, "contain within themselves all that is necessary to their being comprehended and relished," especially when they "convey . . . the personal feelings of their authors" (*PrW* 3:122–23). At most, then, biography should direct the reader how best to "relish" the poet's expression; as the example of Milton's daughter suggests, it should teach a tender passion for the mind embodied in writing.

The opposition of natural life and represented life, living body and poetic corpus, helps to insure that the biographical text does not encroach unduly on the sovereignty of its subject. The temporal lag between the subject's death and the publication of his biography also naturalizes the patrilineal correspondence of subject and biographer exemplified in Boswell's affiliation with Johnson.[13] This model of literary canonization, derived from hagiography, formed a significant context for De Quincey's magazine criticism, which included a number of short evaluative biographies in the Johnsonian mode, three of them on subjects Johnson had treated (Shakespeare, Milton, and Pope), as well as posthumous sketches of Kant, Herder, Schiller, Goethe, and miscellaneous English men of letters.[14] Yet the vulnerability – even of this orthodox practice – to gothic infection is suggested by Boswell's plan to display Johnson "almost entirely preserved."[15] This tone is more marked in De Quincey's memorial essay on "Samuel Taylor Coleridge," written upon Coleridge's death in 1834.

Interrupting De Quincey's autobiographical "Sketches" for four numbers of *Tait's Magazine*, the essay on Coleridge prefigures the generic ambivalence of the Wordsworthian *Reminiscences*. Its casual remarks on biographical method illuminate De Quincey's practice in the later series, but also emphasize the differences between remembering Coleridge and representing Wordsworth. Rejecting the Boswellian formula of "preconceived biographies, which, having originally settled their plan upon a regular foundation, are able to pursue a course of orderly development," De Quincey assumes "the liberty of speaking in the first person"; he describes the essay as a "personal memoir," but one justified solely by the "intellectual claims of Mr Coleridge" (*R* 100–01). This is, in other words, an occasional piece:

It was originally undertaken on the sudden but profound impulse communicated to the writer's feelings, by the unexpected news of this great man's death; partly, therefore, to relieve, by expressing his own deep sentiments of reverential affection to his memory, and partly, in however imperfect a way, to meet the public feeling of interest or curiosity about a man who had long taken his place amongst the intellectual *potentates* of the age. Both purposes required that it should be written almost *extempore*: the greater part was really and unaffectedly written in that way, and under circumstances of such extreme haste, as would justify the writer in pleading the very amplest privilege of licence and indulgent construction which custom concedes to such cases. (*R* 100)

The appeals to custom, profundity of feeling, spontaneity, and the reader's indulgence situate the tribute to Coleridge in the traditionary genre of the epitaph, a form both praised and theorized by Wordsworth.[16] De Quincey's "slight sketch" takes the form Wordsworth particularly recommends, "that in which the survivors speak in their own persons," and his excuse for the essay's informality recalls Wordsworth's defense of idealization. "The writer of an epitaph is not an anatomist, who dissects the internal frame of the mind," Wordsworth argues;

he is not even a painter, who executes a portrait at leisure and in entire tranquillity: his delineation, we must remember, is performed by the side of the grave; and, what is more, the grave of one whom he loves and admires. (*PrW* 2:57)

The ethics and aesthetics of the memorial inscription dictate a pattern of loving emulation between the writer and his predecessor. De Quincey poses his relation to Coleridge as similarity (both "read for thirty years in the same track," both took opium); as repetition (he retells the story of the Maid of Buttermere, he recapitulates Coleridge's plagiarisms); as miniaturization; and as substitution (*R* 40, 66–74). Coleridge's eulogist and also his proxy, De Quincey *represents* his subject in terms that correspond all too well to Boswell's dictum: "Be Johnson."[17] The form of his memoir thus alludes, in more respects than Wordsworth may have foreseen, to the idea of language as "incarnation." A curious figure for praise of the dead, the "incarnation" of language presses yet more exigently upon the living.

However he may duplicate Coleridge, De Quincey neither emulates nor identifies with Wordsworth. Noting one of the few particulars in which he "resembled Wordsworth" – "a peculiar embarrassment and penury of words" in youth – he disclaims the presumption of "compar[ing] myself with so great a man" (*R* 124). Where he should feel love, he confesses instead to an "emotion of ... vindictive hatred"; while the dead Coleridge cannot harm him, Wordsworth not only "drove [him] crazy then," but still "drives [him] crazy now" (*R* 145; *J* 227). These reversals upset the structure of generic authority that De Quincey invokes (and exaggerates to the point of parody) in his essay on Coleridge. He marks the problem by a refusal to "apologize for the most circumstantial notices past or to come of Wordsworth's person and habits," though his salacious parallel with a narrative that would "raise the curtain upon Shakspeare's daily life" (*R* 145) does little to parry the charge of exploitation. The apology is exacted by the Lockean view of property: if all men own their "persons," then the marketing of "personal revelations" (*M* 11:295) may constitute a type of theft. Not merely unseemly, De Quincey's challenge to convention is, moreover, not merely larcenous. Turning transgression to his personal account, he sensationalizes into "public exposure" the *tendresse* Wordsworth urges on biographers of Burns. Far from incarnating an immaterial soul, the representation of a living person strips the "decent drapery" (*C* 1) from what is "properly his."[18]

De Quincey rationalizes this exposure by "the reversionary influence which awaits Wordsworth with posterity" (*M* 11:314). Echoing Boswell's sly allusions to Johnson's "horrour of death,"[19] De Quincey steals Wordsworth's personal effects by reclassifying them as the material of authorship – which always belongs to posterity, however self-possessed the man may be. "Commensurate with the interest in the poetry," De Quincey claims,

will be a secondary interest in the poet – in his personal appearance, and his habits of life, *so far as they can be supposed at all dependent upon his intellectual characteristics*; for, with respect to differences that are purely casual, and which illustrate no principle of higher origin than accidents of education or chance position, it is a gossiping taste only that could seek for such information. (*R* 144–45; De Quincey's emphasis)

De Quincey's prediction echoes Boswell's precedent for "lay[ing] open to posterity" the "domestick privacies" and "minute details of daily life."[20] Yet the *Reminiscences* are presented as criticism, rather than as preservation or even explanatory context: De Quincey is not a biographical critic in the empiricist sense. Instead, he groups facial features with poetry as intellectual *productions* which generate "interest," a kind of dividend on the poet's selfhood.[21] Citing the "volumes [that] have been written upon the mere portraits and upon the possible portraits of Shakspeare" (*R* 145), he displaces pictorial representation by reading. Assimilating the author's private body to his literary corpus, he erases the residual distinction between persons and their works to which Wordsworth inconsistently clings.

The literary portrait, whether painted or published in collections of engraved "heads," was a standard accoutrement of nineteenth-century authorship, intended to establish the canonical image that would unify an attributed set of writings. But though De Quincey, deferring to this fashion, writes pages on Wordsworth's appearance, his descriptions stress the failure of images (even a "real living" face) to capture "Wordsworth in the vigour of his power" (*R* 139–41).[22] His existing portraits mostly "labour under the great disadvantage of presenting the features when 'defeatured' . . . by the idiosyncrasies of old age" (*R* 141); no daughter will recognize her father in these. Wordsworth is to an unusual degree the victim of a "change in personal appearance" that has "usurped upon" his "intellectual expression" (*R* 134–35). "Faces begin soon," De Quincey observes, "to 'dislimn:' features fluctuate: combinations of features unsettle. Even the expression becomes a mere idea" (*C* 116). So true is this of Wordsworth, at least, that in 1809, at the age of 38, he appeared "rather over than under sixty" (*R* 142). The proliferating portraits for mass consumption, now the poet has become famous, *cannot* represent him, because Wordsworth has not waited to be owned by his belated audience.[23] "The self-consuming energies of the brain . . . consumed him"; "in Miss Wordsworth," too, "every thoughtful observer might read the same self-consuming style of thought" (*R* 141). Wordsworth's "dread [of] disfigur[ing] the beautiful ideal of the memories of . . . illustrious persons with incongruous features" is well justified in his own case: where self-possession shades into self-consumption, the owner must preside over the decay of his strength (*PrW* 3:123).

Rather than *picture* the self-defacing poet, De Quincey juxta-poses the "intellectual effects" (*R* 137) of his features with those of other authors. Wordsworth has a better head than Lamb, a longer face than Scott; is more thickset than Southey, thinner than Coleridge. Properly speaking, De Quincey allows, we may only "read a picture of Wordsworth" in his written works (*R* 141). But because interpretation is realized through comparison, De Quincey identifies Richardson's engraving of Milton as the "best likeness of Wordsworth . . . in the prime of his powers" (*R* 142). Thus the defects of self-similarity are compensated by canonical inscription. Wordsworth objects that the "wreath of laurel about the head . . . disturbed the natural expression of the whole picture," but the necessary price of becoming an "English classic" is a deformation of spontaneous feeling (*R* 140, 143). Institutional identity, the imaginary great tradition, supplements natural per-sonhood. In this swerve from empirical preservation, the poet loses himself to the biographer's "conscious and living possession of" the *power* that subordinates casual idiosyncrasies to the require-ments of the author-function.

To crown Wordsworth with Milton's laurels is to reify their shared stature as "great poets who have made themselves necessary to the human heart; who have first brought into consciousness, and next have clothed in words, those grand catholic feelings that belong to . . . life, through all its stages"; who are not "author[s] amongst authors," nor even "poet[s] amongst poets," but "power[s] amongst powers" (*R* 143; *M* 10:399). "It needs no courage, in the year of our Lord 1839, to discover and proclaim a great poet in William Wordsworth," but a rise to fame does not in itself guarantee canonicity (*R* 147). And while Wordsworth's avowed identification with Milton strengthened during his later career, in De Quincey's eyes the resemblance no longer holds true; it characterized only "*that period of his life*" when he retained "the vigour of his power," before anyone thought to take his picture (*R* 143, 141). The respectable, elderly man is not, De Quincey sug-gests, the same poet of "original force" and fervent "intellectual passions" to whom he "paid an oriental homage" thirty years ago (*R* 139, 143). Wordsworth's likeness to Milton consists neither in style nor in beliefs, but designates the "constitutionally sublime" mode of power in which "the poetry [is] incarnated in the poet," and which allies *Paradise Lost* with Wordsworth's brief physical prime (*M* 10:400–01). During this decade or so Wordsworth produced the poetry De Quincey most esteems; flouting the "opinion of the world," for example, De Quincey denigrates *The Excursion*, preferring "those earlier poems which are all short, but generally scintillating with gems of far profounder truth" (*M* 11:314–15). The spiritual expression of De Quincey's Wordsworth, beaming from his eyes as "from depths below all depths," has been obscured by "a premature old age" (*R* 139–41). Wordsworth is canonized, then, by stripping away the accretions of his natural life to reinstate an idealized and immutable great decade, incarnated by De Quincey's recollections.

De Quincey imagines this interpretive gesture as a form of restoration, designed to counteract "the fatal admiration of the amateur" which deprives classic editions of their corresponding canonical portraits (*R* 140). He bids the real Wordsworth live. But so alienated is this *aesthetic* regard from the moral interest he once took in the poet that, exaggerating the Kantian indifference to the existence of an object, his admiration has become inconsistent with the life of the man. One may be reminded of the lovely boys in Wordsworth's poetry, "stopped" and "embalmed" by an art that exempts them from "the years/ That bear us forward to distress and guilt" (*Prelude* 7:400–05). Or, returning to the ethics of genre: where not legitimized by death, biography fatally infringes on the prerogative of self-representation. By anticipating the traditional calendar, De Quincey's *Reminiscences* subvert the poet's singularity, the property in himself inseparable from his originality. Thus De Quincey incarnates Wordsworth's most lurid speculations on language, writing himself into the poet's life like an epitaph graven on a still-warm body. "Language," Wordsworth darkly warns,

if it do not uphold, and feed, and leave in quiet, like the power of gravitation or the air we breathe, is a counter-spirit, unremittingly and noiselessly at work to derange, to subvert, to lay waste, to vitiate, and to dissolve. (*PrW* 2:85)

That counter-spirit, De Quincey tells "William Wordsworth," is at work even now:

if you ever allowed yourself to forget the *human* tenure of these mighty blessings . . . if, in the blind spirit of presumption, you have insulted the less prosperous fortunes of a brother, frail, indeed, but not dishonourably frail, and in his very frailty . . . able to plead that which you never cared to ask – then, if (instead of being 68 years old you were ⁶⁸⁄, I should warn you to listen for the steps of Nemesis approaching from afar; and, were it only in relation to your own extremity of good fortune, I would say, in the case of your being a young man, lavish as he may have been hitherto, and for years to come may still be –

> "Yet fear her, O thou minion of her pleasure!
> Her audit, though delay'd, answered must be,
> And her *quietus* is – to render thee."   (*R* 195–96)

Biography subverts with one figure what it upholds with another. De Quincey "renders" Wordsworth, in the combined senses of payment, portrayal, and dissolution, just the kind of tribute Shakespeare offers in the quoted Sonnet 126, the final poem addressed to his "young man."[24] At length, then, Wordsworth "has gone over to the majority," in "the Roman phrase for expressing that a man had died" (*M* 1:62). Neither "frail brother" nor "surviving daughter," De Quincey haunts him as the living death of his greatness: the presumptuous Semele, duly chastised, has been reincarnated as Nemesis, daughter of Nox. Feeding, but also vitiating, Wordsworth's hopes for "a literary Work that might live" (*PW* 589), De Quincey's biography is the best revenge.[25]

SHELLS AND SILENCE

A tendentious reading of De Quincey's "Wordsworth" might conclude that the biographical subject cannot resemble the poet, or even that Wordsworth's self-similarity hangs on a supplementary *méconnaissance*. The collapse of affiliation, while posing a problem of empirical authority, also suggests that authorship can never be owned singly – that it is always and necessarily both a fractured and a corporate endeavor. Yet while the inadequacies of portraiture may yield an aporia of *self*-resemblance, De Quincey's biography negatively asserts the poet's inimitability. "WORDSWORTH, where he is indeed Wordsworth," as Coleridge strangely cautions, "may be mimicked by Copyists" and "plundered by Plagiarists; but he can not be imitated, except by those who are not born to be imitators" (*BL* 2:141–42). Attempting a radical division of authorial voice or presence from literary property – the poet's chattels may be stolen, but his essence cannot be duplicated – Coleridge nonetheless identifies "Wordsworth" so entirely with "Wordsworth's poetry" that the text takes on the burden of being the man. This claim extends Wordsworth's argument that Burns "has reared a poetic" character "on the basis of his human character" (*PrW* 3:123) to the extreme of collapsing the two terms. The body of work *is* the biography; for Coleridge, Wordsworth's poetry is autobiographical whether or not the poet so wills it, and the strength of this identification constitutes Wordsworth's power. Elided in this critical dictum is the excited recognition that activates the authorial contract: "had I met these lines running wild in the deserts of Arabia," Coleridge famously declared of "There Was a Boy," "I should have instantly screamed out 'Wordsworth!'" (*CL* 1:453). The wandering Arab finds his proper home in the Coleridgean reflection. Imitation is thus disqualified as a problem for poetic authority or for the critical "friend" who ratifies it. The idea lingers, however, as a peculiar challenge to the ontology of personhood and the textual apparatus that supports identity. If the poet's essence is his autobiographical corpus, does an unauthorized representation of the man constitute an *imitation* of "Wordsworth"? Alternatively, one might ask, pursuing Coleridge's caveat: when is Wordsworth *not* Wordsworth, and who decides?

The complications that attend these issues of literary property, mimesis, and personhood surface in a gothic expansion of Coleridge's thesis, interpolated by De Quincey into an essay on Walter Savage Landor. De Quincey refutes an allegation about Wordsworth's envy of Keats by reiterating the rhetorical question asked by "Boswell . . . of Johnson" and by Byron of Scott: "'Of *whom could* you be jealous'"?[26] Wordsworth, De Quincey asserts, is not "capable of descending to envy. Who or what is it that *he* should be envious of? Does anybody suppose that Wordsworth would be jealous of Archimedes if he now walked upon earth, or Michael Angelo, or Milton?" The last two examples surely impinge upon poetic identity, as both the *Reminiscences* and the *Logic of Political Economy* suggest. Nonetheless, De Quincey now insists,

Nature does not repeat herself. Be assured she will never make a second Wordsworth. Any of us would be jealous of his own duplicate; and, if I had a *doppel-ganger* who went about personating me, copying me, and pirating me, philosopher as I am I might (if the Court of Chancery would not grant an injunction against him) be so far carried away by jealousy as to attempt the crime of murder upon his carcase; and no great matter as regards HIM. But it would be a sad thing for *me* to find myself hanged; and for what, I beseech you? for murdering a sham, that was either nobody at all, or oneself repeated once too often. But, if you show to Wordsworth a man as great as himself, still that great man will not be much *like* Wordsworth – the great man will not be Wordsworth's *doppel-ganger*. If not *impar* (as you say), he will be *dispar*; and why, then, should Wordsworth be jealous of him, unless he is jealous of the sun, and of Abd el Kader, and of Mr. Waghorn – all of whom carry off a great deal of any spare admiration which Europe has to dispose of. (*M* 11:460–61)

De Quincey offers this fantasy as a Coleridgean parable: impossible to imagine a man whose genius is identical in kind and degree to Wordsworth's. "Genius," he elsewhere observes, "is always peculiar and individual; one man's genius never exactly repeats another man's" (*M* 3:35). More precisely, though, the notion of a *doppel-ganger* confirms the telling slip from infringements of property to full-scale "personation": if there *were* such a thing as another Wordsworth, the second could only be a copy of the first. The gothic myth of originality eliminates not duplication so much as *accidental* likeness. That is because nature, which manufactures individual souls, is immediately assimilated to the juridical (imposture), to the psychological (imitation), and to the commercial (piracy). De Quincey regards the body-double as a consequence of print technology and expanded networks of distribution. ("What are these doppelgänger of phantom reduplicated lines . . . ?" he once asked an erring compositor [*NLS* MS. 4789].) Thus, by way of demonstrating Wordsworth's uniqueness, he recapitulates the authorial dilemma of his *Confessions* – contemplating his "own self, *materialiter* considered," as the counterfeit of his "own self, *for-maliter* considered" (*C* 25). If nature does not repeat herself, literature may and must.

The threatened invasion of literary property is doubled in the displacement from subject to narrator; the singular Wordsworth becomes De Quincey, meditating the murder of his twin. The slip emphasizes the conflation of profit considerations with attacks on fame, the unicity of the writing self. By subverting the contract between producers and their readers, pirates and hoaxers threaten the extra-textual life of the author, as De Quincey suggests in his countervailing claim that the "sham" cannot be a real person. Literary subjectivity, like individualism more generally, is a form of monopoly – a truth mystified in the superstition of "bodily commerce" by which "*doppelgänger* becom[e] apparent to the sight of those whom they counterfeit" (*M* 8:440). Yet while a man might be justified in killing an image repeated too often, there remains the suggestion that a self can be repeated just often enough. The threat of impersonation simply extends the necessity of *person*ation, that is, the rhetorical doubling that makes the writing subject visible to himself. The "alignment between . . . two subjects" that de Man calls the "specular" or "autobiographical moment" is spectacularly exemplified in the structure of the *Prelude*, the masterpiece Wordsworth alternately called the "poem to Coleridge" and the "poem on my own earlier life."[27] Wordsworth may not be duplicated because he is already self-divided. Romantic self-similarity strongly enacts Johnson's paradox, as recorded by his pale ephebe Boswell: "every man's life may be best written by himself."[28]

In Wordsworth's case, whatever may be true of other authors, "personation" does overlap with piracy. Yet biography impersonates without imitating – stealing the "matter," but not the manner, of the poet's written copy of himself. The generic shift from derivative poetry to mimetic prose eludes Coleridge's qualitative judgment, while disproving its metaphysical principle. Coleridge, that is, champions voice at the expense of form; De Quincey's project represents formal innovation at the expense of voice and individual "substance." Not born to imitation, De Quincey succeeds in it by troping the Coleridgean vindication of originality: rather than shout Wordsworth's name, he loses himself in Wordsworth's Arabia. Neither poet nor critic, he nonetheless pirates the one and plagiarizes the other – both inevitable results of the contradiction between property and rhetoric that he thematizes in his engagement with the *Prelude*.

The second installment of De Quincey's three-part essay on "William Wordsworth" takes its shape, its descriptive color, and many of its incidents from Wordsworth's poem on his own life. The autobiography supplies the deficiencies of De Quincey's empirical knowledge, representing the vigorous poet *as* poet in a way portraits cannot. The point is made explicit when, recapitulating Wordsworth's career at Cambridge, De Quincey interrupts his narrative to quote from the primary text. He has been describing the poet's college rooms, which on one side faced a "statue of Newton 'with his silent face and prism,'" memorials of the abstracting intellect, serene and absolute, emancipated from fleshly bonds," and on the other side echoed to "the shrill voice of scolding," repre-

senting "the world of passion" in all its grossness (*R* 168). The
duality of vocal body and silent intellect is then refigured as the
difference between literature and science so that De Quincey may
"mention appropriately,"

and I hope without any breach of confidence, that, in a great philosophic
poem of Wordsworth's, which is still in M.S., and will remain in M.S. until
after his death, there is, at the opening of one of the books, a dream,
which reaches the very *ne plus ultra* of sublimity in my opinion, expressly
framed to illustrate the eternity and the independence of all social modes
or fashions of existence, conceded to these two hemispheres . . . that
compose the total world of human power – mathematics on the one
hand, poetry on the other.

> "The one that held acquaintance with the stars
> – undisturbed by space or time;
> The other that was a god – yea, many gods –
> Had voices more than all the winds, and was
> A joy, a consolation, and a hope."   (*R* 168–69)[29]

Whether or not De Quincey's pre-emptive interpretation
amounts to a breach of confidence (and that is an open question),
it deviates from its Wordsworthian original in several respects. This
"great philosophic poem" was for Wordsworth merely "tributary"
to the "larger and more important" (*EY* 454) philosophical poem
Coleridge prophesied in the *Biographia Literaria*. De Quincey's
elevation of the unpublished work over the published *Excursion*
repeats his high early estimate of this purportedly "least important" component of the poet's *magnum opus* (*J* 39). More obtru-
sively, his reading of the dream negates Wordsworth's fear, voiced
at the beginning of the *Prelude*'s Book Fifth, that however "worthy
of imperishable life" the works of human spirit may be, "we feel –
we cannot chuse but feel – / That these must perish" (*Prelude*
5:19–21). The dream is "expressly framed" *by De Quincey*, not
Wordsworth, "to illustrate [poetry's] independence of all social
modes or fashions of existence." Envisioning the poetic canon in
its most reified, monolithic form, De Quincey establishes an artificial contrast between the poet's idealized "life" and his own life of
the poet, a narrative framed to provide "circumstantial notices" of
Wordsworth's "appearance and his habits of life . . . personal and
social, his intellectual tastes, and his opinions on contemporary
men, books, events, or national prospects" (*R* 145). By associating
Wordsworth with an essentialist claim he does not actually make

(and which the fragment that follows does not bear out), De Quincey invents absolute distinctions between materialist and idealist accounts of writing, and between thematic and contextual modes of reading, which the *Lake Reminiscences* repeatedly deconstruct. Thus the authorized version of the manuscript comes to represent an idealist conception of poetic originality, while De Quincey's piracies limn an alternative that appropriates the Dream of the Arab as an allegory of his own biographical project.

The tension between De Quincey's circumstantial claim of intimacy and the asserted autonomy of Wordsworth's poem "on the growth of his own mind" betrays itself in a slight misattribution: De Quincey reassigns the dream from a "friend" to "the poet" himself, representing the passage as a reflexive commentary on the poem in progress.[30] Quickly rehearsing the plot – the poet falls asleep reading *Don Quixote*, and dreams that across "some endless Zahara" he sees "'An Arab of the desert, lance in rest,'" carrying two books – De Quincey emphasizes the symbolism of two details: the "troubled" countenance of the Arab, and the second book, "which is . . . yet not a book, seeming, in fact, a shell as well as a book, sometimes neither, and yet both at once" (*R* 169). Holding the shell to his ear, the dreamer hears

> "A wild prophetic blast of harmony,
> An ode, as if in passion utter'd, that foretold
> Destruction to the people of this earth
> By deluge near at hand."   (*R* 170)

"The Arab, with grave countenance," then tells the dreamer of his "charge 'To bury those two books' . . . that is, in effect, to secure the two great interests of poetry and mathematics from sharing in the watery ruin." No sooner has this mission been revealed than "the dreaming poet . . . descries – 'a glittering light' . . . Upon which, the poet sees this apostle of the desert riding off 'With the fleet waters of the world in chase of him'" (*R* 170). This *précis* makes the essential point, repeated in *Prelude* criticism ever afterward, that the Arab's destructive quest may be seen as an attempt to "secure" the two books from another kind of burial.[31] It also poses a remarkable correspondence with De Quincey's avowed interests in dreams and oriental mythology. Not only does Wordsworth's vision recall (imitate?) the "Asiatic scenes" and "silvery expanses of water" evoked in the *Confessions* (*C* 71–72); it also alludes to the "pseudo-men" or "counterfeits" which, "according to the Arab superstition" and De Quincey, haunt solitary travellers through "the wilderness of the barren sands" (*M* 8:437–40).

De Quincey implicitly equates the shell/book with the "short breathings from the Wordsworthian shell" (*M* 11:462) – poetic quotations – that he interpolates into his summary. It is also easy to see in the Arab's "disturb'd" countenance and "reverted" eye the image of a "defeatured," retrospective poet, "twin labourer" (*Prelude* 5:43) to the poet who dreams him. The face-to-face encounter between the "apostle of the desert" and the dreaming poet, then, recapitulates the moment of recognition De Quincey posits in his early reading of Wordsworth. The poet's utterance "for commerce of [his] nature with itself" (*Prelude* 5:18) comes out of another mouth, indicating, as Lacan might observe, that "someone thinks in his place."[32] Commenting on the doublets that pervade this passage, Timothy Bahti argues that the characters of the dreamer and the Arab exemplify a "structure of repetition with a difference," in which "the two aspects of the Wordsworth-poet" are personified as reader and writer.[33] The Dream of the Arab figures its doubleness in a dark conceit of the poet reading *himself* writing, not merely a "poem," but his "own meaning" – in psychoanalytic terms, the unconscious. This is as close as Wordsworth comes in the *Prelude* to encountering a *doppel-ganger*. Does the Arab then personate Wordsworth, or De Quincey? Neither, and both at once. The episode's specular structure reduplicates when De Quincey adapts it for his *Reminiscences*, and becomes further complicated by the ambiguous nature of the Arab's mission. Like the piratical double De Quincey imagines, the Arab presents the poet with his meaning only in order to take it away. Thus, the passage raises further questions about both property and interpretation: does the Arab possess any title to bury the "many gods" who speak through the shell? What is the relationship between the apostle of the desert and the apostle who offers these preludic fragments of Wordsworthian shell to the many readers of *Tait's*?

The Arab might respond by asking, in turn, whether anyone can own an "unknown tongue" (*Prelude* 5:94), or the discourse of the other. The Dream of the Arab is in many senses a palimpsestic text, layered, superscribed, and reappropriated. It is tempting to wonder whether Wordsworth might have owed a part of its inspiration to De Quincey's apocalyptic promise, some months before the passage was written, "that, from the wreck of all earthly things which belong to me, I should endeavour to save [your] work by an impulse second to none but self-preservation" (*J* 33–34).[34] In any case, from the early moments of their correspondence, De Quincey had imagined Wordsworth's "special revelations" (*M* 1:122) to himself in scenes like that in Book Fifth. Wordsworth's second letter had mentioned his commerce with himself in a "Poem on my own earlier life" which he offered to "read . . . to you" (*EY* 454). De Quincey responded ecstatically:

with a view to my individual gratification, the poem on your own life is the one which I should most anxiously wish to see finished; and I do indeed look with great expectation for the advent of that day, on which I may hear you read it, as the happiest I shall see. (*J* 39)

Like Coleridge, De Quincey probably did first hear the *Prelude*'s "voices more than all the winds" in the poet's oral performance.[35] In the *Confessions* he notes that Wordsworth "is the only poet I ever met who could read his own verses" (*C* 64), emphasizing in this otherwise gratuitous remark his own privilege as witness.

A supplement to the biographical trope of the face, Wordsworth's voice sounds for De Quincey both the embodied, living man – since later generations may see his portrait, but can never hear him speak – and also, by a figurative inversion, what is ineffable in the transmission of "memorable effects" (*R* 162) in poetic language. Material yet unlocalized, the form and cadence of poetry bespeak identity but cannot be copyrighted, a paradox illustrated when, after his recitations had inspired similar metrical experiments by Scott and Byron, Coleridge published "Christabel" to rebut "charges of plagiarism or servile imitation from myself" (*CPW* 214). A consideration of voice, in both its literal and figurative senses, hence indicates a solution to the embedded riddle in De Quincey's description of the shell. When "is a book . . . yet not a book"? Perhaps when it is an unpublished "life" that "will remain in M.S. until after [the poet's] death" (*R* 169). The "semi-Quixote" (*Prelude* 5:142) bent on burying his speaking shell may then be read, not only as a commentary on autobiography in general, but as an emblem for the curious literal-mindedness of Wordsworth in secreting his poem while he lives.

De Quincey's misrepresentation of the dream-sequence as a manifesto of Wordsworth's confidence in poetry's "endless triumph over the ruins of nature and time" (*R* 170) ironically accentuates the futility of the Arab's mission. A shell, buried, may be safe from tides and currents, but only at the price of silence and anonymity: this is the submerged "gem of purest ray serene" that was the nineteenth century's byword for poetic obscurity.[36] Inverting the parable of the talents, the analogy between the poet and the Arab parodies Wordsworth's self-withdrawal. More precisely, De Quincey's rendition of the Wordsworthian trope (buried shell/unpublished "life") suggests that to suppress an autobiography until death is to treat it like a corpse, or, indifferently, like the opposite of a corpse: a spirit or essence. Such a manuscript is indeed a "poor earthly casket," by no means "immortal" (*Prelude* 5:164). By establishing so marked and superstitious a symmetry between his natural life and his represented life, Wordsworth has written himself his *own doppel-ganger*; the "image of [his] mighty mind," begun as a form of self-analysis, has become uncanny, involuted, to him.[37] It is the burial of the shell, exemplifying the miser's fantasy of "worth" without circulation, that changes the consolatory voice into a *memento mori*. Thus if, as De Quincey speculates of the palimpsest, the "relation between the vehicle and its freight has gradually been undermined," it becomes the role of the apostle to "kill, but so that a subsequent generation may call back into life; bury, but so that posterity may command to rise again" (*C* 140–41).

In so casually introducing Wordsworth's unpublished poem to the readers of *Tait's*, De Quincey was well aware that if he was not, strictly speaking, breaking a promise, he was certainly inviting Wordsworth's resentment. While at work on the Wordsworth sequence he wrote to Tait:

The part I am now upon in the acct. of W. W. is deeply indebted to my knowledge of his private Memoirs: I violate no confidence, but at the same time I tell what no man could tell, for Coleridge only, besides myself, had ever been allowed to read this most interesting part of his works. (*J* 349)

To enter this twilight ethical territory is to surrender his own authorial presence. De Quincey's claim that he (the proxy of Coleridge's phantom!) "tell[s] what no man could tell" redefines the autobiographical subject as the eerie "sham" of iteration, personifying "everything that ought to have remained secret and hidden but has come to light" (*SE* 17:225). The echo of "Christabel" further inflects his revelation toward the atmospherics of the gothic: "this most interesting part of [Wordsworth's] works," like Geraldine's bosom, glimpsed when "she unbound/ The cincture from beneath her breast," is "a sight to dream of, not to tell" (*CPW* 224:248–53). Either De Quincey too is dreaming, or else he is "no man" but Christabel's double – the equivocal daughter, or minor, cast off by her father.

The other of Wordsworth's dream, De Quincey returns as his "echo augury," a prophetic repetition that inverts chronology and wrests meaning from its primary source. The "daughter of a voice," he explains,

meant an echo, the original sound being viewed as the mother, and the reverberation, or secondary sound, as the daughter. Analogically, therefore, the direct and original meaning of any word, or sentence . . . was the mother meaning; but the secondary, or mystical meaning, created by peculiar circumstances for one separate and peculiar ear, the daughter meaning, or echo meaning. (*M* 1:123)

In this persona De Quincey both hears and conveys "deep messages of admonition . . . through sudden angular deflexions of words, uttered or written, that had not been originally addressed to himself" (*M* 1:122). To a post-Freudian ear, the private, circumstantial meaning is the only one that counts. The daughter meaning's *clinamen* from the original constitutes its interpretive authority, just as "in dreams always there is a power not contented with reproduction, but which absolutely creates or transforms" (*C* 157). In telling what no man could tell, De Quincey circulates a "property," his "separate and peculiar" knowledge, at the cost of the identity that could own it; like a plagiarist, he is ghosted by the voice that speaks through him. At the same time, his "echo" (for what else is the sound of a shell?) supplants the "original" as the *Prelude*'s "mystical meaning": its truth, or its "real."

De Quincey's reliance on the *Prelude* for the facts of Wordsworth's life after Cambridge – his presence in France at the beginning of the Revolution, his friendship with Beaupuy, his complex reaction to the death of Robespierre (*R* 171–84) – strays dangerously close to plagiarism, for in these pages he imitates the "substance" and sequence of another text to appropriate "all that is valuable" in it.[38] Perhaps worse, he embellishes his narrative with substantial quotations from Books Ninth and Tenth, despite his nominal hesitation over "whether I am entitled to quote" (*R* 169); here the question becomes one of piracy, or illegal publication. The legal issues involved in citations from an unpublished text were in fact delicate and ambiguous. Even the "bodily taking" of very long extracts from published material, presented for review, was justified on the grounds that they could not negatively affect sales of the work.[39] But in the case of De Quincey's *Reminiscences*, the popular digest effectually predated the original composition, putting a novel spin on the question of fair use. There were no clear precedents for this mode of paraphrase, though piracies of unpublished works were not unknown.[40] Unpublished manuscripts were clearly the property of their authors; yet they did not enjoy *statutory* protection, so that an author wishing to recover damages on a pirated manuscript could, as De Quincey observed, "obtain redress only for each copy *proved* to have been sold by the pirate" (*M* 1:189).[41] Thus, while De Quincey's excerpts from the *Prelude* were probably not legally actionable, they could have been regarded as verging on infringement – or, in De Quincey's euphemism, as somehow "affect[ing]" the poet's "interests" (*R* 169). Further complicating the issue was the notion, floated by Wordsworth among others, of a "natural," perpetual and inheritable copyright in works either published *or* unpublished, which rather than being reinforced by the statute, had been abridged by it to a finite number of years.[42] According to this line of reasoning, withholding a work from publication would have the paradoxical effect of preserving its legal immortality, though of course the work would also be effectively silenced. An unpublished poem would never lose the authorial imprint represented by copyright; it would never earn money or gain an audience either. By keeping his autobiography out of circulation, Wordsworth retained this absolute but self-negating solitude, independence and eternity, emphatically owning the poem that most emphatically owned him.

The problem of Wordsworth's "property in his works" (*BL* 1:43), as Coleridge calls it, frames the *Prelude*'s status in 1839 not only because De Quincey admitted to pecuniary problems, or because he had accused Coleridge of "palpable plagiarism" (*R* 39) in 1834, or even because his own originality was elsewhere open to challenge.[43] The management of authorial property greatly preoccupied Wordsworth in the late 1830s, and the anxieties attendant on this subject seem to have dictated much of the bitterness of his response to De Quincey's *Reminiscences*. Wordsworth wrote relatively little new poetry during the 1830s; his "memorial volume" of 1835, *Yarrow Revisited*, was his first separate publication for thirteen years. He had, however, been issuing successive revised editions of his collected works (1832, 1836, 1838), a labor representative of his lifelong efforts to control the form and presentation of his literary corpus, and, not incidentally, also an ingenious method for continually reextending the terms of his copyrights.[44] Wordsworth's lobbying for copyright reform reached the point of obsession around 1837, and he remained passionately involved in promoting legislation until the passage of the Copyright Act of 1842.[45]

In late 1838 Wordsworth returned to the poetic corollary of his interest in copyright, the project of editing and revising "his grand autobiographical poem" for posthumous publication. "At this he has been labouring," wrote Isabella Fenwick some months later, "seldom less than six or seven hours in the day . . . it seemed always in his mind – quite a possession."[46] The legal immortality conferred by copyright seems, as Susan Eilenberg suggests, to have been linked in Wordsworth's mind to the "spirit" of the poem; in 1839 he observed to Thomas Noon Talfourd that had the *Prelude* "been published as soon as it was finished, the copyright would long ago have expired in the case of my decease" (*LY* 2:969).[47] Had it been made available twenty years earlier – to extend Wordsworth's anthropomorphic parallel – by now the autobiography might have been nothing but a corpse, bereft of the animating spirit represented by property laws, vulnerable to defacement and "savage violation" (*PrW* 2:49) by literary grave-robbers.

De Quincey's trespass against the *Prelude* cuts to the heart of Wordsworth's concerns because it intrudes on the property that most closely touches his estate in himself. As Mary Jacobus observes, the *Prelude*'s "theme/ Single and of determined bounds" defends the compass of Wordsworth's "single self" (*Prelude* 1:668–69, 3:356); encroachments on the poem may threaten the interiority of the autobiographer.[48] If this is true for all unauthorized citations, De Quincey's reading of the Dream of the Arab glosses its intrusion with an implicit challenge to the poetics of oneness. His double casting of Wordsworth as both dreaming poet and maniacal Arab opens the poem to a multitude of revisionary claims, including the apparently innocuous remark that the apostle's "memory (though not refreshed by a sight of the poem for more than twenty years) would well enable" him to quote "long extract[s]" should he so choose (*R* 169). The excerpts he does include also derive from this graven memory, rather than from the manuscript in Wordsworth's possession.

Quoting from memory, De Quincey in effect quotes *himself* – the picture of his own mind, receiving its "individual gratification" – rather than the manuscript as worked artifact. The poet's property has become De Quincey, realizing the Lockean figure of memory in the lament that frames Wordsworth's dream: "Oh, why hath not the mind/ Some element to stamp her image on/ In nature somewhat nearer to her own?" (*Prelude* 5:44–46). De Quincey's solution proposes the "human brain" as deathless text or "natural and mighty palimpsest," whose every impression, no matter how deeply buried, awaits its "resurrection" with "posterity" (*C* 144–45). However this figure anticipates the topography of the unconscious, it also describes what is, for De Quincey, a *material* fact:

> Rarely do things perish from my memory that are worth remembering. Rubbish dies instantly. Hence it happens that passages in Latin or English poets which I never could have read but once, (and *that* thirty years ago,) often begin to blossom anew when I am lying awake, unable to sleep. I become a distinguished compositor in the darkness; and, with my aërial composing-stick, sometimes I "set up" half a page of verses, that would be found tolerably correct if collated with the volume that I never had in my hand but once . . . this pertinacious life of memory for things that simply touch the ear . . . does in fact beset me. Said but once, said but softly . . . words revive before me in darkness and solitude. (*C* 116–17)

Suspended on the verge of dreams, De Quincey becomes not merely book-maker but book, piratical compositor for a readership of one. Reversing the association of immortality with copyright, his indelible trace of the *Prelude* suggests that while bound volumes decay, greatness is eternal, preserved by a "pertinacious life of memory" that supersedes the lives and wills of individuals. Stamped with the poet's image, in nature near him, yet not his double, De Quincey preserves Wordsworth's memory by *re*textualizing it.

Transferred from book to book, speaker to listener, author to reader, the poem achieves its immortality through its own dispersion. This strange freight "lives," as Wordsworth hoped, only insofar as it is alienable. Read, asked what it "could mean" (*Prelude* 5:84–86), and so absorbed into other memoirs, the autobiography ceases to be the poet's alone. To pose the issue in terms of literary property, De Quincey's memory – both spiritual image *and* material element – undoes the distinction between the book as object (stone or shell) and the "intangible creation of the mind" that underlies modern copyright. More exactly, De Quincey's deep entrancement suggests the fallacy involved in the Lockean division of "material commodity" from "poetic form." His dream prefigures and ironically extends Eaton Drone's contention that

so complete may be the identity of an incorporeal literary composition, that, even when it has no existence in writing or print, it may be preserved in its entirety for ages in the memory; passing from generation to generation . . . It is a creation, without material form, in the realm of the imagination; but so complete is its incorporeal, invisible form, so marked its individuality, so distinctly perceptible to the musical mind, that another will reproduce it "by ear," without the aid of written or printed notes.

Corporeal possessions perish; but time does not destroy or efface what is best in literature.[49]

At this extreme (Drone is defending the rights of authors) the idealist position collapses into the materialist one. The poem's "invisible form" – its meter, cadences, "voice" – *is* its materiality, whether carved in stone or impressed, as Ilay Campbell had argued in 1773, on the minds of readers whose purchase entitled them "to copy, transcribe, and print [it] at pleasure."[50] Inscribed in the palimpsest, however, the creation becomes subject to the vagaries and displacements of the unconscious, for though "once it had been the impress of a human mind which stamped its value upon the vellum," this "secondary element of value" may "come at last to absorb the whole value" (*C* 140).

De Quincey, reproducing (and transforming) a dream "by ear," *substantiates* the "phantom" poet with the "shell to his ear" (*Prelude* 5:141–43; *R* 169), fulfilling his early promise of salvage and self-sacrifice to Wordsworth. Yet to the author, he resembles a thieving Arab, absconding with someone else's treasure. "The everlasting reverberation of a name from a dense population, furnished with the artificial means for prolonging and repeating the echoes, must lead to . . . continual temptations" for "pirating such an author, or for counterfeiting him" (*M* 14:133), De Quincey once remarked of Walter Scott. Is it theft or preservation to unearth a secret hoard? Does the discovery decompose the poet or revive his body of work? "Ghosts," De Quincey observes, are "popularly . . . supposed to rise and wander for the sake of revealing the situations of buried treasures" (*M* 8:436). To read is to plunder, even if the reader wears the same garments as the writer. This recognition is repressed in Wordsworthian self-writing, whose duplicity is always being recuperated – or betrayed – in the continuum of phenomenology. De Quincey's rebarbative "word" gives the poet his "worth," suturing the corpus it materially divides (*Prelude* 5:90). Wordsworth's Arabian knight, he foretells the truth of the poet's fame in both its apocalyptic and consolatory modes: apocalyptic, because canonicity portends the death of the author; consolatory, because the wound to consciousness will be renamed the sublime. Hence it scarcely matters whether one describes the Arab's relation to the poetic speaker as an allegory of the unconscious, or psychoanalysis as a myth of the shell's transmission. The signifier's mutation into "phantom," subjecting the dreamer to "someone else's" unconscious, makes this difference immaterial.[51]

Some reader may say that De Quincey coerces such a recognition by misquoting the *Prelude*. The dream of Book Fifth is not assigned to "the poet . . . himself" in the 1805 manuscript De Quincey knew. In fact, Wordsworth's scrupulous allusions to his "friend"'s "kindred hauntings" (*Prelude* 5:55) set the dream outside the order of self-representation, and its complex textual history makes it a particularly slippery form of property. As is well known, the Dream of the Arab borrows its outline and some of its details from a dream described in Adrien Baillet's *Vie de Descartes*; the anecdote was probably told to Wordsworth by Coleridge or Michel Beaupuy, and was certainly familiar to De Quincey as well.[52] Descartes, who regarded his dream as an indication of "divine blessing upon his philosophic mission," recorded it, along with an interpretation begun while he was still asleep, in his manuscript *Olympica*. The manuscript, unfortunately, "was never published and has long been lost. Baillet, whose life of Descartes appeared in 1691 . . . did, however, have the manuscript before him when he described the dreams."[53]

The Cartesian dream records in its ontology the truth and necessity of biography as the supplementation of philosophical self-knowledge. The surviving canonical text is not Descartes's memorandum, but a paraphrase transposed into the third person and incorporated into Baillet's *Life*. The transcript furnishes a pious precedent for De Quincey's revelation of the Wordsworthian dream, as well as a rationale for construing exposure as preservation. What if, at Wordsworth's death, some accident were to destroy the manuscript *Prelude* as Descartes's manuscript was destroyed? Wordsworth's complaint on the fragility of books is far more urgently appropriate to the vulnerable condition of the poem he so perversely withholds.

Imagining himself as the Baillet to Wordsworth's Descartes, De Quincey controverts the neo-Cartesian discovery that "only in the self-consciousness of a spirit is there the required identity of object and of representation; for herein consists the essence of a spirit, that it is *self*-representative" (*BL* 1:278; my emphasis). Yet vestiges of Baillet's transcription slightly blur De Quincey's summary of Book Fifth: he deemphasizes the visual pun of the naturalized books, while praising the "exquisite skill in the art of composition" by which the dream "is made to arise out of" the poet's immediate situation. De Quincey's synopsis of the dream "cannot in any way affect Mr Wordsworth's interests" (*R* 169) because the poem's value does not inhere in the borrowed plot. Indeed, De Quincey's interpretation resurrects the effaced subtext, in which Descartes's uncertainty about his vocation – "*quod vitae sectabor iter?*" – received its answer in "the union of philosophy with wisdom." The book of which Descartes dreamed was no less than the "*Corpus poetarum,*" the elusive canon of imagination.[54] "The traces of the elder manuscript" (*C* 141) authorize De Quincey's reading of Book Fifth as an omen of transcendence, assimilating a meditation on the lives of artifacts to Descartes's intimation of immortality. Dreaming as Descartes, De Quincey's author reads the translation of his living body into the poetic inheritance. Dreaming as Descartes, then, he becomes "Wordsworth," enacting the displacement of self-knowledge which constitutes literary subjectivity. "*Here, in the field of the dream, [he is] at home*": to paraphrase Lacan paraphrasing the Cartesian *cogito*, Wordsworth dreams where he is not, is where he knows not; where he was, there poetry shall be.[55]

The allusive meaning of the dream attests, for De Quincey's *Reminiscences*, to the restorative effects of biography in the appropriative, intertextual mode he practices. If the face of Milton presents an emblem for Johnsonian life-writing, Baillet depicts biography as the life of the poetic corpus. Judged by the standards to which De Quincey holds Coleridge, the *Prelude*'s *ne plus ultra* would surely count as a plagiarism; its sublimity, then, consists in the way it allegorizes the *many* voices that resurrect the "dry bones" of the Cartesian outline "into the fulness of life" (*R* 37).[56] The incantation De Quincey heard so many years ago speaks through him as a heightened phonocentrism – the apostle's immediate revelation – combined with an insistence on the need for transmission; for a voice is merely cast to the winds unless it is echoed and passed on. Understood as figures for poetic language, the *Prelude*'s "articulate sounds" and "blast[s] of harmony" (5:95–96) suggest an ineffable individuality that precedes and outlives the "psychospherical shell" that would contain it.[57] Animating and displacing the silent face of authorized biography, De Quincey's echo augurs both the impossibility of absolute originality and its apotheosis as transmitted effect.

De Quincey's reading, with its encryption of the biographer as Arab, rests on an unauthorized conflation of the Quixotically haunted dreamer with the empirical Wordsworth – it is, to this extent, a "misprision," or corrective mistake. Yet the mistake found uncanny vindication when, some twelve years later, the *Prelude* was published in a version that, like De Quincey's memory, transposes the dream-narrative from the "studious friend" to the poetic speaker (*Prelude* [1850] 5:50–140). Could De Quincey have influenced Wordsworth's revision? Wordsworth, righteously incensed at De Quincey's exposures, refused even to hear "a word of the contents of those papers," later reiterating that he "never read a word of his infamous production nor ever shall" (quoted in *J* 346–47). This curiously self-cancelling indignation (for if he knew nothing of the essays' contents, what could he resent?) suggests the *unconscious* logic that governed Wordsworth's emendations, completed in July 1839, about five months after De Quincey published his excerpts in *Tait's*. The very idea of such a publication represented to Wordsworth the double or shade of his originality: the confirmation, perhaps, of his fear that he "might almost 'weep to have' what he may lose – / Nor be himself extinguished, but survive/ Abject" (*Prelude* 5:25–27). The revision, his attempted mastery of this loss, reclaimed the Arab's freight "of more worth" as his own imaginative property.[58]

An implicit rebuke to his apostle's self-inscription and an effort to halt the drift of poetic voice, Wordsworth's dream-work is ironized not only by its sanction of De Quincey's error, but by its complicity with the biographical reading. By approving the stabilized version, Wordsworth acknowledges the *doppel-ganger*, who kills in the specular moment of recognition. These gothic tropes mark the irruption into idealism of its material repressed – or rather, the *construction* of such an unconscious in a refusal of interpretation. The result is that De Quincey's reading, which hinges on an initial exaggeration of Wordsworth's autonomy, is incorporated into the *Prelude* as its textual history: in other words, its meaning. To put this point differently, Wordsworth has attempted to *own* his greatness, to stake a claim in his canonical status. But canonicity, bound as it is to the contradictions of the author-function, only masquerades as real estate. Guillory observes that "canonicity is not a property of the work itself but of its transmission, its relation to other works in a collocation of works" like the casketed "Shakespeare" and "Milton."[59] It is, in other words, *not* a property in the Lockean sense Wordsworth imagines. Authors may assert titles in combinations of words, but they cannot own their posterity. Refusing to read the De Quinceyan or readerly *Prelude*, Wordsworth (mis)recognizes the literary prehistory of his own fame.

STRANGE FITS

"A man who can set such an example, I hold to be a pest in society, and one of the most worthless of mankind," Wordsworth ringingly pronounced (quoted in *J* 347). In the *de facto* conclusion of the *Reminiscences*, a brief account of a hysterical illness published in August 1840, De Quincey answers Wordsworth's charge of civil offense by literalizing it. The story's subject and its position in De Quincey's series both suggest that it possesses a theoretical value: it is at once a recapitulation of De Quincey's romance with Wordsworth, and an allegory of his defection to autobiography. A narrative of narrative, it also presents De Quinceyan personification at its most equivocal. In the conclusion to this chapter, I reconsider the imbrications of reading, biography, and sexuality by examining a case history of poetic passion, transferred without mutation to an empirical person.

De Quincey makes no claims for this tale as illustrative of

Wordsworth's personality; it is presented, rather, as "the most memorable 'psychological curiosity' in my life," revealing "a power derived from grief of creating ocular spectra and phantoms" (*NLS* MS. 1670). The story of Catherine Wordsworth was, in other words,

connected . . . with the records of my own life by ties of passion so profound, by a grief so frantic, and so memorable through the injurious effects which it produced of a physical kind, that, had I left untouched every other chapter of my own experience, I should certainly have left behind some memorandum of this, as having a permanent interest in the psychological history of human nature. (*R* 369–70)

The tone and the lexicon immediately recall Wordsworth's "Lucy" poems, but De Quincey's unremarked shift from "*fits* of passion" to "*ties* of passion" figures in little the generic transition from lyrical stasis to narrative contiguity that the following story both enacts and thematizes. This is, he stresses, a *conversion* narrative, in both the Rousseauian and the Freudian senses of that word: a temporally defined moment that initiates an internal change and, moreover, an episode that involves "the translation of . . . psychical excitation into physical terms" and back again into "case history" (*SE* 7:53). The theoretical significance De Quincey attributes to this anecdote stems from the way it "connects" disparate "chapters" in his fragmented, serialized life, both by virtue of its chronological proximity to events he records elsewhere and by the way it condenses the figures that recur again and again in his various fables of origination.[60] A single illustration suggests its power as metaphor *and* metonymy: De Quincey blamed this experience of "frantic" grief for his fall from recreational drug use to addiction, cryptically alluding in his *Confessions* to a "distress of mind" in 1812 as "the point of my narrative on which, as respects my own self-justification, the whole of what follows may be said to hinge" (*C* 52). In addition, the episode marks a decisive point in the "unlinking" of De Quincey's "chains" of friendship with Wordsworth (*R* 384). Thus it buries Wordsworth once again, this time resurrecting his biographer in the guise of addict; it connects addiction to questions of gender and textual transference; and it implicitly queries the assumptions of narrative and therapeutic accounts of the self. The brief life and sudden death of Catherine Wordsworth precipitate and then free De Quincey from another "nympholepsy," reenacting the possession that had "seized upon" him in his first meeting with the poet (*R* 119, 374). The disease of autobiography, then, cures De Quincey of the lyrical fascination that instituted his biographical *Reminiscences.*

Catherine, the "fourth in the series of [Wordsworth's] children," "was not above three years old when she died"; but her "life, short as it was, and [her] death, obscure and little heard of as it was amongst all the rest of the world" (*R* 369–71), made all the difference to De Quincey. Her story, perhaps the strangest, most overheated iteration of the *ur*-narrative "Jane Quincey, aged three years," also provides the starkest example of De Quincey's epitaphic inversions: Catherine counts in his personal history precisely because she died before she could count for herself. In this respect, and in her delicate immunity to the world's indifference, Catherine also resembles the heroine of Wordsworth's Lucy poems, the elliptical lyrics clustered around a telescoped or truncated story: "I loved a (little) girl, and then she died." These poems establish the tone and the itinerary of De Quincey's memoir, and also supply a context for treating the lover's relation to his beloved as a meditation on desire and narrative.

Exercises in virtual plot, the Lucy poems variously suggest or assume a narrative paradigm whose attenuation defines "passion" as an epistemological problem rather than simply an affective one. Wordsworth, De Quincey observes, "always preserved a mysterious silence on the subject of that 'Lucy,'" whose "death" (or "some other fatal event") is "repeatedly alluded to . . . in his poems" (*R* 187–88). "No lover in the proper sense," Wordsworth "does not willingly deal with a passion in its direct aspect, or presenting an unmodified contour, but in forms more complex and oblique, and when passing under the shadow of some secondary passion" (*M* 11:301). It is not so much that Lucy's death is ambiguous as that the epitaphic speaker elides causality and foreshortens temporal sequence, posing riddles that only an impassioned *reader* could expand into story.[61] A comparison of the manuscript version of "She dwelt among th' untrodden ways" with the poem printed in the 1800 *Lyrical Ballads* makes the aesthetic of elision explicit. The manuscript version has five stanzas:

> My hope was one, from cities far,
> Nursed on a lonesome heath;
> Her lips were red as roses are,
> Her hair a woodbine wreath.

> She lived among the untrodden ways
>> Beside the springs of Dove,
> A maid whom there were none to praise,
>> And very few to love;
>
> A violet by a mossy stone
>> Half-hidden from the eye!
> Fair as a star when only one
>> Is shining in the sky!
>
> And she was graceful as the broom
>> That flowers by Carron's side;
> But slow distemper checked her bloom,
>> And on the Heath she died.
>
> Long time before her head lay low
>> Dead to the world was she:
> But *now she's in* her grave, and Oh!
>> The difference to me!   (*EY* 236–37; my emphasis)

The three-stanza printed version renounces the narration of Lucy's "slow distemper," passing directly from the hypothetical "few could know/ When Lucy ceas'd to be" to the terse (and temporally frozen) "But she *is in* her grave, and Oh!/ The difference to me" (*LB* 154; my emphasis). With the recognition of "difference," the abbreviated sketch of Lucy's life yields to an account of the speaker's change in consciousness. That difference, the loss of the poetic referent, represents a gain for memory, the plot of interiority. In his access to what "few could know" about Lucy, the speaker substitutes for the reader, his internal change troping interpretation as the reconstruction and appropriation of a fragmentary story. The "hermeneutic composability" of the story – its *narratability*, or the framework through which it is comprehended – is personified in the lyric speaker.[62] The "negative quest romance" of the Lucy poems, then, allegorizes the story of their own reading.[63] If "Lucy" names the elusive lyric artifact, her lover's lament defines the reader of lyric in terms of transmuted narrative: the subject as *différance*. Thus, as the speaker of "Three years she grew" concludes, Lucy bequeaths a "memory of what has been/ And never more will be" (*LB* 199).

Such a memory is the therapeutic goal of De Quincey's narrative expansion, which participates like its lyric models in a "mixed generic mode – part love [story], part epitaph."[64] Recounting a fit of nympholepsy, De Quincey's story superimposes the interpretive questions raised by the Lucy poems on a story of illicit desire – or does some trespass lurk beneath the cryptic surface of the poems themselves? What fond and wayward thoughts will slide into a reader's head! "I have heard," De Quincey reports, "from gossiping people about Hawkshead, some snatches of tragical story, which, after all, might be an idle semi-fable, improved out of slight materials" (*R* 188). In the hardening of such insinuations into publicly admitted "excess of love" (*R* 372), sexual transgression becomes indistinguishable from the epistemophilia that is both encouraged and proscribed in the Lucy poems. De Quincey's disease is the symptom of this contradiction; its etiology suggests the possible consequences of a narrative antidote to lyrical romance.

For Catherine is less a (remembered) child than "an impersonation of the dawn and the spirit of infancy." The brevity of her life precluded "much room for the expansion of her understanding, or the unfolding of her real character"; dying while still *infans*, Kate remains as much of a cipher as Lucy.[65] De Quincey, compensating for his inadequate psychological account of her fascinations, textualizes her by invoking Wordsworth's "sketch towards her portraiture," "Characteristics of a Child Three Years Old" (*R* 371–72; *PW* 63). The poem confirms his impression of her "all-sufficiency to herself" in language that recalls "Lucy Gray": "solitude to her/ Was blithe society." The "wild" and "radiant spirit of joyousness" that infused the "nature and manners of this innocent child" link her as well with the "fountain of light" incarnated in the "exquisite little poem of 'We are Seven'" (*R* 371; *M* 11:301, 3:461). In short, what appealed to him in the child was the "abstraction seated in her person" (*R* 372). Not only does she personify childhood, she personifies the child as poetry: Wordsworth's poetry. The child whom Wordsworth literally fathered is also the spirit who embodies Wordsworthian abstraction. Loving Catherine, De Quincey acts out a *literary* passion, substituting a "relation to a representation" for the intersubjectivity he could not sustain with her father.[66]

His choice of Kate, despite her "half-hidden" charms, presents De Quincey as a more observant reader of Wordsworth's poetry than the poet himself, "with whom . . . she was noways a favourite." Alone among the Wordsworth circle, De Quincey thought Catherine "beautiful" (*J* 208). Yet a perceptive reading need involve no great delicacy, as the predatory voice of "Nature" in "Three years she grew" suggests. "There was room enough in [Kate's] short life," De Quincey confesses,

and too much, for love the most frantic to settle upon her. The whole vale of Grasmere is not large enough to allow of any great distances between house and house; and, as it happened that little Kate Wordsworth returned my love, she in a manner lived with me at my solitary cottage; as often as I could entice her from home, walked with me, slept with me, and was my sole companion. (*R* 371)

Grotesquely cast as the Leda to De Quincey's swan, Catherine allows her lover to appear "with his tail on," in a virile reversal of his earlier recognition-fantasy. Too young to refuse him, she is a blank slate on which De Quincey writes the text of his choosing. Like the pedagogue of "We Are Seven," De Quincey insisted that Kate "be taught by nobody but *me*"; no one, including her father, was to "insinuate any learning into Catherine – or to hint at primers – to the prejudice of my exclusive privilege" (*J* 185). In this way he fulfilled his longstanding wish to supervise "the education of a child"; her family enthusiastically cooperated, expecting Kate to become a fine scholar (*OE* 136; *J* 22–23). Perhaps, like Wordsworth's "Nature," De Quincey hoped to "rear her" and so to "make/ A Lady of [his] own" (*LB* 198). Shortly after Kate's death he wrote to Dorothy:

Many a time, when we were alone, she would put her sweet arms about my neck and kiss me with a transport that was even then quite affecting to me. Nobody can judge from her manner to me before others what love she shewed to me when we were playing or talking together alone. On the night when she slept with me in the winter, we lay awake all the middle of the night – and talked oh how tenderly together: When we fell asleep, she was lying in my arms; once or twice I awoke from the pressure of her dear body . . . Many times on that night – when she was murmuring out tender sounds of endearment, she would lock her little arms with such passionateness round my neck – as if she had known that it was to be the last night we were ever to pass together. Ah pretty pretty love, would God I might have seen thy face and kissed thy dear lips again! (*J* 265)

De Quincey confirms the aptness of the warning couched in "Three years she grew": "Nature" may be a "child molester."[67] By acting out a possible sequel to poetic encounters like "We Are Seven," De Quincey indicates once again that no representation, even (or especially) of an infant, may be presumed immune from sensationalism. If De Quincey's residence in the Lakes may be read as a lesson in the perils of mistaking rhetoric for psychology – of an imaginary subjection to poetry as friendship with the poet[68] – the record of Catherine Wordsworth's death rewrites the entry into the symbolic as ravishment.

"Poetry is passion," Wordsworth writes in his note to "The Thorn" (*LB* 288); but the reader's complementary passion must be tempered and restrained, lest it "overbalance" into pain or "entire delusion" (*PrW* 1:138–40). Though the poet promises "the company of flesh and blood," his reader must remember that poetry offers only a *resemblance* to "the passions produced by real events"; Wordsworth depends upon the conventions of meter and selection to "remov[e] what would otherwise be painful or disgusting in the passion" (*PrW* 1:130, 138–39). This formal censorship saves poetry from the contradiction of an "ethereal and transcendent" essence that nonetheless requires "sensuous incarnation" (*PrW* 3:65). De Quincey's passion, attuned to the vulnerability of this paradox, respects no boundaries between representations and real persons, collapsing the distinction between aesthetic response and empirical desire in a way that casts the poet of *Lyrical Ballads* as the pander of his infant daughter. Described in rhetorical terms, De Quincey's transference adapts the form of lyric to the real time of mortality. It is the lapse of lyrical stasis into narrative temporality that impels interpretive transgression toward social scandal. De Quincey's transgressive reading thus literalizes the "violat[ion]" of "the canonical script" described as a constituent feature of narrative.[69] As a point of autobiographical departure, his affair with Catherine also confirms the link between narrative and desire identified by Peter Brooks and Jay Clayton.[70] Lucy is to Catherine, as lyric is to narrative, as the abstract love of poetry is to child molestation. Or, to extend this series of equivalences, the canonical breach in the slip from lyrical suspension to narrative enactment luridly dramatizes the appropriation of text by reader that is implicit in all acts of interpretation and that is, moreover, thematized in the Lucy poems. The charge of molestation gives a behavioral name to a textual symptom: the reader's barred imperative to restore a specific chain of causality to Wordsworth's epistemologically attenuated Lucy-lyrics.

Wordsworth may be Kate's father, but only De Quincey relishes her beauties; in the person of little Kate, the child who fell in love with "We Are Seven" finds the reciprocal fantasy of a representation that *recognizes him*. Catherine, he writes, "noticed me more than any other person, excepting, of course, her mother" (*R* 370). De Quincey's passion is redoubled when he can claim that her love for him eclipses her more natural love for her father. He has "entice[d] her from home" and into the "solitary cottage" where her lover now dwells, as did her father of old. The intensity of the transference figures the "blind," "doating," "servile" (*R* 372) reader's theft of the "phrases and figures of speech which from father to son have long been regarded as the common inheritance of Poets" (*PrW* 1:132). This revision of De Quincey's biographical ideal, the ravishing of Milton's daughter, positions De Quincey as Pygmalion (giving brief life to a beautiful idea) and also activates the erotic abnegation of a "senseless self-surrender to passion" to which the masochist "clung . . . as a luxury" (*R* 373).

But how soon my Catherine's race was won! No other solution to the "We Are Seven" quandary can be imagined, and De Quincey has barely related his "devot[ion] to this one affection" when, in the next sentence, he tells how he "learned the terrific news (for such to me it was) that she had died suddenly" (*R* 372). To the inevitable next question, what should s/he know of death, he responds with a story of illicit knowledge as bodily affliction and as aesthetic. De Quincey's transports at Kate's death were indeed so immoderate and so public that they aroused rumors of paternity, as though only the taboo of an incestuous love could generate such extravagance.[71] The shrewdness of this theory notwithstanding, it was a *rhetorical* violation that induced De Quincey's overbalance: the catachresis or involute of "death and its sunny antipole" (*M* 11:302) which he discovered in the death of Elizabeth (*C* 103–06), which he found sublime in "We Are Seven," and which represented, to him, the figure of figuration. His grief for Kate suggests how readily reversible the terms of such conjunctions may be:

[Kate] had gone to bed in good health about sunset on June 4th; was found speechless a little before midnight; and died in the early dawn, just as the first gleams of morning began to appear above Seat Sandel and Fairfield, the mightiest of the Grasmere barriers, about an hour, perhaps, before sunrise.

Never, perhaps, from the foundations of those mighty hills, was there so fierce a convulsion of grief as mastered my faculties on receiving that heart-shattering news . . . the visionary sort of connexion which, even in her parting hours, she assumed with the summer sun, by timing her immersion into the cloud of death with the rising and setting of that fountain of life, – these combined impressions recoiled so violently into a contrast or polar antithesis to the image of death that each exalted and brightened the other. (*R* 372)

De Quincey responds to this news with an ardor born of his appreciation of yoked opposites, each "exalting" and "brightening" the other. "No death is usually half so affecting," he notes with fine discrimination, "as the death of a young child from two to five years old" (*C* 116). But just as origin and tendency are notions inseparably co-relative, masochistic melancholy slides easily into sadism; De Quincey's commiserating letters to Dorothy went so far as to invent torments that Catherine *might* have experienced as she lay ill (*J* 267–68). Hence his record of Kate's death also explores the rivalrous permutation of his recognition-fantasy, in an excess of feeling for the sister who suffers in the rejected daughter's place.[72]

With Kate's death, the story becomes properly De Quincey's. The consciousness of difference initiates a complex process of mourning, which may be understood in general as a mode of narrative by which the subject articulates a break with the past. De Quincey's record of his "distress of mind" and "the bodily illness which it produced" (*C* 52) further suggest that his stages of grief *theorize* narrative as the genre of his poetic disenchantment and autobiographical consolidation. "I returned hastily to Grasmere," he continues, and there

stretched myself every night, for more than two months running, upon her grave; in fact, [I] often passed the night upon her grave; not (as may readily be supposed) in any parade of grief . . . but in mere intensity of sick, frantic yearning after neighborhood to the darling of my heart. (*R* 372)

Laid out on the child's grave, the tiny plot that replaced both her father's and her lover's houses as Kate's permanent home, De Quincey performs a gothic parody of the impulse that brought him to Grasmere in the first place: to live in "neighborhood" with Wordsworth. His action recalls the thematics of property at work in his choice to rent Dove Cottage, which both he and the Wordsworths regarded as an extension of the household at Allan Bank.[73] As the "tenant of that pretty cottage in which I found

them" (*R* 206), De Quincey made himself custodian of the
Wordsworth legend before there was a reputation to protect; Town
End was the site not only of his first visit, but also of Wordsworth's
labor "in the vigour of his power" from 1800 to 1808 (*R* 141).
Thus De Quincey could describe Wordsworth "in connexion with
my own life; for . . . my life flowed on in daily union with" his (*R*
206). Indeed, Wordsworth later complained, De Quincey had
been "7 months an inmate of my house." For Wordsworth, this intimacy defined the *Tait's* essays as a "breach of the laws of hospitality" (quoted in *J* 347) – but, of course, it also made them possible,
just as the *unheimlich* begins at home. De Quincey's tenancy represented the chance of squatter's rights in Wordsworth's "original
literary composition," insofar as such property is "reducible to the
head of occupancy."[74]

The relation between mourning and property is clarified by a
minor poem in the 1800 *Lyrical Ballads* which De Quincey took as
his "canonical script" of grief. "A Poet's Epitaph" particularizes the
traditional *siste viator* by cautioning most passers-by to "turn aside"
and then singling out a "modest" and "retired" supplicant whom
"you must love" before "he will seem worthy of" this regard. The
poem concludes with an ironic transvaluation and an offer of
hospitality:

> But he is weak, both man and boy,
> Hath been an idler in the land;
> Contented if he might enjoy
> The things which others understand.
>
> – Come hither in thy hour of strength,
> Come, weak as is a breaking wave!
> Here stretch thy body at full length;
> Or build thy house upon this grave. – (*LB* 212–14)

The dead poet's childish, weak, and idle second self stakes a claim
to the succession with a monument to his own posture of lament,
thereby effacing the graven inscription beneath. De Quincey personifies himself as the unpromising protégé – "frail, indeed, but
not dishonourably frail" (*R* 196) – who makes his home on the
grave of the poet's surrogate.

De Quincey's churchyard vigil figures both the death of biography conceived as the imitation of life and the impossibility of
reading conceived on the model of the affections.[75] Like the "We
Are Seven" girl, he "cleave[s] to" gravestones "not only as symbols

of [his] passion, but as *things*, active and efficient, which are of themselves part of the passion." The grieving "mind luxuriates in . . . repetition," as Wordsworth observes of "The Thorn" (*LB* 288–89). This stage of unmastered repetition finds its sensory correlative in a version of the "hallucinatory wishful psychosis" that Freud describes in "Mourning and Melancholia" (*SE* 14:244) and that De Quincey calls "the creative faculties awakened in the eye or other organs by peculiar states of passion":

my eye was haunted at times, in broad noonday (oftener, however, in the afternoon), with a facility, but at times also with a necessity, for weaving, out of a few simple elements, a perfect picture of little Kate in the attitude and onward motion of walking. I resorted constantly to these "intacks," as places where I was little liable to disturbance; and usually I saw her at the opposite side of the field . . . uniformly with the air of advancing motion. (*R* 373)

In this early phase of mourning, De Quincey is Kate's visionary portraitist; the simplicity of the "elements" that compose her life graces her with a picturability her father resisted. Also unlike her father, De Quincey has not yet lost "sight [of] that heavenly face," or been, even for a moment, "surprised by joy" (*PW* 204). And yet, countering his melancholy fixation, the ghost's "air of advancing motion" portends the return of narrative time. "I clung to" this vision "as a luxury," De Quincey writes, but "it was reasonably to be expected that nature would avenge such senseless self-surrender to passion." Nature's vengeance restores narrative proper by dramatizing the limits to intentional behavior.[76]

All at once, on a day at the latter end of August, in one instant of time, I was seized with some nervous sensation that, for a moment, caused sickness. A glass of brandy removed the sickness; but I felt, to my horror, a sting as it were, of some stationary torment left behind – a torment absolutely indescribable, but under which I felt assured that life could not be borne. It is useless and impossible to describe what followed: with no apparent illness discoverable to any medical eye – looking indeed, better than usual for three months and upwards, I was under the possession of some internal nervous malady, that made each respiration which I drew an act of separate anguish. I travelled southwards immediately to Liverpool, to Birmingham, to Bristol, to Bath, for medical advice; and finally rested . . . at Clifton, near Bristol. (*R* 373–74)

This "nervous malady" is clearly marked as hysterical or tendentious, miming Catherine's illness – indigestion, "strong convulsions," paralysis, and speechlessness – in the muted register of an "irritation of the stomach," followed by respiratory problems and culminating in a near-inability "to stand or walk" (R 370–74; C 52). De Quincey's identification with Catherine expresses itself through a conversion in which his body tropes the traumatic event elided from the Lucy poems. His illness enacts the "secret" of Wordsworth's poems from the mystified perspective of a reader who "suppose[s] in advance the presence in the other of a certain knowledge." Such a "transference," Slavoj Zizek suggests, "must transpose us into the future, not the past."[77] This attitude makes itself felt as compulsive locomotion, "stationary torment" being literally "left behind" as De Quincey pursues his quest for a cure. His bout of hysteria punctuates his protracted apostasy from lyrical fixation and biographical propriety. Walking through this exaggerated, diagrammatic case-history of mourning, De Quincey proceeds to turn his somatic phenomena into conscious ideas. "At length," he goes on,

my malady began to leave me: it was not quite so abrupt, however, in its departure, as in its first development: a peculiar sensation arose from the knee downwards, about midnight: *it went forwards* through a space of about five hours, and then stopped, leaving me perfectly free from *every* trace of the awful malady which had possessed me. (R 374; my emphasis)

The progress of De Quincey's illness *through* and *out of* his body allegorizes the metonymic displacement that is the basic rhetorical structure of narrative. No longer "possessed," he returns to conclude his "own unattached narration" (R 370).

De Quincey's autobiography originates in extravagant textual response, but that generative moment of desire must ultimately be forgotten for the subject of narrative to achieve his fictive consistency. From this vantage of tranquil recollection,

The remarkable fact . . . is that all grief for little Kate Wordsworth, nay, all remembrance of her, had, with my malady, vanished from my mind. The traces of her innocent features were utterly washed away from my heart: she might have been dead for a thousand years, so entirely abolished was the last lingering image of her face or figure . . . even her little grassy grave, white with snow, when I returned to Grasmere in January, 1813, was looked at almost with indifference, except, indeed, as now become a memorial to me of that dire internal physical convulsion thence arising by which I had been shaken and wrenched; and, in short, a case more entirely realising the old Pagan superstition of a nympholepsy in the first place, and, secondly, of a Lethe or river of oblivion, and the possibility, by one draught from this potent stream, of applying an everlasting ablution to all the soils and stains of human anguish, I do not suppose the psychological history of man affords. (*R* 374)

Here, apparently, ends a strikingly successful instance of mourning, with all the ruthlessness this itinerary implies. Freud calls it "a secondary and theoretical aim" of psychoanalysis "to repair all the damages to the patient's memory" by translating symptoms into continuous narrative (*SE* 7:18). The "catastrophe of [De Quincey's] illness," however, produces its effect of formal closure by substituting a "Lethe or river of oblivion" for the "unnavigable river" of the hysteric (*R* 374; *SE* 7:16). The greatest wound to memory may be memory itself. If De Quincey's cure may be measured by the thematic coherence of his "memorandum," the recuperative power of narrative is purchased by a radical erasure, blinding him to "the real of his desire" that he glimpsed when transfixed by grief.[78]

Now truly buried, Catherine Wordsworth decays into verse, becoming again the "sketch" of a poem De Quincey can safely quote. Stephen J. Spector explains this amnesia as the "loss of the ground of metaphor" that sets De Quincey adrift from the mirror stage.[79] Kate's very grave – "white with snow" like little Jane's – De Quincey regards as "a memorial *to me* [my emphasis]," not as a person or a place to visit. Her grave has become the emblem of a fully internalized plot, establishing the narrator's relation of contiguity with the markers of past moments. Autobiographical subjectivity spatializes an interpretive rupture with the graven former self: what cannot be seen may therefore be read. Yet something has been lost in the translation, for the imaginary, despite its illusory stability, dwells in close conjunction with the "real," that specter "more terrifying than so-called external reality itself." When De Quincey emerges from his infatuation to the daylight reality of his own story, he actually "continue[s] to sleep, to maintain his blindness" with repeated draughts of the Lethe that, renamed "just, subtle, and mighty opium," will propel him continually onward to new "object-causes" of desire (*C* 49).[80]

The autobiographer does not memorialize; he remembers to forget. Kate may then be understood as De Quincey's scapegoat for the real of *reading*, with the thoroughgoing forgetfulness, both of self and of other, that being-in-the-text entails. The challenge

Wordsworth presents to De Quincey's epistemology is solved in this case – precariously and temporarily – by separating the buried child of poetry from its biological and literary father. Wordsworth still passes understanding, but his *poetry*, now gendered feminine, may be "enjoyed." The therapeutic disease of nympholepsy reinstates legible differences between poet and reader, lyric and narrative, personification and person. De Quincey's knowledge of Wordsworth is consequently attenuated, but also positionally empowered – for what father knows everything his daughter gets up to? Yet if, as the sly lover of Wordsworth's poetry, De Quincey finally finds himself in an oedipalized relation to the man, his stance represents the defeat of an earlier strategy rather than an *a priori* challenge to phallic authority.[81] Failing to be ravished by Wordsworth – a frustration that is repeated in the displacement of biography – De Quincey institutes a division between the empirical man and his works; the healing of this breach will then bring him courting again.

If Kate's death limns the real of the minor, her published epitaph may have traumatized Wordsworth, who could not, after all, be expected to enjoy the spectacle of De Quincey's immodest passion. Wordsworth's vehement condemnation of that "infamous" rent in the decent drapery of his privacy *domesticates* the evils of textual promiscuity by reducing them to social *faux pas*. For, as Crabb Robinson summarized the poet's objections, "it is not *what* he writes that excites your indignation but that he should write *anything* – Praise is an insult at such a time and in such a manner" (quoted in *J* 347; original emphasis). The prohibition on writing "anything" reiterates Wordsworth's desire to stabilize the textual dialectic – the poet is to be read, not written – or, at least, to defer his inevitable bereavement. Robinson, who privately called the articles "scandalous, but painfully interesting," compromised with the suggestion that, had they been "published thirty years hence," "a considerable part of the articles . . . would be read with pride & satisfaction by your grand-children" (*J* 346–47; *HCR* 273). Biographical anecdotes released posthumously, under the rubric of the "Memoir," might have served as benign props for the poetic authority of a copyrighted *Prelude*. Those missing years made a great difference to Wordsworth. But the manner of the *Reminiscences* was also to blame, because biography supplied the generic alibi for De Quincey's incorporation of "Wordsworth" into his own career.

Wordsworth may sometimes have feared that the taste he created might end by creating the poet. As a reflection on peculiar genius or character, such an anxiety must have been inconceivable to the apostle who proposed that "if you have occasion to write a life of Lucifer, set down that by possibility, in respect to pride, he might be some type of Wordsworth" (*R* 381). More threatening to Wordsworth than a gothic *doppel-ganger*, though, was the "juvenile Reader" who took literally, as well as literarily, poetry treating "things not as they *are*, but as they *appear* . . . to the *senses*, and to the *passions*" (*PrW* 3:63). In his imaginative grasp, and in his "exertion of a co-operating *power*" of response (*PrW* 3:81), De Quincey vindicated Wordsworth's truth by rendering it appalling. The "world of delusion" he dreaded in De Quincey suggests, then, the topography of *Wordsworth's* "real," stripped of such mystifications as the "embodied spirit of . . . knowledge" he called "the People." However concretely biographical his poetic subjects (and they were too much so, Coleridge complained [*BL* 2:129]), Wordsworth's meditations on reading always remained at the level of generality, as though he had not banished egregious poeticism so much as relocated abstraction in an imaginary audience. In De Quincey, Wordsworth saw the degradation of his ideal posterity into its "erroneous and perverse" (*PrW* 3:66) actuality. As realized in the importunate form of De Quincey – with his conscientious confusion of poetics and pedophilia – the impassioned biographer devolves into a pornographer. His trespasses have less to do with inventoried properties than with poetry's theoretical exemption from embodiment. De Quincey's love was not a crime: he stole Kate's childhood from the father, not the child, and he stole her from literature by seeing her literarily. I have no wish, however, to domesticate this trauma. By exhibiting the flawed correspondence of legal and literary immunities, by exploiting the internal fractures of property and personhood, his *Reminiscences* suggest how little comfort such distinctions afford.

Strictly speaking, the literary tradition preserves writing, not writers, but canonicity is the misrecognition of this fact. De Quincey's *Reminiscences* plot this structural perversion as family-romance, and its erroneousness as the death of a child. Or, to give this figure one more turn, Kate's death *objectifies* De Quincey's minority – the figure of his ravishment – and *naturalizes* the generic distinction that is his own claim to fame. Romantic minority, as I have been insisting throughout this study, represents *at once* a "primary" cathexis of reading and its "secondary" reinscription as the "turning round" of autographic figuration. The burial of De Quincey's figure consolidates both the many lives of the auto-biographer and the life-in-death of the canonical poet, but the irreducibility of the text to this supervention nonetheless leaves its traces. My concluding discussion of "Minor Romanticism" attends to such traces, subordinating questions of subjectivity to the read-ings, or transmissions, in which literary personae take shape. The figure of the minor, I will argue, poses one response to the formal-ization of transmission in Romantic dialectics. The historicity of this figure offers a glimpse into the *institutional* dialectics we inherit, as well as their Romantic resistances.

Epilogue: minor Romanticism

THE CHILD'S EYE

"To carry on the feelings of childhood into the powers of manhood; to combine the child's sense of wonder and novelty with the appearances, which every day for perhaps forty years had rendered familiar": this, Coleridge affirms, "is the character and privilege of genius, and one of the marks which distinguish genius from talents" (*BL* 1:80–81). Defamiliarization takes place through dialectical synthesis, whereby the temporal oscillations and specular reversals that haunt the *Prelude* are recuperated in a narrative of development.[1] Wordsworth can thus claim, in the final book of the *Prelude*, that "we have traced the stream/ From darkness, and the very place of birth," then "given it greeting as it rose once more/ With strength . . . / And lastly, from its progress have we drawn/ The feeling of life endless" (*Prelude* 13:172–84).

The philosophical critic's prescription echoes repeatedly in the memoirs and contemporary portraits of his disciples, from Crabb Robinson's sentimental comment on "how Lamb confirms the remark of the childlikeness of genius" (*HCR* 185) to De Quincey's opiated experience of a "re-awakening of a state of eye generally incident to childhood" (*C* 67). Precisely fulfilling Coleridge's first condition, both Lamb and De Quincey are represented as failing in the second: De Quincey finding himself at the same time "powerless as an infant" (*C* 67), Elia avowing as an "infirmity," to "a degree beneath manhood," his trick of looking "back upon those early days" (*LM* 3:6 [*E* 32]). The Eliacal "half-Janus" – helpless to convert his habitual retroversion into Wordsworthian "Prospectus" – would seem by Coleridge's lights a "half-genius" as well, not fully exemplifying "the creative, and self-sufficing power of absolute *Genius*," yet not simply limited to the "faculty of appropriating and applying the knowledge of others" which Coleridge denigrates as "mere *talent*" (*BL* 1:31).

The notion of stunted genius marks the minor writer's enmeshment in Romantic dialectics of production, and also his status as an apparent contradiction or scandal. It is true that figures of diminishment are a commonplace of early nineteenth-century criticism; John Scott for example regrets the "certain air of *smallness* belonging to" the Cockneys, and chides Leigh Hunt in particular for the "*smallness of soul* . . . apparent in all he does"; Hunt, he alleges, "would convert life into child's play" (*LM* 3:70, 2:516). Epithets like these make reports of De Quincey's actual size read as literalized judgments on his artistic stature; Carlyle described "the dwarf Opium-Eater," who stood a bare five feet tall, as "a pretty creature" resembling "the beautifullest little child" (quoted in *OE* 272; *J* 23).[2] Both Hazlitt and Lamb were also, apparently, rather short men, and the tessellations of this circumstance in Hazlitt's erotic life are suggested by his attachment to a "*little image*" of Bonaparte that Sarah Walker saw as a portrait of his sexual rival (*H* 9:112–14). As a term of evaluation, small size indexes what Elia calls the "order of imperfect intellects" possessing "few whole pieces"; such congenital essayists "are content with fragments and scattered pieces of Truth . . . They seldom wait to mature a proposition, but e'en bring it to market in the green ear" (*LM* 4:152–53 [*E* 68]). Elia imagines becoming "entangled in another man's mind," just as he might be "outpace[d]" when "walking with a tall varlet" like Wordsworth, who, Coleridge warns in a witty inversion, "strides on so far before you" as "to *dwarf* himself by the distance" (*LM* 3:495 [E 61]; *H* 17:111; *BL* 1:37). Diminutiveness signifies, in particular, an imputed lack of creative vitality: Hazlitt claims to be "deficient in the faculty of imagination" (*LM* 3:131), while Elia admits that "for the credit of my imagination, I am almost ashamed to say how tame and prosaic my dreams are grown." Proposing that "the degree of the soul's creativeness in sleep might furnish no whimsical criterion of the quantum of poetical faculty resident in the same soul waking," he resigns himself to his "proper element of prose" (*LM* 4:387 [*E* 79–80]). This quantum is moralized in De Quincey, who dreamed magnificently even while his addiction parodically foreshortened the growth of poetic mind into "mere childish helplessness, or senile paralysis of the judgment."[3]

Yet while no doubt dismissable as the exception that proves the genial rule – or, recurring to Coleridge's terms, the fragment of an anterior whole; or, again, the "grotesque dwarf" that attends "magnitude of intellect" (*BL* 1:301) – the minor professes a counter-discourse of diminishment and fragility *as power* that in some respects eludes idealist explanation. "*A part*," Hazlitt cryptically asserts, "*is greater than the whole*" (*LM* 1:647).[4] Lamb, for example, apologizes in his "Character of the Late Elia" for that phantom's "aversion from being treated like a grave or respectable character" and for his resistance to "the advances of age that should so entitle him" (*LM* 7:21). "He herded always," the memorialist continues,

with people younger than himself. He did not conform to the march of time, but was dragged along in the procession. His manners lagged behind his years. He was too much of the boy-man. The *toga virilis* never sate gracefully on his shoulders. The impressions of infancy had burnt into him, and he resented the impertinence of manhood. These were weaknesses; but such as they were, they are a key to explicate some of his writings. (*LM* 7:21 [*E* 173–74])

Lamb adduces the signs of fixation and effeminacy as evidence of an enlarged sensibility and capacity for response. His fidelity to a past of vanishing manners and "giant" folios (or pre-industrial, non-commodified literature) is represented as a kind of functional atavism, a refusal of entitlement (*LM* 2:624 [*E* 29]); antiquarian knowledge and aesthetic sensitivity are the powers purchased by arrested psychic development.

Hazlitt makes a similar claim in his essay "My First Acquaintance with Poets," an extended gloss on the Intimations Ode in which he contrasts his adult felicity of composition with the stammering attempts of his adolescence, and concludes by asserting the superiority of an expressive silence. "Am I then better than I was then?" he asks; "Oh no . . . Would that I could go back to what I then was!" (*H* 17:114). He dates his vocation of authorship from 1798, when his "dumb and brutish" understanding "found a language to express itself" in veneration of Coleridge, "the light of [whose] genius shone into my soul, like the sun's rays glittering in the puddles of the road" (*H* 17:107). Writing begins not in hydraulic overflow but in passionate reflection, a mock-heroic miniature of St. Paul's conversion. This powerful feeling, originating in an apprehension of weakness, inscribes itself in the adult writer as a palimpsest of his youthful romance: "*Dusse-je vivre des siècles entiers, le doux tems de ma jeunesse ne peut . . . s'effacer jamais dans ma mémoire*"

(*H* 17:108). First as a living impression, then in the body of his work, Hazlitt constitutes a memorial or monument to Coleridge's spirit, just as a plaster cast might preserve his countenance.

Hazlitt's reaction offers the practical proof of his own critical dictum that "taste . . . is strictly the power of being properly affected by works of genius . . . The eye of taste may be said to reflect the impressions of real genius, as the even mirror reflects the objects of Nature in all their clearness and lustre" (*H* 17:57). To appreciate geniuses "is to be so far like them," at the price of having one's self-love "touched . . . with a consciousness of inferiority" – lacking which sense the critic would, ironically, only have betrayed his profound unworthiness of Hazlitt's "enlarged capacity" (*H* 17:63). The *consciousness* of inferiority, then, stands as paradoxical evidence of a real superiority. Deficiency of "imagination" acquires a positive sense of openness and generosity, connoting in*te*riority – as in De Quincey's apprehension, via the "literature of power," of "the infinity of the world within me" (*M* 10:49) – and, hence, the possibility of a "likeness" between the production of literature and its reception. As Lacoue-Labarthe and Nancy have suggested, "Romantic criticism . . . constitutes *the* poetic reflection"; it is above all "a *literary criticism*, according to the double value, subjective and objective, of the epithet." The critic's reactive sense of imperfection is redeemed as the "putting-into-form" of a literature that produces, and produces itself as, its own theory. Like the fragment, "the genre of generation" which occasions "the thinking of identity through the mediation of non-identity," the reflection offers itself "as an analogon of the work," while also manifesting the incompletion of literature, or the canon *per se*. The minor, "an author to the second power," objectifies the lack *within* the imaginary totality of the "creative" or "primary" work.[5] The relation of the critical fragment to this unfolding totality – the subject-form of *writing* – hence recapitulates the dialectic of child and man in the hypothesis of organic development.

Hazlitt's vaunted adherence to the opinions and impressions of his youth finds a more explicitly ideological statement in De Quincey's exaggerated reverence for the "special revelations" of "truth, or beauty, or power" that are the prerogative of infancy.

Childhood, therefore, in the midst of its intellectual weakness, and sometimes even by means of this weakness, enjoys a limited privilege of strength. The heart in this season of life is apprehensive; and, where its sensibilities are profound, is endowed with a special power of listening for the tones of truth – hidden, struggling, or remote . . . That mighty silence which infancy is thus privileged by nature and by position to enjoy, co-operates with another source of power – almost peculiar to youth and youthful circumstances – which Wordsworth also was the first person to notice. It belongs to a profound experience of the relations subsisting between ourselves and nature – that not always are we called upon to seek; sometimes, and in childhood above all, we are sought. (*M* 1:121–22)

Childhood is to adulthood as Hazlitt is to Coleridge: the weaker party listens; the adult or the genius speaks. Not *seeking*, for this is an act of the undeveloped "discursive understanding" (*M* 11:54), the child is called by a voice too pure for the coarsened organs of a wiser generation. The child as writer, then, attains the eloquent silence of a reverberating shell, echoing back the "mystical word" (*M* 1:123) whose worth was once known to him alone.

The child's limited privilege is his election, the assurance that Bourdieu calls a natural "nobility" or "capacity for inspired encounters" with the works of nature and the fine arts.[6] Nor is it self-evident that the receiver must be subordinated to the producer, for the "literature of power" teaches, De Quincey claims, "as infancy teaches, – viz. by deep impulse, by hieroglyphic suggestion." Its "teaching is not direct or explicit, but lurking, implicit, masked in deep incarnations" (*M* 11:88). Literature must, as De Quincey writes of his own childhood, be "decipher[ed]" (*C* 113); like subjectivity, it lacks self-transparency. Here the terms of the analogy shift: immaturity is to maturity as literature is to culture at large. The enigmatic infant and the "lurking, implicit" fine arts both communicate "*power*, or deep sympathy with truth. What is the effect, for instance, upon society, of children? . . . A purpose of the same nature is answered by the higher literature, viz. the literature of power" (*M* 11:55).

While De Quincey's revision of the Intimations Ode attributes receptivity to the child, the idea of "impassioned books" as collective prehistory, "like forgotten incidents of . . . childhood," equates infancy and literature as such: both are known in reflex, by their capacity "to *move*" or transfigure the perceptions of the unremembering adult (*M* 11:54, 60). To glimpse the master-light of all our seeing will demand the intervention of an analyst. We might then identify the child-writer with what De Quincey calls "the *minor* key of literature, in opposition to the *major* as cultivated by Shakespere, Spenser, Milton" (*M* 11:61). Minor writing possesses a bifurcated literary identity: on the one hand, as production, it resembles that "*tertium quid*" or "mixed form" in which "threads of direct *instruction* mingle in the texture with . . . threads of *power*" (*M* 11:59); on the other, conceived as reception, it releases the power implicit in major poetry. To carry on the feelings of child-hood, even or especially in the absence of the powers of manhood, would be to preserve one's access to the "unconscious" of genius proper; for, Hazlitt asserts, "no one ever approaches perfection except by stealth, and unknown to themselves."[7]

De Quincey's transvaluation of infantile passivity thus intimates his birthright in what Ortega y Gasset would later call the "espe-cially gifted minority" capable of identifying and responding to great art. "Some possess an organ of understanding which others have been denied," Ortega writes; "the young art helps the 'best' to know and recognize one another in the greyness of the multi-tude and to learn their mission, which is to be few in number and to have to fight against the multitude."[8] The tautology of this account (to be few is to be few) suggests that the figure of the child may be read as a conceptual or ideological pun, conveying a sub-jective disenfranchisement – the minor's thirst for recognition ("one of the miseries of intellectual pretensions," Hazlitt com-plains, "is, that nine-tenths of those you come in contact with do not know whether you are an impostor or not" [*H* 8:284]); his posture of beleaguered solitude; his reluctance to become his "own master" – that belies his objective privilege, the possession of cultural capital. "Taste," writes Hazlitt, "is a luxury for the privi-leged few" (*LM* 2:251 [*H* 12:27]). Bourdieu defines the "aesthetic disposition" as the ability "to maintain for a long time, sometimes a whole lifetime, a child's relation to the world." His point has less to do with the alleged virtues of children than with a mystified class relation toward the "adult" possessors of *economic* capital. What Bourdieu calls, based on its "essentialism," the "aristocracy of culture" announces itself in the interchangeable tropes of preco-city and anachronism; "aristocracy is the form par excellence of precocity since it is nothing other than the seniority which is the birthright of the offspring of ancient families."[9] (De Quincey traced his "aristocratic" family name to the Norman invasion [*M* 3:457–59]).

Aristocrats neither in law nor in letters, De Quincey, Lamb, and Hazlitt were paid writers in a milieu, the periodical industry, which represented criticism both as extra-judicial court (Francis Jeffrey, William Gifford) and as the unproductive play of the *Blackwood's* writers' "youthful indiscretions" and the "Academy of Taste for Grown Gentlemen, or The Infant Connoisseur's Go-Cart" instituted by that "Bucolical Juvenile" Janus Weathercock (*LM* 2:88, 2:510, 6:445). The conceit of juvenilia reinforces one pole of these symmetrical misrecognitions, through a symbolic self-embalming that preserves the writer in the state of "promise" rather than fulfillment. The magazines, so influential in shaping the modern conception of professional authorship, also marked the obsolescence of the classical career with its orientation toward the epic – then still viable for the book-market author, as Wordsworth's career attests.[10] De Quincey never produced the *magnum opus* he intermittently promised, and the only writings for which he tendered high claims were his works-in-regress, the *Confessions* and *Suspiria*. Even so, he made "haughtier pretensions in right of their *conception* than . . . their *execution*" (*M* 1:14; De Quincey's emphasis). The gesture bears comparison with Lamb's rejection of "the man, Elia" for "the child Elia – that 'other me,' there in the background." "I do not want to be weaned by age," Elia complains; and so "I turn back upon memory, and adopt my own early idea, as my heir and favorite" (*LM* 3:6 [*E* 32–34]). Promoting the "idea" above its textual embodiment as the "heir" to the empirical person, the writer canonizes the child as the emblem for discontinuity and compression, "sketch" and "essay."

Thus while the evaluative terms "minor" – and "talent" – are to some extent synonymous with "journalism," a sub-literary discourse destined "to be immediately consumed and forgotten,"[11] the minor as (dwarfed or arrested) *figure* construes limitation at once as his exemption from purely commercialist dictates and as a crypto-scholarly blindness and insight: the contradictory union of empirical attentiveness and its transcendence by inspired intuition. Hazlitt boasts, with characteristically double-edged irony, that he is "just able to admire those literal touches of observation and description, which persons of loftier pretensions overlook and despise" (*LM* 3:132 [*H* 12:226]). The child's "specific power of contemplating" the fleeting and the evanescent (*C* 127) supplies De Quincey's touchstone for the viability of a lesser literary genre, the reminiscence, "pretend[ing] to little beyond that sort of amusement which attaches to any real story, thoughtfully and faithfully related" (*M* 1:9). The journalist's *mere* empiricism even furnishes the occasion to invert Coleridge's standards altogether, as when, facing an alleged deficit of new material to review, the *London*'s Drama critic (Hazlitt) proposes,

Now would be the time for Mr. Coleridge to turn his talents to account, and write for the stage, when there is no topic to confine his pen, or "constrain his genius by mastery." "With mighty wings outspread, his imagination might brood over the void and make it pregnant" . . . He is the man of all others to swim on empty bladders in a sea, without shore or soundings: to drive an empty stage-coach without passengers or lading, and arrive behind his time; to write marginal notes without a text . . . Alas! we have no such creative talents: we cannot amplify, expand, raise our flimsy discourse, as the gaseous matter fills and lifts the round, glittering, slow-sailing balloon, to "the up-turned eyes of wondering mortals." (*LM* 2:687 [*H* 18:369–70])

A telling satire on the "self-sufficing power of absolute Genius," Hazlitt's portrait of the gaseous Coleridge unmasks imagination as a hoax: the humble reporter implies his ethical superiority to the obsessive monologist. Yet the idea of modesty as self-restraint depends for its honorific meaning on the concept of inflation; moreover, the passage is itself an example of the digressive filler it criticizes. The journalist cannot simply be situated at the opposite pole from genius; in some ways he represents its parody. One might recall the frequent complaints of De Quincey's "diffuseness, want of concentration," and digressiveness; his "extraordinary incidence of narrative repetition"; his "exaggerations, forced emphases, bizarre points of view, and all the other stimulants that the journalist uses."[12] Though the notion of genius undoubtedly includes among its ideological motivations the task of distinguishing journalism from high literature, Hazlitt's portrait suggests that this impulse may come from below as well as above: the brilliant windbag cuts a figure enabling a cautious and ironized claim of *professional* conscientiousness.

The epithet "minor," then, rectifies the pejorative connotations of periodical text (which becomes the truthful, spontaneous sketch); offers a variant on the aesthetic of fragmentation (with its promise of transcendence); suggests a name for "prose" that links it genetically with "poetry" (both are literature, not information); and designates a creative mode of consumption that *supplements* the work of form. At the same time, and somewhat incongruously, the figure of the minor incarnates the professionalist ethos which found its first expression in Coleridge's systematic attempt, in the *Biographia Literaria,* to wed the fortunes of poetic genius to its critical augury.[13] Both these (competing) modes of inscription imply that minority should be understood as one aspect of the "auto-production of the Work-Subject," or a point in the constellation of authorship.[14] Neither foil nor mirror, the minor *produces* majority. The canonical Coleridge, for example, may be understood as the real impersonation of Hazlitt's rhetorical balloonist; the satirical description, part of the "context" through which we read Coleridge's poetry, is more accurately viewed as Coleridgean text than as testimony to an autonomous effect. Hazlitt's prose, one might say, *is* Coleridge's "canonicity," a term that designates the form of the text's transmission. While this insight both relies on and corroborates Guillory's account of canon-formation, its derivation from Romantic dialectics permits a more specialized attention than Guillory's to the various modalities of canonical presence, to the relation between these taxonomies and the constitution of "periods," and to the homologies between literary subjectivity (or ideological "content") and the *forms* of institutional transmission.

My final section on "The Secret History" attempts to address one of these problems – the particularity of a canonical mode – without reintroducing the binarisms of inclusion and exclusion which Guillory has persuasively debunked.[15] For now we may notice how the author-function reifies *both* Coleridge's singularity *and* the essayist's clear-sightedness. Associated for the Romantics with periodical prose, this corrective stance would by the twentieth century be more narrowly identified with what F. R. Leavis called the "minority culture" of the university, where Eliot's "minor poet," charged with preserving "the continuity of literature," is transmuted into the academic critic.[16] The widening of dialectical antagonisms into institutional divisions begins, I suggest, in the minor Romantic's identification, against all empirical measures, with a purified version of reading that occludes its own *writing* as prose. Lamb, as Mary Jacobus observes, "is of all writers the most self-confessedly bookish"; Hazlitt, perhaps the most allusive, wins fame and the epithet "mind of a critic" for his biographical series *The Spirit of the Age*; De Quincey proposes himself as "*praegustatore*" (pre-taster), or "vicarious reader for the public" (*M* 11:53).[17] The professionalism that originates in the self-division of the minor persists in the generic shorthand of academic "readings," or, more precisely, reproductions.

THE SECRET HISTORY

It is no news that any account of minority must entail a critique of canon-formation, yet whatever their disparate agendas, the most influential theorists of this issue have assumed an essentially static view of the canon as a device of (objective or subjective) domination. Regardless of the case in point, minor writing can only appear, in such a view, as a version of marginality, with the givenness of the canon substituting for the givenness of social relations.[18] This assumption forces David Lloyd into the contradictory claims that "the primary feature of" any minor literature "is its exclusion from the canon," even while "this literature [must] remain in an oppositional relationship to the canon and the state from which it has been excluded." By this account, the minor work must have been excluded before it came into existence, its critical energies driven by the judgment it presupposes. The ontology of the canon, in turn, recapitulates the imperative that "the [major] work . . . be autonomous," just as it should be "in some manner directed toward the production of an autonomous ethical identity for the subject."[19] Elided by this homology is an account of "the effect of monumentalization by which a canon of works confronts an author over against the contemporary social conditions of literary production."[20] The "autonomy" of the literary work, however thematically overdetermined, is finally an effect of its *transmission*, which resurfaces in Lloyd's suggestive list of the minor's "writing strategies," including parody, translation, and citation, that are "defined by their dependence on prior texts."[21] Lloyd's conflation of "unanxious" intertextuality with (political) opposition does not obscure the perceptions that invest the category of the minor with more specificity than Guillory's analysis, by itself, permits. In the brief rehearsals that follow, therefore, I will focus primarily on the insights that may be abstracted from the very different orientations these theorists represent.

Deleuze and Guattari begin their manifesto, *Kafka: Toward a Minor Literature*, with the claim that "only the possibility of setting up a minor practice of major literature from within allows one to define popular literature, marginal literature, and so on."[22] The terms of their argument suggest both a provocative reading of De Quincey and a clarifying contrast with the account of transmission sketched in the last section. The ambiguously literary Opium-Eater might indeed be described as a "machine-man" or "becoming-minor" that "hate[s] all languages of masters." The characteristics of such "a minor, or revolutionary, literature" are threefold: its "language is affected with a high coefficient of deterritorialization"; "everything in [it] is political"; and "everything takes on a collective value."[23] Posed at this level of abstraction, the Deleuzian critique implies the political endorsement, as "desiring machine," of the demonized and pathologized Opium-Eater: his text marks "a collective [magazine] enunciation," and therefore "a movement from the individual [author] to . . . a collective multiplicity"; it is identified by "a deterritorialization of the mouth, the tongue and the teeth." The addict's self-starvation and "debauches of opium" represent a variation on the "permanent obsession with food" and fasting that signals the competition between content and expression in Kafka; the Piranesian scene of reproduction evokes "machines that dismantle into gears, gears that make up a machine in turn."[24]

Deleuze and Guattari's notion that Kafka "kills all metaphor" to neutralize representation or *meaning* might be extended into a defense of the derivativeness, speciousness, or hollow ingenuity many readers have lamented in De Quincey. In losing "meaning" and "originality," De Quincey meets the condition that language stop "*being representative in order to now move toward its extremities or its limits.*"[25] These limits are dramatized, in De Quincey as in Kafka, by a fetishism of the signifier: while Kafka's "language torn from sense . . . no longer finds its value in anything but an accenting of the word, an inflection," De Quincey compares literary style to musical structure, praising "the iteration and ingemination of a given effect" (*M* 10:136) exemplified in the "Dream-Fugue" of "The English Mail-Coach."[26] "Impassioned prose," no less than poetry, demands intricate rhythmical variations, "as [his] Alcaics and

Choriambics remain to testify" (*C* 132). Such a perverse elevation of technics over substance can be construed as the trace of a linguistic deterritorialization and as the formal counterpart of the drive toward becoming-*child*, or minor. Finally, De Quincey's complacent mastery of English idioms and the learned tongues might be seen as the symmetrical complement of Kafka's alienated relation to his written language, insofar as both writers *thematize* their investments in linguistic capital.[27] Thus De Quincey the Tory pariah, and Kafka the obscure bureaucrat, may both be made instrumental for a critique that eschews opposition for subversion from within.

At this point, however, the comparison founders on its own formal success. While the Deleuzian reading offers an "intensive" De Quincey, a full appropriation must surely devolve into aestheticism – valorizing, as *ipso facto* "revolutionary," a thematic deconstruction of the subject and a preoccupation with the artifactuality of language. If "minor" is taken to have any institutional content for Deleuze and Guattari – a questionable idea, given Kafka's undoubted fame – a revaluation along these lines might simply establish what Guillory calls "alternative canons – canons of the non-canonical," pedagogic constructions which, as he notes, "do not escape the formal features of canonicity."[28] Further, the Deleuzian association of minority, avant-gardism, and revolution might have the effect of justifying an ossified syllabus by pseudo-political criteria, a well-established practice of late twentieth-century criticism.[29] Indeed, the attempt to translate Deleuze and Guattari's analysis points out its peculiarity as a critical gesture. Either they regard Kafka as "intrinsically noncanonical . . . intrinsically antihegemonic," or the "minor" writer simply gives a name to their larger antioedipal project.[30] To escape this kind of circularity, the critic must avoid too readily conflating literary institutions (including "meaning") with social institutions (including the autonomous subject), lest the vehicle of critique become an all-purpose icon of "subversion." Thus, while I argue for a kind of deterritorialization in De Quincey, the implications of his resistance to Wordsworth's politics (for example) may not be construed into an "antihegemonic" stance *per se*.

The question then recurs: is it possible to imagine a *textual* identity, valued relationally, that is also ineluctably minor? Though this idea puts a good deal of stress on what is admittedly "an undeconstructed critical category," De Quincey's minority must be defined quantitatively, not merely qualitatively, if it is to be viewed in its significance for the ideology of the canon.[31] "Can one," to re-echo Leslie Brisman, "wish to be small" and "succeed *in a small* *way?*" Further, "can the image of diminutive stature impel, and not merely mark a diminishment in, creative process?" Brisman's avatar of minority is George Darley, an English poet of the 1830s and 1840s now chiefly remembered for a few "small, sometimes exquisite lyrics." "Darley's smallness," Brisman argues,

> is not merely a judgment of literary history or a painful realization in the history of the poet's own consciousness; it is a *seminal* theme . . . Underlying Darley's best work is what we might call a myth of weakness: that the poet is of diminutive scale, and that he stands as a minor to the major or full-grown poets before him.[32]

The canon is the poet's myth writ large, just as literary history confirms the dependency and parasitism thematized in De Quincey. For Brisman, though, Darley's diminutive scale constitutes an authentic recognition of belatedness – modernity *is* minority – that, troped in the allegedly dialectical pairs early vs. late, great vs. small, and active vs. passive, paradoxically becomes a

> *generation* of poetic voice. The turn from the mighty to the mild is a generational turn, embodying Darley's myth of his own genesis. He derives his originality from this posture of weakness and makes it his "virtue" – his power – to confront smiling rather than frowning forms.[33]

Brisman's Darley weakly acquiesces to linear time, sinning against the Bloomian imperative of misprision, yet converts this very weakness into a powerful revisionary ratio. In Brisman's view, the generational turn finally insures that Darley's is not weak poetry, but poetry *about* weakness. As Renza comments, the quest for diminution must fall short if Brisman's reading is to succeed.[34] By devoting forty pages of *Romantic Origins* to a reading of Darley, that is, Brisman commits the poet to critical resuscitation within a model of literary history in which the minor is thinkable only as the *opposite* of majority, rather than as its generic double or its invisible condition.[35] A truly minor poet would be a forgotten poet, rather than, like De Quincey, the dark interpreter of the majors.

Nonetheless, Darley's poetics of miniaturization present a number of instructive parallels with De Quincey. Darley may be described as an ethical emblem of the minor: what the small poet loses in "voice," he gains by transforming "an experiential anxiety into literary event." Thus Darley, like De Quincey, "retains his prime identity as derivative," though not as "masochistic," in the gendered "We Are Seven" sense.[36] Darley's derivativeness, however stoically recognized, must always be cause for anxiety, rather than an enabling condition or an occasion of textual pleasure. A masochistic myth of genesis, by contrast, would construe the discovery of temporality as an explicitly erotic event, in which "power" identifies *both* the source of pleasure *and* the subjective sensation. In the fantasy of election – Brisman's model of literary history – the choice of an object does not, of course, presume its greatness-for-itself (whatever that might mean), nor does fantasy require an extra-fantastic statement of consent: the precursor is generated, as such, in the subject's ravishment. (Masochism is the domain of erotic freedom par excellence, since the sadist's very refusal to act sadistically – as in the Semele episode of the *Lake Reminiscences* – can itself be interpreted as a source of painful satisfaction.) De Quincey imagines such a possibility in the "bonds of connection" that "typify the affinity betwixt metrical and prose composition," a relation whose principle of "similitude in dissimilitude" is linked for Wordsworth with the origin of "the sexual appetite" (*PrW* 1:135, 149).

Such a redoubling of binary genres may certainly be constructed as a genealogy. Prose, "the one great intellectual machine of civil life," *attends* poetry, in the dual sense of following and protecting (*M* 10:171). Its modernity, however, constitutes proof of originality rather than belatedness; it is a "celebrated thing" (*M* 10:169). "Originally, and whilst man was in his primitive condition of simplicity," De Quincey explains,

it must have seemed an unnatural, nay an absurd, thing to speak in prose ... At first ... it is mere nature which prompts metre. Afterwards, as truth begins to enlarge itself – as truth loses something of its sanctity by descending amongst human details – that mode of exalting it, and of courting attention, is dictated by artifice, which originally was a mere necessity of nature raised above herself. For these reasons, it is certain that men challenging high authentic character will continue to speak by metre for many generations after it has ceased to be a mere voice of habitual impulse. Whatsoever claims an oracular authority will take the ordinary external form of an oracle ... Those people are, therefore, mistaken who imagine that prose is either a natural or a possible form of composition in early states of society . . . Prose . . . strange as it may seem to say so, was something of a discovery. (*M* 10:171–73)

While the descent from impassioned poetry to the light of common day might seem to condemn prose once again to a problematic of inferiority, De Quincey does not distinguish it typologically from poetic language. It differs, rather, as generations of the same species differ, or as genders differ. Poetry's coquettish way of "courting attention," like a woman "raised above herself," converts into the masculine "oracular authority" that loves, needs and recognizes an heir who, in turn, lovingly preserves the continuity of the inheritance. What prose loses in "high authentic character" it gains in extension, without the stigma of "artifice" that attaches to the anachronistic use of "exalted" forms or "poetic diction." The prose writer is original in the sense of "stand[ing] close to origins" while "feel[ing] that a more original power is being diffused *through* him," and beyond him: this is the sexuality of reproduction.[37]

The Darleyan response to literary history is an essentialist one; like Harold Bloom's and his ephebe Brisman's, it consists of fathers and sons on the two sides of an immutable historical divide. The "old tremendous dead" are forces of nature, begotten, not made; they may "smile" at the diminished modern, but they never compromise their mythic autonomy.[38] De Quincey discovers, instead, that the daughter's seduction is "father" of the canon: literary precursors are not precursors *until* they have begotten, just as the fact of a child defines the condition of fatherhood. If we change registers, De Quincey's figures of minority present several departures for a sociological critique of Bloomian "influence," beginning with the question of form itself: "prose," as the narrative of "Style" implies, is another name for what Bakhtin calls "literary language," the matrix of generic mutation. Darley's belatedness might be regarded, from a sociolinguistic perspective, as his resistance to a vernacular program that achieved its widest dispersion in the prose forms of the periodical essay and the novel. The poetic canon's monumentality, De Quincey further suggests, may be seen as the displacement of quite another threat: the technological advances that multiply the "growing weight of books" into "an unmanageable excess," and that produce a correspondingly large and amorphous readership (*M* 11:52–53).

To this flood of information, the literature of power opposes "a Jacob's ladder from earth to mysterious altitudes above the earth."[39] Discerning "selection" is troped as an escape from the mathematical to the dynamical sublime, from "a million separate items . . . on the same plane" to the gigantic "ancients" towering over them (*M* 11:56). If the promiscuous hack would seem the information glut's worst symptom, as "vicarious reader" he basks in the half-created glory of his perceptions: the canon's autonomy, in this view, is the fiction that *allows* more "power" to be produced.

De Quinceyan minority is a relationship of mutual generation with majority. Unlike Brisman's Darley, De Quincey neither self-immolates nor achieves the negative truth of belatedness, because – represented as the context and test-case of great writing – he is inscribed in the history of genius as a mystified version of "contemporary social conditions." His autobiographies, the literary lives of a man of letters, constitute identity as the allegory of reading. The mere fact of literary admiration, as Guillory insists, "does nothing in itself to preserve th[e] work, unless that judgment is made in a certain institutional context, a setting in which it is possible to insure the *reproduction* of the work, its continual reintroduction to generations of readers."[40] The short term for this setting is in De Quincey's case "the magazines," but the more telling context I have been articulating is the *Romantic* institution of the institution's absence, whether it be imagined as an untutored child or as an architecture of the mind. De Quincey's institutional authority derives from his apparent exemption – as autodidact, immethodical autobiographer, and equivocally literary author of "impassioned prose" – from the provincialism of the schools and the ephemerality of mere knowledge.

A last glimpse of this reader's life will retrace the figures of his autotelic institution. In one of his later *Lake Reminiscences*, for example, De Quincey recounts the tragedy of George and Sarah Green, the subjects of an unpublished poem by Wordsworth and also of Dorothy Wordsworth's "George and Sarah Green, A Narrative." Such an overloaded theme would induce repression in a Bloomian strong poet, but De Quincey responds by ironizing narrative repetition – not only textualizing the story's setting, but gratuitously "remind[ing]" the reader of the "memorial stanzas" that he was first to print. The Greens, writes De Quincey, lived in the "little valley of Easedale," a "little area" containing "small fields," "a little, sparkling, pebbly 'beck' . . . not too broad for a child's flying leap," a "little mountain lake," "little hedge-rows," and "miniature fields, running up like forest glades into miniature woods," from which "little columns of smoke" are sent up in silence by the "two or three picturesque cottages" among them (*R* 249–51). As toylike as anything in Darley, De Quincey's description of Easedale evokes a parodically diminished "Tintern Abbey." The picture of the mind is domesticated, commodified, and reduced to a figure of intertextuality; Easedale

is a chamber within a chamber, or rather a closet within a chamber – a chapel within a cathedral – a little private oratory within a chapel. For Easedale is, in fact, a dependancy of Grasmere – a little recess lying within the same general basin of mountains . . . There is one door into it from the Grasmere side; but that door is hidden; and on every other quarter there is no door at all . . . Such is the solitude . . . so rich in miniature beauty – of Easedale. (*R* 251–53)

"There are no miniatures in nature," Susan Stewart observes; "the miniature is a cultural product, the product of an eye performing certain operations."[41] A place, like a poet, can only look small in comparison with something else. Easedale is a miniature *Grasmere*, a dollhouse "dependancy" of Dove Cottage and the mythology of Wordsworth. De Quincey's text, therefore, bears the same relation to Wordsworth's "as the ante-chapel has to the body of a gothic church," or as "the little cells, oratories, and sepulchral recesses" might bear to that chapel (*PW* 589). Its connection with "Wordsworth" becomes, in the poet's terms, as inevitable as the transition from the *Prelude* to *The Excursion*. This palimpsest, moreover, not only preserves but resurrects the ballad Wordsworth himself never printed (*R* 268–69; also see *PW* 487). The obscurity of Easedale signifies De Quincey's special insight into the construction of Wordsworth's career. "A lurking paradise" (*R* 252), Easedale is De Quincey's little secret: a "daydream of life inside life, of significance multiplied infinitely *within* significance."[42] The little place, moreover, supplies the aesthetic "measure" by means of which, as Kant observes, we approximate the idea of the "*absolutely great*," or sublime (*K* 86). Correspondingly, the *Lake Reminiscences* accrue a density of meaning that demands an allusive, literary decoding, to which Wordsworth supplies the master-key. The introduction of a new scene also implies that the larger valley cannot close upon itself: Easedale pictures the logic of supplementarity, whereby one representation grounds another. The major text can always sponsor a satellite. Finally, the mystique of secrecy and limited access created by a "sufficient partition" (*R* 252) between the two valleys suggests how textuality as copia devolves into text as property – or, in Guillory's terms, how the history of literature becomes "a history of writers and not of *writing*."[43]

De Quincey anticipates the Easedale effect in his memorial essay on Coleridge, with its explicit reference to the problem of literary transmission. Interrupting his account of Coleridge's residence in the lakes, De Quincey turns to the *inner* narrative of "a romantic and somewhat tragical affair" which had drawn "the eyes of all England" some thirty years ago, when Coleridge, then writing for the *Morning Post*, "unintentionally furnished the original clew for unmasking the base impostor who figured as the foremost actor in this tale" (*R* 66–67). The plight of the Maid of Buttermere, serially unfolded in Coleridge's articles on "Romantic Marriage," was later incorporated into Book Seventh of the *Prelude* and retailed in several popular novels and melodramas. Hardly virgin territory, this story calls up another miniature, "one of the most secluded Cumberland valleys, so little visited previously, that it might be described almost as an undiscovered chamber of that romantic district" (*R* 67). The notion of an "undiscovered" work presents a quintessential scholarly paradox; how can something *printed* be unknown? "Other generations," De Quincey answers, "have arisen since that time, who must naturally be unacquainted with the circumstances; and, on their account, I shall here recall them" (*R* 67). Coleridge's journalistic scoop is less imposing "original" than pretext for repetition; as the fate of *The Friend* sadly showed, "printed" is not synonymous with "published," or only in the sense that "it had been well for the unfortunate author, if it had remained in manuscript" (*BL* 1:175; *R* 79–82). *The Friend* stood in need of an "*Enemy* . . . to follow . . . in the wake of its leader" and force it "out into a large display" (*R* 305). True publicity requires *re*publication, here naturalized by the appeal to "generations." A learned elder addressing "youthful mind[s]" on the esoteric "productions of [his] contemporary genius" (*BL* 1:12), De Quincey articulates a *pedagogic* relation to the readership of *Tait's*.[44] In scholarly research, as in literary invention, the imperative of originality is wedded to the rhythm of dialectical return.

De Quincey's version of the tale, in which a rustic beauty is seduced by a bigamous forger, centers on a fantasy that associates the heroine with "the little mountain chapel of Buttermere," where her false marriage may or may not have taken place. "If it were," De Quincey speculates,

> I persuade myself that the most hardened villain must have felt a momentary pang on violating the altar of such a chapel, so touchingly does it express, by its miniature dimensions, the almost helpless humility of that little pastoral community . . . It is not only the very smallest chapel by many degrees in all England, but is so mere a toy in outward appearance, that, were it not for its antiquity . . . the first movement of a stranger's feelings would be towards loud laughter; for the little chapel looks not so much a mimic chapel in a drop scene from the Opera House, as a miniature copy from such a scene. (*R* 69)

De Quincey's fetish of the very smallest chapel, with its implicit contrast to the *Biographia*'s image of "one of our largest Gothic cathedrals" (*BL* 1:301), initially reads as joke directed at De Quincey himself, the miniature edition of Coleridge who studies "in the same track" (*R* 40) and rehashes the great man's ideas in essay after essay. Yet the Kantian "contempt, for what we simply call 'small'" is easily reversed, for the identification with minuteness suggests the position of the *subject* from whose perspective the natural world appears large, and whose "attitude of thought . . . introduces sublimity into" the object which, great or small, possesses no such quality in itself (*K* 84–88). If the Coleridgean cathedral offers a conventionally sublime set-piece, the epithet applies more strictly to the reader small enough to fit inside a chapel and unfold its allusive intertextual details. Further, the image of a copy *from a copy* directs the reader's laughter away from the De Quinceyan replica toward the very mythology of belatedness as diminishment: De Quincey's text may be a repetition, but Coleridge's earlier version is only "a mimic chapel in a drop scene," representation rather than source. The reflexive or "theatrical" quality of the miniature reminds future exegetes that it is reproduction which creates origins, the continuity of culture which demands the fiction of nature.[45] Yet the generational metaphor that sponsors De Quincey's text also bounds and qualifies the potential for tertiary commentary: De Quincey, Coleridge's heir *within* the text, is a credentialed authority as other mere readers are not. Like the tragedy of the Greens, this story tells

242 De Quincey's Romanticism

how it is produced by, and reproduces, its Romantic conventions.

The allegory of reading glosses itself in the passage, discussed earlier, where De Quincey describes the "flash of sublime revelation" transmitted to him from the Boy of Winander (*R* 161). Beginning from the aestheticization of his response, De Quincey goes on to theorize that response as the subject of the poem. Its "very object," he writes,

> is not the first or initial stage of the boy's history – the exercise of skill which led him, as an occasion, into a rigid and tense effort of attention – not this, but the second stage, the consequence of that attention. Even the attention was an effect, a derivative state; but the second stage, upon which the poet fixes his object, is an effect of that effect; and it is clear that the original notice of the boy's talent is introduced only as a *conditio sine qua non* – a notice without which a particular result (namely, the tense attention of expectation) could not have been made intelligible; as, again, without this result being noticed, the reaction of that action could quite as little have been made intelligible. Else, and but for this conditional and derivative necessity, but for this dependency of the essential circumstances upon the boy's power of mimicry, it is evident that the "accomplishment" – which Lord Jeffrey so strangely supposes to have been the main object of the poet in recording the boy, and the main subject of his reverie by the side of his grave – never would have been noticed. (*R* 162)

De Quincey's ridicule works to disqualify an interpretation with a certain *prima facie* appeal: the boy's mimetic "talent" may be understood as a figure of Romanticism in its weak sense as nature-poetry. For De Quincey, the poem proper begins at the "second stage," when the joyful noise of production is silenced to permit a reflection, or reception, conditioned upon a "rigid and tense effort of attention." In this paradoxical moment of tense reverie, prefiguring the New Critical emphasis on "close reading" and the de Manian requirement of "rigor," the boy is translated from the position of poet to *institutional* reader, prepared by his strenuous disciplinary training for a rarified experience which De Quincey cannot explain in essential terms.[46] Thus the "original notice" of natural correspondence is revealed as a critical fiction, posited to ground the effect of reading and, more pointedly, of a particular kind of reader. De Quincey wins the poem from Jeffrey the way all great critics do, by turning a previous reading on its head. And while the boy's class still apparently has a text – he perceives a "visible scene," the spectacle of "that uncertain heav'n received/

Into the bosom of the steady lake" (*R* 161) – De Quincey reads this text as a "reaction of" the boy's own "action," or attention. At this point, De Quincey replaces the boy as the subject of the poem: the "very expression . . . by which space and its infinities are attributed to the human heart," he writes, "has always struck *me* as with a flash of sublime revelation" (*R* 161; my emphasis).

In the accession of power experienced by the reader, De Quincey recognizes his "possession," a text that may now be called "De Quinceyan" (*M* 10:48–49). While the "essential circumstance" of a reader would seem to depend upon the prior circumstance of a text (and therefore of an author), De Quincey discovers with Kant that the poem consists in "our own state of mind in the estimation of it" (*K* 94), and with Freud that the literary object displays the ontology of a primal scene. Literature is a way of reading – itself, paradoxically, a "derivative state." It is the textualized "effect of that effect," however – the reactive reinscription of the origin – that confers "intelligib[ility]" on revelation. Thus Wordsworth's poem *carries* De Quincey from his reading to the instruction of later generations, and in particular my own, that the subject of the poem is the act of critical reflection it induces.

Insofar as De Quincey's text is conditional and derivative, Wordsworth must be original, but that "notice" serves here not to derogate but to justify its further reproduction. If the concept of literary tradition, to invoke T. S. Eliot's terms, requires a cognate notion of original talent, so criticism (a department of the institution of schooling) exacts the original notice of a tradition worth defense. Such a notice, I suggest, may be found in De Quincey's antithetical defense of Wordsworth. Wordsworth's canonical majority is performed in the *Lake Reminiscences* by De Quincey's sublime experience, "a quasi-creative power which sets the aesthete apart from the common herd by a radical difference which seems to be inscribed in 'persons.'"[47] De Quincey claims his authorial property in the name of this power, which, migrating to the text of his "reading," identifies both his canonical privilege and his minority. We may then reaffirm with Guillory that canonicity is "a property" of the work's transmission, but we must now add that this institutional effect can never be disentangled from the "work itself." This work, the *iterable* work of formal closure, is the material trace of a reproduction whose surplus value precipitates (or fragments) into *Reminiscences*. Wordsworth's "Boy" fathers not only De

Quincey, but the Romantic form of disciplinary English, with what Guillory has dubbed its supplementary "canon of theory."[48]

By this account, the canon is a burgeoning but self-divided entity resembling the New Critical "concrete universal," a poem which, as Frances Ferguson summarizes, was "continually expanding, through an understanding of reception that incorporated reception into the text itself." The minor, I have been arguing, prefigures this view of interpretation as "a multiplying double of the literary work, the multiple other self to its [imaginary] physical unity" – a view which is in fact correlative with the *literary* canon "itself."[49] It is worth emphasizing that the De Quinceyan allegory of transmission takes nothing away from the poem (how could it?), whatever crimes De Quincey may have committed against mere mortals. Such a claim would merely invert the Kantian "subreption" or cheat, returning the sublimity usurped by distinguished readers to some reified greatness-in-itself.[50] As Guillory shows, one effect of post-Romantic literary instruction has been to do just this. De Quincey's sublime pedagogy represents less of an alternative to this mystique than a transvaluation of it: the expression of awe for the poem becomes interchangeable with awe for the reader, masochistic defeat with proud vaunting of the soul.

Every restatement, though, marks the beginning of a difference. While the minor by no means threatens the *subversion* of Romantic majority, he nonetheless offers a point of access to the *divisions* within the poetic institution and its academic double. The ideology of the canon, we may observe, builds in its own set of resistances. If "becoming-minor" must finally be seen as a critical fiction, "becoming-canonical" is, subjectively speaking, an impossibility too. The focus on the minor allows us to perceive the vulnerability and the mutual inconsistencies of such canonical tenets as prescriptive influence and intrinsic value, formal and authorial autonomy, voice and representativeness. But further, while these Romantic fictions may be consolidated by an abjection of reading, the case of De Quincey suggests that they sponsor an *interest* in their exposure. Though we cannot opt out of this dialectic at will, we may conclude with the fiction of a glimpse at the minor's "unconscious," and whatever faint traces it may offer to resistant scrutiny. The text comes from a passage in the *Logic* where De Quincey glosses Ricardo's "doctrine of rent." Revising his earlier accounts of "dependencies," De Quincey explains that increasing population dictates the use of progressively worse land for agriculture; rent is the difference (measured in produce) between one quality of land and a less productive one.

> Here is, at first sight, a perplexing question . . . There is a singular delusion which takes place here. Because the increment takes place on occasion of the inferior soil being called up, there is a natural *subreptio intellectus*, a hasty impression left on the mind that the inferior soil actually causes the increment – actually *produces* the addition which becomes available for rent. So far from that, so far from adding anything, every descent of this kind upon a lower soil *takes away* something. It *seems* to add – and for the landlord's benefit it *does* add – for it makes *that* a portion of his share which previously had been the share of other people. But, *absolutely* (that is, in relation to the *aggregate* claims of capitalist, farmer, labourer), this increment is manifestly a decrement, and never anything else. Fast as these increments travel *westwards* on the diagram, exactly in that ratio does the residuum – the portion available for the other shares on the land – grow ever narrower and narrower. (*M* 9:244–45)

To turn from the domain of reading back to the economy is to see the analytic of the sublime revised. The *subreptio intellectus* – the reader's self-deceit – has less to do with a misplaced "respect" for external things (*K* 96) than with a complicitous blindness to the landlord's disproportionate gains. If Ricardo's landlord may be equated with the canonical text, the minor or "inferior" writer's incorporation *seems* to "produce [an] addition" to poetic grandeur – and where the author-function is concerned, this is undoubtedly true. The motif of self-robbery or self-stunting has its economic corollary, however, in the effect of making the text more "expensive," that is, of demanding greater and greater investments of educational capital from subsequent readers. Since De Quincey, the Romantic reader needs "a far greater culture," as Kant puts it (*K* 104), to encounter textualized sophistication with a corresponding nuance. For some readers, this sophistication is embodied by the latter-day literature of knowledge, which, in Thomas McFarland's plangent complaint, "overwhelms" the poetic object "by repetition and exponentially increasing commentary," until "what used to be forms definingly related to other forms are . . . transformed to a congeries of unrelated and self-referential shapes." But this scenario, recapitulating De Quincey's in "The Poetry of Pope," merely scapegoats as "secondary" the history of transmission as such, with its absorption of "commentary" into the power of the original "form." More intimidating, perhaps, is the poetic form which has so naturalized its lessons that it appears, again in McFarland's terms, as the pedagogue's "possession."[51] The argument against commentary, or critical history, is ultimately the same as the argument against the scrutinies of formalism – and both are alike fallacious and reactionary. It is as undesirable to compromise rigor and critical self-consciousness as it is unavailing (and, as such, inappropriate) to attempt mastery of "the canon." "One should of course," as Guillory notes, "read as much as one can," and with as much power and subtlety as one can muster.[52]

Missing from McFarland's account of reading, as from De Quincey's, is a credible version of the social as anything but distraction – and this is the silenced presence that reasserts itself in the Ricardian anecdote. Less problematic than the revisionary ratio between older and newer – or superior and inferior – fields of cultivation is the relation between *both* kinds of land and the "aggregate claims" of the economy they found. Similarly, we may say, it is less important whether we regard Wordsworth or Romanticism as single, multiple, or even infinite than that we take account of the tensions, fractures, and fissures consequent on the efforts of writers and readers – first generation, second, or seventh – to make language their own. What the study of the minor text, in itself anything but revolutionary, has to offer this project is an insight into the *madeness* of "cultural forms," and a glimpse at the involutes of ideology, desire, and the sheer waywardness of signification that contribute to their making. Perhaps a practice that attended to these appropriations and deflections might even return to new readers some of the "respect" for their own powers of engagement and resistance, and for the powers of language to resist them in turn, that is the best lesson literary study has to teach. In the minor we may read the allegory of our own elaborated practices, tracing if not their origins at least their interests and investments: to interrogate, not to reverse, the "barbarism of transmission" that is canonical majority itself.[53]

Notes

INTRODUCTION

1 See David Perkins, *Is Literary History Possible?* (Baltimore: Johns Hopkins University Press, 1992), 85–105, for an attempt to historicize the "English Romantic Movement" without considering its prose writers or the major/minor distinction.

2 On "development" as biographical and literary-historical trope, see Clifford Siskin, *The Historicity of Romantic Discourse* (New York: Oxford University Press, 1988), 1–14, 164–78.

3 For a symptomatic account of Romantic prose, see Thomas McFarland, *Romantic Cruxes: The English Essayists and the Spirit of the Age* (Oxford: Clarendon Press, 1987), 15 *passim*.

4 Faced with proof of De Quincey's reliance on "literary source materials in something like sixty percent of his writings," Albert Goldman demotes the unoriginal essayist to the status of "literary journalist" (*The Mine and the Mint: Sources for the Writings of Thomas De Quincey* [Carbondale: Southern Illinois University Press, 1965], 159–60). In *De Quincey's Disciplines* (Oxford: Clarendon Press, 1994), Josephine McDonagh sophisticates this approach, describing De Quincey as "a popularizer and disseminator of other people's ideas" whose work "lies on the interface between pure knowledge and . . . social contexts" (5–6). Criticism of De Quincey's "imaginative prose" has been speared by the opposite horn of this dilemma. V. A. De Luca begins *Thomas De Quincey: The Prose of Vision* (University of Toronto Press, 1980) by apologizing for the paucity of "wholly satisfying works" in De Quincey's corpus of poetry *manqué* (ix-x). Robert Lance Snyder's introduction to Robert Lance Snyder (ed.), *Thomas De Quincey: Bicentenary Studies* (Norman: University of Oklahoma Press, 1981) blames "conventional taxonomy" for De Quincey's "marginal or idiosyncratic" reputation (xix–xx); in the same volume, E. M. Thron suggests that this "minor figure" on "the borders of the canon" illustrates "how Literature is created from a form that is not Literature at all" (3–6, 17). Alina Clej, finally, proposes to cure De Quincey's minority by reclassifying him as "a modernist *avant la lettre*" (*A Genealogy of the*

Modern Self: Thomas De Quincey and the Intoxication of Writing [Stanford: Stanford University Press, 1995], 1).

5 In addition to the works cited above, I refer to the following single-author studies of De Quincey: Edmund Baxter, *De Quincey's Art of Autobiography* (Edinburgh University Press, 1990); John Barrell, *The Infection of Thomas De Quincey: A Psychopathology of Imperialism* (New Haven: Yale University Press, 1991); Charles J. Rzepka, *Sacramental Commodities: Gift, Text, and the Sublime in De Quincey* (Amherst: University of Massachusetts Press, 1995). Also see the chapters or discussions in Mary Jacobus, *Romanticism, Writing, and Sexual Difference: Essays on The Prelude* (Oxford: Clarendon Press, 1989); Annette Wheeler Cafarelli, *Prose in the Age of Poets: Romanticism and Biographical Narrative from Johnson to De Quincey* (Philadelphia: University of Pennsylvania Press, 1990); Joel Black, *The Aesthetics of Murder: A Study in Romantic Literature and Contemporary Culture* (Baltimore: Johns Hopkins University Press, 1991); and Nigel Leask, *British Romantic Writers and the East: Anxieties of Empire* (Cambridge University Press, 1992).

6 See for example Duncan Wu (ed.), *Romanticism: An Anthology* (Oxford: Basil Blackwell, 1994), and Anne K. Mellor and Richard E. Matlak (eds.), *British Literature 1780–1830* (Fort Worth, Texas: Harcourt Brace, 1995). James M. Garrett, in an unpublished statistical study, has shown that while Wordsworth's quantitative representation in popular teaching anthologies has remained relatively constant or even increased since the early twentieth century, De Quincey's has notably declined.

7 Marilyn Butler, "Plotting the Revolution: The Political Narratives of Romantic Poetry and Criticism," in Kenneth R. Johnston, Gilbert Chaitin, Karen Hanson, and Herbert Marks (eds.), *Romantic Revolutions: Criticism and Theory* (Bloomington: Indiana University Press, 1990), 142. Indices to the state of the canon and the teaching profession in Britain include Butler's essay and a recent issue of *Critical Quarterly* (35 [1993]) devoted to the teaching of English.

8 Samuel Weber, *Institution and Interpretation* (Minneapolis: University of Minnesota Press, 1987), 144.

9 For readings that stress De Quincey's "prefiguration" of de Man, see Jacobus, *Romanticism*, 264–66 and Jerome Christensen, "From Rhetoric to Corporate Populism: A Romantic Critique of the Academy in an Age of High Gossip," *Critical Inquiry* 16 (1990): 438–65. Leask claims De Quincey for materialism, arguing that he challenges "the idealism – and voluntarism – of the 'High Romantic argument'" (Leask, *Anxieties*, 170).

10 Gilles Deleuze and Felix Guattari, *Kafka: Toward a Minor Literature*, trans. Dana Polan (Minneapolis: University of Minnesota Press,

1986), 31 and *passim*; Louis A. Renza, *"A White Heron" and the Question of Minor Literature* (Madison: University of Wisconsin Press, 1984), 37–38, 42.

11 Renza, *"White Heron"*, 167, 178.

12 John Guillory, *Cultural Capital: The Problem of Literary Canon Formation* (University of Chicago Press, 1993), 133.

13 Peter T. Murphy, "Climbing Parnassus, and Falling Off," in Mary A. Favret and Nicola J. Watson (eds.), *At the Limits of Romanticism: Essays in Cultural, Feminist, and Materialist Criticism* (Bloomington: Indiana University Press, 1994), 53.

14 One might witness the post-New Critical career of Blake. In this context, Butler's remark that the "exemplary" poet Robert Southey lacks "the dense linguistic texture," "so characteristic of advanced written culture, which invites close reading" ("Plotting," 144–45) helps distinguish the marginal from what Murphy calls the (critically) "boring" non-canonical figure, personified by Samuel Rogers ("Parnassus," 52–55). On the Romantic "prose" standard of literacy, see Guillory, *Cultural Capital*, 124–33.

15 Guillory, *Cultural Capital*, 30.

16 Indeed De Quincey was, with Lamb, among the first English authors to achieve the *institutional* centrality of becoming a university examination text: see Franklin E. Court, *Institutionalizing English Literature: The Culture and Politics of Literary Study, 1750–1900* (Stanford University Press, 1992), 149.

17 Guillory, *Cultural Capital*, 63.

18 Grevel Lindop, "English reviewers and Scotch professors: De Quincey's debts to Edinburgh life and letters," *Times Literary Supplement*, 4839 (29 December 1995), 10.

19 Though the first professorship in English literature was not established until 1828, by the end of the century English held a prominent place in British university education. On this transformation, see Gerald Graff, *Professing Literature: An Institutional History* (University of Chicago Press, 1987), 19–80, and Court, *Institutionalizing*; on the periodicals as institutions that fostered a specifically literary "reading habit," see Jon P. Klancher, *The Making of English Reading Audiences, 1790–1832* (Madison: University of Wisconsin Press, 1987), 1–52, 135–70.

20 Philippe Lacoue-Labarthe and Jean-Luc Nancy, *The Literary Absolute: The Theory of Literature in German Romanticism*, trans. Philip Barnard and Cheryl Lester (Albany: State University of New York Press, 1988), 111–17.

21 For an opposing view of De Quinceyan belatedness, see Clej, *Genealogy*, 212–67.

22 Lacoue-Labarthe and Nancy, *Literary Absolute*, 111.

23 The alternatives of "origin" and "reception" are sketched by Perkins, *Literary History*, 13–15; it will be apparent that I systematically violate his ideal of "objectivity."

24 Guillory, *Cultural Capital*, 55, 62–63, 129.

25 Guillory, *Cultural Capital*, 176–98.

26 Weber, *Institution*, 142. See Peggy Kamuf, "The Division of Literature" (*Diacritics* 25 [1995]: 58–71), for an argument that enlists Weber in a more extended critique of Guillory; her account has influenced my position here.

27 Weber, *Institution*, 144.

28 Jerome Christensen, *Practicing Enlightenment: Hume and the Formation of a Literary Career* (Madison: University of Wisconsin Press, 1987), and *Lord Byron's Strength: Romantic Writing and Commercial Society* (Baltimore: Johns Hopkins University Press, 1993). Also see William H. Epstein, *Recognizing Biography* (Philadelphia: University of Pennsylvania Press, 1987); and William H. Epstein (ed.), *Contesting the Subject: Essays in the Postmodern Theory and Practice of Biography and Biographical Criticism* (Purdue University Press, 1991).

29 Diagnoses of De Quincey began with the appearance of the *Confessions*, which was reviewed in the *Medical Intelligencer* as well as in literary periodicals. More recently, pathology has been the mode of such diverse studies as Barrell's *Infection* and Alethea Hayter's *Opium and the Romantic Imagination* (London: Faber and Faber, 1971). On the relation between pathology and literary discourse, see Siskin, *Historicity*, 179–94.

30 See Frances Ferguson, "On the Numbers of Romanticisms," *ELH* 58 (1991): 471–98.

1 CONVERSIONS: WORDSWORTH'S GOTHIC INTERPRETER

1 The poem's first brush with critical notoriety came in 1798, when James Tobin ("dear brother Jim") entreated Wordsworth to cancel "We Are Seven," lest it make the poet "everlastingly ridiculous." Foiled by Wordsworth's maidenly obduracy, Tobin "left [him] in despair." Quoted in W. J. B. Owen (ed.), *Lyrical Ballads 1798*, 2nd. edn (Oxford University Press, 1969), 137.

2 De Quincey might have encountered "We Are Seven" in several contexts. James Losh records having seen "a curious but fine little poem of Wordsworth's" in manuscript during a visit to Bath in 1798. Joseph Cottle, original publisher of the *Lyrical Ballads*, presented a copy to Hannah More, of whom De Quincey's mother was a disciple. "We Are Seven" was also reprinted anonymously, along with several other *Lyrical Ballads*, in contemporary periodicals. See *OE* 31, 49. Also see Mary Moorman, "Wordsworth's Commonplace Book," *Notes & Queries*

202 (1957): 400–05; Robert Mayo, "The Contemporaneity of the *Lyrical Ballads*," in Alun R. Jones and William Tydeman (eds.), *Lyrical Ballads. A Casebook* (London: MacMillan, 1972), 79–126.

3 This letter was written about two years after the events recorded in the *Confessions*. De Quincey's early letters never allude directly to the winter of 1802, nor does he mention this period in his 1803 *Diary*.

4 See De Quincey's *Diary* for a sample of his prolific reading during this period. Along with numerous gothic romances and works by Schiller, Burns, and Southey, he mentions *Dramatic Pieces from the German*. A ranked list of his twelve favorite poets is headed by "William Wordsworth!!!". Horace A. Eaton (ed.), *A Diary of Thomas De Quincey 1803* (London: Noel Douglas, 1927), 145–46, 171, *passim*.

5 Eve Kosofsky Sedgwick, "The Character in the Veil: Imagery of the Surface in the Gothic Novel," *PMLA* 96 (1981): 266.

6 For a fuller statement of this thesis, see Margaret Russett, "Narrative as Enchantment in *The Mysteries of Udolpho*," *ELH* (forthcoming).

7 For example, De Quincey asserts that "the primary effects of opium are always . . . to excite and stimulate the system" (*M* 3:388). By his own account, De Quincey first sampled opium about six months after writing this letter.

8 The most sophisticated account of De Quincey's gothicism is Eve Kosofsky Sedgwick's thesis that he links "classic gothic conventions with the subject of language" (*The Coherence of Gothic Conventions* [New York: Arno Press, 1980], 66; see also 41–103). My understanding of those conventions and Wordsworth's use of them is also indebted to Karen Swann, "Public Transport: Adventuring on Wordsworth's Salisbury Plain," *ELH* 55 (1988): 811–34. The extent of De Quincey's knowledge, in 1804, of Wordsworth's early poetic experiments is uncertain. "Salisbury Plain" and "The Borderers," the most explicitly gothic and Schillerian of these, were of course his secret. But De Quincey, whose bibliophilia was only less ardent than his hero-worship, may already have read *An Evening Walk* and *Descriptive Sketches* by this time; see *R* 173–74.

9 De Quincey discusses the *sortes Biblicae* and its derivative, the *sortes Virgilianae*, in *M* 1:125–26.

10 Geoffrey Hartman's canonical account of the Wordsworthian memory poem stipulates that "even in 'Tintern Abbey'" the "mind is moved more by itself, by its own recollection, than by the original event" (*Wordsworth's Poetry 1787–1814* [New Haven: Yale University Press, 1977], 366). Freud's explication of the "primal scene" ambiguates the original event in a more De Quinceyan way: see *SE* 17:3–122.

11 Mary Jacobus, in *Tradition and Experiment in Wordsworth's Lyrical Ballads (1798)* (Oxford: Clarendon Press, 1976), remarks on the "grotesque" perseverance of the speaker in "We Are Seven" (101–03). Hartman

notes the poem's similarities to that most lurid of *Lyrical Ballads*, "The Thorn," suggesting that the narrative be read as a refutation of the first (Coleridgean) stanza (*Wordsworth's Poetry*, 44–46, 374).

12 On visual fragmentation of feminine subjects as a technique of mastery in the traditional blazon, see Nancy Vickers, "The Body Remembered: Petrarchan Lyric and the Strategies of Description," in John D. Lyons and Stephen G. Nichols (eds.), *Mimesis: From Mirror to Method, Augustine to Descartes*, (Hanover: University Press of New England for Dartmouth College, 1982), 100–09. In *Romanticism*, Jacobus offers readings of "Nutting" and the Lucy poems that investigate the occluded role of gender in Wordsworthian scenes of instruction (250–59).

13 My understanding of Wordsworthian "quasi-allegorical" figures is indebted to Stephen Knapp, *Personification and the Sublime: Milton to Coleridge* (Cambridge, MA: Harvard University Press, 1985), 98–106 *passim.*

14 For a sophisticated critique of readings that "defend the child and abuse the man," see Frances Ferguson, *Solitude and the Sublime: Romanticism and the Aesthetics of Individuation* (New York: Routledge, 1992), 164–67; to Ferguson, "perhaps the most curious aspect of the poem is . . . how much they agree on" (164).

15 In describing De Quincey's characteristic "suspensions" of textual identification I have learned from Jerome Christensen's reading of De Quincey and "There Was a Boy"; see his "Rhetoric," 438–44.

16 The phrase is Hartman's: *Wordsworth's Poetry*, 145.

17 Adela Pinch, "Female Chatter: Meter, Masochism, and the *Lyrical Ballads*," *ELH* 55 (1988): 843; Jean Laplanche, *Life and Death in Psychoanalysis*, trans. Jeffrey Mehlman (Baltimore: Johns Hopkins University Press, 1976), 88. These paragraphs are much indebted to Pinch's gendered account of masochism in relation to literary representation, and to her reading of "Goody Blake and Harry Gill" as an allegory of the transaction between *Lyrical Ballads* and its readers (835–52). Both Pinch and I rely on Jean Laplanche's discussion of masochism as paradigmatic of the emergence of subjectivity (85–102). While Laplanche, Pinch and Freud elucidate De Quincey's masochism, Freud can only be described as De Quinceyan when he describes the asymmetry of pleasure and unpleasure in masochistic sexuality, invoking "the rhythm, the temporal sequence of changes, rises and falls in the level of stimulus" (*SE* 19:160).

On gender transfer as a feature of De Quincey's literary persona, see his two letters of 1799 and 1800 signed "your affectionate sister, Tabitha Quincey" (*OE* 27); see also Barrell, *Infection*, 46–47, 78–79. For a discussion of De Quinceyan masochism focusing on fantasies of beating, see Sedgwick, *Coherence*, 79–90.

18 On "We Are Seven" and the uncanny, see also Jay Clayton, *Romantic Vision and the Novel* (Cambridge University Press, 1987), 108–11.

19 For a phenomenological account of the "relationship between the consciousness and the projections of an extraconscious agency," see Curtis Perry, "Piranesi's Prison: Thomas De Quincey and the Failure of Autobiography," *Studies in English Literature* 33 (1993): 809–24.

20 Robert M. Maniquis's discussion of the De Quinceyan "unconscious" as "a linguistic structure of self-substantiating signs" has influenced my own understanding. See "The Dark Interpreter and the Palimpsest of Violence" in Snyder (ed.), *Bicentenary Studies*, 109–39.

21 Laplanche, *Life and Death*, 87–94. See also Jean Laplanche and J. B. Pontalis, *The Language of Psychoanalysis*, trans. Donald Nicholson-Smith (New York: Norton, 1973), 9.

22 De Quincey uses the "Lucretian word" *clinamen* in the general sense of divergence (or *différance*) and more specifically as a synonym for the Coleridgean "desynonymy" (*M* 10:72–73). See also Harold Bloom, *The Anxiety of Influence* (New York: Oxford University Press, 1973), 14, 30, 42.

23 Pierre Bourdieu describes, in a way that theorizes deferred action without countenancing the Freudian unconscious, how accident and design converge to produce "witticisms." The "objective" meaning of a successful joke (or of an intervention like De Quincey's) always "outruns . . . conscious intentions" because it realizes the structure of the *habitus,* or interpretive horizon: "the *trouvaille* appears as the simple unearthing, at once accidental and irresistible, of a buried possibility. It is because subjects do not, strictly speaking, know what they are doing that what they do has more meaning than they know." *Outline of a Theory of Practice,* trans. Richard Nice (Cambridge, MA: Harvard University Press, 1977), 79.

24 The only existing text for De Quincey's third letter is a fragmentary copy entered by Dorothy into William's commonplace book. Though it is unattributed by Dorothy, internal and external evidence clearly identifies its sender as De Quincey. See Moorman, "Commonplace Book," 403–05, and *J* 19–20, 35.

25 Marcel Mauss, *The Gift: Forms and Functions of Exchange in Archaic Societies,* trans. Ian Cunnison (New York: Norton, 1967), 39, 45. For an extended analysis of gift-exchange and sacrifice in De Quincey's *Confessions* and autobiographies, see Rzepka, *Sacramental,* 16–28, 52–58, 166–201.

26 Wilson had written to Wordsworth in May 1802, anticipating De Quincey by about a year. The text of his letter may be found in Mary Wilson Gordon, *"Christopher North": A Memoir of John Wilson,* 2 vols. (Edinburgh: Edmonston and Douglas, 1862), 1: 26–32, and in Jones and Tydeman (eds.), *Casebook,* 58–64. Less hyperbolic than De Quincey, Wilson similarly applies ideas from Wordsworth's "Preface" to the poems of *Lyrical Ballads.* Wordsworth replied punctually and copiously (*EY* 352–58), but the exchange did not prompt a sustained correspondence.

27 Biblical citations are from the authorized King James edition.

28 On the Augustinian and Pauline roots of eighteenth-century spiritual autobiography, see M. H. Abrams, *Natural Supernaturalism: Tradition and Revolution in Romantic Literature* (New York: Norton, 1973), 47–48, 133–39, *passim*. De Quincey belongs at the head of the line of Wordsworthian converts that Abrams traces through John Stuart Mill and William Hale White.

29 I offer here an adjustment to Abrams's teleological account of Wordsworth's secular evangelism: see Abrams, *Natural Supernaturalism*, 21–28, *passim*.

30 On the character of De Quincey's love for "the poetry of the Bible," which he read in English, Latin, Greek and Hebrew, see particularly his 1803 *Diary*, 172–73, and the first section of *Suspiria de Profundis*, C 103–19.

31 Harold Bloom, *A Map of Misreading* (Oxford University Press, 1975), 51.

32 Siskin, *Historicity*, 12.

33 Louis Althusser, "Ideology and Ideological State Apparatuses (Notes Toward an Investigation)." *Lenin and Philosophy and Other Essays*, trans. Ben Brewster (New York: Monthly Review, 1971), 171 *passim*.

34 De Quincey's letters disparage Francis Jeffrey's reviews of the "new school," which the *Edinburgh Review* began publishing in October 1802 and continued running for many years thereafter. It was Crabb Robinson who described De Quincey himself as a "pupil": see *HCR* 137.

35 Augustine, *Confessions*, trans. R. S. Pine-Coffin (Harmondsworth: Penguin, 1961), 166–79.

36 On the "jurisdiction" as "the central phenomenon of professional life," see Andrew Abbott, *The System of Professions: An Essay on the Division of Expert Labor* (University of Chicago Press, 1988), 1–31, 315–26. The concept enables Abbott to show that "professions both create their work and are created by it" (316).

37 Bourdieu, *Outline*, 6.

38 Jacques Lacan, "Seminar on 'The Purloined Letter,'" trans. Jeffrey Mehlman, in John P. Muller and William J. Richardson (eds.), *The Purloined Poe: Lacan, Derrida, and Psychoanalytic Reading* (Baltimore: Johns Hopkins University Press, 1988), 43–44, 53.

39 Magali Sarfatti Larson, *The Rise of Professionalism: A Sociological Analysis* (Berkeley: University of California Press, 1977), 80. See Larson more generally for an analysis of the professional movement's conflicted affiliations with evangelical Christianity, democratic politics, and aristocratic ideology.

40 On the sociology of "reception" as a class-specific practice, see Klancher, *Reading Audiences*, 19–38.

41 Siskin, *Historicity*, 141–44.

42 "Confessions of an English Opium-Eater," *The Eclectic Review* (April 1823): 367.

43 Ferguson, *Solitude*, 164.

44 Jacques Lacan, *The Four Fundamental Concepts of Psycho-Analysis*, ed. Jacques-Alain Miller, trans. Alan Sheridan (New York: Norton, 1977), 20.

45 Jacques Lacan, "Of Structure as an Inmixing of an Otherness Prerequisite to Any Subject Whatever," in Richard Macksey and Eugenio Donato (eds.), *The Structuralist Controversy: The Languages of Criticism and the Sciences of Man* (Baltimore: Johns Hopkins University Press, 1972), 192.

46 My understanding of "formalism" and "empiricism" relies on Ferguson's account (*Solitude*, 156–69).

47 Slavoj Zizek, *For They Know Not What They Do: Enjoyment as a Political Factor* (London: Verso, 1991), 218.

48 On "counting as ostensiveness" in relation to the set, the serial, and the name, see Ferguson's reading of "We Are Seven" in *Solitude*, 164–69.

49 The practice of assigning identical names within one generation was particularly common in aristocratic households, where it served as insurance that tradition would be maintained despite high mortality rates. Lawrence Stone, *The Family, Sex and Marriage in England 1500–1800*, abridged edn (New York: Harper & Row, 1979), 257–58. See also Philippe Aries, who contends in *Centuries of Childhood: A Social History of Family Life*, trans. Robert Baldick (New York: Knopf, 1962), that in Renaissance Europe "nobody thought, as we ordinarily think today, that every child already contained a man's personality" (39).

50 Jane II, who died in 1873, was in fact De Quincey's only living sibling by 1821, though she barely figures in his published writings; see *OE* 12, and Alexander H. Japp, *De Quincey Memorials*, 2 vols. (London: William Heinemann, 1891), 2: 68.

51 Lindop rehearses this information without much remarking on De Quincey's error (*OE* 3–8). De Quincey's earlier biographer, Horace Ainsworth Eaton, takes his subject's account at face value, giving two separate dates for Jane's death (1786 and 1790) within a few pages; see his *Thomas De Quincey: A Biography* (New York: Octagon, 1972), 8–14. The record is corrected by Judson S. Lyon, in *Thomas De Quincey* (New York: Twayne, 1969), 188; Lyon also notes that if William was, as De Quincey claimed, five years older than Thomas, he must have been born before their parents' marriage. It seems unlikely that De Quincey was simply unconscious of these inconsistencies; in the 1853 *Sketches* (*M* 1:33) he lengthens the age gap between himself and the first Jane from one year to two (making himself one-and-a-half when

she died), having apparently noticed the impossibility that Jane could be older than Mary but only *one* year older than himself, the youngest of the three.

52 Lacan, "Of Structure," 188–91. J. Hillis Miller's important phenomenological essay on De Quincey in J. Hillis Miller, *The Disappearance of God: Five Nineteenth-Century Writers* (Cambridge, MA: Belknapp Press, 1975) begins by positing Elizabeth's death as elementary rupture (17–18). See also Lacan's thematic articulation of the "imaginary" as the domain of "specular ego" in Lacan, *Ecrits: A Selection*, trans. Alan Sheridan (New York: Norton, 1981), 1–7.

53 Lacan, "Of Structure," 191–93.

54 Ferguson, *Solitude*, 157–61.

55 Lionel Trilling reads "We Are Seven" as "an ontological poem" asking what a "person *is*"; see "Wordsworth and the Iron Time" in M. H. Abrams (ed.), *Wordsworth: A Collection of Critical Essays* (Englewood Cliffs, NJ: Prentice-Hall, 1972), 57. For readings of "We Are Seven" that address questions of representation, see Don H. Bialostosky, *Making Tales: The Poetics of Wordsworth's Narrative Experiments* (University of Chicago Press, 1984), 117 ff., and Frances Ferguson's essential discussion in *Wordsworth: Language as Counter-Spirit* (New Haven: Yale University Press, 1977), 23–27, 66–68.

56 I summarize here Paul de Man's argument about Locke in "The Epistemology of Metaphor," in Sheldon Sacks (ed.), *On Metaphor*, (University of Chicago Press, 1979), 16.

57 Lacan, "Of Structure," 192.

58 This is the point of Ferguson's reading in *Wordsworth*, 26–27.

59 Ferguson, *Wordsworth*, 150.

60 See Robert Lance Snyder, "'The Loom of *Palingenesis*': De Quincey's Cosmology in 'System of the Heavens,'" in Snyder (ed.), *Bicentenary Studies*, 338–59. For Freud's definition of mourning, see *SE* 14:245–56.

61 For an interpretation of the sacrificial object that enlists psychoanalysis to rather different ends, see Barrell, *Infection*, 25–47 *passim*. Treating the "involute" of Elizabeth's death as "a particularly grotesque version of the primal scene" (35), Barrell discusses De Quincey's conflation of sexuality and xenophobic fantasies of aggression. I am interested, by contrast, primarily in how De Quincey articulates the *temporality* (or Lacanian "structure") of psychoanalysis, thereby both extending and problematizing the autobiographical project he shares with Wordsworth and others.

62 Epstein, *Recognizing Biography*, 35; see also 34–51 for a deconstructive account of relations among the natural "fact," the pre-discursive "event," the statement, the genre, and the cultural metanarrative.

63 Lacan, "Of Structure," 193.

64 For a less critical statement of a similar point, see De Luca, *Prose of Vision*, 60.

65 My skepticism about psychoanalytic "explanation" is shared by Clej, who argues that such set-pieces of "the hermeneutic sublime" as the bedroom scene in *Suspiria* should be understood as self-conscious fictions. Her discussion focuses on the literary sources from which De Quincey constructs his teasing conundrum (*Genealogy*, 236–49).

66 On the seven Ages of Man and their survival in common law, see Aries, 21; *The Laws Respecting Women* (New York: Oceana, 1974 [rpr. of London, 1777], 428); and James Walvin, *A Child's World: A Social History of English Childhood* (Harmondsworth: Penguin, 1982), 159. While minority lasted (for males) to the age of 21, the law distinguished three phases of responsibility within that period.

67 On perceptual seclusion see Ferguson, *Solitude*, 114–28; on the "fragmentary exigency," see Lacoue-Labarthe and Nancy, *Literary Absolute*, 39–58.

2 TRANSMISSIONS: COMPOSING
THE CONVENTION OF CINTRA

1 Quoted in Charles Cuthbert Southey, *The Life and Correspondence of Robert Southey* (New York: Harper & Bros., 1851), 242. The later course of the war proved the Convention on the whole a strategic success. In retrospect, Southey toned down his criticisms to a contrast between military advantages and political weaknesses; see Robert Southey, *A History of the Peninsular War*, 6 vols. (London, 1823), 2: 221–44. Other influential nineteenth-century accounts of the Convention include W. F. P. Napier, *History of the War in the Peninsula*, 6 vols. (Philadelphia: Carey and Hart, 1842), 1: 112–43, and Charles Oman, *A History of the Peninsular War*, 7 vols. (Oxford: Clarendon Press, 1902–30), 1: 263–300.

2 "Childe Harold's Pilgrimage," canto 1, stanzas 25–26; in Frederick Page (ed.), *Byron: Poetical Works* (Oxford University Press, 1970), 184–85.

3 Southey, *History*, 2: 268. The Wordsworth circle was not unusual in considering the Convention "one of the most important events of our time" (*PrW* 1:224). Documenting the "opinions and feelings" to which the poet alludes, Owen and Smyser note that numerous demands by town and city leaders for inquiry into the Convention were lodged throughout October and November of 1808 (*PrW* 1:380). For Oman, as for later historians, the "wave of indignation which swept across England" seems "a little hard to understand" (*History*, 291).

4 For a more extended intellectual–historical account of the continu-

ities between Wordsworth's "Foxite stance" in the 1790s and his endorsement of the Peninsular uprising, see Dierdre Coleman, "Reliving Jacobinism: Wordsworth and the Convention of Cintra," *Yearbook of English Studies* 19 (1989): 151 *passim.*

5 On the question of "apostasy," compare *Cintra* (*PrW* 1:226) with Wordsworth's 1821 letter rejecting the names of "Renegado, Apostate etc" and countering that his accusers "have been deluded by Places and Persons, while I have stuck to Principles." He cites *Cintra* as evidence of his "dissatisfaction with the mode of conducting the war" (*LY* 1:97). Studies of Wordsworth's politics that consider *Cintra* as a career turning-point include Michael Friedman, *The Making of a Tory Humanist: William Wordsworth and the Idea of Community* (New York: Columbia University Press 1979), and James K. Chandler, *Wordsworth's Second Nature: A Study of the Poetry and Politics* (University of Chicago Press, 1984). Friedman perceives *Cintra* as the last gasp of Wordsworth's revolutionary sympathies, while for Chandler it initiates the poet's "strong commitment to Burkeanism" (31). Noting the "bewildering polarization of . . . responses" *Cintra* has received, Coleman adjusts Chandler's thesis to suggest that Wordsworth "clothe[s] 'the bare idea of a revolution' in Burkean rhetoric." For Coleman, Wordsworth's Burkean language indexes his differences from, as well as his debts to, Burke's representation of the French Revolution ("Jacobinism," 145, 161, *passim*). I regard Coleman's emphasis on the influence of Burke as the complement to my stress on the French connection.

6 Quoted in Ronald Paulson, *Representations of Revolution (1789–1820)* (New Haven: Yale University Press, 1983), 287. On this question Coleridge agreed with the *Edinburgh Review*'s "jacobinical" "Don Cevallos" articles, which praised the Revolution as a rising of the lower orders. It had become possible "once more [to] utter the words *liberty* and *people*, without . . . looking round the chamber for some spy or officer of the government" (quoted in Paulson, *Representations*, 287; see also Geoffrey Carnall, *Robert Southey and His Age: The Development of a Conservative Mind* [Oxford: Clarendon Press, 1960], 97).

7 Peter J. Manning, *Reading Romantics: Texts and Contexts* (New York: Oxford University Press, 1990), 174. See also Coleman's account of "the French Revolution *redivivus*" ("Jacobinism," 149).

8 Quoted in Carnall, *Southey*, 82.

9 De Quincey argues that Coleridge and Southey changed parties because of Whig foreign policy during the war years (*R* 101–11, 225–27). In a review of *Cintra*, Crabb Robinson praised Wordsworth's commitment to the rebellion without, like him, idealizing English sympathy with Spain ("On the Spanish Revolution," in Donald H. Reiman (ed.), *The Romantics Reviewed* [New York: Garland, 1972], part C, 1: 631–53). Wordsworth discussed Wrangham's sermon on

Spain in a letter describing his own intention to publish a tract (*MY* 1:277–78).

10 Quoted in Southey, *Life*, 246. Also see *PrW* 1:196–98, 380. On the "Jacobin" idea that "a government is . . . the instrument and means of purifying and regulating the national will by its public discussions," see *CW* 3[2]:396.

11 Southey visited Portugal in the fall of 1795–96. In 1808, he was already at work on his multi-volume *History of Portugal* and had recently published *Letters from England*, purportedly translated from the Spanish of Don Manuel Alvarez Espriella (see Carnall, *Southey*, 37–83, 67–69). His library at Keswick consisted of the "great cardinal classics" of "English, Spanish and Portuguese" (*R* 237–38). Notwithstanding these qualifications, he believed he had "not the sort of talent requisite for writing a political pamphlet upon the state of Spain," although "no public event ever distressed [him] so greatly" as the Cintra Convention (Southey, *Life*, 244; John Edwin Wells, "The Story of Wordsworth's 'Cintra'," *Studies in Philology* 18 [1921]: 22).

12 Coleridge complained of De Quincey's "marvellous slowness in writing a note to the Pamphlet when at Grasmere, the sum and meaning of which I had dictated in better & more orderly sentences in five minutes" (*CL* 3:206). Sara Coleridge rather differently recalled seeing "my father and Mr. De Quincey pace up and down the room" as they both "discussed the affairs of the nation" with Wordsworth (quoted in Wells, "Story," 20).

13 Coleridge contributed eight "letters" on Spanish affairs to the *Courier* in December and January 1809–10; these he described as "a kind of supplement to Wordsworth's pamphlet." Wells discusses his substantive contributions to *Cintra*, citing H. N. Coleridge's remark that "a very brilliant portion of Mr. W.'s pamphlet . . . is Coleridge's" (Wells, "Story," 22, 28). In an early political essay of *The Friend*, Coleridge recommended *Cintra* as the work of "a fellow-labourer in the same vineyard" (*CW* 4[1]:183).

14 Among Whigs, initial enthusiasm about the Spanish uprising did not necessarily translate into support for military intervention. Later the Tory ministry pursued the war over severe opposition criticism. Arthur Wellesley's role in the Convention was exploited as a way of weakening the position of his brother, the Marquis of Wellesley (Carnall, *Southey*, 87). The fantasy of a pure war of liberation also became increasingly difficult to sustain as the rebels' goals became better understood. For a brief account of Whig policy during the war, see Godfrey Davies, "The Whigs and the Peninsular War, 1808–14," *Transactions of the Royal Historical Society* 4th series, 32 vols. (London, 1919), vol. 2; for an early (Whiggish) critique of the prevailing Whig "state of mind," see Robinson, "Spanish Revolution."

15 See Celeste Langan's distinction between "negative and positive

liberty" (civil and substantive rights) in *Romantic Vagrancy: Wordsworth and the Simulation of Freedom* (Cambridge University Press, 1995), 18.

16 François Furet, *Interpreting the French Revolution*, trans. Elborg Forster (Cambridge University Press, 1981), 51–52.

17 Furet, *Interpreting*, 27, 35.

18 Jean-Jacques Rousseau, *The Social Contract*, trans. Maurice Cranston (Harmondsworth: Penguin, 1968), 61.

19 On the political significance of "The English Mail-Coach," see Robert M. Maniquis, "Lonely Empires: Personal and Public Visions of Thomas de Quincey," in Eric Rothstein and Joseph Anthony Wittreich (eds.), *Literary Monographs*, 9 vols. (Madison: University of Wisconsin Press, 1967–78), 8:47–127; and Robert Hopkins, "De Quincey on War and the Pastoral Design of *The English Mail-Coach*," *Studies in Romanticism* 6 (1966–67): 129–51. Maniquis stresses De Quincey's vision of "the multitude spiritually joined – but in historical individuation" (66–67); Hopkins contextualizes De Quincey's politics in relation to Kant's writings on war, Wordsworth's *Poems Dedicated to National Independence and Liberty*, the establishment of peace societies, and technological change; he also alludes briefly to *Cintra* (144, *passim*). Also see Baxter, *Autobiography*, 125, 152, *passim*.

20 Hence the abiding Revolutionary obsession with conspiracy; see Furet, *Interpreting*, 53–55 *passim*.

21 Chandler describes attacks on "abstract rights" as the central tenet of Burkean ideology (*Second Nature*, 32–35 *passim*).

22 On the idea of popular "opinion," see Furet, *Interpreting*, 30–39.

23 I borrow this phrase from Chandler, *Second Nature*, 216–34.

24 Rousseau, *Social Contract*, 75.

25 This brief summary of De Quincey's political allegory elaborates on suggestions in Barrell, *Infection*, 8–11; and (especially) Arden Reed, "'Booked for Utter Perplexity' on De Quincey's *English Mail-Coach*" (in Snyder [ed.], *Bicentenary Studies*, 295–98).

26 See J. L. Austin, *How To Do Things With Words*, ed. J. O. Urmson and Marina Sbisa (Cambridge, MA: Harvard University Press, 1975), 14–15, on the prerequisites for "the smooth or 'happy' functioning of a performative."

27 Chandler asserts antithetically that "the effort to subject barbarous reading to the discipline of oral performance is central to Wordsworth's literary program" (*Second Nature*, 143). Wordsworth's discourse of embodiment, more explicitly articulated in the "Essays Upon Epitaphs," shares the Jacobin Revolution's distrust of representation as such. The ideal of *incarnating* the popular voice was most convincingly realized in the career of Robespierre (Furet, *Interpreting*, 56–61).

28 See *PrW* 2: 84, and pp. 80–82 of this chapter.

29 Reed, "'Booked,'" 281.

30 Furet uses the term "absolutist" to signify both "a perfect 'fit' [*transparence*] between . . . action and the general meaning attributed to it by the protagonists," and the "imaginary absolute power" (a "legacy of the monarchy") that the philosophical societies wielded over "opinion." On the tension between the concept of general will and bureaucratic delegation, see Furet's reading of Rousseau (*Interpreting*, 19, 30–31, 38–39). On Wordsworth's Rousseauism, see also Chandler, *Second Nature*, 69–85, 105–116.

31 Rousseau, *Social Contract*, 69.

32 Furet, *Interpreting*, 29.

33 Lynn Hunt, *Politics, Culture, and Class in the French Revolution* (Berkeley: University of California Press, 1984), 25–26.

34 Compare Furet's reading of Sieyes' tract *Qu'est-ce que le Tiers Etat?* as "a discourse on exclusion and a discourse on origins" arguing with "staggering tautology" that "what could be represented was precisely what the citizens had in common" (*Interpreting*, 44).

35 On anachronism as the disguise of ideological "content," see Karl Marx, *The Eighteenth Brumaire of Louis Bonaparte* (New York: International Publishers, 1990), 16–18.

36 Furet, *Interpreting*, 20.

37 For more documentation of perceived continuities between Robespierre and Napoleon, see Alan Liu, *Wordsworth: The Sense of History* (Stanford University Press, 1989), 379, 419, 440.

38 See Liu, *Sense*, 418–28, on the series of reversals (variously troped as apostasy or dialectic) by which Coleridge maintained his "opposition" stance from the 1790s onward. Also see Jerome Christensen's observation that "the difference between Jacobin revolution and Burkean counterrevolution is negated by their shared ambition to abolish all differences" ("*Ecce Homo*: Biographical Acknowledgment, the End of the French Revolution, and the Romantic Reinvention of English Verse," in Epstein [ed.], *Contesting*, 58).

39 Furet, *Interpreting*, 39.

40 Furet, *Interpreting*, 37.

41 Rousseau begins *The Social Contract* by announcing his lack of professional qualifications: "I may be asked whether I am a prince or a legislator that I should be writing about politics. I answer no: and indeed that that is my reason for doing so" (49).

42 Friedman characterizes *Cintra* as a "statesman's manual," but sees this function as paradoxically defeated by its "deracination" of professional statesmen and courtiers (*Tory*, 270, *passim*).

43 Also see Langan, *Vagrancy* 31–32, on the distinction between "subject" and "citizen."

44 See Rousseau, *Social Contract*, 62–64.

45 Rousseau, *Social Contract*, 79.

46 Furet, *Interpreting*, 61–72.

47 Paul de Man, *The Rhetoric of Romanticism* (New York: Columbia University Press, 1984), 92. See also Ferguson, *Wordsworth*, 31. At one point in *Cintra* Wordsworth hazards a numerical figure for "feeling": "a force of two hundred thousand men or more . . . The advantages of this plan would be – that the power, which would attend it, must . . . insure unity of effort" (*PrW* 1:311). For another argument on the relation of "actual death" to death in language, see Neil Hertz, "Lurid Figures," in Wlad Godzich and Lindsay Waters (eds.), *Reading de Man Reading* (Minneapolis: University of Minnesota Press, 1989), 93–95.

48 *The Correspondence of Henry Crabb Robinson with the Wordsworth Circle*, ed. Edith J. Morley (Oxford: Clarendon Press, 1927), 2: 125.

49 Manning argues along similar lines that *The Convention of Cintra* attempts a "foreclosure of history," completing the "deflection" or "revulsion from historical actuality his experience of the French Revolution produced in Wordsworth" (*Reading*, 190, 186).

50 Langan, *Vagrancy*, 38, 193–200 *passim*.

51 I use the terms "prefigure" and "prefiguration" in Christensen's sense; see "Rhetoric," 448–50.

52 Epistemological confidence is posited in terms of voice throughout *The Borderers*. For exemplary readings that link these issues to the theater of the French Revolution, see two related essays by Reeve Parker, "'O Could You Hear His Voice': Wordsworth, Coleridge, and Ventriloquism," in Arden Reed (ed.), *Romanticism and Language* (Ithaca: Cornell University Press, 1984), 125–43, and "Reading Wordsworth's Power: Narrative and Usurpation in *The Borderers*," *ELH* 54 (1987): 299–331.

53 Jean-Jacques Rousseau, *Reveries of the Solitary Walker*, trans. Peter France (Harmondsworth: Penguin, 1979), 38–39.

54 Rousseau, *Social Contract*, 61.

55 I owe this last remark to a seminar with Neil Hertz.

56 The cairn or pile of stones at Dunmail Raise was thought to commemorate the defeat of Dummail, "last king of rocky Cumbria," by Edmund of England, *c.* 945. Cumbria, previously an independent kingdom, became a fief of the English crown (M. J. B. Baddeley [ed.], *The Lake District* [London: Ward, Lock, n.d.], 84; W. G. Collingwood, *The Lake Counties* [London: Dent, 1949], 158).

57 Anticipating "rhetorical" deconstruction, De Quincey ridicules the notion of "sentimental correspondence" in his dismissal of Jeffrey's reading of the poem. Several recent discussions of "There was a boy" have influenced my account. See especially Paul de Man, "Time and History in Wordsworth," in Cynthia Chase (ed.), *Romanticism* (London: Longman, 1993), 55–77; Jerome Christensen, "Rhetoric" and "*Ecce Homo*" (*passim*); and Jacobus, *Romanticism*, 264–66.

58 Marx, *Eighteenth Brumaire*, 18.

59 Quoted in Baxter, *Autobiography*, 124.

60 For a subtle account of how "presence" is dislocated by past and future, and how the "suddenness of action" is mimed by "retarded" language, see Reed, "'Booked,'" 290–94.

61 Rousseau, *Reveries*, 38.

62 Homer, *The Iliad*, trans. Robert Fitzgerald (Garden City, New York: Anchor/Doubleday, 1975), book 16, lines 814–67; book 19, lines 1–78.

63 See also McDonagh, *Disciplines*, 25 *passim*, for a discussion of De Quincey's reactionary politics as belated revolutionary anxiety.

64 Quoted in McDonagh, *Disciplines*, 27.

65 In January 1809 De Quincey wrote an elaborate letter to *The Times* (his first publication, apparently) urging support of a public subscription for the "Spanish Patriots." A year later he remained keen enough to contemplate a trip to Spain for the purpose of observing developments there at close range (*R* 364; *OE* 163; see also *CL* 3:247–49).

66 On the question of resemblance see Christensen, "Rhetoric," 441–43. My account of the turn from personification to biography echoes his definition of biography as "the impression of a transient affect that continues, transiently, to be affecting; a life written as the cadenced suspension of the identity we know it 'must' become" (Christensen, "*Ecce Homo*," 77).

67 In balancing these claims, I intend an adjustment to the narrative of a turn from the "historical" to the interiorized "natural and transcendent" described by some recent Romanticists. See, in particular, Siskin's Foucaultian argument that the historical swerve from mimetic continuity is exemplified in a "lyric turn," a "social gesture ... followed by ... a personal confession of the writer's *need* to proceed in a more private direction," which denies history in the name of "individual ... 'progress'" (*Historicity*, 12–15). While Siskin's thesis has influenced my reading of *Cintra*'s resistance to "history," it should be noted that this resistance is most intense when Wordsworth is most deeply engaged in topical polemics.

68 Southey, *Life*, 246.

69 For another account of De Quincey's presswork on the *Cintra* pamphlet that focuses on his "Christological" self-sacrifice, see Rzepka, *Sacramental*, 194–201. In general, Rzepka regards De Quincey's relation to Wordsworth as a version of the Oedipal narrative. See my chapter five for a counter-argument on the gender of De Quincey's sacrificial persona.

70 Byron, "Childe Harold" Canto 1, stanzas 24–25, in Page (ed.), *Byron: Poetical Works*, 184–85.

71 See Austin on signature as substitute for bodily presence in performative enunciations (*Words*, 60–61).

72 See Paulson, *Representations*, 222–42, on the "Frankenstein syndrome" in gothic fiction as a disguised critique of the Revolution. Furet argues

that the problematics of the gothic were integral to Revolutionary ideology: "the *abbé* Barruel had only to follow in the Thermidoreans' footsteps to arrive at his global interpretation of the Revolution as a plot by the *philosophes* and freemasons" (*Interpreting*, 58).

73 Quoted in Simon Schama, *Citizens: A Chronicle of the French Revolution* (New York: Random House, 1989), 674, my emphasis. Schama translates Robespierre's circular on the execution: "il a imprimé un grand caractère à la convention nationale."

74 This phrase was deleted from the published text of *The Convention of Cintra* upon Wordsworth's expressing the fear that it might be libellous (see *MY* 1:327–34, 336–7). "The sentence passed upon them by the voice of their countrymen" appears in *PrW* 1:282.

75 Thus, Wordsworth not only shows how the treaty "misfires," in Austin's terms, but *performs* its failure. Though most of the treaty is quoted or paraphrased in *The Convention of Cintra*, Wordsworth was also eager to "print . . . the armistice and Convention in the notes" (*MY* 1:295). By appending the (well-known) text of the Convention to his response, Wordsworth transferred authorship from Wellesley and Dalrymple to himself (as spokesman). Derrida similarly incorporates nearly every word of John R. Searle's "Reiterating the Differences" into his rebuttal, *Limited Inc* (trans. Samuel Weber and Jeffrey Mehlman [Evanston, IL: Northwestern University Press, 1990]).

76 For a more detailed biographical narrative and textual history of De Quincey's contributions, see Wells, "Story"; for his blow-by-blow record of daily labors, see *J* 47–202.

77 Wordsworth never did send a satisfactory answer: every time De Quincey posed a query, Wordsworth would respond that "the passage about knowledge is '*as [you] wrote it*,'" but, as De Quincey observed, "I wrote it 2 ways" (*J* 137).

78 Wordsworth adds tactlessly: "I regret that I did not request the Pamphlet to be sent down when the Body of it was printed, as I might have reasonably concluded that there must have been blunders in the manuscript which could be known to nobody but myself" (*MY* 1:347–48). Thus, taking his hatred of delegation to its logical conclusion, he casually negates all De Quincey's unpaid work in London.

79 In the event, *The Convention of Cintra* failed even to sell out its first edition of 500 copies. Christopher Wordsworth records that "many copies were disposed of by the publishers as waste paper, and went to the trunkmakers" (*Memoirs of Wordsworth*, 2 vols. [London: Edward Moxon, 1851], 1: 405).

80 Southey attributes "Wordsworth's lack of perspicuity to two causes – his admiration of Milton's prose, and his habit of dictating instead of writing . . . in dictating, his own thoughts are to himself familiarly intelligible, and he goes on . . ." (quoted in Wells, "Story", 63). Wells

defends De Quincey's punctuation, comparing the full text of *Cintra*
with the segments that appeared in the *Courier* to argue that the published version "is very much better in consistency both from sentence
to sentence and within the given sentence; in the accurate location of
the pointing; and notably in clearness" (Wells, "Story," 65–66).

81 "Peter Quince" was Sara Hutchinson's unfriendly nickname for De
Quincey (*J* 218, 221).

82 Wordsworth even imagined that De Quincey's editorial decisions
might have made *Cintra* vulnerable to prosecution for libel, hence
silencing it completely; see *J* 79–84, 196–99.

83 Michel Serres, *The Parasite*, trans. Lawrence R. Schehr (Baltimore:
Johns Hopkins University Press, 1982), 68.

84 On the categories of "people" (the projection of an ideal readership)
and "public" (an index of withdrawal from actual readers) as
Wordsworth's mystification of his reception history, see Manning,
Reading, 171, 190.

85 See Owen and Smyser for textual commentary and drafts of De
Quincey's Postscript and the note on Saragossa (*PrW* 1:369–70,
410–15). The Postscript was acknowledged by the Wordsworth circle
as De Quincey's work; Coleridge, for example, praised "our young
friend's note on Sir J. Moore & his Dispatches – it was excellently
arranged & argued" (*MY* 1:347–49; *CL* 3:214). The main lines of
argument were elaborated in a letter of Wordsworth to De Quincey
(*MY* 1:305–09). Though it is De Quincey's first known publication
(except for a letter to *The Times* mentioned above and in *OE*, 163–64)
the Postscript is not included in the Masson collective edition of his
works.

86 Serres, *Parasite*, 66.

87 The case for De Quincey's "pathology," at once psychological and cultural, has been forcefully made by Barrell, who portrays the "myth of
[De Quincey's] childhood" as both symptom and cause of his "fear of
the oriental" (20): see Barrell, *Infection*, especially 1–24. I borrow the
phrase "typical aberration" from Susan Stewart's *Crimes of Writing:
Problems in the Containment of Representation* (New York: Oxford
University Press, 1991), 39.

3 IMPERSONATIONS: THE MAGAZINIST AS MINOR AUTHOR

1 Charles Pollit, *De Quincey's Editorship of the Westmoreland Gazette*
(Kendal: Atkinson and Pollit, 1890), 29, 70.

2 Eaton, *De Quincey*, 262–63.

3 Neither the *Blackwood's* nor the *Westmoreland Gazette* articles are
included in *M*. For examples of De Quincey's writing in 1818–19 see
Pollit, *Westmoreland Gazette*.

4 This long minority refers ostensibly to the interval between the death of De Quincey's father (when Thomas was seven) and the son's achievement of legal majority at twenty-one. Fourteen years also elapsed between De Quincey's first meeting with Wordsworth, in 1807, and the publication of the *Confessions* in 1821.

5 Also see Rzepka, *Sacramental,* for an interpretation of the *Confessions* "as a literary commodity" that mystifies the "traumatic repetition" of De Quincey's first bid for independence. I regret that I read Rzepka's work too late to do much more than indicate (here and elsewhere) some points of intersection between our accounts of the *Confessions*. Both are concerned with De Quincey's articulation of an "author-function," which Rzepka sees in terms of De Quincey's "imaginative transformation of his commercial exchange relationship with his audience" into "a form of gift-relationship" with the author as "transcendental anonymity." (4, 58, 67 *passim*). Two differences in emphasis follow from this definition. While Rzepka regards De Quincey as a particularly diagrammatic instance of authorial mystification as such, I begin by premising an anomaly: De Quincey's status as *literal* anonymity. Therefore, while Rzepka treats the *Confessions* as a formally autonomous work, I focus on its continuities with the magazine text of which it forms a part.

6 Like the elusive *De emendatione humani intellectûs* and the *Prologomena to all future Systems of Political Economy* (*C* 64–66), *Confessions* is a great work evermore about to be (or, recurring to chapter one, a case of arrested development). Its textual history may be compared to the structure of George Darley's *Nepenthe* (1835), which appeared in two cantos, with a promised (never published) third. Leslie Brisman takes this self-diminishing text as paradigmatic of Darley's self-dwarfing career; see Brisman, *Romantic Origins* (Ithaca: Cornell University Press, 1978), 211.

7 Josephine Bauer, *The London Magazine, 1820–29* (Copenhagen: Rosenkilde and Bagger, 1953), 40–42, 68; *HCR*, 275–76.

8 Lindop points out that De Quincey "would have had to produce eighty pages of the magazine" just to pay the annual rent of his house at Fox Ghyll (*OE* 262).

9 Karl Marx, *Capital: A Critique of Political Economy*, trans. Samuel Moore and Edward Aveling, ed. Frederick Engels (New York: Modern Library, 1906), 187–91.

10 Bourdieu, *Outline*, 78–86.

11 Bauer, *London*, 42, 45.

12 On this trope, see for example Jacobus, *Romanticism*, 226, and the revealing exchange noted in *CW* 3[1]:252–53. While my reading of what Jacobus calls "the loss of integrity between body and name" is indebted to hers, I would note that it is less the high-literary "author" who suffers this fate than the writer for newspapers and periodicals.

The connection between the readership of periodicals and the growing population of prostitutes is admittedly more speculative. In fact there were probably many more prostitutes than buyers of magazines in London during the 1820s. Jacobus cites estimates of the number of metropolitan prostitutes in 1803 at 50,000 to 70,000 (208). Klancher puts the total readership of "the most significant journals," including the *London*, at about 20,000 (*Reading Audiences*, 50).

13 Two *London* signatures cited from Frank P. Riga and Claude A. Prance, *Index to the London Magazine* (New York: Garland, 1978), 242–43.

14 Klancher, *Reading Audiences*, 51.

15 Michel Foucault, *Language, Counter-Memory, Practice: Selected Essays and Interviews*, ed. Donald F. Bouchard, trans. Donald F. Bouchard and Sherry Simon (Ithaca: Cornell University Press, 1977), 126.

16 Jacques Derrida, *Of Grammatology*, trans. Gayatri Chakravorty Spivak (Baltimore: Johns Hopkins University Press, 1976), 112.

17 Peter T. Murphy, "Impersonation and Authorship in Romantic Britain," *ELH* 59 (1992): 630.

18 Peter T. Murphy, *Poetry as an Occupation and an Art in Britain, 1760–1830* (Cambridge University Press, 1993), 120. See 117–24, and Murphy's essay cited in note 17, for the best combined account of the exchanges between empirical persons and fictional personae in *Blackwood's*.

19 Gordon, *"Christopher North"*, 268.

20 Jean Baudrillard, *For a Critique of the Political Economy of the Sign*, trans. Charles Levin (St. Louis: Telos Press, 1981), 104–07.

21 J. G. Lockhart, *The Life of Sir Walter Scott* (London: Dent, 1906), 254.

22 Baudrillard, *Critique*, 106; original emphasis.

23 Klancher, *Reading Audiences*, 51.

24 Baudrillard, *Critique*, 105.

25 Walter Scott, *Waverley; Or, 'Tis Sixty Years Since*, ed. Claire Lamont (Oxford University Press, 1986), 355–56.

26 According to Bauer, "the *London* editor was the first to hazard in print . . . the identity of the *Great Unknown*" (*London*, 206).

27 Gordon, *"Christopher North"*, 251; my emphasis. Gordon denies that Wilson edited *Blackwood's*, blaming this mistake on the propensity to "attribut[e] specific powers to specific persons."

28 On vituperation in *Blackwood's*, see also Kim Wheatley, "The *Blackwood's* Attacks on Leigh Hunt," *Nineteenth-Century Literature* 47 (1992): 1–31.

29 Quoted in Gordon, *"Christopher North"*, 269.

30 Foucault, *Language*, 121–23.

31 Other portions of this letter are quoted in *OE* 242.

32 On this see also Murphy, "Impersonation," 625–26. The ironies of Scott's death include the fact that he was eventually killed by James

Christie, Lockhart's friend. Lockhart was by no means immune from the contradictions of Scott's position: it was apparently the mention of his legal name in the *London* that incited him to the challenge, and before he would agree to fight he published a disclaimer in the *New Times* stating, with evident falsity, that he had never received financial compensation from Blackwood. For a full and even-handed account of this exchange, see Leonidas M. Jones, "The Scott–Christie Duel," *Texas Studies in Literature and Language* 12 (1971): 605–29.

33 Psalmanazar's *Memoirs* were published in 1765; Ireland's *Confessions*, in 1805. For a fascinating discussion of Psalmanazar's career as faux-ethnographer, see Stewart, *Crimes*, 31–65.

34 Joshua Wilner, "Autobiography and Addiction: The Case of De Quincey," *Genre* 14 (1991): 501. Wilner's account of the *Confessions* as a generically problematic autobiography has influenced my reading here: see especially his remarks on the "*delay* which intervenes between the assertion of identity and its concession" (500–02). See also Mark Schoenfield, "The Shifting Relic: Thomas De Quincey's 'Samuel Taylor Coleridge,'" *Nineteenth-Century Contexts* 12 (1988): 105–21. On physiognomy as legibility, see Sedgwick, "Character," 255–70.

35 Stewart, *Crimes*, 69. Note that the hero of the *Confessions* is never, strictly speaking, credited with an identity – only with a "connection" that the money-lenders deem potentially profitable (*C* 26).

36 [Thomas De Quincey], *Walladmor: "Freely Translated Into German From the English of Sir Walter Scott." And Now Freely Translated From the German Into English*, 2 vols. (London: Taylor and Hessey, 1825), 2: 300.

37 [De Quincey], *Walladmor*, 2: 125.

38 Ibid., 1: xviii–xx.

39 Ibid., 2: 308–09.

40 Edmund Spenser, *The Fairie Queene*, ed. Thomas P. Roche, Jr. (New Haven: Yale University Press, 1981), Book 4, Canto 5, stanzas 14–15.

41 Lacan, *Four Fundamental Concepts*, 89.

42 Reiman, *Romantics Reviewed*, part C, 1: 201.

43 Quoted in Pollit, *Westmoreland Gazette*, 15.

44 The hypothesis that the Opium-Eater postulates a certain history to ground a marketable persona is strengthened by the dearth of independent evidence for how he spent the winter of 1802. Biographers emphasize this period as "a formative episode in his life," but in the absence of letters or financial records, they must rely almost exclusively on "De Quincey's own account," as Lindop admits (*OE* 81, 87). See also Eaton, *De Quincey*, 78–88.

45 Leask characterizes the *Confessions* as "a materialist 'assassination' of Coleridge's *Biographia Literaria*" (*Anxieties*, 171, 186). This account transvalues Leslie Stephen's estimate of De Quincey as "the adjective, of which Coleridge was the substantive": "De Quincey," quoted in

Laurie Lanzen Harris and Sheila Fitzgerald (eds.), *Nineteenth-Century Literature Criticism*, 57 vols. (Detroit: Gale Research, 1983), 4: 68.

46 Lindop incorrectly states that the signature "X. Y. Z." accompanied both installments of the "Confessions" (*OE* 247).

47 De Quincey was hereafter known to the *London* circle (and to the Wordsworths) as "the Opium-Eater" (see *OE* 254–55). Later he carried both this title and the by-line "X. Y. Z." over to his work for *Blackwood's* and *Tait's*.

48 See Bauer, *London*, 333, on the magazine's pseudo-Elizabethan idioms.

49 Jacobus remarks of the "poetics of quotation" shared by Hazlitt, Lamb and De Quincey that "the language of books *is* the language of the past, and the writing of the past is the language of books" (*Romanticism*, 130). See also David Bromwich, *Hazlitt: The Mind of a Critic* (New York: Oxford University Press, 1983), on Hazlitt's habit of quotation and its relations to "echo and allusion" (275–313, 349).

50 Guillory, *Cultural Capital*, 66–67.

51 That these "major" titles possess no more *intrinsic* value than magazine writing does not, of course, vitiate their legitimating function; see Guillory, *Cultural Capital*, 65.

52 Stewart, *Crimes*, 22.

53 Peter J. Manning, "Charles Lamb, Elia, and the *London Magazine*," unpublished essay delivered at the Modern Language Association convention, December, 1992. Jacobus comments in a similar spirit that "Lamb makes another's matter his own by an innocent form of plagiarism – quotation" (*Romanticism*, 144).

54 Foucault, *Language*, 130.

55 Guillory, *Cultural Capital*, 69–70; Manning, "Elia," 7.

56 See Bauer, *London*, 154–59, for a fuller account of the interplay among the subjects undertaken by various contributors; Lamb often appropriated suggestions from Elia's imitators. In his "Voices Together: Lamb, Hazlitt, and the *London*," *Studies in Romanticism* 29 (1990): 257–92, Mark Schoenfield invokes Bakhtinian "heteroglossia" to examine how, in one issue of the *London*, Lamb's "The Old and the New Schoolmaster" is "pressured" by Hazlitt's essay "On Antiquity."

57 Roy Park (ed.), *Lamb as Critic* (Lincoln, NB: University of Nebraska Press, 1980), 300–01.

58 Christensen, *Byron's Strength*, 89.

59 Jean Baudrillard, "The Structural Law of Value and the Order of Simulacra," in John Fekete (ed.), *The Structural Allegory: Reconstructive Encounters with the New French Thought* (University of Minneapolis Press, 1984), 63.

60 Park (ed.), *Lamb*, 302–03.

61 Baudrillard, "Simulacra," 62.

62 Lacan, *Four Fundamental Concepts*, 73.
63 Rzepka similarly remarks of this passage that the "disembodied speech" of the "invisible" author "brings all visible things into phenomenal existence" (*Sacramental*, 14–15).
64 Marx, *Capital*, 213–17.
65 Park (ed.), *Lamb*, 300.
66 Foucault, *Language*, 129.
67 Barbara Johnson, "My Monster/My Self," in Harold Bloom (ed.), *Modern Critical Interpretations: Mary Shelley's Frankenstein* (New York: Chelsea House, 1987), 57–58.
68 Marx, *Capital*, 205–09; my emphasis.
69 Murphy, *Occupation*, 118–19.
70 Guillory, *Cultural Capital*, 103. Guillory illustrates this point by citing an early anthology appearance of Gray's "Elegy," hard by another poem that "reads [it] and so enacts its reception" (103–07).
71 McDonagh remarks on the "contagion that spreads through reading. Thus De Quincey's *Confessions* provoked a proliferation of writing" (*Disciplines*, 171).
72 Hayter, *Opium*, 105.
73 James Hogg, *The Private Memoirs and Confessions of a Justified Sinner* (Oxford University Press, 1991), 240–41, 253.
74 John Wilson [as "Christopher North"], *Noctes Ambrosianae*, ed. Shelton MacKenzie, 5 vols. (New York: Redfield, 1855), 1: 362–63, 375.
75 Wilson, *Noctes*, 362, 376.
76 On mimetic opium-eating (at least one experimenter died of an overdose) see Hayter, *Opium*, 105–08, and *OE* 248. Wilkie Collins has his addicted character Ezra Jennings cite "the far famed *Confessions of an English Opium Eater*" as his oracle on the drug's effects in *The Moonstone* (Harmondsworth: Penguin, 1988), 442.
77 Wilson, *Noctes*, 365, 383.
78 See Murphy's analysis of the corresponding problem in the career of Hogg (*Occupation*, 122–24).

4 REPRODUCTIONS: OPIUM, PROSTITUTION, AND POETRY

1 Quoted in Eaton, *De Quincey*, 262.
2 Quoted in Hayter, *Opium*, 115–17, 230.
3 Guillory, *Cultural Capital*, 319.
4 On the concepts of "aesthetic disposition" and "cultural capital" see Pierre Bourdieu, *Distinction: A Social Critique of the Judgement of Taste*, trans. Richard Nice (Cambridge, MA: Harvard University Press, 1984), 1–96, 260–67.
5 Laplanche, *Life and Death*, 15–17. For De Quincey's interest in "patten," see Pollit, *Westmoreland Gazette*, 49, 57.
6 In the *Noctes* the Opium-Eater is peculiarly abstemious, consuming

only muffins and coffee amidst the other characters' Rabelaisian gluttony (Wilson, *Noctes*, 370). One symptom of opium withdrawal, De Quincey noted, was an awareness of "digestion itself, – which should naturally go on below the consciousness, but which . . . [had] become distinctly perceptible" (*M* 3:469). Friends such as Woodhouse, Robinson and Hogg remarked on De Quincey's spartan diet, which he traced to his nursery days.

7 Bourdieu, *Distinction*, 56, 486. On the "ascetic form of the aesthetic disposition" as cultural capital, see 260–95.

8 Laudanum, or "tincture of opium" (solid opium dissolved in alcohol) was popularized by the physician Thomas Sydenham in the 1660s; see Virginia Berridge and Griffith Edwards, *Opium and the People: Opiate Use in Nineteenth-Century England* (New Haven: Yale University Press, 1987), xxiv, 24, 63.

9 On lactation as the nexus of economic production and sexual reproduction, see Gayatri Chakravorty Spivak, *In Other Worlds: Essays in Cultural Politics* (New York: Routledge, 1988), 247–52.

10 Adam Smith, *An Inquiry into the Nature and Causes of the Wealth of Nations*, ed. R. H. Campbell, A. S. Skinner, and W. B. Todd (Indianapolis: Liberty Classics, 1981), 44–45.

11 See Baudrillard's account of "the ideological genesis of needs," *Critique*, 63–87 *passim*.

12 In *The Wealth of Nations*, Smith posits use value as the prehistory of exchange value (that is, economy). De Quincey makes value in use synonymous with Ricardo's notion of wealth (comfort), which depends upon "natural agents, such as the sun, the air, the pressure of the atmosphere, etc." (David Ricardo, *The Principles of Political Economy and Taxation* [London: Dent, 1957], 190). Wealth is "the true polar antagonist to the idea of value in exchange," a point essential to "the entire doctrine of Ricardo concerning value" – the "superstructure" that rests on this founding distinction (*M* 9:127–28). Nonetheless, De Quincey views wealth as a purely "regulative" concept or theoretical fiction which "though inert, keeps in their proper places other ideas more tangible and constitutive" (*M* 9:129). De Quincey's caveat is magnified in the Baudrillardian critique of use value as "the condition for the *retroactive construction* of the use of an object as an expression of its value" (quoted in Guillory, *Cultural Capital*, 301; my emphasis).

13 Ricardo, *Principles*, 6; my emphasis.

14 For a lucid account of the paradoxes involved in the notion of "natural" (labor) price, see Kurt Heinzelman, *The Economics of the Imagination* (Amherst: University of Massachusetts Press, 1980), 178. These inconsistencies are particularly clear in De Quincey's early, orthodox Ricardian "Dialogues of the Three Templars on Political Economy" (*M* 9:37–112).

15 De Quincey's anachronistic notion of "affirmative" value may be

viewed as an attempt to revive the "aesthetic" economy Smith described in *The Theory of Moral Sentiments*, published seventeen years before *The Wealth of Nations*. Consumption is propelled, according to this model, by the surplus of the commodity's beauty over its sheer utility. See Guillory, *Cultural Capital*, 310–15. On De Quincey's peculiar relation to political economy as it was practiced at mid-century, see McDonagh, *Disciplines*, 50–53.

16 Guillory, *Cultural Capital*, 318.

17 Ibid., 311.

18 On empirical versus transcendental representation see Ferguson, *Solitude*, 55–96.

19 See John Milton, *Paradise Lost*, ed. Scott Elledge (New York: Norton, 1975), book 11, lines 445–47.

20 See Kant's taxonomy of colors and their corresponding ideas (K 144).

21 J. S. Mill's famous awakening from lassitude is exemplary. In Wordsworth's poems, Mill recalls, he found "a source of inward joy" which would "be made richer by" his own labor for "improvement in the physical or social condition of mankind." This type of "exchangeable value" corresponds to De Quinceyan affirmative value: Mill "value[d] Wordsworth less according to his intrinsic merits, than by the measure of what he had done for" him. What might have seemed "mere outward beauty" was "coloured by" the exchange of feelings, and hence "a medicine for my state of mind" (quoted in Heinzelman, *Economics*, 81, 232).

22 Guillory, *Cultural Capital*, 321.

23 Heinzelman compares Smith's definition of exchange value as "the extent of th[e] power which it conveys to the owner" to Wordsworth's economy of reading in the 1815 "Essay Supplementary" (*Economics*, 208–10).

24 See Guillory, *Cultural Capital*, 320.

25 De Quincey's narcotic account of use value is to political economy what his aesthetic of murder is to philosophy. Black argues that "On Murder Considered as One of the Fine Arts" subverts the Kantian tradition, which "assumed a coherent, nonproblematic relation between ethics and aesthetics, and . . . between the experiential forms of the beautiful and the sublime" (*Aesthetics*, 15).

26 Jacques Derrida, "The Rhetoric of Drugs: An Interview," trans. Michael Israel, *Differences* 5 (1993): 2. On the related question of poisons and cures, see Jacques Derrida, "Plato's Pharmacy," in *Dissemination*, trans. Barbara Johnson (Chicago: University of Chicago Press, 1981), 70–75, 95–117.

27 My thinking on this issue is indebted to Jerome Christensen's remark that "De Quincey's answer" to the question of how "sameness [can] be made to do what difference has always done" "will be, by tincturing it." Christensen, "The Color of Imagination and the Office of Romantic

Criticism," in Christine Gallant (ed.), *Coleridge's Theory of Imagination Today* (New York: AMS Press, 1989), 233. See this essay generally for a fuller account of color in the discourse of political economy.

28 Reiman, *Romantics Reviewed*, part C, 1: 417; "Confessions of an English Opium-Eater," *The Monthly Review*, London, n.s. vol. C (March, 1823), 295.

29 Bourdieu, *Distinction*, 1.

30 See Milton, *Paradise Lost*, book 11, lines 411–49.

31 The metaphor of containment refers, of course, to the New Critical version of this (Kantian) argument. See Frances Ferguson's reading of the "concrete universal" in terms of an "understanding of reception that incorporated reception into the text itself." (Ferguson, "Numbers," 482).

32 On the Coleridgean notion of the "clerisy," see Christensen, "Color," *passim*; Klancher, *Reading Audiences*, 150–70; for an application to De Quincey, see McDonagh, *Disciplines*, 78–79.

33 See Kurt Heinzelman, "Economics, Rhetoric, and the Scene of Instruction," *Stanford French Review* 15 (1991): 363–66, for an excellent account of De Quinceyan rhetoric as "theatrical" and "exhibitional," in contrast to Smith's axiomatically "transparent" and "value-neutral" style.

34 Baxter notes De Quincey's concern with "the exchange value of language" in the *Logic* (*Autobiography*, 159). See also Heinzelman, *Economics*, 89–90. On De Quincey's theory of criticism, see McDonagh's remark that "the power of the literary text now depended on the existence of a particular reader" (*Disciplines*, 78).

35 Quoted in Heinzelman, "Scene of Instruction," 367.

36 Marx, *Capital*, 649.

37 Heinzelman quotes Foucault's dictum: "The analysis of thought is always *allegorical* in relation to the discourse that it employs" (Heinzelman, *Economics*, 91).

38 See Christensen on "the key word 'office'" as marking the professionalist *simulation* of difference, or "theoretical" production of wealth ("Color," 233).

39 On Coleridge's desynonymy of property and propriety, see Jerome Christensen, *Coleridge's Blessed Machine of Language* (Ithaca: Cornell University Press, 1981), 138–41.

40 Sir James Steuart, 1767, exemplifying "the complaint against language [that] runs like a refrain throughout economic writing" (Heinzelman, *Economics*, 73).

41 I am indebted to Matthew Becker for this discrimination.

42 Heinzelman connects this term with surplus value in "Scene of Instruction," 368.

43 For a related discussion of "The Household Wreck" that has influenced my account, see McDonagh, *Disciplines*, 130–33.

√ 44 See De Quincey's division of "Rhetoric" into the "fine art" of *conscious ornament*" and the "utility" value of "fraud" (*M* 10:81–82).

45 Bourdieu, *Distinction*, 85–86.

46 Ricardo, *Principles*, 48–49; my emphasis.

47 Ricardo, *Principles*, 49.

48 François Rabelais, *The Histories of Gargantua and Pantagruel*, trans. J. M. Cohen (Harmondsworth: Penguin, 1955), 74.

√ 49 Bourdieu cites Rabelaisian parody as a populist inversion of (bourgeois) aesthetic distantiation (*Distinction*, 491).

50 Quoted in Bourdieu, *Distinction*, 229.

51 See Michel Foucault, *The Archaeology of Knowledge and the Discourse on Language*, trans. A. M. Sheridan Smith (New York: Pantheon, 1972), 21–36.

52 Bourdieu defines literary style as the concrete form of a social "relation" "whose whole value lies in an *écart*, i.e., a distance." "Cultural (or linguistic) competence . . . function[s] like a sort of 'trade-mark,' and . . . help[s] to define the value of its products in the various markets" (*Distinction*, 226, 65).

53 This connection is also made by McDonagh, *Disciplines*, 57–59.

54 Neil Hertz, *The End of the Line: Essays on Psychoanalysis and the Sublime* (New York: Columbia University Press, 1985), 48, 53. Also see Stewart, *Crimes*, 132–72.

55 Leask suggests that the echo of the *Biographia* represents a "plagiarism of the plagiarist," Coleridge (*Anxieties*, 188). In *Romantic Weather: The Climates of Coleridge and Baudelaire* (Hanover: University Press of New England for Brown University Press, 1983), 217 *passim*, Arden Reed brilliantly reads the Piranesi passage as a reflection on "abysmal influence," recursively mediating De Quincey's relation to precursor and translator.

56 Reed, *Romantic Weather*, 211.

57 On the practice and cultural associations of engraving, see for example Morris Eaves, "Blake and the Artistic Machine: An Essay in Decorum and Technology," in Nelson Hilton (ed.), *Essential Articles for the Study of William Blake, 1970–1984*, (Hamden, CT: Archon Books, 1986), 175–209.

58 Thomas Weiskel, *The Romantic Sublime: Studies in the Structure and Psychology of Transcendence* (Baltimore: Johns Hopkins University Press, 1976), 28.

59 Barrell's excellent contextual gloss on this phrase demonstrates how literally it may be understood; see *Infection*, 5.

60 See, for example, Reed's assertion that "De Quincey's text constitutes a critique of Romantic imagination from within" (*Romantic Weather*, 212).

√ 61 Joshua Wilner makes a similar point when he argues that these lines from *The Excursion* represent "the elevation of their own language" ("The Stewed Muse of Prose," *Modern Language Notes* 104 [1989]: 1088).

62 For a literary-historical account of the De Quinceyan commodified sublime, see Clej, *Genealogy*, 172–211.

63 Nicholas Abraham and Maria Torok, "Introjection – Incorporation: Mourning *or* Melancholia," in Serge Lebovici and Daniel Widlocher (eds.), *Psychoanalysis in France* (New York: International University Press, 1980), 4–8.

64 This brief reading of the *Biographia* owes much to Reed (*Romantic Weather*, 186–95), and more to Christensen (*Blessed Machine*, 168–75).

65 Stewart Kyd, *A Treatise on the Law of Corporations*, 2 vols. (New York: Garland, 1978 [rpr. of 1793–94]), 1:13; William Blackstone, *Commentaries on the Laws of England*, 4 vols. (Philadelphia: J. B. Lippincott, 1908), 1: 467; original emphases.

66 Blackstone, *Commentaries*, 1: 468–69.

67 See Guillory, *Cultural Capital*, on the "professional imaginary" (178 *passim*).

68 Guillory, *Cultural Capital*, 56–57.

69 Derrida, *Limited Inc*, 36–37.

70 See *J* 349.

71 See Geoffrey Hartman's sacralizing account of how Wordsworth "keep[s] *The Prelude* in reserve," in *The Unremarkable Wordsworth* (Minneapolis: University of Minnesota Press, 1987), 116.

72 Quoted in Marx, *Capital*, 646.

73 Walter Benjamin, *Illuminations*, ed. Hannah Arendt, trans. Harry Zohn (New York: Schocken, 1969), 221.

74 [anon.] "Confessions of an English Opium-Eater," *The Monthly Review* (March 1823): 289–90, 296.

75 Edgar Allan Poe, *Letters*, ed. John Ward Ostrom (New York: Gordion, 1966), 58.

76 Roland Barthes, *Image, Music, Text*, trans. Stephen Heath (New York: Farrar, Straus, and Giroux, 1977), 148.

77 See Clej, *Genealogy*, for the most theoretically sophisticated indictment of De Quincey's "arid" writings, which encrypt "the 'secret' of modern literary production – the secret that the modern authorial subject, even in its high Romantic mode, is a rhetorical construct made out of echoes." While I endorse the substance if not the tone of her conclusion, it has been a project of this book to contest the inevitable accompanying discovery of an "anxiety of influence that pervade[s]" De Quincey's works (*Genealogy*, 249, 254–55, *passim*). Regarding De Quincey as the theorist of reproduction rather than a guilt-ridden "scriptor," I suggest that the diagnosis of "anxiety" remains caught in a pseudo-dialectic of authenticity and imitation.

5 APPROPRIATIONS: THE COUNTER-LIVES OF THE POET

1 I rely on de Man's account of autobiography as "a figure of reading" that depends on "a substitutive exchange" between two subjects (*Rhetoric*, 70).

2 Like most of De Quincey's work, the essays collected in *R* have a complicated publication history. The ones discussed here, "William Wordsworth" (I–III) and "Society of the Lakes – IV" (*R* 119–206, 362–74), first appeared in four numbers of *Tait's Edinburgh Magazine*, 1839–40, under the group title "Lake Reminiscences." *Tait's* had been publishing an occasional series by De Quincey since February 1834, when it began running "Sketches of Life and Manners from the Autobiography of an English Opium-Eater," interrupted by the four-part "Samuel Taylor Coleridge," beginning September 1834. The expressly autobiographical series concluded in 1836, and in February 1837 De Quincey began again with "Literary Novitiate," reprinted *M* 2:113–37. *Tait's* ran eighteen more essays by De Quincey, including the Wordsworth sketches, up through February 1841. De Quincey described the "Lake Reminiscences" as "by much the most interesting chapters of my Autobiography" (*NLS* MS. 1670). Ticknor and Fields published the series of 1837–41, plus the essay on Coleridge, as a bound text titled *Literary Reminiscences* in 1851. Annette Wheeler Cafarelli argues that the essays in the 1851 volume should be considered as "as a unified narrative sequence" – in effect, as a book – despite their miscellaneous publication ("De Quincey and Wordsworthian Narrative," *Studies in Romanticism* 28 [1989]: 121). Mark Schoenfield makes the opposite argument ("Shifting Relic," 116–18). On "recognition" as shorthand for cognitive and representational problems in biography, see Epstein, *Recognizing Biography*, 1–6.

3 See Cafarelli, "Wordsworthian Narrative," 126–29, on De Quincey's rejection of Boswellian filiation.

4 John Milton, *Poems*, ed. Laurence D. Lerner (Harmondsworth: Penguin, 1985), 39. These two lines form the centerpiece of de Man's argument on prosopopeia as the figure of autobiography (*Rhetoric*, 78–80).

5 Freud observes that male subjects of this fantasy "invariably transfer themselves into the part of a woman," enacting an "inverted" Oedipal scenario of being loved by the father (*SE* 17:197–99). De Quincey's fantasy, however, corresponds more precisely to Freud's "feminine" version, suggesting that this inflection of the masochistic scene belongs to De Quincey's superseded idea of becoming Wordsworth's daughter. As Barrell shrewdly notes, it is not De Quincey but the nymphs who are threatened by nympholepsy (*Infection*, 38).

6 John Locke, *Treatise of Civil Government and A Letter Concerning Toleration*, ed. Charles L. Sherman (New York: Irvington, 1965), 19.

7 Quoted in Jerome Christensen, *Practicing Enlightenment*, 54. The union of Zeus and Semele produced Dionysus, whom Zeus carried to term in a pocket of his thigh.

8 Jacobus brilliantly identifies this passage as the key to De Quincey's figure of the biographer as "chosen daughter" (*Romanticism*, 229–30). Subsequent portions of this chapter indicate where I diverge from Jacobus's reading, to which mine is indebted.

9 See Renza, *"White Heron"*, 15–17, on the bourgeois thematics of naming and property in Bloom's revisionary ratios.

10 See Christensen on the "scurvy spots" Hume contracted from reading Cicero and Plutarch (*Practicing Enlightenment*, 56–59).

11 Stephen Gill, *William Wordsworth: A Life* (Oxford: Clarendon Press, 1989), 388.

12 James Boswell, *Life of Johnson*, ed. R. W. Chapman (Oxford University Press, 1983), 802–03.

13 See Epstein, *Recognizing Biography*, 68–80, on affiliation, similitude, and patronage in eighteenth-century biography. On the "canon" of biography, see Epstein, 4–5 *passim*, and Cafarelli, *Prose, passim*.

14 Many of the essays reprinted in *M* 4 and *M* 5 conform to a well-established practice of short magazine biography. On the basis of these and "such little known projects as" *The Caesars*, Cafarelli proposes classifying De Quincey "primarily as a biographer" ("Wordsworthian Narrative," 123–24).

15 Boswell, *Life*, 22.

16 De Quincey had read all three *Essays Upon Epitaphs*, which he describes as "very valuable" (*R* 82); he invokes the figure of "incarnation" frequently in his essays on literary theory, and mentions having learned it from Wordsworth in his essay "Style" (*M* 10:229–30); see also *M* 10:262, 5:301.

17 Quoted in Cafarelli, "Wordsworthian Narrative," 128.

18 Locke, *Treatise*, 19.

19 Boswell, *Life*, 839.

20 Boswell, *Life*, 22–24. Wordsworth takes pointed exception to Boswell, who "had broken through many pre-existing delicacies" (*PrW* 3:120).

21 On the economy of biography, see Epstein, *Recognizing Biography*, 74.

22 For de Manian reflections on face and figure in De Quincey, see Jacobus, *Romanticism*, 229, and Stephen J. Spector, "Thomas De Quincey: Self-effacing Autobiographer," *Studies in Romanticism* 18 (1979): 508 *passim*.

23 Epstein discusses commercial portraiture and the proliferation of "copies" in eighteenth-century enterprise (*Recognizing Biography*, 67).

24 For the text of the sonnet, which De Quincey slightly misquotes, see

G. Blakemore Evans *et al.* (eds.), *The Riverside Shakespeare* (Boston: Houghton Mifflin, 1974), 1772.

25 De Quincey's fiction is notable for the recurrent motif of a disguised son who avenges a violent crime inflicted on his parents. See especially "Klosterheim; or, The Masque," and "The Avenger," *M* 12:5–156, 234–85.

26 Quoted in Sonia Hofkosh, "The Writer's Ravishment: Women and the Romantic Author – The Example of Byron," in Anne K. Mellor (ed.), *Romanticism and Feminism* (Bloomington: Indiana University Press, 1988), 103.

27 De Man, *Rhetoric*, 70.

28 Boswell, *Life*, 19.

29 The quotation is given as in De Quincey; the 1805 text reads in full, " . . . stars,/ And wedded man to man by purest bond/ Of nature, undisturbed . . . " (*Prelude* 5:104–06).

30 The 1805 *Prelude* assigns the dream to a "friend," while the 1850 version narrates the dream in the first person. See *Prelude* (1805) 5:49–165, (1850) 5:50–165; also see Jane Worthington Smyser, "Wordsworth's Dream of Poetry and Science: *The Prelude*, V," *PMLA* 71 (1956): 274–75.

31 On this see J. Hillis Miller, *The Linguistic Moment: Wordsworth to Stevens* (Princeton University Press, 1985), 107.

32 Lacan, *Four Fundamental Concepts*, 36.

33 Timothy Bahti, "Figures of Interpretation, The Interpretation of Figures: A Reading of Wordsworth's 'Dream of the Arab,'" *Studies in Romanticism* 18 (1979): 614–17. I am indebted to several other excellent deconstructive readings of the *Prelude*'s Book Fifth; see especially Miller, *Linguistic Moment*, 59–103; and Jacobus, *Romanticism*, 97–125, which connects the Arab with De Quincey's Dark Interpreter (118–20).

34 De Quincey made this declaration in August 1803; the Dream of the Arab was composed in February–March 1804.

35 De Quincey's first responses to the *Prelude* are not recorded, and the extent of his access to it is unclear. He may, as he boasted to Carlyle, once have had part of the manuscript in his possession and made his own copy, or he may only have heard it recited. See *J* 358; *OE* 187.

36 On Gray's "Elegy," the canon, and questions of literacy, see Guillory, *Cultural Capital*, 85–133. This phrase from the "Elegy" is routinely cited in the *London Magazine*'s many essays on neglected or uneducated poets.

37 On "involutes," "perplexed combinations of *concrete* objects . . . in compound experiences," see *C* 103–05.

38 Eaton S. Drone, *A Treatise on the Law of Property in Intellectual Productions in Great Britain and the United States* (Boston: Little, Brown, 1879), 386.

For the Lockean position represented by Drone, "the controlling question always is, whether the substance of the work is taken without authority"; for obvious reasons, "substance" remains an undefined term, though Drone regards it as impervious to paraphrase and translation (385–86).

39 Benjamin Kaplan, *An Unhurried View of Copyright* (New York: Hafner Press, 1967), 17. As a survey of the Reiman collection demonstrates, periodical reviews during the early century routinely quoted much more extensively than would be permissible now. The question of "fair abridgment" revolved, Kaplan explains, around whether the excerpt might be perceived to interfere with "the normal economic exploitation of the copyright" (11–17).

40 The publication of *Wat Tyler* in 1817 (see Southey vs. Sherwood) is the famous example. Southey failed to get an injunction against the publisher, *not* because he had surrendered possession of the manuscript, but because it was judged to be seditious, hence unprotected (Drone, *Treatise*, 112).

41 On the other hand, according to Drone, common-law literary properties (i.e. unpublished works) were more narrowly restricted; reading a manuscript in public could constitute an infringement of common-law property (*Treatise*, 100).

42 See Susan Eilenberg, *Strange Power of Speech: Wordsworth, Coleridge, and Literary Possession* (New York: Oxford University Press, 1992), 202–05, 262–67, on the "confusion of copyright with authorial property" that generated the argument for "restoration" of perpetual copyright. For a later defense of Wordsworth's position, see Drone, *Treatise*, 22–23 *passim.*

43 De Quincey began his memorial series on Coleridge with a discussion of four Coleridgean plagiarisms; his alleged motive was to "break the force of the discovery" (*R* 36–43). Response to this exposure spurred him to a long explanatory footnote in which he defended himself against the appearance of having *forged* German titles in order to accuse Coleridge (*R* 392–93). De Quincey's appropriations – and even plagiarisms – in his miscellaneous historical and biographical essays are the subject of Goldman's *The Mine and the Mint.*

44 Gill, *Wordsworth*, 373–90.

45 Eilenberg, *Strange Power*, 192–93 *passim.*

46 Quoted in W. J. B. Owen (ed.), *The Fourteen-Book Prelude* (Ithaca: Cornell University Press, 1985), 6. For details of dating and textual changes to *The Prelude*, see 5–10 *passim.* A brief account of Wordsworth's revisions may be found in Gill, *Wordsworth*, 391.

47 Also see Eilenberg, *Strange Power*, 208.

48 Jacobus, *Romanticism*, 216.

49 Drone, *Treatise*, 7.

50 Ilay Campbell, "Information for A. D. and J. Wood, booksellers in Edinburgh, 1773," in Stephen Parks (ed.), *The Literary Property Debate: Six Tracts, 1764–1774* (New York: Garland, 1975), 7.

51 See Nicholas Abraham, "Notes on the Phantom: A Complement to Freud's Metapsychology," quoted in Swann, "Public Transport," 826–28.

52 De Quincey quotes Baillet's *Vie* in his essay "On Murder," *M* 13:24–26. For an English translation of Descartes' three dreams on November 10, 1619 – "the major crisis of his life" – see Jack Rochford Vrooman, *René Descartes: A Biography* (New York: G. P. Putnam's Sons, 1970), 53–60.

53 Smyser, "Wordsworth's Dream," 270–71.

54 Vrooman, *Descartes*, 57–58.

55 Lacan, *Four Fundamental Concepts*, 44 *passim*.

56 See De Quincey's account of how Coleridge transformed a poem whose premise and "framework" he borrowed from Frederica Brun (*R* 37).

57 Lacan, *Four Fundamental Concepts*, 47.

58 Owen dates these revisions of the 1832 MS. D, including the transposition of the dream into the first person, to early summer, 1839 (*Fourteen-Book Prelude*, 8–9, 581–91). See also Smyser, who concludes that the parallel between De Quincey's mistake and the textual changes must be coincidental ("Wordsworth's Dream," 274).

59 Guillory, *Cultural Capital*, 55.

60 For different interpretations of this episode see also Spector, "Self-effacing," 503 *passim*; Rzepka, *Sacramental*, 204–11; and E. Michael Thron, "The Significance of Catherine Wordsworth's Death to Thomas De Quincey and William Wordsworth," *Studies in English Literature* 28 (1988): 559–67.

61 See also Eilenberg, *Strange Power*, 110–11, on narrative in the Lucy poems.

62 Jerome Bruner, "The Narrative Construction of Reality," *Critical Inquiry* 18 (1991): 9.

63 Ferguson, *Wordsworth*, 177.

64 Ferguson, *Wordsworth*, 176. On the connection between the Lucy poems and Kate Wordsworth, see also Spector, "Self-effacing," 503–06.

65 De Quincey emphasizes the parallel with "Three years she grew" at the price of slight chronological strain: Kate, who was born on September 6, 1808, would have been nearly four when she died in the summer of 1812, though De Quincey remembers her as a year younger (*R* 371).

66 Pinch, "Meter," 843.

67 Ferguson, *Wordsworth*, 188–89.

68 This is the moral De Quincey elucidates in "On Wordsworth's Poetry," *M* 11:295.

69 Bruner, "Narrative," 5.

70 Peter Brooks "attempt[s] to describe the work of desire as the subtending dynamic of narrative" ("Storied Bodies, or Nana at Last Unveil'd," *Critical Inquiry* 16 [1989]: 1). Jay Clayton juxtaposes this thesis with the work of Teresa de Lauretis and Leo Bersani in "Narrative and Theories of Desire," *Critical Inquiry* 16 (1989): 33–53.

71 In 1821 De Quincey denied to Crabb Robinson "that he was himself the father of Cathy Wordsworth." Robinson had observed in 1812 that, when news of her death reached London, De Quincey "burst into tears on seeing Wordsworth and seemed to be more affected than the father" (*J* 294, 209).

72 Laplanche notes that the version of the Oedipal complex involved in the beating fantasy takes the form of a "'fraternal complex': ego–parents–brother or sister" (*Life and Death*, 102).

73 On the Wordsworths' proprietary attitude toward their old home, see *J* 218–20; Dorothy complained as late as 1817 that the De Quinceys were "spending their honeymoon in our cottage."

74 Blackstone, *Commentaries*, 2: 405.

75 See Ferguson, *Wordsworth*, 41–56, for a discussion of the affections and metaphor.

76 On intentionality, see Bruner, "Narrative," 6 *passim.*

77 Slavoj Zizek, *The Sublime Object of Ideology* (London: Verso, 1989), 56.

78 Zizek, *Sublime*, 45.

79 Spector, "Self-effacing," 507.

80 Zizek, *Sublime*, 45.

81 Rzepka argues, to the contrary, that "the opium-eater's extravagant grief at Kate's death is but a skirmish" in his "epic Oedipal struggle with Wordsworth" (*Sacramental*, 211).

EPILOGUE: MINOR ROMANTICISM

1 Siskin, *Historicity*, 114–24.

2 Carlyle's remark is also quoted in John Weeks' introduction to [Thomas De Quincey], *Klosterheim, Or: The Masque* (Santa Barbara: Woodbridge Press,1982), vi.

3 Quoted in Hayter, *Opium*, 114.

4 On the ideological function of "parts and wholes," see Siskin, *Historicity*, 67–147.

5 Lacoue-Labarthe and Nancy, *Literary Absolute*, 105, 114, 45–49, 117.

6 Bourdieu, *Distinction*, 29.

7 William Hazlitt, *Sketches and Essays*, ed. Harold Bloom (New York: Chelsea House, 1983), 178.

8 Quoted in Bourdieu, *Distinction*, 31.

9 Bourdieu, *Distinction*, 54, 70.

10 For another argument relevant to the study of Romantic periodical prose as a minor form, see Schoenfield, "Voices Together." McDonagh's account of De Quincey as a "popularizer and disseminator of other people's ideas" (*Disciplines*, 5) presumes his minority while offering a helpful intellectual context for the practices that define it. Bromwich, on the other hand, attempts in his full-length study, *Hazlitt*, to rectify the "refinement and diminishment of our idea of" his subject by "offer[ing] a story about his genius in relation to the literature he cared for," an approach that admittedly "gives little evidence of development" (3, vii). A writer of ephemera that "outlasted its intended span" (347), Bromwich's Hazlitt simply emerges as the greatest *minor* writer of his time. For a similar estimate of Hazlitt, see Cafarelli, *Prose*, 113–15 *passim*.

11 Foucault, *Language*, 123.

12 These judgments derive, respectively, from MacKenzie (ed.), *Noctes Ambrosianae*, 362; Barrell, *Infection*, 208; Goldman, *The Mine and the Mint*, 8.

13 For the best accounts of Coleridge's relation to professionalism, see Christensen, *Blessed Machine*, 96–185, and especially "Color," *passim*.

14 Lacoue-Labarthe and Nancy, *Literary Absolute*, 55.

15 For Guillory's critique of the synonymy between the "noncanonical" and the "excluded," see especially *Cultural Capital*, 3–82.

16 See Guillory, *Cultural Capital*, 134–55.

17 Jacobus, *Romanticism*, 143. On De Quincey as "professional reader or critic," charged with facilitating the circulation of commodified literature, see also McDonagh, *Disciplines*, 71–81. As McDonagh observes, this notion implies a transfer of agency from the poet to the critic.

18 On the canon-debate in relation to social identity, see Guillory, *Cultural Capital*, 3–55.

19 David Lloyd, *Nationalism and Minor Literature: James Clarence Mangan and the Emergence of Irish Cultural Nationalism* (Berkeley: University of California Press, 1987), 19–21.

20 John Guillory, "Canonical and Non-Canonical: A Critique of the Current Debate," *ELH* 54 (1987): 503.

21 Lloyd, *Nationalism*, 22.

22 Deleuze and Guattari, *Kafka*, 18.

23 Ibid., 16–17, 26–28.

24 Ibid., 18–21, 57.

25 Ibid., 21–23.

26 Ibid., 21.

27 De Quincey's linguistic "deterritorialization" may be plotted according to Deleuze and Guattari's adaptation of the Gobardian tetralin-

guistic model. First, there is the vernacular or territorial language, represented by the "mother tongue" spoken among "well-educated women not professionally given to literature" (*M* 10:142–43). The second level of vehicular, commercial, bureaucratic language corresponds to the Latinate "bookishness" of the newspapers (see *M* 10:148–54). German (the language of Kant and Richter) is the third-level "language of sense and culture," while Greek is the "mythic" fourth-level language "on the horizon of cultures."

28 Guillory, "Canonical," 483.
29 Renza speculates interestingly on this possibility, taking as his test case Poe's story "Berenice." Renza, whose study focuses on a short story by Sarah Orne Jewett, criticizes Deleuze and Guattari on the grounds that they would make Poe, a canonically major author, *more minor* than Jewett – and so reinstate the traditional canonical hierarchy in new terms. See *"White Heron"*, 29–38.
30 Guillory, *Cultural Capital*, 52.
31 Renza, *"White Heron"*, 3.
32 Brisman, *Romantic Origins*, 184.
33 Ibid., 193.
34 See Renza, *"White Heron"*, 12–13: the over-compensation revealed in the strategy of smallness derives ultimately from a wish to be great.
35 The other authors considered in Brisman, *Romantic Origins*, are the standard six poets: Coleridge, Keats, Byron, Shelley, Wordsworth, Blake.
36 Brisman, *Romantic Origins*, 211, 222.
37 Ibid., 207, my emphasis.
38 Ibid., 192.
39 See also McDonagh, *Disciplines*, 73.
40 Guillory, *Cultural Capital*, 28.
41 Susan Stewart, *On Longing: Narratives of the Miniature, the Gigantic, the Souvenir, the Collection* (Durham, NC: Duke University Press, 1993), 55.
42 Stewart, *On Longing*, 54.
43 Guillory, *Cultural Capital*, 63.
44 See Bourdieu, *Distinction*, on the metaphor of "inheritance" that naturalizes the access to culture regulated by the school (76–83, *passim*). On the demographics of periodical subscribers and the projection of a class-instituting "reading habit," see Klancher, *Reading Audiences*, 18–75.
45 See Stewart, *On Longing*, 54.
46 See Guillory, *Cultural Capital* 134–75, on the New Criticism's program of restricting access to specifically literary experience by situating it within a discipline practiced at the university level.
47 Bourdieu, *Distinction*, 31.
48 Guillory, *Cultural Capital*, xii.

49 Ferguson, "Numbers," 482.

50 I borrow this analogy from Weiskel, who glosses the Kantian term "subreption" as "suppression of the facts, concealment, deception" (*Romantic Sublime*, 46).

51 Thomas McFarland, *William Wordsworth: Intensity and Achievement* (Oxford: Clarendon Press, 1992), 1, 28.

52 Guillory, *Cultural Capital*, 33.

53 Ibid., 55.

Index

CAMBRIDGE STUDIES IN ROMANTICISM

GENERAL EDITORS

MARILYN BUTLER, *University of Oxford*

JAMES CHANDLER, *University of Chicago*